Handbook
of
Mineral Law

Field Edition

by
TERRY S. MALEY

Mineral Land Publications
P.O. Box 1186
Boise, Idaho 83701
(208) 343-9143

i

PREFACE TO THE FIELD EDITION

This field edition is a practical reference for attorneys, land managers, prospectors, geologists, engineers and government resource managers whose work involves the acquisition and management of mineral resources. It should be particularly useful to those who are overwhelmed by the proliferation of laws and regulations that govern mineral activities and need a single up-to-date reference that offers an concise and readable review of the subject.

This book was written for those who need convenient and reliable advice on the field aspects of mineral law. Emphasis is placed on field-related topics such as surveys, land and mineral status records, effect of the various types of land and mineral conveyances and withdrawals on the availability of mineral lands, claim location procedures and maintenance of mining claim titles. The chapters on recording and maintaining mining claims as required by section 314 of the Federal Land Policy and Management Act of 1976 are current and reflect the latest Interior and Federal court decisions.

Terry S. Maley

THE AUTHOR

Terry Maley received B.S. and M.S. degrees in geology from Oregon State University and a Ph.D. in economic geology from the University of Idaho. He has taught graduate-level courses on mineral law and mineral title at several universites and has presented mineral law courses nationwide to more than 1200 mineral industry professionals since 1978. Most courses have been awarded continuing legal education units by state bar associations. Dr. Maley is currently an affiliate faculty member at the University of Idaho. He has served four years as Administrator of the Idaho Division of Earth Resources with responsibility over all State research and regulatory programs concerning geology and mineral resources. He has worked for the Bureau of Land Management in Washington, D.C., Arizona, Nevada and most currently in the Idaho where he is Branch Chief of Mining Law. Dr Maley has authored 40 articles and 5 books on mineral law including the highly regarded *Handbook of Mineral Law* (3 editions), *Mineral Title Examination* and *Mining Law from Location to Patent*. He keeps the last two volumes current with annual cumulative supplements. Dr. Maley was the recipient of the Gold Quill Award for the Outstanding paper published in the Journal of the American Society of Farm Managers and Rural Appraisers; and in 1987 he chaired the *Mineral Law* session at the 93rd Annual Convention of the Northwest Mining Association.

CONTENTS

NAVIGABLE WATERS

The beds of navigable waters are owned by the individual states and are not public domain. However, these beds are not to be sold by the states as they must be open as common highways. Whether or not a body of water is considered navigable depends on its condition at the date of a state's admission into the union. Those who wish to appropriate lands for mineral deposits should be very familiar with the rules that govern boundaries to the some 84 million acres of submerged lands.

Definition of Navigability

Now that we have established that the individual states own the beds of navigable waters, what is navigability in terms of the law? Where there is a controversy concerning navigability, it must be decided by the courts based on the facts and conditions of each water body as it exists at the date of statehood. The Federal test for navigability was first articulated in **Daniel Ball**, 77 U.S. 557, 563 (1870):

> Those rivers must be regarded as public navigable rivers in law which are navigable in fact. And they are navigable in fact when they are used, or are susceptible of being used, in their ordinary condition, as highways for commerce, over which trade or travel are or may be conducted in the customary modes of trade or travel on water.

The Supreme Court has held that a title navigability determination cannot be made to depend upon the relative development or lack of development at the time of its admission to the Union.[1] Therefore neither the extent nor the nature of commerce in the region at the time of statehood is relevant and title need not be determined by how commerce was conducted at statehood.[2] The requirement that title navigability be determined at the time of statehood means only that when making a title navigability determination, the **Daniel Ball test** is to be applied to the physical dimensions and configuration of the river existing at the time of statehood.[3] The paramount consideration is whether the water body is susceptible to use as a route for transportation rather than undue concern about its susceptibility to use as a highway for commerce.[4]

Equal-Footing Doctrine

In the United States it has long been established that each new state created out of the public domain automatically, upon its admission to the union, becomes the owner of the beds of all waters then navigable and not previously conveyed by the Federal Government into private ownership under the equal-footing doctrine.

1

The equal-footing doctrine is the basis for each new state to have sovereignty over the beds of navigable waters as it is admitted into the union. In **U.S. v. Texas**, 339 U.S. 707 (1950), the equal-footing doctrine is clearly explained:

> Yet the "equal-footing" clause has long been held to have a direct effect on certain property rights. Thus the question early arose in controversies between the Federal Government and the States as to the ownership of the shores of navigable waters and the soils under them. It was consistently held that to deny to the States, admitted subsequently to the formation of the Union, ownership of this property would deny them admission of an equal footing with the original States, since the original States did not grant these properties to the United States, but reserved them to themselves.

Submerged Lands Act of 1953

In addition to the numerous Federal court decisions which affirm the state's sovereignty over the beds of navigable waters, the U.S. Congress enacted the Submerged Lands Act of May 22, 1953 (43 U.S.C. 1301 et. seq.) with a legislative statement on the same principle. This Act declared title and ownership of the lands and natural resources within such lands and waters be vested to the respective states. "Natural resources" is defined in the Act as including without limitation, "oil, gas, and all other minerals." The Act also authorized the states "to manage, administer, lease, develop, and use the said lands and natural resources all in accordance with applicable state law..."

Ordinary High-Water Mark

Navigable bodies of water are segregated from the public lands at the ordinary high-water elevation. The ordinary high-water mark or elevation is the line which the water impresses on the soil by covering it for sufficient periods to cause a lack of vegetation. The ordinary high-water mark of a river is a natural physical characteristic placed upon the bank by the action of a river. This mark is placed during the ordinary flow of the river and is not the effects or marks caused during peak or flood stage. On the other hand it is not established by a river running below normal flow.[5]

Meander Line

The meander line in a government survey of public lands bordering a body of navigable water is not a true boundary but is established to mark the sinuosities of the stream bank.[6] A meander line is established by traversing the margin of a permanent natural body of water. Again, meander lines are not surveyed to represent boundaries, but to define the sinuosities made by the high-water mark of the water body. When the bed of the body of water migrates, the ownership of the adjoining land migrates with the mean high water line.

2

Although it is commonly presumed that those water bodies that have been meandered by the cadastral surveyor are navigable, the question of navigability may only be answered by the facts in a specific case and not from any action on the part of the surveyor.[7] Rivers are meandered at the ordinary mean high-water mark on both banks where the right-angle width is 3 chains or greater. However, shallow streams and intermittent streams are not meandered even if they exceed 3 chains in width. Lakes with a surface area of 50 acres or more are also meandered. Shallow or seasonal lakes are not meandered even though they may exceed 50 acres.[8]

Boundary Lines Versus Meander Lines

Where a patented tract of land is riparian to a navigable body of water, the water line is the boundary line rather than the meander line. In other words, the patent conveys all land beyond the meander line to the water line.[9] A meander line is run for the purpose of computing the acreage of fractional lots. If these lots are patented and the government survey plat shows that small areas of land lie outside the lot between the meander line and the water line, the water line is still the boundary and the riparian owner would have title to the small areas of land outside the fractional lot. These small areas of land go with the lot only if failure to include them was not due to fraud or mistake, but was consistent with a reasonably accurate survey.[10]

However, this rule does not apply when it is conclusively shown that no body of water exists or existed at or near the place indicated or where there was no effort to survey the lands situated between the meander line and the water line.[11] Also, where the area of land between the meander line and the water line is large compared with the fractional lot surveyed, it is not included in the patent.[12]

Title to Bed of Many Rivers in Dispute

Where there is a controversy on the navigability of a water body, the issue may only be settled by the Federal courts, based upon the facts and conditions in a specific case as they existed at the date of statehood.

In many parts of the west, ownership of the beds of many major rivers is in dispute between the state and Federal Governments. For example, the main Salmon River in central Idaho is an excellent example of such a controversy. Although there are several Idaho State Supreme Court cases holding that the state owns the river bed, no Federal Court case has decided the matter - consequently, the issue is not settled.

3

Accretion, Reliction, Avulsion and Erosion

There are four types of water action that cause a physical change in the bed of a navigable water body:

1. **Accretion** is the gradual and imperceptible deposition of material along the bank of a body of water and the lands formed by this process.

2. **Reliction** is the gradual uncovering of land cause by the recession of a body of water.[13]

3. **Avulsion** is the sudden and rapid change of a stream channel, or some other body of water forming a boundary. In the event that a navigable river finds a new channel, the bed of the new channel resulting from avulsion continues to belong to the owner of the land encroached upon; whereas, the bed of the former river still belongs to the state.

4. **Erosion** is the washing away or removal of the land by the sea or a river's flow. Usually considered to be an imperceptible action, the rate of erosion may be quite rapid in total effect and may be distinguished from avulsion by the absence of identifiable upland between former and new channels.

Navigable Waters within Indian Reservations

The United States hold title to the bed of navigable waters in trust for future states. Upon admission of a state to the union, the United States relinquishes to the state the ownership of the beds of navigable waters. Indian tribes do not have title to the beds of navigable waters that exist within their reservations.[14]

Conveyances Made Before Statehood Do Not Preclude State from Acquiring Navigable Waters

Two Supreme Court decisions hold that conveyances made by the United States before statehood do not convey navigable waters unless such intention was clearly and specifically declared to convey navigable waters.[15]

Mineral Rights Included in Navigable Waters Title

At the time a state enters the union, title to navigable waters including tidelands passes to the state. No mineral rights in such lands are reserved to the United States.[16]

Mining Claims Contiguous to Navigable Water Bodies

If a mining claim abuts against a navigable body of water, the water line is the boundary of the claim rather than the meander

4

line as shown on the mineral survey plat.[17] This of course presumes that the meander line follows as nearly as practicable the water line. All accretions and relictions that form after the patent is issued become the property of the patentee or his successors in interest.[18]

Federal Minerals within Meander Lines of Water Body

Lands within the meander lines of a water body may be leased for oil and gas even though such lands are surveyed. The applicable regulations[19] require that the lands be described by metes and bounds connected to an official corner of the public land surveys.

In **David A. Province**, 85 I.D. 154 (1978), the Board considered the question of whether the oil and gas deposits within the meander lines of the Yellowstone are covered by an existing lease that covers the lot bounded by the meander line. The Board determined that the issue is the same regardless of whether the leased lands contiguous to the meander line are public domain or patented surface with Federally-owned oil and gas deposits. In several earlier decisions it was established that where the United States has patented lands subject to an oil and gas reservation, lands accreting to the patented lands are also subject to the reservation.

In **Province**, the Board held that the lease extends only to the meander line and not the water line. This conclusion was primarily based on an examination of the Mineral Leasing Act which suggests that the intention of Congress that a lessee should receive only a specific acreage is so dominant that there is no room for the common law doctrine of riparian rights.

Unsurveyed Island in Navigable Waters

In **Scott v. Lattig**, 227 U.S. 229 (1913), the Supreme Court held that an error in omitting to survey an island in a navigable stream does not divest the United States of title or preclude surveying it at a later date. An island within the public domain in a navigable stream and actually in existence both at the time of the survey of the banks of the stream and also upon admission to the union of the state within which is situated remains the property of the United States. Even though omitted from the survey, such land does not become part of the fractional subdivision on the opposite banks of the stream. Conversely, if an island in a navigable stream, which is public land, washes away totally before statehood and then forms again in the same place after statehood, title to the island is in the state.

5

Accretion to Islands

Although as a general rule the island owner owns accretion to the island, there are limitations on that rule depending on how far the accretions run and whether the accretions are deposited on a streambed owned by one other than the island owner.[20]

Navigability of Lakes

Navigability of lakes comes under the same rules as the navigability of streams. A lake must, at the time of statehood, have been used or been susceptible to commercial use in its natural condition without modification of the lakebed.[21]

Patent Conveys Only Surveyed Lands

A patent conveys only land which is surveyed, and when the surveyors have carried a survey only to a certain line, a grantee may not successfully challenge the correctness of their action or claim lands beyond that line under a patent issued in accordance with that survey.[22] Also, a patent of public lands has ownership according to the actual survey on the ground, even though the official survey plat may not show the tract as it is located on the ground, or the patent description may be in error.[23]

Nonnavigable Bodies of Water

Under certain conditions, nonnavigable bodies of water may be meandered and, of course, title to the beds of such lakes or rivers vests in the United States until sold.[24] If the government conveys title to a fractional subdivision fronting upon a nonnavigable body of water, the patent generally gives ownership to the middle of the bed in front of the fractional subdivision.[25] The fact that a body of water is meandered does not necessarily mean that it is a navigable body of water or that the meander line is a boundary line. As mentioned above, meander lines are not run as boundaries, but to define the sinuosities of the banks of the stream or lake, and as a means of ascertaining the quantity of land embraced in the survey.

Under Federal common law, the bed of a nonnavigable lake belongs to the shore owners in a pie-shaped fashion to the center of the lake.[26] The beds of meandered nonnavigable water bodies are subject to appropriation under the United States mining and mineral leasing laws only when the abutting upland is unappropriated Federal land.[27] The Interior Board of Land Appeals has held that the common law of accretion and relictions do not apply to determine the boundaries of oil and gas leases bordering nonnavigable waters.[28] Therefore, the boundary of the lease is the meander line indicated on the official plat.[29]

6

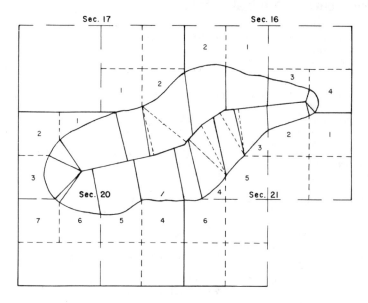

Apportionment of the bed of a nonnavigable lake
(from *Manual of Survey Instructions,* 1973, Bureau of
Land Management).

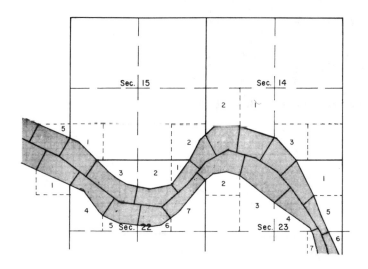

Apportionment of bed of nonnavigable lake (from
Manual of Survey Instructions, 1973, Bureau of Land
Management).

References - Navigable Waters

1. U.S. v. Utah, 283 U.S. 64 (1931).
2. State of Alaska v. U.S., Civil No. A80-359 (Feb. 9, 1987).
3. Supra at 14.
4. Utah v. U.S., 403 U.S. 9 (1971).
5. U.S. v. Claridge, 279 F. Supp. 87 (D.C. Ariz 1966), affirmed 416 F.2d 933, cert. denied 397 U.S. 961.
6. Hórne v. Smith, 159 U.S. 40 (1895); U.S. v. Elliott, 131 F.2d 720 (CCA Okl 1942).
7. Oklahoma v. Texas 258 U.S. 574 (1922).
8. Manual of Surveying Instructions, 1973. Department of the Interior, Bureau of Land Management.
9. Chester Ferguson, 20 IBLA 224, 231 (1975); U.S. v. Lane, 260 U.S. 662 (1923).
10. U.S. v. Lane, supra; Producers Oil Co. v. Hanzen, 238 U.S. 325. 338 (1915).
11. Jeems Bayou Club v. U.S., 260 U.S. 561 (1923); Security Land & Exploration Co. v. Burns, 193 U.S. 167 (1904).
12. Land v. Brockett, 110 So. 740, 162 La 519, cert denied 273 U.S. 757.
13. Fontenelle v. Omaha Tribe of Neb., 298 F. Supp. 855 (DC Neb. 1969), affirmed 43 F.2d 143.
14. Kootenai Tribes v. Namen, 380 F.Supp. 452 (DC Mont 1974), affirmed 534 F.2d 1376, cert. denied 429 U.S. 929.
15. U.S. Holt State Bank, 270 U.S. 49, 55 (1926); Montana v. U.S., 45 U.S. 544, 552 (1981).
16. Charles B. Reynolds, 56 L.D. 60 (1937).
17. Alaska United Gold Mining Co. v. Cincinnati Alaska Mining Co., 45 L.D. 331 (1916).
18. Id.
19. 43 CFR 3101.1-3 and 3101.1-4.
20. Houston v. United States Gypsum Co., 569 F.2d 880, 883 (5th Cir.) rehearing denied, 580 F.2d 815, 818 (5th Cir. 1978).
21. U.S. v. Utah, 183 U.S. 64 (1931).
22. Chester Ferguson, 20 IBLA 224 (1975).
23. U.S. v. Heyser, 75 I.D. 14, 18 (1968).
24. U.S. v. Oregon, 295 U.S. 1 (1935).
25. Oklahoma v. Texas, 261 U.S. 345 (1923).
26. Bougeois v. U.S., 545 F.2d 727, 730 (Ct. Cl. 1976).
27. Lawrence F. Baum, 67 IBLA 239 (1982).
28. Sam K. Viersen, Jr., 72 ID 251 (1965).
29. James L. Harden, 15 IBLA 187 (1974).

GRANTS OF SWAMP AND OVERFLOWED LANDS

Introduction

The Act of March 2, 1849 (9 Stat. 352) granted all public domain swamp and overflowed lands to the State of Louisiana for reclamation purposes. The Act of September 28, 1850 (9 Stat. 579) extended this grant to Alabama, California, Florida, Illinois, Mississippi, Missouri, Ohio, Indiana, Iowa, Michigan and Wisconsin. Minnesota and Oregon were later included in this grant by the Act of March 12, 1860. These grants included all swamp and overflowed lands which at the date of the granting Act were unappropriated public domain. Also at the date of the Act, these lands were required to be unfit for agriculture without construction of levees or drainage canals.

Mineral Lands Not Excluded from Swamp Land Grant

The Supreme Court[1] has held that mineral lands were not excluded from the Swamp land grant to Louisiana, and the Secretary could not refuse to issue a patent to such land pending his determination of mineral character.

References - Grants of Swamp and Overflowed Lands

1. Work v. Louisiana, 269 U.S. 250 (1925)

PUBLIC LAND SURVEYS

Introduction

Public land surveys are essential for proper management and identification of the public domain. These surveys establish, on the ground, boundaries of subdivisions of the public lands in units that can easily be identified and recorded on official field notes and plats. At one time the public domain included approximately 1.8 billion acres or about 78 percent of the total land area of the continental United States. Thus far, approximately 1.3 billion acres of land have been surveyed by the rectangular system of surveys. As of 1970, approximately 460 million acres remained to be surveyed.

The Bureau of Land Management was established in the Department of the Interior on July 16, 1946. The functions of the General Land Office were then placed in the new Bureau of Land Management. The Cadastral Survey program, administered by the BLM, includes branch offices responsible for field surveys in each of the BLM state offices. The Cadastral Survey creates or reestablishes marks and defines boundaries of tracts of land. The components of a cadastral survey include (1) field note record of the observations, (2) monuments, and (3) plat of the survey. From time to time, the public lands may be resurveyed at the discretion of the Director of the BLM; however, after the United States passes title, the survey is permanent and may not be changed.

Original Public Domain Land Was Surveyed

The original public domain was acquired by the Federal Government by cession from the states, treaty and purchase. This original public domain land is now embraced by the states of Alabama, Alaska, Arizona, Arkansas, California, Colorado, Florida, Idaho, Illinois, Indiana. Iowa, Kansas, Louisiana, Michigan, Minnesota, Mississippi, Missouri, Montana, Nebraska, Nevada, New Mexico, North Dakota, Oklahoma, Ohio, Oregon, South Dakota, Utah, Washington, Wisconsin and Wyoming. The rectangular system of surveys has been extended or is now in progress over this area and is the basis for the identification, administration and disposal of the public lands. The rectangular system of surveys is the basic cadastral reference system for all states except for 18 eastern states and the States of Hawaii and Texas.

Definition of Resurvey

A **resurvey** is a reconstruction of land boundaries and subdivision accomplished by rerunning and re-marking the lines represented in the field note record or on the plat of a previous official survey.

Original Survey Controls Over More Accurate Resurvey

After a tract of land has been resurveyed and patented by the United States, a subsequent and more accurate survey does not affect ownership boundaries.[1] Although the United States may resurvey the lands it owns and reestablish boundaries, such resurveys are only done for its own information and cannot affect the rights of owners on the other side of the line established by prior survey.[2] Therefore, where two surveys conflict, the senior survey controls.[3]

The Interior Department has no power to correct errors in a survey of the public lands after the lands have been sold to purchasers in good faith. The only remedy to such a mistake is for the Government to initiate a suit in the courts.[4]

Mineral Segregation Surveys

Mineral segregation surveys are made to delineate the boundary between public land and one or more claims by a metes-and-bounds survey. This is not to be confused with a mineral survey as the mineral segregation survey is made only where there is insufficient information to properly segregate mining claims from nonmineral public land. Mineral segregation surveys are generally initiated by two circumstances: (1) the official mineral survey is faulty; and (or) unsurveyed mining claims must be segregated because of a pending administrative action.

Protracted Surveys

The Bureau of Land Management has developed a system for protracted surveys to augment the public land survey system. Protracted surveys consist of lines drawn on maps that follow the public land survey system but are not based on a field survey with monumentation. The purpose of the protracted surveys is to provide a means for recording actions concerning the public lands and also provide a basis for land management. Although eventually lands under protracted surveys will be given an official survey, the Federal Government, in the meantime, is able to issue mineral leases for the vast unsurveyed areas in such states as Alaska.

Monuments Control Over Description

The purpose of monumentation of a survey is to fix the corner positions so the position of the survey may be indefinitely known.

11

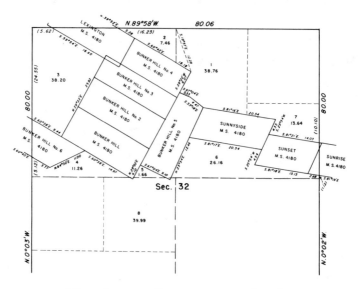

Mineral segregation survey; note that the outer perimeter of the claim group is surveyed by a metes and bounds survey.

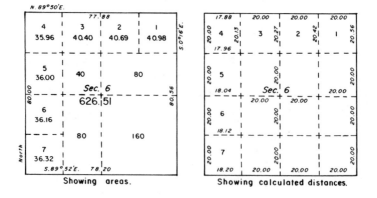

Showing areas.　　Showing calculated distances.

Examples of subdivision by protraction (from *Manual of Survey Instructions*, 1973, Bureau of Land Management).

The position and existence of monuments have been given considerable legal significance by the courts. The best evidence of the location of a corner is the corner monument. Field survey monuments are given controlling preference over the recorded direction and lengths of lines as shown by the official plat and field notes.[5]

Monuments Control Over Description with Mining Claims

Where a discrepancy exists, it is a well established general rule that the position of the monuments on the ground prevails over the description of the claim on the location notice. This same rule applies in a mineral patent where the position of the mineral monuments controls over the patent description.[6]

Location Monument

When a mineral survey is situated in a district where there is no corner of the public survey and no other monument within 2 miles, a location monument is established. The site, when practicable, should be some prominent point, visible from every direction, where the permanency of the monument will not be endangered by snow, rock, or land movements or other natural causes.

The monument consists of an iron post similar to the type used for rectangular surveys or a stone not less than 30 inches long, 20 inches wide, and 6 inches thick, set three-fourths in the ground. The letters "USLM" followed by the number of the survey are marked on the brass cap or plainly chiseled upon the stone. The exact reference point is indicated on the top of the monument by a cross.

Specification for Monuments

The Bureau of Land Management has authorized that a special post be used to monument public surveys. The post consists of a zinc-coated iron pipe, 30 inches in length with an outside diameter of 2.5 inches. A brass cap is fastened to the top and the bottom is split. Brass tablets are also attached to rock outcrops and set in concrete monuments. The tablet is 3.25 inches thick and 3.5 inches long. Under certain conditions deviations from the standard monument may be allowed.

Miscellaneous Types of Monuments

A **reference monument** is used where a monument cannot be established because of potential destruction such as on a road bed. The site of the true corner will be marked and at least two reference monuments will be established outside the roadway.

13

A **witness point** has no particular relation to a regular corner; it is a monumental station on a line of survey used to mark an important position.

Tree Monuments - If the true point of a corner is occupied by a living tree, the tree is made the monument. If the tree is too small to be marked, it is removed.

Corners

A **witness corner** is established only under circumstances where it is not practical to position the monument at the site of the corner. The witness corner is monumented and generally placed as closely as possible to the corner and on a line of the survey. The terms corner and monument are not synonymous. A "**corner**" is a point established by a survey; whereas, a "**monument**" is the physical structure such as a pot or pipe which marks the corner.

Marks on Monuments

A **brass cap monument** is marked so that it must be read while standing on the south side of the monument. The year the monument was positioned is marked on the south side. Section or township boundaries are indicated by grooves on the surface of the brass cap and the appropriate section, townships and ranges are marked on the plate in their proper position relative to the boundary lines.

Marks on **stone monuments** are cut on the exposed faces or sides of the stone - never on its top or end. In section corners located along the boundary of the township, the notches and grooves give the number of miles to the adjoining township corners. All other section corners in the township give the number of miles from the monument to the south and east boundaries of the township.

Approval of Plat and Field Notes

The public lands are not considered surveyed or identified until approval of the survey and filing of the plat in the administering land office by direction of the Bureau of Land Management.[7] Once the plat and field notes are approved, in matters involving disposal or sale of the surveyed lands, the surveys are conclusive and binding on all parties concerned, including the Government.[8]

Survey Plat

The survey plat is a drawing which represents the lines surveyed, established, or resurveyed, showing the bearing and length of each line. Also shown are the description of the boundaries and

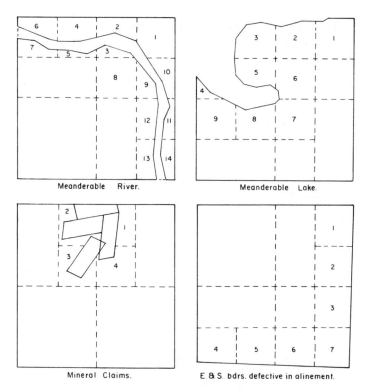

Examples of Subdivision of fractional sections (from *Manual of Survey Instructions,* 1973, Bureau of Land Management).

Marks on old stone section corners; the grooves indicate the number of miles from the south and east boundaries of the township, respectively. *Restoration of Lost or Obliterated Corners,* 1974, Bureau of Land Management.

Legend of markings common to all monuments:

AM	Amended Monument	R	Range
AMC	Auxiliary Meander Corner	RM	Reference Monument
AP	Angle Point	S	Section
BO	Bearing Object	S	South
BT	Bearing Tree	SC	Standard Corner
C	Center	SE	Southeast
CC	Closing Corner	SMC	Special Meander Corner
E	East	SW	Southwest
EC	Electronic Control	T	Township
LM	Location Monument	TR	Tract
M	Mile	W	West
MC	Meander Corner	WC	Witness Corner
N	North	WP	Witness Point
NE	Northeast	¼	Quarter Section
NW	Northwest	1/16	Sixteenth Section

Examples of Section Corner Marks

Standard Township corner:

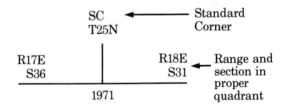

Closing Township corners:

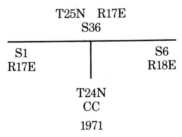

16

Corners common to four townships:

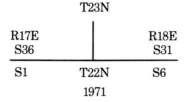

T23N

R17E		R18E
S36		S31
S1	T22N	S6

1971

Corners common to two townships:

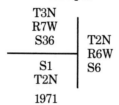

T3N
R7W
S36 | T2N
| R6W
S1 | S6
T2N

1971

Corners referring to only one township:

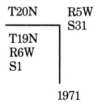

T20N R5W
        S31
T19N
R6W
S1

1971

Standard section corners:

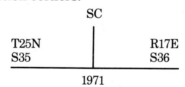

SC

| T25N | | R17E |
| S35 | | S36 |

1971

Closing section corners:

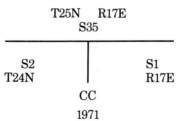

T25N R17E
   S35

| S2 | | S1 |
| T24N | | R17E |

CC

1971

17

Corners common to four sections:

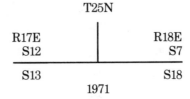

T25N

R17E		R18E
S12		S7
S13		S18

1971

Section corners common to two sections:

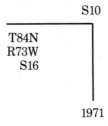

T27N		R17W
S31		S32
T26N		R17W

S6

1971

Section corners referring to one section only:

S10

T84N
R73W
S16

1971

Standard quarter-section corners:

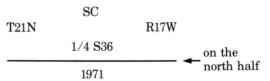

SC

T21N · R17W

1/4 S36

◄ on the north half

1971

Manual of Surveying Instructions 1973 at 109-112.

18

area of each tract of land including the relationship to contiguous official surveys. Topography and cultural features may be shown where practical.

Field Notes

The field notes are the written record of the survey. This record identifies and describes the lines and corners of the survey and the procedures by which they were established or reestablished. The new subdivisions to be platted (or replatted in the case of some resurveys) and the quantity of land in each unit are derived from the field notes.

Field Notes and Plat as Evidence

The subdivisions are based upon and are defined by the monuments and other evidences of the controlling official survey. As long as these evidences are in existence, the record of the survey is an official exhibit and, presumably, correctly represents the actual field conditions. If there are discrepancies, the record must give way to the evidence of the corners in place. In the absence of evidence, the field notes and plat are the best means of identification of the survey and they will retain this purpose. In the event of a resurvey they provide the basis for the dependent method and the control for the fixation of the boundaries of alienated lands by the independent method.

Original Survey Plats Maintained by BLM

The original plats of survey are maintained on 35 mm aperture cards and held in the various state offices of the Bureau of Land Management. Paper copies of the microfilm may be purchased at a moderate price. The original township survey plat should not be confused with the master title plats or other survey plats. The master title plat is a composite of all the survey plats for a given township but is not a "survey" plat. It will also contain special surveys, mineral surveys, homestead surveys as well as many other types of surveys.

References - Public Land Surveys

1. State of New Mexico v. State of Colorado, 267 U.S. 582.
2. Lane v. Darlington, 249 U.S. 331, 333 (1919).
3. U.S. v. Doyle, 468 F.2d 633 (CA colo 1972).
4. Murphy v. Kirwan, 103 F. 104 (CC Minn 1900).
5. Sala v. Crane, 221 P. 556 (1923), error dismissed 267 U.S. 585.
6. Cardoner v. Stanley Consol. Mining & Milling Co., 193 F. 517 (CC Idaho 1911).
7. U.S. v. Cowlinshaw, 202 Fed. 317 (1913).
8. Mann v. Tacoma Land Co., 44 F. 27 (CC Wash 1980), affirmed 153 U.S. 273.

caused because of the existence of meanderable bodies of water or mineral claims. In order to make as many sections as possible represent square miles or 640 acres, north-south lines parallel to the east boundary of the township and at intervals of one mile are surveyed successively from east to west.

East-west lines parallel to the south boundary of the township and at intervals of one mile are surveyed successively from south to north. Thus if the township is not six miles square, the excess or deficiency is added to or deducted from the six sections along the northern boundary and the six sections along the western boundary of the township. So if there is an excess or deficiency area along these boundaries, 25 sections may each contain 640 acres and 11 sections may each contain more or less than 640 acres. Along the boundary where an excess or deficiency of acreage occurs, the area is lotted so as to provide a maximum number of aliquot parts (40-, 80-, and 160-acre parcels). Lots are numbered counterclockwise within a single section, beginning in the northeast part of the section. The total acreage is given in each lot, generally slightly more or less than 40 acres at west and north boundary corrections. Fractional sections, which are invaded by meanderable bodies of water or by approved mining claims which do not conform to regular legal subdivisions, are also lotted.

Subdivision of Townships

The square mile, or section, is the unit of subdivision of a township. The normal township includes 36 sections of which only 25 contain 640 acres each. Sections against the north and west boundaries, except section 6, contain regular aliquot parts totaling 480 acres. The balance of these sections consists of a row of four fractional lots along the township boundary.

The amounts by which a section or its aliquot parts may vary from the ideal section (which is a square 5,280 feet on each side) and still be considered regular are referred to as the rectangular limits. For alignment the section's boundaries must not exceed 21 feet from cardinal in any part, nor may the opposite boundaries vary more than 21 feet. The distance between corners, to be normal, must not exceed 25 links in 40 chains.

The south boundary of a township is generally the controlling latitudinal boundary, except where such boundary has a defective alignment. New corners are established by starting at the southeast corner of the township and are placed at regular intervals of 40 chains, counting from east to west. The excess or deficiency is placed in the west half mile. A sectional correction line is established if the south boundary is defective.

20

TERMINOLOGY USED IN PUBLIC LAND SURVEYS

Initial Points - There are 37 independent initial points in the United States, each of which serves as the origin for public land surveys. The principal meridians and base lines originate from the initial points.

Principal Meridian - The Principal meridian coincides with the true meridian, extending both north and south in both directions from the initial point. There are 36 principal meridians in the United States.

Base Line - The base line extends both east and west from the initial point on a true parallel of latitude crossing the principal meridian at right angles.

Standard Parallels - Standard parallels or correction lines are east-west lines, parallel to the base line and placed at intervals of 24 miles both north and south of the base line; they correct for convergence at the north and south poles.

Guide Meridians - Guide Meridians are north-south lines, parallel to the principal meridian and placed at intervals of 24 miles both east and west of the principal meridian.

Township Lines - Township lines are east-west lines parallel to the base line and the standard parallels. Township lines are placed at intervals of six miles and are numbered to the east or west beginning with number 1 at the base line.

Range Lines - Range lines are north-south lines parallel to the principal meridian and guide meridians. Range lines are placed at intervals of six miles and are numbered to the east or west beginning with number 1 at the principal meridian.

Township - The primary limit of the rectangular survey is the township, six miles square. Townships are subdivided into 36 sections by placing parallel lines through the township from south to north and from east to west at intervals of one mile. The sections are numbered beginning with number 1 in the northeast section and proceeding west and east alternately through section 36.

Section - A section consists of one mile square or 640 acres. It is divided into quarter sections by straight lines connecting established quarter-section corners on opposite boundaries. Eight monuments are placed on each section - one on each corner and one midway between corners along the boundary lines.

Lots - Lots are fractional units caused by correction of survey error along the western and northern borders of the township or

The east boundary of a township is generally the governing meridional boundary, except where it is defective in alignment. New corners of the sections of the township are established by county from south to north along the eastern boundary of the township at 40 chain intervals. A sectional guide meridian is required if the east boundary is defective in alignment.

The purpose of the above procedure is to establish the maximum number of normal sections that do not need to be lotted.

Subdivision of Sections

Under the general land laws, the unit of administration is the quarter-quarter section of 40 acres. However, sections are not subdivided in the field by the Bureau of Land Management cadastral surveyor except under special circumstances. However sections are commonly subdivided upon the official plat by protraction.

Subdivision by Protraction

Boundaries of quarter sections are shown on the plat by broken straight lines connecting the opposite quarter-section corners. With the exception of section 6, sections which are bounded by the north or west boundary of a normal township are subdivided by protraction into two regular half-quarter sections and four lots. Section 6 has 7 lots protracted against both the north and west boundaries.

Along the northern and western boundaries of the section, lots are numbered consecutively from east to west and from north to south, beginning with lot No. 1 at the east or north corner of each section. The lots in section 6 are numbered starting with No. 1 in the northeast, then progressing in a counterclockwise direction to No. 7 in the southwest corner of the section.

Sections containing meanderable water bodies or approved claims which do not fit regular legal subdivisions are subdivided by protraction into regular and fractional parts. The lines subdividing the section are terminated at the meander line or claim boundary. In general, fractional sections are subdivided so as to contain as many aliquot parts as possible.

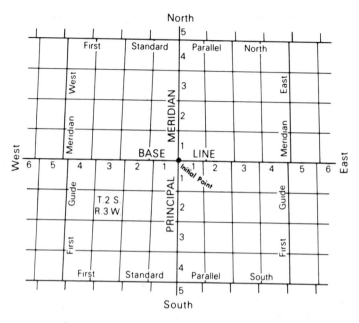

Survey of quadrangles, each embracing 16 townships bounded by standard lines, showing the coordinate system of numbering townships.

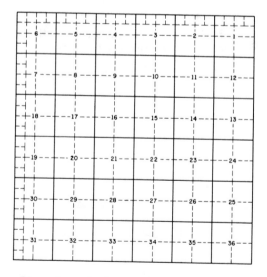

Plan of numbering sections in a township.

23

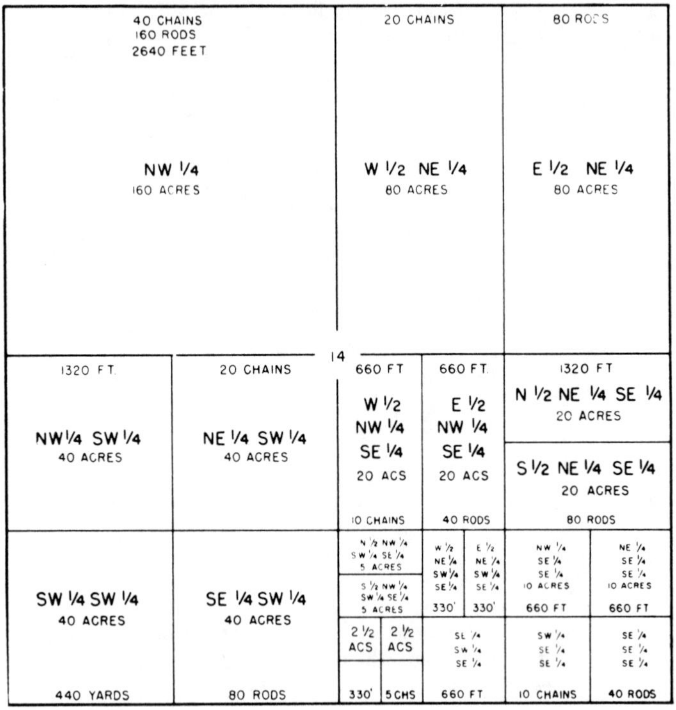

40 CHAINS
160 RODS
2640 FEET

20 CHAINS

80 RODS

NW 1/4
160 ACRES

W 1/2 NE 1/4
80 ACRES

E 1/2 NE 1/4
80 ACRES

14

1320 FT.

20 CHAINS

660 FT

660 FT.

1320 FT

NW1/4 SW1/4
40 ACRES

NE 1/4 SW 1/4
40 ACRES

W 1/2
NW 1/4
SE 1/4
20 ACS

E 1/2
NW 1/4
SE 1/4
20 ACS

N 1/2 NE 1/4 SE 1/4
20 ACRES

S 1/2 NE 1/4 SE 1/4
20 ACRES

10 CHAINS

40 RODS

80 RODS

SW 1/4 SW 1/4
40 ACRES

SE 1/4 SW 1/4
40 ACRES

N 1/2 NW 1/4
SW 1/4 SE 1/4
5 ACRES

S 1/2 NW 1/4
SW 1/4 SE 1/4
5 ACRES

2 1/2
ACS

2 1/2
ACS

W 1/2
NE 1/4
SW 1/4
SE 1/4

E 1/2
NE 1/4
SW 1/4
SE 1/4
330'

SE 1/4
SW 1/4
SE 1/4

NW 1/4
SE 1/4
SE 1/4
10 ACRES

SW 1/4
SE 1/4
SE 1/4

NE 1/4
SE 1/4
SE 1/4
10 ACRES

SE 1/4
SE 1/4
SE 1/4

330'

330'

660 FT

660 FT

440 YARDS

80 RODS

330'

5 CHS

660 FT

10 CHAINS

40 RODS

Figure 11. Normal subdivision of a section with annotations showing how various subdivisions are described.

24

WRITING LEGAL DESCRIPTIONS

Description of lands within the scope of the public-land rectangular surveys should conform to the accepted nomenclature of that system, citing the name of the proper reference meridian, the appropriate township and range numbers and, where necessary, the section and sectional subdivisions shown upon the official plat of survey. Each reference meridian has its own base line; and, therefore, the words "and base line" are usually omitted. The name of the reference meridian should be spelled in full. If the lands have not been surveyed, the description should conform to the legal subdivisions that will, when established, include the lands.

Abbreviations

When used in a narrative, such words as township, range, section, north, south, east, etc. may be written in full, but when such words are used in a land description, they should be abbreviated and capitalized as follows:

Township(s)	T., Tps.
Range(s)	R., Rs.
Section(s)	sec., secs.
North	N.
Southwest	SW.

If two or more townships are contained in a description and all the townships have the same number north or south of the baseline, the plural abbreviations "Tps." should be used.

Example: Tps. 4 S., Rs. 15 and 16 E.

However, the term "range" is abbreviated as singular or plural depending on the meaning.

Example: Tps. 2 and 3 N., R. 11 W.
Tps. 7, 8 and 9 N., Rs. 3, 4, and 5 E.

Preferred Order of Listing

In writing the description for a tract of land, the proper order of listing is to begin with the lowest numbered section in each township. First give the lot numbers in order, then the subdivisions within each quarter section, beginning in the NE, then NW, SW and SE in a counterclockwise manner.

The order for giving townships, if more than one is included, is determined by the range number; begin with the lowest range number. However, within each range, begin with the lowest township number.

Where townships must be described that are both north and
south of the base line and east and west of the reference
meridian, it is preferred that those northeast of the initial point
be described first followed by northwest, southwest and southeast.

Area

It is generally desirable to give a statement of the total land
area following the description. If the lands have been surveyed,
the acreage as given on the plats should be indicated. If the
lands were not surveyed, the approximate area should be given
in even acres.

The following statement should be used:

The area(s) described aggregate(s)_____acres.

Land Descriptions

Where NE¼NW¼ sec. 22 and SE¼NW¼ sec. 22, are included,
the resulting 80-acre unit can be designated E1/2NW¼ sec. 22.
In using symbols, the usual punctuation is omitted. Note that
the period is omitted after N, NE, S, SE, etc., and that there is no
comma and no space between symbols indicating a quarter-
quarter section (NE¼SE¼ sec. 10).

Sample Description

Lots 2 and 4, NW¼NE¼, S½NE¼NW¼, and SE¼, sec. 31, T.
3S., R.1E., Black Hills Meridian. The areas described aggregate
255 acres.
(Note: no space or comma between symbols indicating a quarter-quarter section.)

METES AND BOUNDS SURVEYS

Metes-and-bounds surveys are required to define the boundaries of irregular areas of land which are not conformable to legal subdivisions. This type of survey may involve mineral claims, small-holding claims, private-land grants, forest-entry claims, national parks and monuments, Indian reservations, light house reservations, trade and manufacturing sites, homestead claims in Alaska, or the like.

In a metes and bounds survey, a tract of land is defined by a description of its boundary. This is done by utilizing natural or artificial monuments located at the corners and along the boundary lines. The lengths and directions of the lines connecting successive monuments are the basis of the description. If the described tract makes a common boundary with an adjoining tract of land, then the adjoining tract should be identified by the name of the owner and the survey designation. The bearings and distances of the lines connecting the corners of a tract are given in order around the perimeter, with the final traverse indicating a return to the point of beginning. If the point of beginning is an established corner of an official survey, it should be described by corner and survey number or other appropriate designation. The latitude and longitude are given unless the beginning point is a corner of the public land surveys or connected by survey to such a corner.

Monuments

A monument may consist of a natural or artificial object located at a corner of the tract. Objects used as monuments include lakes, rocks, peaks, trees, fences, ditches, posts, pipe and the confluence of two rivers or streams.

Direction of Lines

The direction of a line is normally established by giving the angle from the meridian within one of the four quadrants. This direction or "bearing" of the line may be given from the north or south point, depending on the direction (north or south) that you take to describe the successive monuments.

Lengths of Lines

Horizontal distances are generally measured in land surveys at the mean elevation of the ground. In geodetic surveys, however, horizontal distances are adjusted to sea level. The foot unit is generally used in most metes and bounds surveys and in townsite and city subdivisions. The chain is the unit of length used in public land surveys although in certain special cases the meter is used.

Sequence and Closure

The bearings and distances of the courses connecting successive monuments or corners of a tract are given in a regular order. It is generally desirable to give each course on a separate line. If the course or corner of one tract should coincide with the course or corner of another, this should be specifically mentioned.

Point of Beginning

The position of a tract of land must be stated in relation to established natural or artificial monuments of known position or by stating its geographic position in terms of latitude and longitude. When possible, it is desirable to tie a corner of a tract of land to a cadastral survey monument by giving the direction and distance from a specific corner of the tract to the cadastral monument.

Natural and Artificial Boundaries

In certain cases, the boundary of a tract may be defined by streams, lakes, divides and straight lines connecting topographic features. Where a river is used as a boundary, generally the middle of the channel or one bank is made the boundary. If you face downstream, the bank on your left side is termed the left bank and the one to your right is termed the right bank.

If rivers, lakes and tidal waters are used as boundaries, the elevation or level of the water should be specified (e.g., mean high-water line, low water mark, mean high tide). Artificial monuments such as roads, railroads, and ditches are commonly used.

Area

It is a good practice to state the area of the tract in acres, following the description. For example, "the tract as described contains 35 acres."

Units of Distance Measurement

The law prescribes the chain as the unit of linear measure for the survey of the public lands. All returns of measurements in the rectangular system are made in the true horizontal distance in miles, chains, and links.

Units of Linear Measure
1 chain = 100 links = 66 feet
1 mile = 80 chains = 5,280 feet

Units of Area
1 acre = 10 square chains = 43,560 square feet
1 square mile = 640 acres

Examples of Metes and Bounds Descriptions

Example No. 1

Beginning at corner No. 1, a hemlock post, 4 in. square, 24 in. above ground, located on the Takotna Highway about 1/4 mile southeasterly from its intersection with the left bank of Kuskokwim River and in approximate latitude 62° 52′ N., longitude 155° 40′ W. Corner No. 2 of U.S. Survey 999 bears N.26° 59′ W., 327.6 ft.

From corner No. 1, by metes and bounds,
S. 25°43′ W., 1900 ft., to corner No. 2;
S. 57°30′ W., 3000 ft., to corner No. 3;
S. 32°30′ E., 830 ft., to corner No. 4;
N. 57°30′ E., 4000 ft., to corner No. 5;
N. 25°43′ E., 1650 ft., to corner No. 6;
N. 34°17′, W., 550 ft., to corner No. 7;
S. 85°38′ W., 871.6 ft., to corner No. 1, the place of beginning.

The tract as described contains 121.66 acres.

Example No. 2

Beginning at corner No. 1, on the south shore of Humboldt Harbor, at mean high tide, in latitude 55°19′12″ N., longitude 160°31′07″ W., from which U.S. Location Monument No. 1146 bears S. 79°32′51″ W., 28.44 chs. distant.

From the initial point
South, 13.44 chs. to corner No. 2, identical with corner No. 3, U.S. Survey No. 1400;
N. 67°41′ E., 15.93 chs. to corner No. 3;
North, 13.44 chs. to corner No. 4 on south shore of Humboldt Harbor at mean high tide;
Thence with meanders of Humboldt Harbor at mean high tide,
S. 70°26′ W., 2.60 chs.,
S. 0°15′ W., 1.50 chs.,
S. 59°31′ W., 1.50 chs.,
S. 73°02′ W., 5.00 chs.,
S. 75°22′ W., 2.50 chs.,
S. 77°39′ W., 3.90 chs. to corner No. 1, the place of beginning. The tract as described contains 18.65 acres.

SURVEY OF MEANDER LINES

The U.S. Supreme Court has stated many times that meander lines established by the cadastral surveys are not ownership boundaries, but are lines that delineate the banks of a stream or lake so as to determine the amount of water in the survey. When the bed of the body of water changes, by action of water, the high-water mark changes, and the ownership of the adjoining land migrates with it.

Meander Line

All navigable bodies of water, including important rivers and lakes, are segregated from the public lands at the **mean high water line or elevation**. A **meander line** may be defined as the traverse of the margin of a permanent natural body of water. Meander lines are run to determine the amount of land segregated by the water body. In order for a line to be called a meander line it must define the bank of a river or lake. The high water mark is the line which the water impresses on the soil by covering it for sufficient periods to denude it.

Meander Corner

A meander corner is established at every point where a standard, township, or section line intersects the bank of a navigable stream or other meanderable body of water.

Rivers

All rivers which have a right-angle width of 3 chains or greater (1 chain = 66 feet) are meandered on both banks, at the ordinary mean high-water mark. Shallow streams and/or intermittent streams that lack well defined channels or banks are not meandered even though the right-angle width may be greater than three chains.

Lakes

All lakes are meandered if they contain an area of 50 acres or more. Artificial lakes and reservoirs are generally not segregated from the public lands but such water bodies are delineated on the plat to show their true position. Shallow or poorly-defined lakes such as desert playas or lakes that occur seasonally from wet weather are not meandered, even if such water bodies include more than 50 acres.

Islands

All islands are meandered above the mean high-water elevation if they are surrounded by a body of navigable water. However, islands surrounded by a body of navigable water, but created after the state was admitted into the union, are not meandered. If an island was not part of the bed of a navigable body of water at statehood, the island remains public land, even though it may have been omitted from the original survey.

Marks on meander corners:

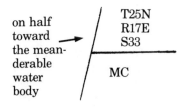

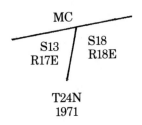

MINERAL SURVEY

Mineral surveys are used to delineate the legal boundaries of mineral lands on the public domain where the boundaries are established by lines that deviate from standard subdivisions and lots. All lode mining claims must receive a mineral survey prior to application for patent. Placer mining claims and mill sites must also receive a mineral survey if their boundaries are described by metes and bounds instead of by legal subdivision. A mineral survey should accomplish the following:

1. Monument the claim corners.
2. Witness the location in the field.
3. Show all conflicts with earlier surveys and other prior locations that should be excluded.
4. Show all workings on the claim.

Claims Requiring a Survey

A mining claim must be surveyed if (1) the claim is a lode location, (2) the claim covers land which is not surveyed in accordance with the rectangular survey system, and (3) the boundaries of the claim do not conform to the legal subdivisions of the rectangular survey system.[1]

If a placer claim is located on surveyed land and conforms to legal subdivisions, a mineral survey is not required. Even though the lands are surveyed, if the description of the claims does not conform to legal subdivision, a survey and plat must be prepared. Conversely, even if the lands conform to legal subdivisions and the area was not surveyed by the government, a mineral survey and plat are required.[2]

Sequence of Survey

The mineral survey and plat must be made after recordation of the notice of location as required by state law;[3] however, the survey must be completed and approved before filing the patent application.[4] And two copies of the plat and field notes must be filed with the patent application.

If Break in Chain of Title, New Survey Is Required

The official survey of a mining claim must be in accordance with the recorded notice of location as of record at the time of the order authorizing the survey.[5] So if there is a break in the chain of title to a claim after a mineral survey is approved, that survey could not apply to a relocation of the claim.

Cancellation of Surveys

Once a mining claim is patented, the survey can never be cancelled. However, if an unpatented mining claim is declared null and void through contest proceedings or is void for failure to comply with the recordation requirements of the Federal Land Policy and Management Act, it may be cancelled by the same officer of the BLM who approved the survey. The plat of survey is then annotated to show the cancellation.[6]

Survey Plat Becomes Official Record of BLM

A mineral survey, once recorded on a plat of survey and approved by the proper official, becomes an official record of the BLM. At any time after approval, the survey plat may be submitted with the patent application, so long as the lands described in the patent application are the exact lands covered by the mineral survey.

The original plat and field notes are maintained in the public room of the BLM and are available for inspection. Copies of these records can also be purchased.

Mineral Surveyor

The first step in the patent process is to secure a mineral surveyor. This is done by acquiring a list of approved and active mineral surveyors from the State Office of the BLM. Any surveyor on the list is qualified to conduct mineral surveys in all states. Fees, which may be negotiable, depend on many factors such as accessibility to the claim, existing survey monuments, vegetative cover, conflicts with other claims, workings, etc.

Ties to the Public Survey System

Ties are made to the public land survey, U.S. location monuments (formerly called mineral monuments), adjacent mineral surveys and conflicting claims. A solar or polaris observation is made to establish the true bearings of the claim lines. The corner of a location which is used to make a tie to a public survey corner is generally designated corner number 1, with the remaining corners numbered in consecutive order.

In areas where there is no corner of the public survey system within two miles of the mineral survey, a location monument is established. The site for such a monument should be a prominent point, easily visible from all directions and reasonably free from destruction by natural causes. The monument may consist of an iron post or a stone with the letters "USLM" followed by the number of the survey marked on the brass cap of the pipe or chiseled on the stone.

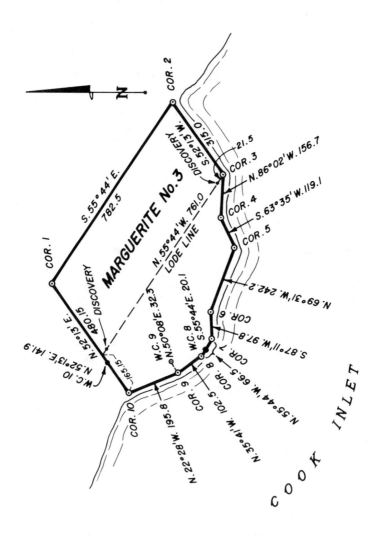

Mineral survey of a lode mining claim bounded on the south by a navigable body of water. *Mineral Procedures Guide,* 1980, Bureau of Land Management.

Survey Monuments

Monuments are established by sinking a 24 to 30-inch large iron post, ranging from 3/4 inch to one inch in diameter, in concrete. A brass cap, 2 inches in diameter, is placed on top of the pipe which is left approximately 12 to 16 inches above the ground. All monuments, whether claim corners or angle points, are numbered consecutively, beginning with number one. The mineral survey number as well as the claim number are given on each brass cap.

Mining Claims Bounded by Navigable Water

In a mineral survey where a mining claim is bounded by a navigable water body, it is proper to run such a boundary as a meander line and the field notes of the mineral survey should state that it is a meander line of the mean high water line and that the corners of such line are meander corners. However, the water line rather than the meander line is taken as the boundary of the claim when patented. Where one of the boundaries of a patented mining claim is a navigable body of water, all accretions formed after survey and prior to entry and patent of the claim pass under the patent. Furthermore, all accretions that form after patent become the property of the riparian owner.

If one entire end of a lode claim is delineated by a meander line, the end line is protracted parallel to the inland end line at the farthest seaward point so as to determine and qualify for extralateral rights.

References - Mineral Survey

1. 43 CFR 38611.1-1.
2. 43 CFR 3863.1(a).
3. 43 CFR 3861.1-2.
4. 43 CFR 3861.1-3.
5. Walter Bartol, 19 IBLA 82 (1975).
6. Add-Ventures, Ltd., 95 IBLA 44, 50 (1986).
7. Victor A. Johnson, 33 LD 693 (1905).
8. Alaska United Gold Mining Co. v. Cincinnati Alaska Mining Co., 45 LD 330 (1916)

PUBLIC LAND RECORDS

BLM initiated a new land status records system for most of the 16 western states in 1955. This system, which replaced the old tract books and status plats, consists of (1) a master title plat for each township (a status diagram at the scale of the survey plat, but not a survey plat), (2) an historical index for each township, and (3) use plats for each township. The new land status records have been recognized as the official records of the land offices by the administrative decisions of the Interior Board of Land Appeals. This land status system was not extended to the BLM Eastern States Office which serves the 13 easternmost public land states.

Each State Office of the Bureau of Land Management is the source of all records for that state regarding the title of Federal lands. This is also the source of information concerning public land surveys by the Cadastral Engineers.

Filing Documents with the BLM

The state offices of the BLM are open to the public for the filing of applications and other documents and inspection of records on Monday through Friday during regular business hours, except holidays. Applications and other documents may not be filed out of regular office hours.[1] Each office is furnished with a receipting machine for date-time receipting. When applications are filed in person during public filing hours, the exact date-time of receipt is stamped on the copies. It is a good practice when filing such documents as mining claim location notices or assessment work affidavits to get a copy of the filed instrument with the date-time stamp. Filings made before and after public filing hours are stamped when the office officially opens for filing. Most filings received during office hours are stamped with the date-time when received; however, mail filings received during closed office hours are stamped when the office opens.[2]

Types of Information

The BLM records system includes the following items: (1) ownership or master title plat; (2) historical index; (3) use plat; (4) serial register; (5) case file; (6) control document index; (7) survey records; and (8) status maps. The title and status records consist of 35mm microfilm aperture cards which have been filmed from the original master township plats. These cards are available for viewing on a microfilm reader in the public room of the state land office. If desired, paper copies made from the microfilm may be purchased at a nominal charge. A few states do not have these master title plats on microfilm; however, the title information may be obtained by inspection of plat books. Plat books are generally acknowledged to be more convenient to use during a title search than microfilm aperture cards.

Survey Records

The State Office of the BLM maintains survey records for all public lands in the state. The BLM also maintains survey and ownership records for the entire United States in Washington, D.C. Copies of the survey plat and related field notes are available for inspection or purchase by the public. Mineral survey plats and associated field notes are also available for inspection or purchase.

Serial Register Books

The **serial register** is a case control record consisting of loose leaf serial pages bound in volumes. It is a daily record of the applications received in the land office. These **serial registers** also show all the actions taken on each application including the issuance of a lease or patent. If the application is withdrawn or rejected, the records are so annotated.

The **serial register** was established on July 1, 1908, as a digest of each serialized case. It is maintained in the public room of each state office and is available for inspection by the public. However, should it be ascertained that any person is using the serial register books for improper purposes, access to the books may be denied to such person.

Serial Register Page

Each serial register page has a serial number which corresponds to a case file that contains all the documents that relate to a case. The serial page is prepared and filed in the register as soon as possible after the filing receives a serial number. A time lag of no more than one working day is the maximum allowed, except for filings subject to special procedures. Most BLM offices have serial register pages microfilmed and available for viewing or purchase of paper copy.

The serial number is a reference to a file which consists of a one or two letter prefix showing the office location and is followed by a number. On July 1, 1966, all state offices began numbering new cases consecutively starting with the number 1. Certain types of actions on a case require notation on the serial register pages; whereas certain cases do not.

Master Title Plat

A master title plat is prepared by first making a copy of the official township survey plat at a scale of 30 chains to the inch. However, the master title plat is not the official survey plat. The ownership or title information portrayed on the master title plat was collected from a variety of Federal documents, including withdrawal orders, patents and state selection lists. Microfilm copies of these documents are generally kept on file in the land office so that they may be inspected by the public and paper copies purchased, if desired.

The master title plat portrays the land which has been patented, with reservations, to the United States. This plat also shows withdrawals of all types (National Forests, Indian Reservations, rights-of-way, etc.) state grants, navigable waters, acquired lands, and, of course, vacant public domain land. The title information is shown by use of various weights and shapes of lines. Each action that affected title has a particular type of line that contains the affected area. The annotation, which gives the nature of the action, is placed within the bounds of the line and at the lower extremity of the area involved.

Supplemental Master Title Plat

The supplemental master title plat depicts a congested section or sections of a master title plat at a scale providing the greatest utility in the records to adequately and clearly reflect current status. The same notations are shown on the supplemental master title plat as would have been shown on the master title plat.

Use Plat

Information concerning temporary uses does not appear on the master title plats. Applications for mineral leases and permits are shown on use plats. Use plats are reproductions of the master title plats, containing all permanent title information, with the pertinent use information overprinted. For example, the boundary of the lands embraced by an application or lease will be shown on the plat together with the application or lease numbers. Generally, the land office maintains a special microfilm aperture card for each use, e.g., oil and gas leases, phosphate, geothermal resources, etc. No use plat will be maintained unless the township contains a mineral lease or application.

Historical Index

The historical index is an important tool for title history as it contains a chronological history of all actions that affect the use of or title to the public lands and resources within a township. This index shows all the transactions in any chain of title or change of status of the public lands. In addition, it contains material which will further explain or clarify annotations on the master title plats.

Mineral Location and Contest Index

The location and contest index is a listing, using historical index format, by township and range of (1) mineral location notices filed under special mining claim recording laws, (2) abandonments and relinquishments of mining claims secured by the Government, and (3) actions initiated to determine the validity of mineral, agricultural and other claims.

Case Files

Case files contain a record or copy of all the actions made affecting a given case. Generally each case has a summary sheet attached to show all the actions taken. Most BLM state offices have a card index by name of applicant to assist in locating case records.

Examination of Case Files by Public

As a general rule the case files are open to inspection by the general public. BLM procedure requires that a form be completed giving the date and identity of the person examining the file. This form is placed in the case file as a permanent record of the inspection. If a person wishes to review a case that has been sent to the National Archive Records, the requestor must write directly to the following address:

National Archives and Records Service
8th and Pennsylvania Avenue, N.W.
Washington, D.C. 20409

Control Document Index

The control document index consists of copies of patents and deeds which convey title to and from the United States. It also includes copies of documents which affect or have affected the availability of right or title to lands within the township. Copies of patents and other documents are on 35 mm film mounted on aperture cards. These cards are arranged by state, meridian, range,

SAMPLE TOWNSHIP PLAT

TOWNSHIP O SOUTH RANGE OO WEST

NAME OF COUNTY IN WHICH TOWNSHIP IS LOCATED.
IF THE TOWNSHIP IS LOCATED IN MORE THAN ONE COUNTY,
THE COUNTY NAMES ARE NOT SHOWN HERE.

COUNTY

NAME OF DISTRICT OFFICE WHERE LANDS ARE LOCATED,
AND DESIGNATION OF SECTION 3 OR SECTION 15 LANDS
AS DEFINED BY TAYLOR GRAZING ACT.

DISTRICT OFFICE SEC 3

LOT NUMBERS

ADA COUNTY   ELMORE COUNTY

SCALE in Chains

40

STATUS OF PUBLIC DOMAIN
LAND AND MINERAL TITLES

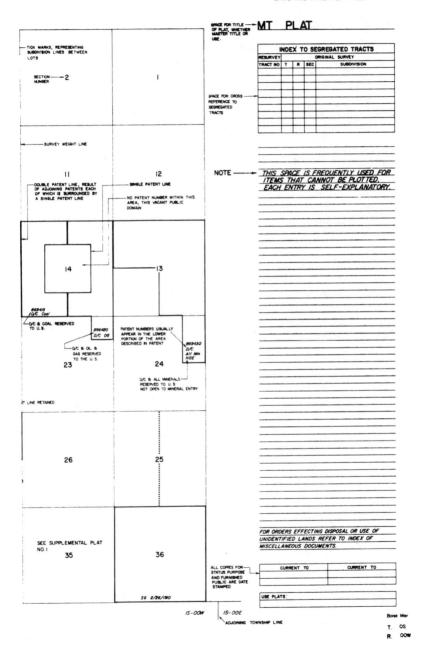

SPACE FOR TITLE → **MT PLAT**
OF PLAT, WHETHER
MASTER TITLE OR
USE.

INDEX TO SEGREGATED TRACTS

RESURVEY	ORIGINAL SURVEY			
TRACT NO	T	R	SEC	SUBDIVISION

SPACE FOR CROSS
REFERENCE TO
SEGREGATED
TRACTS

TICK MARKS, REPRESENTING
SUBDIVISION LINES BETWEEN
LOTS

SECTION ─── 2
NUMBER

1

SURVEY WEIGHT LINE

11

DOUBLE PATENT LINE, RESULT
OF ADJOINING PATENTS EACH
OF WHICH IS SURROUNDED BY
A SINGLE PATENT LINE

12

SINGLE PATENT LINE

NO PATENT NUMBER WITHIN THIS
AREA, THIS VACANT PUBLIC
DOMAIN

NOTE ───── *THIS SPACE IS FREQUENTLY USED FOR*
ITEMS THAT CANNOT BE PLOTTED.
EACH ENTRY IS SELF-EXPLANATORY.

14

13

063415
D/C Coal

D/C & COAL RESERVED
TO U.S.

896420
D/C OG

D/C & OIL &
GAS RESERVED
TO THE U.S.

23

PATENT NUMBERS USUALLY
APPEAR IN THE LOWER
PORTION OF THE AREA
DESCRIBED IN PATENT

24

063430
D/C
All Min
NOE

D/C & ALL MINERALS
RESERVED TO U.S
NOT OPEN TO MINERAL ENTRY

T LINE RETAINED

26

25

FOR ORDERS EFFECTING DISPOSAL OR USE OF
UNIDENTIFIED LANDS REFER TO INDEX OF
MISCELLANEOUS DOCUMENTS.

SEE SUPPLEMENTAL PLAT
NO.1
35

36

SG 2/26/1940

ALL COPIES FOR
STATUS PURPOSE
AND FURNISHED
PUBLIC ARE DATE
STAMPED

CURRENT TO	CURRENT TO

USE PLATS:

IS-00W

IS-00E

ADJOINING TOWNSHIP LINE

Boise Mer

T. 0S
R. 00W

41

township and chronologically within townships. This is the most important source of title documents necessary to support a chain of title.

BLM Records of Unpatented Claims

Section 314 of the Federal Land Policy and Management Act of 1976 (43 U.S.C. 1744) and the regulations published in 43 CFR Subpart 3833 require recordation of unpatented mining claims with the state offices of the BLM and the local recording office. To meet the demands of the recordation requirements and to improve efficiency , the BLM has installed computers in the state office that are tied into a data bank in BLM's Denver Service Center. Information on claims is available by serial number, township and range, name of the claimant and name of the claim. Now it is possible to examine up-to-date microfiche containing the basic elements of a mining claim title. The microfiche as well as copies of the actual case files may be examined either in the public room of the BLM state office or ordered for home or office review. For example, one may wish to monitor mining claims in certain geographic areas to determine if they are properly maintained under the annual filing requirements. With updated microfiche copies available every two or three months, it is now possible to ascertain that an area is open to mineral entry with a fair degree of confidence before expending exploration money or staking a claim. Of course, it is still necessary to examine local records because FLPMA requires filing location notices and annual filings with **both** the BLM and the local recorder.

Automated Land and Mineral
Record System (ALMRS)

In 1970 the BLM developed a plan to modernize and automate the public land record system. In July of 1982, the Director of the BLM signed an order to implement the Automated Land & Minerals Record System (ALMRS). The automation of this system is an enormous undertaking and is not scheduled for completion until 1991.

The automated system replaces the manual historical index and master title plat system of the western states and a comparable system in the eastern states. The system covers all land records activity where the Federal Government has an interest. For example, if the United States issued a patent to lands but reserved an interest in oil and gas, the retained interest would be covered in the new record system.

The system includes the automated examination of lands and minerals cases currently affecting the Federal title as well as use authorizations to determine if conflicts exist relative to the adjudication of a case. The possibility of conflicts should be lessened by the faster updating and better maintenance of status records. Many elements of a case are entered into the system to provide for case counting, statistical reports and case adjudication. The data in one case can be compared for conflicts against all other cases, land description, or status information in the system.

Computer generated master title plats will allow storage, retrieval and updating of geographic data and land status information in graphic form. All BLM offices will have the ability to retrieve and display both alphanumeric and plat graphics data. Land descriptions, land and mineral status and geographic position data will be available in a variety of formats including screen display, printing list, plotted map, and map display on a terminal screen. All of this information will be available to the general public at "user stations" set up in the BLM offices. Also, because ALMRS is a Bureau-wide system, files from one state will be available in another.

Products Available from ALMRS

The following types of products are available from the Automated Land and Mineral Record System:

1. Master title plats plotted on mylar or paper for a township, group of townships, group of sections or a section. Information is displayed on a graphics computer terminal with user control of scale, line type, shading and annotation.

2. Case counts by case type, pending action, and agency/organization where case is pending.

3. Progress reports and data summaries.

4. Case Abstract: A summary of the important elements of a case; similar to the serial register page.

5. Indexes: Four different indexes are now available for most cases; a case can be accessed in the computer by the serial number, geographic location and proprietor or owner:

    a. **Serial Register Pages:** The format is similar to the manually- typed documents previously used; however, more specific information has been added and the current status of each case is shown.

    b. **Location Index:** The location index is a list by township and range of every pending, authorized, patented and closed file in ALMRS.

    c. **Proprietor Index:** The alphabetical index of all

applicants, leases, assignees, etc., that are in the system. The index includes addresses, serial numbers, a brief land description and the case disposition.

d. **Serial Number Index:** This index is a numerical listing of all serial numbers in ALMRS. The index includes the individuals that have current interest in the case along with a brief land description and the case disposition.

Land Status Maps

A land Status Map at a scale of 1:5,000,000 is available for most of the western states in each state office of the BLM. Although this map may not be up to date and land status may be generalized, it is very useful for planning purposes. The BLM and Forest Service both have status maps for limited areas at a scale of one-half inch to the mile and one inch to the mile. These maps may be available at BLM district offices. The BLM also has status maps at a scale of 1:100,000 overprinted on USGS 15 minute quadrangles. These BLM Surface/Mineral Management Quads are available for sale at some BLM state and district offices in the area served at the cost of $2 per quad. Maps depict surface ownership in color and ownership of the mineral estate by line symbols and cross hatching.

County Land Status Information

The following county officials are standard sources of title information:

1. **County Recorder** - the county recorder maintains records of deeds, assignments, leases, mortgages, location notices and assessment work affidavits for unpatented mining claims.

2. **County Tax Assessor** - the tax assessor maintains records of land owners and addresses, land valuation and appraisal data and other tax-related information.

3. **County Planning Commission** - the planning commission is the organization responsible for administering zoning regulations and ordinances. Many counties require permits for mining activities.

State Land Status and Title Information

Most states have an agency or executive department responsible for maintaining title and status records on lands that are presently or were ever in state ownership. This includes ownership of mineral interests, easements, permits, use authorizations, leases, etc. Generally ownership and use plats are maintain in a manner similar to the master plats of the Federal Government. The following state agencies should be contacted for title information concerning state-owned lands:

Alaska
Department of Natural Resources
Division of Lands
323 E. 4th Avenue
Anchorage, Alaska 99501
(907) 279-5577

Arizona
Arizona State Land Department
State Office Building
Phoenix, Arizona 85007
(602) 271-4621

California
State Lands Commission
1020 12th Street, Second Floor
Sacramento, California 95814
(916) 445-5488

Colorado
Department of Natural Resources
Columbine Building
1845 Sherman Street
Denver, Colorado 80203
(303) 892-3451

Idaho
Department of Lands
State Capitol Building
Boise, Idaho 83720
(208) 384-3280

Montana
Department of State Lands
State Capitol
Helena, Montana 59601
(406) 449-2074

Nebraska
Board of Educational Lands and Funds
Box 4815, State Capitol Building
Lincoln, Nebraska 68509
(402) 471-2015

Nevada
State Land Register
Room 216, Nye Building
Carson City, Nevada 89701
(702) 885-4363

New Mexico
State Land Office Building
P.O. Box 1148
Santa Fe, New Mexico 87501
(505) 827-2881

North Dakota
State Land Commissioner
State Capitol Building
Bismarck, North Dakota 58501
(701) 224-2801

Oklahoma
Commissioners of the Land Office
of the State of Oklahoma
Room 101, State Capitol Building
Oklahoma City, Oklahoma 73105
(405) 521-2757

Oregon
Division of State Lands
502 Winter St., N.E.
Salem, Oregon 97310
(503) 378-3805

South Dakota
Commissioner of School and
Public Lands
State Capitol Building
Pierre, South Dakota 57501
(605) 224-3303

Texas
General Land Office
1700 N. Congress
Austin, Texas 78701
(512) 475-4303

Utah
Division of State Lands
Room 105, State Capitol
Salt Lake City, Utah 84114
(801) 328-5381

Washington
Department of Natural Resources
State Office Building
Olympia, Washington 98504
(206) 752-5317

Wyoming
Commissioner of Public Lands
and Farm Loans
·113 State Capitol Building
Cheyenne, Wyoming 82001
(307) 777-7331

References - Public Land Records

1. 43 CFR 1821.2-1.
2. BLM Manual 1274.13.

WITHDRAWALS

PreFLPMA Withdrawals

Withdrawals may segregate completely, partially, or not at all. The authority used to establish the withdrawal determines the amount of segregation that may be established. There are four general sources for preFLPMA withdrawals:

1. the implied Executive authority of the President;

2. the Pickett Act; and

3. Act of Congress authorizing withdrawals -
   a. in particular fields of activity, or

   b. for specific land to be used for specified
      purposes.

Implied Executive Authority

In 1909 President Taft withdrew as oil reserves more than 3 million acres of public lands from mining location using no statutory authority. These withdrawals were vigorously criticized by Congress as a usurpation of the legislative power by the executive Branch. However, Congress never did pass legislation to rescind the withdrawals. The courts have consistently held that the President has the right to withdraw lands from entry, settlement, or other forms of appropriation without consent from Congress. **U.S. v. Midwest Oil Co.**, 236 U.S. 459 (1914). And that withdrawals by the Secretary of the Interior have the same effect as those by the President.[1] This inherent right of the Executive also applies to withdrawal of public lands from appropriation under the mining law.[2]

The Pickett Act

The Pickett Act of June 25, 1910, as amended by the Act of August 24, 1912 (43 U.S.C. 141-43) was enacted as an outgrowth of the exercise of the "implied authority" used by president Taft. Congress felt the President needed authority to temporarily withdraw lands to protect the public interest; however, it believed that certain limitations should be placed on the President by restricting the amount of segregation to certain specific minerals. The Act provides that all such lands "shall at all times be open to exploration, discovery, occupation, and purchase under the mining laws of the United States, so far as the same apply to metalliferous minerals."

The Pickett Act has been used for numerous types of withdrawals. To determine the segregative effect of such a withdrawal, it is necessary to read the specific withdrawal order. For example, an order for a specific withdrawal may not withdraw the land from the location of non-metalliferous minerals even though the authority is available. Under the Pickett Act, mill sites on nonmineral lands in connection with metalliferous deposits may be located on withdrawn land. Section 704(a) of FLPMA repealed Presidential authority under the Pickett Act.

By Executive Order No. 9337 of April 24, 1942, the President delegated all his withdrawal authority vested in him by the Pickett Act and all other sources to the Secretary of the Interior. Executive Order No. 10, 355 of May 26, 1952.

Withdrawals Under FLPMA

In response to a growing concern over the lack of statutory guidance on withdrawals, Congress established a comprehensive withdrawal procedure in Section 204 of the "Federal Land Policy and Management Act of 1976." Because land withdrawals substantially limit the availability of mineral lands, the future direction of the Federal Government in this area is of great interest to those concerned with the management of mineral resources. Congress granted the Secretary broad withdrawal authority, including the explicit authority to withdraw land from the operation of the mining and mineral leasing laws. This authority is subject to Congressional control and a number of statutory requirements must be satisfied.

Publication of Proposed Withdrawals

Within thirty days of receipt of an application for withdrawal, and whenever he proposes a withdrawal on his own motion, the Secretary of the Interior shall publish a notice in the **Federal Register** stating that the application has been submitted for filing or the proposal has been made and the extent to which the land is to be segregated while the application is being considered by the Secretary. Upon publication of the notice, the land is segregated from the operation of the public land laws including the mining laws for two years from the date of publication of the notice, unless terminated sooner.[3]

Withdrawal Distinguished from Segregation

A published notice serves only to temporarily segregate the land from operation of the public land laws under 43 U.S.C. 1714(b); whereas, a withdrawal may be for a period of 20 years.[4]

Withdrawals Over 5,000 Acres

On and after October 21, 1976 (FLPMA), a withdrawal aggregating five thousand acres or more may be made only for a period of not more than twenty years by the Secretary on his own motion or upon request by a department or agency head. The Secretary shall notify Congress of such withdrawal no later than its effective date. Congress may terminate the withdrawal within 90 days by concurrent resolution. The Department of the Interior must also submit an extensive report to support the withdrawal.

Withdrawals Less Than 5,000 Acres

A withdrawal aggregating less than five thousand acres may be made by the Secretary on his own motion or upon request by a department or an agency head. Depending on the use, the withdrawal may be for a period of up to twenty years.

Emergency Withdrawals

When the Secretary of the Interior or the Congress determines that an emergency situation exists and that extraordinary measures must be taken to preserve values that would otherwise be lost, the Secretary shall immediately make a withdrawal and file notice of such emergency withdrawal with the Congress. Such emergency withdrawal shall be effective when made but shall last only for a period not to exceed three years.

Review of Existing Withdrawals

Existing withdrawals in the eleven contiguous western states must be reviewed within 15 years. Certain withdrawals are excluded from the review: (1) withdrawals of BLM and National Forest lands that did not close the land to mining or mineral leasing; (2) withdrawals of BLM and National Forest lands in wilderness, natural, primitive, or national recreation areas, regardless of whether the withdrawals closed the land to mining and mineral leasing; and (3) withdrawals of land within certain systems as of October 21, 1976 (Indian reservations, National Forests, National Parks, Wildlife Refuges, Wild and Scenic Rivers, and National Trails).

National Wildlife Federation Lawsuit: Injunction Affecting Withdrawal Revocations

On July 15, 1985, the National Wildlife Federation (NWF) filed suit in the District Court for the District of Columbia Challenging the Department's procedures for terminating, revoking, or modifying withdrawals or classifications of public lands. The District Court granted the preliminary injunction requested by NWF in a memorandum opinion dated December 4, 1985. **National Wildlife Federation v. Burford**, 676 F. Supp. 271 (D.D.C. 1985). In accordance with the direction of the Court, the Department had the injunction published in the **Federal Register**. 50 FR 51609 (Dec. 18, 1985). The Court stayed its injunction on December 19, 1985. 50 FR 52565 (December 24, 1985).

Subsequently, by memorandum opinion dated February 10, 1986, the District Court denied reconsideration of the injunction and modified the injunction to clarify that it only applied to Federal defendants, not third parties, and that terminations of classifications and revocations of withdrawals which had taken place since January 1, 1981, were suspended, not voided. **National Wildlife Federation v. Burford**, 676 F. Supp. 280 (D.D.C. 1986), aff'd, 835 F.2d 305 (D.C. Cir. 1987). Although the preliminary injunction was filed on February 10, 1986, it did not become effective until February 18, 1986. **Harold Bennett**, 107 IBLA 291, 294 (1989).

On November 4, 1988, U.S. District Court Judge Pratt ruled in favor of the Bureau of Land Management in the lawsuit. **National Wildlife Federation v. Burford**, Civil No. 85-2238 (D.D.C. Nov. 4, 1988). Judge Pratt vacated the preliminary injunction and dismissed the case on the basis that the National Wildlife Federation did not have standing to bring suit.

Where the above-mentioned preliminary injunction has the effect of suspending the termination of a withdrawal which segregated the land from mineral entry, a mining claim located before the effective date of the preliminary injunction (February 18, 1986) is not null and void ab initio because the lands are open to location. **Harold Bennett**, supra. Conversely, where a mining claim is located after February 18, 1986, on lands subject to the preliminary injunction, the claim is null and void ab initio. **Art Marinaccio**, 107 IBLA 303 (1989).

References - Withdrawals

1. Wilbur v. U.S. ex. rel. Barton, 46 F.2d 217, affirmed 283 U.S. 414.
2. Portland Electric Co. v. Kleppe, 441 F.Supp. 859 (DC Wyo 1977).
3. 43 CFR 2310.2(a).
4. Stephen W. Fox, 50 IBLA 186 (1980).

NOTING WITHDRAWALS ON
LAND RECORDS

Noting Withdrawals or Reservations on Federal Land Status Records

The noting of the receipt of an application for land action that would ultimately segregate the lands from entry on the tract books or official plats has the effect of temporarily segregating such lands from location, lease or entry under the mining and mineral leasing laws, to the extent that the withdrawal or reservation applied for, if effected, would prevent such forms of disposal. Action on all existing permit and lease applications would be discretionary; however, any mining claim in existence at the date of the records notation could maintain valid existing rights.

Once the lands are segregated from entry, lease and permit, applications are accepted for filing but are rejected through the adjudication process. Applications cannot be held pending the possible availability of lands in the future.[1] If lands are available for leasing, but are not notated on the public land records, a non-competitive offer to lease the lands must be rejected until the record has been rectified.[2]

Notation Rule Does Not Apply to Withdrawals After FLPMA

Withdrawal applications filed before the enactment of FLPMA are subject to the notation rule. However, section 204 of FLPMA (43 U.S.C. 1714) provides for a segregative effect to terminate in 2 years from the date of the **Federal Register** notice regarding the filing of a withdrawal application. Therefore if there is no acceptance or rejection of the application, the segregative effect automatically terminates at the end of the two year period, regardless of the notation rule.

Where a public land order, published in the **Federal Register**, revokes a withdrawal on a specified future date, the revocation is effective even though the BLM serial register page, master title plat and use plats and historical indices were not noted to show the restoration. In other words the "notation" or "tract book" rule does not apply in cases where lands are open to the mining laws at a future date specified in public land orders published in the **Federal Register**.[3]

Notation Segregates Even Though Application Defective

The Interior Board of Land Appeals has consistently held that the posting of an application to the records effects the segregation of the described land even though the application for the withdrawal was defective and did not comply with the regulations.[4]

Parties are Charged with Knowledge of Public Records

The Bureau of Land Management maintains an elaborate system of public records of the status of the public lands. The Board has held in many cases that "one who fails to inspect the status of public land in which he is financially interested is negligent at his peril, as he is charged with knowledge of their content."[5]

Notation Rule Upheld by 9th Circuit Court of Appeals

In **Shiny Rock Mining Corporation v. United States**, 825 F.2d 216 (9th Cir. 1987), the Court upheld the notation rule. Shiny Rock Mining Corporation had located claims in an area that was previously withdrawn from appropriation under the mining laws by a 1964 Public Land Order. The Court held that if the "the BLM records have been noted to reflect the devotion of land to a particular use that is exclusive of another conflicting use, no incompatible rights in the land can attach by reason of any subsequent application until the record has been changed to reflect the availability of the land for the desired use."[6]

Effect of a Withdrawal on the Materials Act

Most withdrawal or segregation orders close land to one or more of the following by express reference: the public land laws, the mining laws or the mineral leasing laws. Although there is a variety of other language used in withdrawals, it is very rare for a withdrawal order to specifically refer to the Materials Act of 1947.

A recent Interior Solicitor's opinion (July 28, 1988) stated that "any withdrawal or segregation that closes lands to the operation of the public land laws, and expressly includes the mineral leasing laws, should be construed to close lands to the operation of the Materials Act..." Furthermore, if the segregation is silent as to mineral leasing but has been construed to prohibit it, the land should be considered closed to the Materials Act also. Otherwise, withdrawn or segregated land remains open to the Materials Act.

Notation of Mineral Patent Application Does Not Segregate

The notation of a mineral patent application on the BLM records does not segregate the land from mineral entry.[7] The notation of an application on the proper BLM records has a segregative effect only a statute or Departmental regulation provides that the filing of the application segregates the land. **Scott Burnham**, 102 IBLA 363, 364 (1988).

References - Noting Withdrawals on Land Records

1. 43 CFR 2091.1.
2. R.E. Puckett, 14 IBLA 128 (1973).
3. Mary E. Brown, 62 ID 107 (1955); David W. Harper, 74 ID 141 (1967).
4. U.S. v. Foresyth, 15 IBLA 43 (1974).
5. U.S. v. Alexander, 17 IBLA 432 (1974).
6. Id. at 218.

EFFECT OF WITHDRAWALS ON LEASING

Withdrawals Closed to Leasing if Specified in Withdrawal Authority

Unless a withdrawal or reservation of public domain land specifically provides otherwise, the land withdrawn or reserved is presumed to be available under the Mineral Leasing Act of 1920, as amended.[1] The primary reason that most withdrawals are not specifically closed to the mineral leasing act is that the issuance of a lease is discretionary, unlike an appropriation under the Mining Law of 1872. Therefore, the Secretary may consider each lease application on a case-by-case basis.

Lease Offers on Segregated Lands Suspended Until Withdrawal Application Canceled

If a lease offer is filed while land has been segregated by a withdrawal application, the offer should be suspended pending final action of the withdrawal application. In the event the withdrawal application is canceled, the lease may be processed on its merits.[2]

Secretarial Discretion to Issue Lease

The discretionary authority of the Secretary of the Interior to refuse to issue oil and gas leases for public domain lands applies even where the lands have not been withdrawn from operation of the mineral leasing laws.[3] A decision of the BLM refusing to issue a lease will be upheld provided it sets forth the reasons for doing so and provided the background data and facts of record support the conclusion that the refusal is required in the public interest.[4]

Authority of Secretary to Cancel Lease

It is clear that the Secretary of the Interior generally has the authority to cancel any lease issued contrary to law because of the inadvertence of his subordinates.[5] An example of this occurred recently where lands that were currently embraced within a valid lease were erroneously offered in a simultaneous drawing. The Board[6] held that the lands were not available for leasing and that the second lease was void.

Lease Stipulations

BLM has the authority to require execution of special stipulations to protect environmental and other land use values when deciding to issue a lease. Rejection of a lease offer is a more severe measure than the most stringent stipulation. The record where leasing has been refused should ordinarily reflect that BLM has considered whether leasing subject to clear and reasonable stipulations would be sufficient to protect the public interest concerns raised by the surface management agency.[7]

As a general rule a stipulation should not be so restrictive as to preclude enjoyment of the lease. However, a no surface occupancy stipulation may be appropriate if it is justified by the record and the applicant is willing to accept it.[8]

References - Effect of Withdrawals on Leasing

1. Esdras K. Hartley, 54 IBLA 38 (1981).
2. Trent J. Parker, 49 IBLA 209 (1980).
3. Esdras K. Hartley, supra.
4. Cartridge Syndicate, 25 IBLA 57 (1976).
5. Boesche v. Udall, 373 U.S. 472 (1963).
6. Husky Oil Co., 52 IBLA 41 (1981).
7. Howard L. Ross, 49 IBLA 87 (1980).
8. Esdras K. Hartley, supra.

MINING CLAIMS
IN WITHDRAWALS

The Mining Law Does Not Apply to All Lands Owned by the United States

Although section 1 of the Act of May 10, 1872, is expansive in scope, declaring that "all valuable mineral deposits in lands belonging to the United States...shall be free and open to exploration and purchase," it has long been recognized that the general mining law does not apply to all land "belonging to the United States." Rather, "only where the United States has indicated that the lands are held for disposal under the land laws does the section apply; and it never applies where the United States directs that the disposal be only under other laws." **Oklahoma v. Texas**, 258 U.S. 574. 600 (1922).

Mining Claims on Withdrawn Lands Are Void

No property rights are created by the location of mining claims on lands that are not open to mineral entry and location, and such claims are void as a matter of law. No contest proceeding or hearing is required, and such claims may be declared null and void by a BLM administrative decision which is appealable to the Interior Board of Land Appeals. **U.S. v. Consolidated Mines & Smelting Co.**, 455 F.2d 432 (9th Cir. 1971).

Mining Claims Not Validated by Revocation of Withdrawal

Mining claims located on land withdrawn from operation of the mining laws are null and void ab initio and will not be validated by modification or revocation of the order of the withdrawal.[1]

Segregation from Mineral Entry without Mention of the Mining Laws

Pathfinder Mines Corporation (Pathfinder) located 22 lode claims in the Grand Canyon National Game Reserve in Kaibab National Forest on November 20, 1981. When Pathfinder recorded the claims as required by section 314 of FLPMA (43 U.S.C. 1744), BLM determined that the lands located were closed to entry under the mining laws and declared the claims null and void ab initio.

The Grand Canyon National Game Reserve was withdrawn by a proclamation dated November 28, 1906, by President Roosevelt pursuant to the authority given him under the Act of June 29, 1906. The proclamation, which substantially incorporates the provisions of the authorizing statute, makes no mention of whether the land is open to mineral entry.

The case was eventually affirmed by the Ninth Circuit Court of Appeals. In **Pathfinder Mines Corp. v. Hodel**, 811 F.2d 1288 (9th Cir. 1987), the Court stated:

The absence of an express withdrawal does not cure the fundamental incompatibility of entry under the General Mining Law with the protection and propagation of game animals. A tenuous inference from Congressional silence may not defeat the express purpose of the Preserve. Indeed, the IBLA has ruled (in this case and others) that game preserve lands are withdrawn from entry where full exercise of rights under mining laws would "jeopardize or impair or destroy the usefulness of the reserve as a wildlife refuge."

In a number of recent cases where there was no express reference to the withdrawal of minerals, the Interior Board of Land Appeals has consistently held that "the location of mining claims on such lands would be inconsistent with or might materially interfere with the purpose for which the land was segregated." **O. Glen Oliver**, 73 IBLA 56 (1983).

Mining Claims Located on Outer Continental Shelf

From time to time, there are attempts to appropriate lands on the Outer Continental shelf under the mining law. In **Ford Mac-Elvain**, 50 IBLA 303 (1980) the Board affirmed a BLM decision declaring 105 mining claims null and void because they were located on the Outer Continental Shelf. The Board said that claims for mineral deposits on the Outer Continental Shelf cannot be established under the general mining law because the Outer Continental Shelf Lands Act provides the exclusive authority for the development of minerals. 43 U.S.C. 1331-56 (1982).

Claimant Responsible for Knowledge of Withdrawal

Claimants are charged with constructive knowledge of the existence of withdrawals. BLM is not required to promptly check the legal status of every claim to advise locators they are on lands not open to entry under the mining laws. In **John F. Malone**, 89 IBLA 341, 344 (1985), the Board said the "BLM cannot be expected to promptly determine the legal status of each individual claim, considering the volume of records for unpatented mining claims it is expected to review."

Prestaking Mining Claims in Withdrawals

When a withdrawal is to be revoked, a notice is placed in the **Federal Register** giving the time, date and description of lands to be available. Where highly sought after lands are to become available, there are, in many cases, hundreds of locators attempting to locate mining claims over the same lands at the same time. In order to get an advantage or priority in right, many locators attempt to accomplish as much of the location work as possible before the lands are opened. The practice of prestaking is widely recognized as an unsettled issue in mining law.

Discovery Required at Withdrawal Date and at Present

Although the claim may have been valid in the past because of a discovery of a valuable mineral deposit, it must be shown, as a present fact, at the time of the hearing that the claim is still valuable for minerals. The loss of the discovery, either through exhaustion of the minerals, changes in economic conditions, or other circumstances, results in the loss of the location. [2]

Amended Location Relates Back to Prewithdrawal Location

In order to establish possessory rights to a mining claim predating a withdrawal, a claimant must be able to establish that a location that postdates the withdrawal date is an amended location rather than a relocation. This is because an amended location would generally relate back to the date of an original location only if no adverse rights have intervened. Withdrawal of the land subject to valid existing rights will not prevent the amended location from relating back to the original location; a relocation, however, will not relate back to the date of the original location because a relocation is in effect a new location.[3]

A location that was valid when the land was withdrawn cannot be enlarged by amendment after the date of the withdrawal.[4] To establish that a location is an amendment of a location made before a withdrawal, a claimant must show that the earlier location included that portion of the claim subject to the withdrawal. A claimant must also establish that the location predating the withdrawal was properly made, and that the persons making the amended location have an unbroken chain of title with the original locators.[5]

A hearing is required where there is a disputed issue of fact whether the interests of the present mining claimant are adverse to the interests of the prior locators (a relocation); or whether instead, the present owner was the successor to the earlier interest (an amendment).[6] Before a hearing is held, however, a claimant should be required to submit a copy of the location filed prior to the withdrawal date which the new location is said to amend. A claimant should also be able to establish an unbroken chain of title from the location which predates the withdrawal date and continues to the new amended notice of location.[7]

Section 38 Applied to Claims in Withdrawals

There is a provision of the mining law, 30 U.S.C. 38 (1976), under which a person who has held and worked his mining claim for a period of time equal to the time prescribed by the statute of limitations for mining claims of the state where the claim is situated is considered to have made a location.[8] The holding and working of a mining claim in open, notorious adverse possession for the period of time required to establish adverse possession of a mining claim while the land is open to mining location is regarded as tantamount to a new location or relocation. Under such a location there is no requirement for proof of location notices, recorded or otherwise.[9]

For example, if a withdrawal which closed lands to mineral entry was established on June 1, 1970, a claimant who did not have a location notice properly recorded prior to that date, might be able to establish that he had a valid existing claim at the date of the withdrawal. To do this, he would have had to have held and worked his mining claim for a period of time equal to the time prescribed by the statute of limitations for mining claims of the state where the claim is situated (generally 5 to 7 years). The entire period would have to run while the land was open to location. In addition, a discovery of a valuable mineral deposit must exist within each claim at the date of the withdrawal. However, if possessory title is to be based on 30 U.S.C. 38, a claim still must have been recorded with the BLM on or before October 22, 1979 pursuant to section 314 of FLPMA (43 U.S.C. 1744).[10]

You Cannot Drill or Excavate to Make Discovery

You cannot drill, sample, excavate or conduct any activities to make a discovery after the date of withdrawal. However, such activities may be allowed to the extent they "may tend to support an assertion that valuable deposits of minerals had been physically disclosed within the boundaries of each of the claims prior to that date.[11]

Assays and drilling may be allowed after a withdrawal to confirm a discovery made before the withdrawal.[12] It is still necessary for the mining claimant to show at the time of a hearing on the claim's validity that a discovery of a valuable mineral deposit was made as of the date of the withdrawal and had been maintained as a present fact.

The thousands of mining claims that exist within lands withdrawn from mineral location on December 31, 1983, pursuant to the Wilderness Act of 1964, will all be subjected to the requirement that a discovery be exposed within the limits of each claim as of December 31, 1983. Because any operations for future work on these will require an approved plan of operations, it is to be expected that the Forest Service will wish to verify the discovery prior to approval of such a plan. In the event a discovery is not verified, the Government would intitiate contest proceedings to invalidate a claim.

Loss of Option to Patent Claims Is Not Unconstitutional Divestiture

The case of **Freeze v. U.S.**, 639 F.2d 754 (Ct. Cl. 1981) involved a claimant who owned five unpatented lode mining claims with lands withdrawn as the Sawtooth National Recreation Area under the authority of the Act of August 22, 1972 (16 U.S.C. 460) also known as the Sawtooth Act. The Sawtooth Act expressly provides that, "Subject to valid existing rights, all Federal lands located in the recreation area are hereby withdrawn from all forms of location, entry, and patent under the mining laws of the United States." The Act further provides that, "patents shall not hereafter be issued for locations and claims heretofore made in the recreation area under the mining laws of the United States." Therefore, while the right of possession and enjoyment attaching to valid claims existing upon the effective date of the Act is expressly recognized and preserved, the ability to obtain patents upon unpatented claims is expressly denied.

The plaintiff contended that he suffered an unconstitutional taking by virtue of the denial of his ability to obtain patents upon the five unpatented claims which he held on the effective date of the Act, even though he had not initiated an application for patent by the date of the Sawtooth Act. The Court of Claims concluded that "at best, plaintiff has suffered a denial of the opportunity to obtain greater property than that which he owned upon the effective date of the Sawtooth Act. This cannot fairly be deemed the divestment of a property interest, save by the most overt bootstrapping."

References - Mining Claims in Withdrawals

1. Kelly B. Healey, 60 IBLA 115 (1981); David W. Harper, 74 ID 141 (1967).
2. U.S. v. Lee Western Inc., 50 IBLA 97, 98, 105 (1980).
3. R. Gail Tibbetts, 86 ID 538, 547 (1979).
4. United States Phosphate Co., 43 LD 432
5. R. Gail Tibbetts v. Bureau of Land Management, 62 IBLA 124 (1982).
6. U.S. v. Consolidated Mines and Smelting Co., 455 F.2d 432, 441 (9th Cir. 1971).
7. Grace P. Crocker, 73 IBLA 78 (1983).
8. W.E. Wicks, 14 IBLA 356, 359 (1974).
9. U.S. v. Guzman, 81 ID 685, 695-96 (1974).
10. U.S. v. Haskins, 59 IBLA 105, 106 (1981).
11. U.S. v. Gunsight Mining Co., 5 IBLA 62, 64 (1972); U.S. v. Porter, 37 IBLA 313, 316 (1978).
12. U.S. v. Foresyth, 15 IBLA 43 (1974).

FEDERAL ACTIONS AFFECTING MINERAL STATUS

Alaska Native Claims Settlement Act

The Alaska Native Claims Settlement Act[1] (ANCSA) authorizes the Secretary to withdraw from all forms of appropriation under the public land laws, including the mining and mineral leasing laws...up to, but not to exceed, eighty million acres. ANCSA provides that certain lands surrounding and adjacent to Native Villages are withdrawn, subject to valid existing rights, from all forms of appropriation under the public land laws, including the mining and mineral leasing laws, and from selection under the Alaska Statehood Act.

Mineral patent applications may continue to be filed after December 18, 1976, on land selected by village or regional corporations until the land is actually conveyed. ANCSA prohibits the filing of such an application after December 18, 1976, only if the land had been conveyed before the patent application was filed. Therefore, the statutory provision establishing the 5 year limit affects only conveyed lands, not lands which have merely been selected but not yet conveyed.[2]

Classification and Multiple Use Act

The Classification and Multiple Use Act of September 19, 1964[3] (78 Stat. 986), authorizes the Secretary of the Interior to review the public lands to determine which lands shall be classified as suitable for disposal and which lands he considers to contain such values as to make them more suitable for retention in Federal ownership. Publication of notice in the **Federal Register** of a proposed classification has the effect of segregating such land from settlement, location, sale, selection, entry, lease, or other formal disposal under the public land laws, including the mining and mineral leasing laws.[4] Mining claims located after the land has been segregated from appropriation under the mining laws by a notice of proposed classification under the Classification and Multiple Use Act of 1964 are properly declared null and void ab initio.[5]

Exchanges

Both preFLPMA and postFLPMA exchange applications segregate the land from appropriation under the mining laws at the time the formal application is filed with BLM.[6] Regulations issued pursuant to FLPMA provide for segregation of lands covered by an exchange proposal only upon publication in the **Federal Register** of notice to that effect and only for a period of 2 years from the date of publication.[7] A pending land exchange does not segregate the selected lands from availability for mineral leasing, regardless of whether the exchange application is filed before or after FLPMA.[8]

Indian Lands

Indian land ownership has been acquired by various tribes by treaty, act of Congress, executive action, purchase and aboriginal possession. Although the United States generally holds title to the reservations, the Indians have the right to use and occupy the land. Unless the Federal Government reserved mineral rights in the reservation grant, the general mining laws and mineral leasing laws do not apply to reservations.

Material Sale Contracts

Materials sale contracts do not segregate the land from mining location, but such locations are subject to the outstanding contract of sale.[9]

Military Withdrawals

Military lands are set aside for military and naval purposes and are normally not open to any of the public land, mining, or mineral leasing laws,[10] but a valid location made before the effective date of a withdrawal can maintain valid existing rights.[11] Lands that have been withdrawn or reserved for the use of any agency of the Department of Defense are not subject to leasing under the terms of the Mineral Leasing Act without the consent of the Secretary of Defense.[12]

Multiple Mineral Development Act

Prior to the Act of August 12, 1953 (30 U.S.C. 501), and the Multiple Mineral Development Act of August 13, 1954 (30 U.S.C. 521 et. seq.), mining claims located after the Mineral Leasing Act of February 25, 1920 (30 U.S.C. 181 et. seq.), for lands which were known to be valuable for such minerals were regarded as null and void ab initio. This conclusion was based on the rationale that a tract of public land could not simultaneously be subject to leasing under the Mineral Leasing Act and be subject to a valid mining claim, which would embrace all minerals. The basis for this is there was no authority to reserve the leasable minerals withdrawn from mining location by the Leasing Act.[13] The Multiple Mineral Development Act authorizes the location of mining claims on lands

63

covered by a mineral permit or lease, or application for permit or lease, or which are known to be valuable for leasable minerals. However, the leasable minerals are reserved to the United States in such a mineral patent.

For example, land which in 1946 was included in an oil and gas lease issued under the Mineral Leasing Act was not subject to mining location after that date. If there was no compliance with the Acts of August 12, 1953, or of August 13, 1954, mining claims located on such land are invalid.[14] When a mineral patent application is adjudicated, it is examined for compliance with the Acts.

The Act of August 12, 1953, applies to mining claims located after July 31, 1939, and before January 1, 1953, which were at the time of location on lands (1) included in a Federal lease or permit; (2) covered by application for federal permit or lease; or (3) known to be valuable for one or more of the Federal Leasing Act minerals. Such lands would be considered open to location under the mining laws if the owner of the claim had prepared within 120 days of August 12, 1953, an amended notice of location and posted a copy on the claim and filed a copy with the office of record. The notice must contain a statement that the notice is filed pursuant to the provisions of the act.

The Act of August 13, 1954, provides that any claim is validly located if located after July 31, 1939, and before February 10, 1954, on lands that at the time of location were (1) included in a Federal mineral lease or permit, (2) covered by an application for permit or lease, or (3) known to be valuable for leasing act minerals. In order to qualify under this Act, the claimant must comply with the following:

1. The owner of a mining claim filed before January 1, 1953 must have posted and recorded an amended location notice as required by Pub. L. 250.

2. The owner of a mining claim located after December 31, 1952 and before February 10, 1954 must have posted and recorded an amended location notice within 120 days of August 13, 1954. The notice must contain a statement that the amendment is filed pursuant to the requirements of Pub. L. 585.

Mining claims and mill sites (1) that were located between July 31, 1939, and February 10, 1954, and qualified under Pub. L. 250 and (or) Pub. L. 585, or (2) that were located after August 13, 1954 are subject, before issuance of a patent, to a reservation of all leasing act minerals. If patent should issue for any such mining claim or mill site, it should contain a reservation to lands which at the time of issuance of patent were (1) included in a permit or lease issued under the mineral leasing laws, (2) covered by an application for permit or lease under the mineral leasing laws, or

(3) known to be valuable for minerals subject to disposition under the mineral leasing laws.

It is possible to establish entitlement to a patent pursuant to 30 U.S.C. 38 if a claim were located while lands were under a mineral permit, lease or application for lease or permit. To do this a claimant, in recognizing that the initial location was void, would need to establish that he has held and worked his claim for a period equal to the time prescribed by the statute of limitation for mining claims of the state or territory in which they are situated. However, the land must be open to location during the entire period of time the statute of limitations is running. Evidence of such possession and working of the claims for such period is sufficient to establish a right to a patent under the mining laws.

Effect of P.L. 250 and P.L. 585 on the Validity of a Claim Location

Location Date of Claim	Validity of the Claim Location
Between February 25, 1920 and July 31, 1939.	Invalid location.
After August 13, 1954.	Valid location (because leasing act minerals may be reserved in patent).
Between July 31, 1939 and December 31, 1952.	Valid location only if compliance pursuant to Public Law 250.
Between December 31, 1952 and January 1, 1953.	Valid location only if compliance pursuant to Public Laws 250 and 585.
Between January 1, 1953 and February 10, 1954.	Valid location if compliance pursuant to Public Law 585.
Between February 10, 1954 and August 13, 1954.	Invalid location.
After August 13, 1954 even though covered by mineral lease, permit or application after the location date.	Valid location.

National Forests Open to Mining and Mineral Leasing Laws

Lands within the National Forests are subject to location and entry under the general mining and mineral leasing laws pursuant to the Act of June 4, 1897. Mining claims cannot be located on lands in national forests acquired under the Act of March 1, 1911 (16 U.S.C. 513-515), known as the Weeks Act. However, the Department of the Interior is vested with jurisdiction to convey title to lands within a national forest and to grant easements running with the lands.[15]

By the Transfer Act of February 1, 1905 (33 Stat. 628), Congress transferred administration of the forest reserves to the Department of Agriculture. After the transfer, responsibility for surveying and for all mineral entries within the forests remained with the General Land Office (now Bureau of Land Management).

National Parks and Monuments

Each national park has been withdrawn through a specific act of Congress. National monuments are established by Congressional action and Executive authorization. Many national monuments have been established by presidential proclamation under the Antiquities Act of June 8, 1906.[16] Lands in national parks and national monuments are generally not subject to mining location, except where specifically authorized by law. The Act of September 28, 1976, closed Crater Lake National Park, Mount McKinley National Park, Death Valley National Monument, Coronado National Monument and Organ Pipe Cactus National Monument to location under the Mining Law of 1872.

Lands in the National Park System are withdrawn from leasing, location, entry and patent under the mining and mineral leasing laws of the United States, unless the language creating the area specifically makes lands within the area subject to the mining laws.[17]

POWER SITE WITHDRAWALS

Pickett Act of 1910 Superseded by Federal Power Act

Many of the power site withdrawals established prior to the Federal Power Act of 1920, 16 U.S.C. 818 (1982), were accomplished under the authority of the "Pickett Act" of June 25, 1910 (43 U.S.C. 142). Because the Pickett Act provided that withdrawn lands "shall at all times be open to exploration, discovery, occupation, and purchase under the mining laws of the United States, so far as the same apply to metalliferous minerals...," many locators of metalliferous minerals in power site withdrawals contended that these locations were valid.[18] However, if claims were located after the Federal Power Act of June 10, 1920, which closed such lands to mineral location until enactment of the Mining Claims Rights Restoration Act of August 11, 1955, the claims would be null and void ab initio because the Pickett Act was superseded by the Federal Power Act.

The Federal Power Act provides that any lands of the United States included in an application for power development under that Act shall, for the date of filing of an application, be reserved from entry, location or other disposal under the laws of the United States until otherwise directed by the Federal Energy Regulatory Commission (FERC) or by the Congress.

Mining Claims Rights Restoration Act

The purpose of the "Mining Claims Rights Restoration Act" (P.L. 359; Act of August 11, 1955) was "to permit the mining, development, and utilization of the mineral resources of all public lands withdrawn or reserved for power development..." After enactment of the statute on August 11, 1955, such lands were "open to entry for location and patent of mining claims and for mining, development, beneficiation, removal and utilization of the mineral resources of such lands under applicable Federal statutes."

However, lands under license, permit or preliminary permit are not opened to entry by the Act.[19] Mining claims which were located before August 11, 1955, in a power site withdrawal were null and void from their inception and the Mining Claims Rights Restoration Act, did not operate retroactively to validate claims which were void when located.[20]

As a general practice, when a mining claim is recorded pursuant to the Mining Claims Restoration Act, the BLM adjudicator sends a letter to FERC to determine if the lands embraced by the location are under a license, permit or preliminary permit. If FERC reports that the claim is located within such an area, the adjudicator issues a decision declaring the claim null and void ab initio. The Board of Land Appeals[21] has held that even though the notice of the application for the permit, and application for a license was not made on the land office records of public land status, the claims must be declared null and void ab initio because they were located when the land was within the area under preliminary permit.

Recordation of Location Notice

The owner of unpatented claims located prior to the Mining Claims Rights Restoration Act of August 11, 1955, must record the location notice within one year of the date of the Act in the BLM state office that has jurisdiction over the lands on which the claim is located. However such a claim must have been located at a time when the lands were open to location such as prior to the effective date of the power site withdrawal.

The owner of an unpatented claim located after August 11, 1955, in a power site withdrawal must record the location notice within 60 days of the location date. For identification purposes only, the copy of the location notice or certificate, filed in the land office should contain a notation that it was filed under the act of August 11, 1955.[22]

Within 60 days after the expiration of the annual assessment year, the claimant must file a statement as to the assessment work done or improvements made during the previous assessment year.[23]

In **McDonald v. Best**, 186 F.Supp. 219 (DC ND Cal. 1960) the District Court held that the Mining Claims Rights Restoration Act of 1955 did not authorize forfeiture of mining claims because of failure of the claim owner to file for record in the land office within a year after August 11, 1955, a copy of the location notice of the claim. Although the Act required the filing of such notice within one year, it provides no penalty for failure to file. The Court then determined that actual notice is an adequate substitute for recordation.

Since the Federal Land Policy and Management Act of 1976 requires that a location notice be filed for record with the BLM within 90 days of the date of location, failure to notify the BLM is not a fatal defect. The 60-day period for prohibition of mining on placer claims starts when the BLM discovers that the placer claims is located in a power site withdrawal.

Options and Limitations on Mining

If a hearing is to be held, mining operations shall be suspended until after the hearing and an administrative law judge issues an order providing for one of the following:

1. a complete prohibition of placer mining;

2. a permission to engage in placer mining upon the condition that the locator shall, following placer operations, restore the surface of the claim to the condition in which it was immediately prior to those operations; or

3. a general permission to engage in placer mining.

The Milendar Cases

In **U.S. Forest Service v. Milender**, 104 IBLA 207 (1988), the Board affirmed in part, reversed in part and modified in part its earlier decision of **U.S. Forest Service v. Milender**, 91 I.D. 175 (1985). This most recent **Milender** decision represents a major interpretation of the Mining Claim Rights Restoration Act.

In these two cases, the Board reversed a long-standing Departmental interpretation of the Act of August 11, 1955. The presumption had been under earlier decisions that the Secretary under the Act could not limit or condition the claimant's right to mine thus engendering the term "unrestricted placer mining." If it were determined at a hearing that unrestricted placer mining would substantially interfere with the lands other uses and/or values, a complete prohibition of mining would be ordered.

The Board recognized that there is no such thing as unrestricted placer mining on the public lands of the United States. Today, placer mining statutes and regulations as well as judicial and administrative precedent restrict mining. The proper standard of evaluating the potential effect of placer mining on other land use is the extent to which legal, normal, operations, subject to regulatory restraint, might interfere with such uses.

General Permission to Engage in Placer Mining

The most liberal alternative under PL 359 is "general permission" to engage in placer mining. A "general permission" to engage in placer mining means that mining, development, beneficiation, removal, and utilization of the mineral resources of such lands are to be carried out under existing laws regulating such activities.[24]

Mining with Reclamation

Under Section 2 of the Mining Claims Rights Restoration Act, the Interior Department has the authority to precondition mining plan approval on the return of mined acreage to its pre-mining condition.[25] The issuance of an order requiring restoration of the surface to the condition that existed before mining may prevent the most damaging effects of mining precisely because the costs of conducting the clean-up operation would exceed any profit obtained. By requiring restoration, the Department forces the mining claimant to absorb certain environmental costs. His right to mine the claim is made subordinate to his obligation to restore the surface upon the completion of mining. The Board[26] also indicated that "no costs can be attributable to the ultimate destruction of the surface because the claimant is required to restore the surface to the same condition which existed prior to mining.

Prohibition of Mining and Substantial Interference

In determining whether placer mining should be allowed under PL 359, the United States must sufficiently establish such a substantial use of the land for uses other than mining which warrants a prohibition of mining.[27] But even should the Secretary find there to be substantial interference with other uses, nothing in the Act or in the legislative history of the Act prevents the Secretary from granting general permission to engage in placer mining, provided such an order be appropriate. Such an order would be appropriate when the competing surface use has less significance than a proposed placer mining operation. This requires that the importance of the competing interests be compared and judged on whatever grounds are relevant in the individual case. The question in each case must be whether the relative value of the land for full-scale mining can be calculated so as to exceed the value of the land for other purposes.[28]

Hearing Held to Determine if Placer Mining Will Interfere with Other Uses of the Land

The Act provides that the locator of a placer claim shall conduct no mining operation for a period of sixty days after filing of a notice of location. Upon receipt of a notice of location of a placer claim, a determination is made by the BLM on whether placer mining operations on the land may substantially interfere with other uses of the land included within the placer claim.[29]

If it is determined that placer operations may substantially interfere with other uses, a notice of intention to hold a hearing will be sent to each of the locators by registered or certified mail within 60 days from the date of filing of the location notice. If the claimant is not notified of a notice of intention to hold a hearing within 60 days of recording the notice of location, the BLM will probably take no further action on the case.

The mining claimant bears the ultimate burden of showing by a preponderance of the evidence that benefits resulting from placer mining outweigh the injuries caused by mining to other uses of the land. The Government is required to put on a prima facie case that placer mining will substantially interfere with other uses of the land and then the burden devolves to the claimant to overcome this showing by a preponderance of the evidence. If he or she is unable to do so, for any reason, placer mining operations may properly be prohibited.[30]

Bonding Where Mining with Reclamation

If a limited order (mining with reclamation) is issued by the Judge, the regulations require the mining claimant to provide a

70

bond. The amount of the bond is to be set for the purpose of assuring surface reclamation after mining is complete.[31]

RECLAMATION WITHDRAWALS

Section 3 of the Reclamation Act of June 17, 1902 (43 U.S.C. 416) provided for withdrawal of land for irrigation projects. Although these withdrawals segregated the land from mineral entry, the Act of April 23, 1932 (43 U.S.C. 143) authorized the Secretary of the Interior, at his discretion, to open reclamation withdrawals to mining location and patent under the general mining laws. Before locating a mining claim within a reclamation withdrawal, an application to open land to location must be made according to the procedure given in 43 CFR 3816.

First Form Withdrawals Closed to Mineral Entry

"First form" reclamation withdrawals made under the authority of the Reclamation Act of June 17, 1902, withdrew land from location, entry and patent under the general mining laws. Any mining claim located subsequent to the effective date of the withdrawal is null and void ab initio.[32] Withdrawals under the "second form" apply to those lands that are not needed for the construction and maintenance of irrigation works, but may possibly be irrigated from such works. Because "second form" withdrawals permitted homesteads, and since homestead lands were subject to mineral entry, all "second form" lands would be subject to mineral entry.[33]

Location Is Subject to Contract and Reservations in Patent

The Act of April 23, 1932,[34] authorizes the Secretary of the Interior, at his discretion, to open lands withdrawn under the federal reclamation laws to location and patent under the general mining laws if such lands are known or believed to be valuable for minerals. To protect the interests of the Federal government, the Secretary is authorized to reserve "such ways, rights, and easements over or to such lands as may be prescribed by him," and may require the execution of a contract by the intending locator before vesting in rights in him if necessary to protect the irrigation interest. Any subsequent location made on such lands shall be subject to the terms of the contract and (or) reservations and any patent issued shall contain a reference to the contract and (or) reservations.

Agency Processing of Application

When the application is complete as required by 43 CFR 3816.2, the Bureau of Land Management transmits the case to the Bureau of Reclamation with a request for report and recommendations. If the Bureau of Reclamation makes an adverse report on the application, the application will be rejected, subject to the right of appeal. If the withdrawal is terminated or partially terminated, it is accomplished by a public land order signed by the Secretary of the Interior and published in the **Federal Register.**

Lands Must Be Known or Believed Valuable for Minerals

The Act of April 23, 1932, as amended,[35] authorizes the Secretary "in his discretion" to open to "location, entry, and patent under the general mining laws" public lands which have been withdrawn "for possible use for construction purposes under the Federal reclamation laws." Before the Secretary may exercise his discretion, the statute requires that the land must be "known or believed to be valuable for minerals" and that the rights of the United States must not be prejudiced.

Recreation and Public Purposes Act

The Act of June 14, 1926, as amended by the Act of June 4, 1954 (43 U.S.C. 869) commonly known as the Recreation and Public Purposes Act, authorizes the Secretary of the Interior to lease or convey public lands for recreational and public purposes. These public lands may be determined to be suitable for lease or sale under the Act by BLM motion in response to demonstrated public needs for public lands for recreational or public purposes during the planning process as described in section 202 of FLPMA.[36]

A classification of land for disposition under the Act segregates the lands from mineral location even if the classification is not published in newspapers or the Federal Register and is only noted on the land office supplemental plat.[37] Leasable minerals are not affected by classification under the Recreation and Public Purposes Act and such minerals may be leased even if the lands are patented.

Small Tract Act

Lands classified under the Small Tract Acts of June 1, 1938, as amended by the Act of June 8, 1954 (43 U.S.C. 682a) are segregated from location or entry under the mining laws unless provided otherwise in the order of classification.[38] However, leasable minerals may be leased as provided by 30 U.S.C. 181 et seq.

Forest Service Special Use Permits

Special use permits issued by the Forest Service are open to entry under the mining and mineral leasing laws unless formal action by the Secretary of the Interior or some statutory authority is involved. The Interior Board of Land Appeals has held that the Secretary of Agriculture is neither expressly nor impliedly authorized to withdraw unimproved national forest lands from mineral location.[39]

Stock Driveways

The reservation of driveways for stock is authorized by the Act of December 29, 1926, as amended by the Act of January 29, 1929 (43 U.S.C. 300) to insure access by the public to watering places and areas needed for the movement of stock to summer and winter ranges or shipping points. Stock driveways are open to mineral leasing and are subject to mineral entry under the mining law; however any claim located after the effective date of a stock driveway withdrawal, would be subject to the stock driveway.[40]

Wild and Scenic Rivers System

The Wild and Scenic Rivers Act (16 U.S.C. 1271 et seq.) was passed to preserve in a free-flowing condition selected rivers which, with their immediate environments possess outstandingly remarkable scenic, recreational, geologic, fish, and wildlife, historic, cultural or other similar values. In the law, eight rivers were designated as components of the system and 27 more rivers were designated for potential addition to the Wild and Scenic Rivers System.

Lands constituting the bed or bank or within one-quarter mile of the bank of any designated or potential additional river are specifically withdrawn from mineral entry. Patents issued for valid existing claims at the date of the Act will convey only title to the mineral deposits with rights to use only that part of the surface necessary for mining operations.

Wilderness Act of 1964

The Wilderness Act of September 3, 1964 (16 U.S.C. 1131) provided that effective January 1, 1984, the wilderness would be withdrawn from all forms of appropriation under the mining and mineral leasing laws. Valid existing rights on January 1, 1984, will be preserved.

To qualify for a mineral patent in the Wilderness System, a claim must have been located and have valid and existing rights (a discovery) on or before December 31, 1983. Also, the claim must continue to have a discovery until patent issues. Two types of patents may be issued, depending on when the claim was located and when the discovery was perfected: (1) claims located on or before September 3, 1964, with valid existing rights of that date, qualify for a patent to both mineral deposits and the surface; and (2) claims located after September 3, 1964, and on or before December 31, 1983, qualify for a patent to only the mineral deposits.

It is important to point out that lands subsequently covered by wilderness areas established after September 3, 1964, will have different dates than those given above. Unless a specific statute establishing a wilderness area provides otherwise, a claim with valid existing rights at the date the wilderness area is established will qualify for a patent to both the surface and the mineral deposits.

Wildlife Refuges

Fish and wildlife refuges are administered by the Fish and Wildlife Service. Although most of these refuges are withdrawn from the mining and mineral leasing laws, several are at least partially open. The pertinent executive order or public land order authorizing the withdrawal and the Interior Department regulations should be consulted. Although Congress has passed a few laws authorizing withdrawals for refuges, most have no statutory basis. Approximately 27 million acres of public land have been withdrawn for fish and wildlife refuges.

Reference - Federal Actions Affecting Mineral Status

1. 43 USC 1610 (1982).
2. Doyon, Ltd., Mint, Ltd., (On Reconsideration), 78 IBLA 327 (1984).
3. 43 USC 1411 (1982).
4. 43 CFR 2462.2.
5. Rudolph Chase and Raymond Voss, 8 IBLA 351 (1972).
6. Charles A. Morriss, 36 IBLA 372 (1978).
7. 43 CFR 2201.1(b).
8. Kerr-McGee Corp., 46 IBLA 156 (1980); Lane Lasich, 63 IBLA 192, 194 (1982).
9. 43 CFR 3610.1-d and 3611.
10. Scott v. Carew, 196 U.S. 100.
11. Fort Maginnis, 1 LD 552.
12. Joseph E. Thompson, A-28107 (Aug. 26, 1960).
13. Arthur L. Rankin, 73 ID 305, 309 (1966); U.S. v. United States Borax Co., 58 ID 426, 432 (1943).
14. Clear Gravel Enterprises, 64 ID 210 (1957).
15. U.S. v. Grimaud, 220 U.S. 506.
16. 34 Stat. 225.
17. Gene R. Blaney, A-30894 (June 11, 1968); Mining in the Nation Park Service Areas, 78 ID 352 (1971).
18. See Henry Stagnaro, 31 IBLA 317 (1977) and George Hawkins, 66 IBLA 390 (1980).
19. 30 USC 621(a).

20. John C. Farrell, 55 IBLA 42 (1981); Day Mines, Inc., 65 ID 145 (1958).
21. Foster Mining & Engineering Company, 7 IBLA 305 (1972).
22. 43 CFR 3734.1(c).
23. 43 CFR 3734.1.
24. U.S. Forest Service v. Milendar, 104 IBLA 207, 214 (1988).
25. Id. at 230.
26. Id. at 231.
27. 92 ID 175, 262.
28. Id. at 216.
29. 30 USC 621(b).
30. U.S. Forest Service v. Milendar, 104 IBLA 207, 236-37.
31. Id. at 231.
32. William C. Reiman, 54 IBLA 103 (1981); Susan E. Mitchell, 53 IBLA 42 (1981).
33. M.G. Johnson, 78 ID 107 (1971).
34. 43 USC 145 (1982).
35. Id.
36. 43 CFR 2741.4.
37. R.C. Buch, 75 ID 140 (1968).
38. 43 CFR 2091.3-2.
39. See generally U.S. v. Foresyth, 15 IBLA 43, 49-54 (1974); U.S. v. Gergdal, 74 ID 245, 249-52 (1967).
40. 43 CFR 3815.2.

RIGHTS-OF-WAY

Rights-of-way are generally open to mining location, but mining rights are subject to use of the land for purposes of the right-of-way. Section 706(a) of FLPMA repealed on the date of the Act (October 21, 1976) portions of a number of statutes that relate to rights-of-way. However, existing rights-of-way at the date of FLPMA remain in effect.

44 LD 513 Easements

The authority for 44 LD 513 easements to Federal agencies is authorized by **Secretary's Instructions**, 44 LD 513 (January 13, 1916). These instructions provide that where Federal facilities have been constructed or where funds have been appropriated and the area needed for such improvements has been fixed and construction will take place immediately, the land is protected from adverse claims. Although mining claims may be located over such an existing easement, mining or prospecting operations must not interfere with the purposes of the easement, and mineral patents will contain a reservation of the easement.

Title to Railroad Rights-of-Way Remained in United States

In **Great Northern Ry. v. U.S.**, 315 U.S. 262 (1942), the U.S. Supreme Court held that the right-of-way granted by the 1875 Act[1] was "but an easement" granting no right to the underlying oil and minerals." The Railroad Act of July 1, 1862[2] granted a right-of-way 400 feet in width and every alternate section of land for 10 miles on either alternate section of land for 10 miles on either side of the road. The Railroad Act of July 2, 1864[3] granted a right-of-way 400 feet in width and every alternate section of land for 20 miles on either side of the road in states and for 40 miles on either side of the road in territories. The General Railroad Right-of-Way Act of March 3, 1875,[4] granted a right-of-way 200 feet in width.

The railroads acquired no mineral interest other than coal and iron beneath rights-of-way granted under all acts before March 3, 1871.[5] This is true even where the right-of-way passes through sections which were patented as place lands.[6]

The railroad acquired no mineral interest beneath rights-of-way granted between 1871 and 1875.[7] Minerals contained beneath rights-of-way passed to subsequent patentees providing minerals were not reserved in the patent under a mineral reservation such as the Stock-Raising Homestead Act.[8]

Because rights-of-ways under the 1875 Act are only easements, the railroad acquired neither the surface nor the mineral estate.[9] Therefore a subsequent homestead patentee with a patent subject only to the right-of-way[10] acquires all minerals beneath the 1875 right-of-way. Similarly, where lands containing post-1871 rights-of-way are patented, the patentee owns the minerals.

In the case of rights-of-way issued before March 3, 1871, all leasable minerals may be leased from the federal government under the 1920 Act, except coal and iron which may be leased from the owner of the right-of-way.[11] Pre-1871 rights-of-way should be open to mining claim location; however there is no specific case on this. Many early Interior cases indicate that mining claims cannot be located on limited fee rights-of-way.

The Act of May 21, 1930 (30 U.S.C. 301 et seq.) and regulations, 43 CFR 3109.1-1, authorize leasing oil and gas to the owner or assignee of the right-of-way.

Material Site Rights-of-Way

Grants of rights-of-way are made to state governments for the removal of materials for the construction and maintenance of highways under the Federal Aid Highway Act of August 27, 1958. 23 U.S.C. 317 (1982). It is well established that material site rights-of-way withdraw the lands affected from entry and location under the mining laws.[12]

Rights-of-Way to Mining Claims

The General Mining Law of 1872 gives to the locators and owners of mining claims, as a necessary incident, the right of ingress and egress across public lands to their claims for the purposes of maintaining the claims and as a means toward removing the minerals. Therefore, a right-of-way permit is not required.[13] However, ingress and egress across public lands to a patented claim for purposes other than mining or to other patented property does require a right-of-way permit. In certain cases, isolated tracts of public land containing mining claims are completely surrounded by patented lands. If there is no right-of-way or easement specifically reserved by the Federal government across the patented land to the mining claims, then the claimants must negotiate with the owners of the surrounding lands for access to the claims.

References - Rights-of-Way

1. 18 Stat. 482.
2. 12 Stat. 489.
3. 13 Stat. 358.
4. 18 Stat. 482.
5. U. S. v. Union Pacific R. Co., 353 U.S. 112 (1957).
6. Brown W. Cannon, Jr., 24 IBLA 166 (1976).
7. Great Northern R. Co. v. U.S., 315 U.S. 262 (1942).; U.S. v. Union Pacific R. Co., 353 U.S. 112 (1957).
8. Denver & Rio Grande R. Co., 198 F. 137 (D. Colo. 1912), aff'd 222 F. 481 (8th Cir. 1915).
9. Great Northern Ry Co. v. U.S., supra.
10. Amerada Hess Corp., 83 ID 194 (1976).
11. Solicitor's Opinion, 67 ID 225 (1960).
12. Pepcorn and Reddekopp, 50 IBLA 415 (1980); A.W. Schunk, 16 IBLA 191, 81 ID 401 (1974).
13. Mosch Mining Co., 75 IBLA 153 (1983).

MINERAL IN CHARACTER

Legal Basis

The legal basis for reserving mineral lands from disposal under the public land laws originates in the Act of July 4, 1866, where it is stated "in all cases lands valuable for minerals shall be reserved from sale, except as otherwise expressly directed by law."[1]

Rule-of-Thumb for Mineral Reservations

The general rule-of-thumb concerning the reservation of mineral lands in patents was established by the United States Supreme Court in 1918.[2] The Court held that "every grant of public lands whether to state or otherwise should be taken as reserving and excluding mineral lands, unless it is expressly stated that they are to be included."

Definition of Mineral in Character

There is no definition of "mineral in character" in the statutes; however, over the years, the courts have defined it in a variety of ways. Perhaps the most authoritative and enduring test for determining the mineral character of land was announced by the United States Supreme Court in **Diamond Coal & Coke Co. v. United States**, 233 U.S. 236, 239-40 (1914). The Court said:

> [I]t must appear that the known conditions...were plainly such as to engender the belief that the land contained mineral deposits of such quality and quantity as would render their extraction profitable and justify expenditures to that end.

Definition May Include Evidence for Determination

In **Southern Pacific Co.**, 71 ID 224, 233 (1964), the Secretary published a definition that not only included the language used in **Diamond Coal & Coke Co.**, but also included the type of evidence that may be used to establish mineral in character. The basis for this evidence of mineral in character was derived from earlier Supreme Court cases. The Secretary of the Interior stated:

> It is not essential that there be an actual discovery of mineral on the land. It is sufficient to show only that known conditions are such as reasonably to engender the belief that the land contains mineral of such quality and in such quantity as to render its extraction profitable and justify expenditures to that end. Such belief may be predicated upon geological conditions, discoveries of minerals in adjacent land and other observable external conditions upon which prudent and experienced men are shown to be accustomed to act.

Mineral in Character and the Ten Acre Rule
(Placer Claims Only)

Each 10-acre subdivision of a placer claim must be mineral in character; if a 10-acre tract is nonmineral in character, it must be excluded from the patent.[3] In **McCall v. Andrus**, 628 F.2d 1185 (9th Cir. 1980), cert. denied 450 U.S. 996 (1981), the Ninth Circuit Court of Appeals upheld the ten-acre rule and also the rule that only one discovery is required for a claim, regardless of size.

Distinction between "Discovery" and
"Mineral in Character"

A small number of Interior and Federal court cases have distinguished between "discovery" and "mineral in character."[4] Proof of discovery requires a showing of an exposed mineral deposit on the claim, whereas, mineral in character may be proved by geological inference. The marketability test is applied to both discovery and mineral in character.[5] Discovery is the higher standard because lands may be mineral in character but still lack a discovery.

Ten-Acre Rule Applies to Individual Placer Claim

The 10-acre rule is equally applicable to individual and association placer claims.[7] Therefore, every placer claim subjected to a validity examination will have at least two tracts examined for mineral in character, unless the claim is less than 10 acres in size.

Ten-Acre Rule Applies to All Validity Examinations

The 10-acre rule applies to every placer claim examined for validity. This is true for patent applications as well as validity examinations in connection with multiple-use conflicts (e.g., mining claims in wilderness areas).[8]

Ten-Acre Rule Applies to Placer Claims
Described by Metes and Bounds

The 10-acre rule applies to all placer claims described by a metes and bounds survey, regardless of whether the land is surveyed or unsurveyed.[9] See chapter on "Placer Claims" for additional information.

Quantity of Mineral

Mineral lands do not include those vast areas of the country that contain precious metals in small quantities, but not in sufficient value to justify their exploitation.[10] Where land is shown to contain minerals in such limited quantities that their extraction would not justify the cost, the land is not mineral in character.[11]

Agricultural v. Mining Purposes

To determine whether land is agricultural or mineral in character depends on whether the land is more valuable for agricultural or mining purposes.[12] In an 1894 case the Supreme Court said that "...if the land is worth more for agriculture than mining, it is not mineral land, although it may contain some measure of gold or silver."[13]

It has never been the policy of Congress to dispose of mineral lands under the agricultural or nonmineral laws.[14] Title to known mineral land cannot be acquired under an agricultural or nonmineral entry.[15]

Known to Be Valuable at Time of Sale

The exception of mineral lands from a grant in the acts of Congress applies only to lands that were known to be valuable for their minerals at the time of the grant. Minerals should exist in such quantity as to justify expenditures in the effort to extract them.[16]

No Retroactive Effect if Minerals Later Found

A decision by the Interior Department that lands are nonmineral in character will not be disturbed if the lands are patented and are later found to be mineral in character.[17] In **Deffenback v. Hawk**, 115 U.S. 392 (1885), the Court stated:

It is quite possible that lands settled upon as suitable only for agricultural purposes, entered by the settler and patented by the government under the preemption laws, may be found, years after the patent has been issued, to contain valuable minerals. Indeed, this has often happened. We, therefore, use the term **known** to be valuable at the time of sale to prevent any doubt being cast upon titles to lands afterwards found to be different in their mineral character from what was supposed when the entry of them was made and the patent issued.

Mineral in Character Established by Economics

In the 1981 **Oneida Perlite** case,[18] the Interior Board of Land Appeals described the two different situations that can be a basis for mineral in character:

Geologic conditions - The lands may be non-mineral in character where the mineral does not exist in sufficient quality and (or) quantity for a 10-acre subdivision to be of commercial value.

Economic conditions - The lands may be non-mineral in character where there is a superabundant supply of a mineral that has no market and therefore no commercial value. In other words a mineral deposit would exist that is so large that only a small part of it could conceivably be marketed in the foreseeable future. Some these cases have involved deposits so enormous that they alone could satisfy the entire needs of the United States for several hundred years. Construction minerals such as sand, gravel, pumice, cinders, building stone, perlite and clay are common examples of minerals with reserves for which there is no market.

Marketability Applied to Mineral in Character

Mineral in character may be proved by geological inference coupled with marketability.[19] The application of marketability means that there must not only be a mineral deposit on the property but that it can be extracted, processed and marketed at a profit.

Final Certificate Is Not Evidence of Mineral Character

The issuance of a "final certificate" in connection with a mineral patent application is neither evidence that a discovery has been made nor that the land is mineral in character.[20]

Mineral Patent Is Prima Facie Evidence of Mineral Character

A mineral patent is prima facie evidence that a discovery exists and that the land is mineral in character. Similarly, the issuance of a nonmineral patent is prima facie evidence that the land is nonmineral in character.[21]

References - Mineral in Character

1. 30 USC 21 (1982).
2. U.S. v. Smith, 245 U.S. 563 (1918).
3. Ferrell v. Hoge, 29 ID 12, 13, 15 (1889).; U.S. v. Meyers, 17 IBLA 313 (1974).
4. State of California v. Fodeffer, 75 ID 176, 178-79 (1968); U.S. v. Bechthold, 25 IBLA 92 (1972); McCall v. Andrus, 628 F.2d 1185 (1980), cert. denied 450 U.S. 996 (1981); Schlosser v. Pierce, 93 ID 211, 226 1986).
5. U.S. v. Meyers, 17 IBLA 313, 317 (1974).
6. Laden v. Andrus, 595 F2d 482, 487 (9th Cir 1979).
7. Lara v. Secretary of the Interior, 820 F.2d 1535, 1538 (9th Cir. 1987).
8. Id. at 1539.
9. Id.

10. Davis v. Weibbold, 138 U.S. 507, 519 (1891).
11. Id.
12. Barden v. Northern Pacific R. Co., 154 U.S. 288 (1894).
13. Davis v. Weibbold, supra at 521.
14. Ivanhoe Mining Co. v. Consolidated Mining Co., 102 U.S. 167 (1880).
15. Deffeback v. Hawke, 115 U.S. 392, 402 (1885).
16. Davis v. Wiebbold, supra at 524.
17. Lane v. Watts, 41 App DC 139 (1913), affirmed 234 U.S. 525.
18. Oneida Perlite, 57 IBLA 167 (1981).
19. McCall v. Andrus, supra at 1188.
20. U.S. v. Harper, 8 IBLA 364 (1972).
21. U.S. v. McCall, 7 IBLA 31 (1972).

RESERVATION OF SPECIFIC MINERALS

Until 1909, as a general rule there was no mineral reservation in United States land patents issued under the homestead laws. Since it has long been the policy of Congress to not allow disposal of mineral lands under the public land laws, lands classified as mineral lands were not available for entry under the homestead acts. However, because so much highly sought after lands were precluded from entry under this policy, Congress passed a series of laws that authorized patenting of lands if certain valuable specified minerals were reserved to the United States.

Coal Reservations by 1909 and 1910 Statutes

The Act of March 3, 1909 (30 U.S.C. 81) provides that persons who enter, in good faith, lands which after the date of entry are determined to be valuable for coal may receive a patent to such entry. However, the patent will contain a reservation to the United States of all coal in the lands with the right to prospect for, mine and remove the coal. This 1909 Act was the first statute authorizing a severance of the mineral title under the homestead acts.

The Act of June 22, 1910 (30 U.S.C. 85) provides that lands, exclusive of Alaska, which have been withdrawn or classified as coal lands, or are valuable for coal, are subject to entry under the homestead desert land laws. In a nonmineral patent, the coal is reserved to the United States, together with the right to prospect and mine. The Act gives the owner of the coal deposits the right to enter and occupy as much of the surface as required for all purposes reasonably incident to mining and removal of the coal. The coal owner may either pay the surface owner for damages caused to the surface or post a bond.

Phosphate, Nitrate, Potash, Oil, Gas or Asphaltic Minerals Reservation Authorized by 1914 Statute

Section 1 of the Act of July 17, 1914 (30 U.S.C. 121), as amended, authorized the issuance of patents under the nonmineral land laws for lands which were withdrawn or classified as phosphate, nitrate, potash, oil, gas, or asphaltic minerals, or which are valuable for those deposits. Nonmineral patents issued for lands which were withdrawn, classified, or reported as valuable for one of these minerals contained a reservation of the specific mineral(s), together with the right to prospect for, mine, and remove the same. The Act of July 17, 1914 applies to all public land states except the State of Alaska.

The Act of July 17, 1914, gives the owner of the mineral deposits the right to enter and occupy as much of the surface as required for all purposes reasonably incident to mining and removal of the coal. The coal owner may either pay the surface owner for damages caused to the surface or post a bond.

Sodium and Sulphur Reservation

The Act of March 4, 1933 (30 U.S.C. 124) provided that lands withdrawn, classified, or reported as valuable for sodium and/or sulphur may be patented under the nonmineral land laws under the same conditions as described in the Act of July 17, 1914. This 1933 Act does not apply to Alaska, and sulphur lands are limited to the State of New Mexico.[1]

Reservation of All Minerals in Stock Raising Homestead Patents

Section 9 of the Act of December 29, 1916 (43 U.S.C. 299) requires that patents issued under the Stock Raising Homestead Act shall contain a reservation to the United States of all coal and other minerals, together with the right to prospect for, mine, and remove the same.

Coal, Oil, and Gas Reservations Authorized in Alaska by 1922 Statute

The Act of March 8, 1922, as amended by the Act of August 23, 1958 (43 U.S.C. 376) authorized the issuance of nonmineral patents for homesteads and certain other entries even though the lands are known to contain workable coal, oil or gas deposits or may be valuable for coal, oil or gas. Patents issued for such lands contain a reservation to the United States of all the coal, oil, or gas in the land patented together with the right to prospect for, mine and remove the same.

The Act of March 8, 1922, gives the owner of the coal, oil or gas the right to enter and occupy as much of the surface as required for all purposes reasonably incident to mining and removal of the minerals. The mineral owner may either pay the surface owner for damages caused to the surface or post a bond.

General Rules Regarding Mineral Reservations in Patents

As a general rule it is important to remember that specific and general mineral reservations were not contained in United States patents until the particular statute authorized such reservation. The following table shows the earliest dates that specific minerals were reserved in patents issued under the homestead acts:

Earliest Date	Reserved Mineral(s)
March 3, 1909*	Coal
July 17, 1914*	Phosphate, Nitrate, Potash, Oil, Gas, or Asphaltic Minerals
December 29, 1916	All Minerals
March 4, 1933	Sodium and Sulphur

*The earliest date in Alaska would be March 8, 1922 for coal, oil and gas.

For example, by examining the above table, one may easily ascertain that you would not expect any mineral reservation in homestead patents issued prior to March 3, 1909. Also you would not expect to find that phosphate was reserved in any patent issued prior to July 17, 1914.

References - Mineral Interests

1. Fleming Foundation v. Texaco, 337 SW2d 846 (Tex Civ App 1960).
2. Santa Fe Railroad Co., 64 IBLA 27, 30-31 (1982).
3. Id.

RAILROAD GRANTS

Congress made two types of grants to the railroad companies to encourage the building of railroads: (1) outright grants in fee and (2) a right-of-way. The grants in aid were made by giving a railroad company so many odd-numbered sections within 10 miles on each side of their right-of-way. In some cases this was extended by granting the odd-numbered sections within 20 miles of the railroad line. The extent of the grant, whether it be 10 or 20 miles, was called the "place limits" and the odd-numbered sections within these limits were called the "place land. " Patents were issued in some cases where the railroad completed certain requirements. However, a patent is not necessary to accomplish the grant.

When the Department has issued a patent to a railroad under its grant, title vests in the railroad and the Department has no further jurisdiction over the patented land. An unrestricted patent to a railroad under its grant includes the title to the surface of the land and the mineral deposit under it. If a reservation should exist in a railroad patent which purports to reserve the minerals to the United States, such reservation is void. Under the Act of July 1, 1862, as amended by the Act of July 2, 1864, the railroads were granted alternate sections of public land within a belt extending for a designated number of miles on either side of the railroad's line to be built in the future. It was recognized early that the land office may not always make the proper classification of lands involved in railroad grants; however, the discovery of minerals after issuance of a patent would have no retroactive effect on the conveyance.[1]

To compensate for lost "place lands," the railroads were given indemnity lands. These lands were also limited to lands that were nonmineral in character and the lieu selection had to be from odd-numbered sections not more than 10 miles beyond the "place limits," but were not always limited to the odd-numbered sections. Although patents were generally issued for indemnity lands, in some cases the certification of the indemnity list conveyed the title without issuance of a patent.

Reference - Railroad Grants

1. Barden v. Northern Pacific Railroad Railroad Co., 154 U.S. 288, 330 (1894).

STATE LAND GRANTS

The purpose of most of the land grants to the states by the Federal government was to establish a source of support for public education. Through the Ordinance of May 20, 1785, Congress provided the first authorization of grants of public domain lands to states. In addition to requiring a rectangular system of surveys for public lands, this Ordinance also provided for reservation of lot number 16 of every township to be used to maintain public schools. The Act of April 30, 1802, which authorized the entry of Ohio into the Union, provided that section 16 of every township be granted to the inhabitants of each township for public schools. The Act of August 14, 1848, which provided for the organization of the Territory of Oregon, authorized both sections 16 and 36 to be granted to the states for use of schools. Certain states such as Utah and Arizona and New Mexico were granted four sections in each township for school purposes.

School Land Grants Extended to Include Mineral Sections

Section 1 of the Act of January 25, 1927 (43 U.S.C. 870) provided that grants to states of numbered sections for the support of schools are extended to also include numbered sections that are mineral in character. The states of Arizona, California, Colorado, Idaho, Montana, Nebraska, New Mexico, North Dakota, Oregon, South Dakota, Utah, Washington, and Wyoming benefited from this grant. This additional grant applies to school section lands known to be of mineral character at the effective date. It does not include school-section lands that were nonmineral in character at the time of the grant, but were later found to contain mineral deposits. The Act of 1927 does not apply to indemnity of lieu selections or exchanges or the right to select indemnity for numbered school sections in place lost to the state.

State Indemnity Selections

As a general rule, grants made by the Statehood Acts to the various states of sections 16 and 36 (also sections 2 and 32 in Arizona, New Mexico and Utah) become effective on the date of acceptance of approval of the plat of survey. If the acceptance or approval occurred before the date of admission of the state into the union, the grant attaches either on the date of approval of the plat or the date of admission into the union, whichever is the later date. However, if the land is appropriated at the date the grant would attach, the state does not receive the land and is entitled to indemnity for the lost lands.

Department Has No Jurisdiction If Lands Conveyed to State

In the case of state indemnity selections where title is conveyed to a state by patent or approved clearlist, the Department is divested of jurisdiction and authority to make any determination of rights to the land.[1] This includes the maintenance of mining claim recordation files and acceptance of a mineral patent application.[2] The United States loses jurisdiction even if the claim is valid at the date of conveyance.

In the case of state school grant sections, if title to the land was conveyed either by the Statehood Act or by the Act of January 1927, the Department would have no jurisdiction over the land. Therefore mining claim recordation files could not be maintained or mineral patent applications could not be considered.[3] However if it could be shown that a prior valid claim existed at the date of the enabling act or on January 25, 1927 (if the section were mineral in character), then the Department would have jurisdiction over lands embraced by the claim.[4]

Mining Claims in State Selection

What is the remedy for a mining claimant who owns a mining claim with valid existing rights on lands conveyed to a state? A claimant, after obtaining a judicial determination that the claim is a valid existing right contemplated by the Act conveying lands to a state could apply for a patent to the claim. If the Department were to then reject the application because the lands were no longer owned by the Federal Government, a claimant could properly seek a court order directing the Government to set aside the conveyance to the state to the extent the conveyance conflicts with the claim.[5]

Filing of State Selection Application Segregates the Land

The filing of a state indemnity selection segregates the affected land from entry under the mining laws for a period of 2 years from the date the application is filed.[6]

References - State Land Grants

1. Gernamnia Iron Co. v. U.S., 165 U.S. 379, 383 (1897).
2. Rosander Mining Co., 84 IBLA 60, 63-64 (1984); Ed Bilderback, 89 IBLA 263, 269 (1985).
3. State of Idaho, 101 IBLA 340, 347 (1988).
4. Id.
5. Ed Bilderback, supra at 269.
6. 43 CFR 2091.3-1(a); Leo Rhea Partnership, 80 IBLA 1 (1984).

PUBLIC LAND DISPOSALS

Preemption Statutes

The Act of March 2, 1799 provided the first general authority for contract purchasers to buy land from the government. Although this was the first preemption statute, many others were subsequently enacted by Congress. A preemption statute is an act that confers special privileges to purchase the public lands. The preemption laws were repealed by the Act of March 3, 1891 which predated the Act of March 3, 1909. Since the 1909 Act was the first statute to provide for a specific mineral reservation in a land patent issued under another statutory authority that had no provision for a mineral reservation, patents issued under the authority of the preemption acts will generally contain no reservation of minerals.

General Land Sale Acts

The Act of April 24, 1820 (43 U.S.C. 672) was one of the earliest public land sale acts that provided authority for issuance of a large number of patents. The Act of April 24, 1820, as well as other early land disposal statutes, contained no provision for reservation or exception for minerals. However, if public lands were sold under the authority of the Act of April 24, 1820, and the enactment of one of the statutes that authorize a mineral reservation (see Acts of March 3, 1909, June 22, 1910, July 17, 1914 and March 4, 1933), the patent issued may contain such reservation even though the Act of April 24, 1820 authorizing the sale made no provision for a reservation. Therefore, when examining patents, not only is the date of the granting act important, but the date the patent was issued is also important to ascertain whether it should contain a mineral reservation.

Small Tract Act

Lands classified under the Small Tract Acts of June 1, 1938, as amended by the Act of June 8, 1954, are segregated from location or entry under the mining laws, unless provided otherwise in the order of classification. However, Leasable minerals may be leased.

The Act also provides that all tracts patented under the Act shall contain a reservation to the United States of "the oil, gas, and all other mineral deposits, together with the right to prospect for, mine and remove the same under the applicable law and such regulations as the Secretary may prescribe." However, no such regulations have been established, so the reserved minerals are not open to location.[1]

Mining Claim Occupancy Act

The Mining Claim Occupancy Act of October 23, 1962, authorized the Secretary of the Interior to convey to any occupant of an invalid mining claim, up to and including a fee simple title for up to five acres of occupied land. For all interests conveyed under the Act, the mineral interests of the United States are reserved for the term of the estate conveyed. Locatable and salable minerals are withdrawn from all forms of entry and appropriation for the term of the estate. The underlying oil, gas and other leasable minerals of the United States are reserved for exploration and development purposes, but without the right of surface ingress and egress, and may be leased under the mineral leasing laws.

Town Site Act

Land embraced within a town site reservation on the public domain, when unoccupied, was open to the location of mining claims.[2] However, once the United States granted a town site patent to a private individual, the land is no longer open to entry.[3]

Desert Land Entry

The Act of March 3, 1877, as amended by the Act of March 3, 1891, authorizes desert-land entries in the States of Arizona, California, Colorado, Idaho, Montana, Nevada, New Mexico, North Dakota, Oregon, South Dakota, Utah, Washington and Wyoming. In order to be subject to entry under the desert-land law, public lands must be surveyed, unreserved, unappropriated and nonmineral in character. Lands patented under the authority of the Act may have a possible reservation of coal, phosphate, nitrate, potash, oil, gas, sodium, sulphur, or asphaltic minerals as authorized by the Acts of 1909, 1910, 1914 and 1933. However locatable minerals are not reserved in Desert Land Entries.

Recreation and Public Purposes Act

Lands classified for lease or disposition or patent under the Recreation and Public Purposes Act of 1926, as amended, 43

U.S.C. 869 (1982), are not open to mineral entry. The R&PP Act makes minerals reserved under its provisions subject to disposition only under applicable laws and "such regulations as the Secretary may prescribe." However because the Secretary has not issued regulations to cover mineral entry on lands patented under the R&PP Act, "the Secretary has in effect, prescribed that there shall be no prospecting for or disposition of the reserved deposits at this time."[4] However, leasable minerals may be leased even if the lands are patented.

Alaska Homestead Laws

A number of land disposal laws apply only to Alaska. However, the homestead laws were extended to Alaska by the Act of May 14, 1898. In general it was required that such lands be surveyed and nonmineral in character. A patent for such lands would include all mineral rights unless specifically reserved.

References - Public Land Disposals

1. Dredge Corporation v. Penny, 362 F.2d 889 (9th Cir. 1955).
2. Steel v. Smelting Co., 106 U.S. 447.
3. Davis v. Weibbold, 193 U.S. 507, 528 (1890).
4. Gloria Ann Sandvik, 73 IBLA 82, 84 (1983); Ronald R. Graham, 77 IBLA 174, 177 (1983); R.C. Buch, 75 ID 140, 146 (1968), affirmed Buch v. Morton, 449 F.2d 600, 605 (9th Cir. 1971).

HOMESTEAD ACTS

Before enactment of the first Homestead Act on May 20, 1862, public lands had been sold to the highest bidders, and to those who had a preemption claim. Under the homestead acts the intent of Congress was to encourage settlement of the public domain by rewarding the settlers with the land after they had proved up on it.

With the exception of the Stock-Raising Homestead Act of 1916, none of the homestead acts contained a provision for reservations or exceptions of minerals in the patent. However no entry was allowed if the lands were mineral in character.

With the exception of the Stock-Raising Homestead Act, lands patented under the authority of the homestead acts may have a possible reservation of coal, phosphate, nitrate, potash, oil, gas, sodium, sulphur, or asphaltic minerals. However, no other mineral can be reserved to the United States in a patent, including minerals locatable under the Mining Law of 1872.

STOCK-RAISING HOMESTEAD ACT

The Stock-Raising Homestead Act of December 29, 1916 (39 Stat. 862) provided for homestead entry of 640 acre tracts of nonirrigable land for the purpose of raising livestock. The lands were to be "chiefly valuable for grazing and raising forage crops, to not contain merchantable timber, are not susceptible of irrigation from any known source of water supply and are of such character that six hundred and forty acres are reasonably required to support a family."

Mineral Reservation Authorized by SRHA

Section 9 of the Act of December 29, 1916 provides that patents issued under the Act shall contain a reservation to the United States of "all coal and other minerals in the lands so entered and patented together with the right to prospect for, mine, and remove the same." The Act also provided that the reserved minerals are subject to disposal in accordance with the mineral land laws in force at the time of disposal. Therefore, minerals subject to the Mining Law of 1872 may be located and minerals subject to the Mineral Leasing Act of 1920, as amended, may be leased.

What Minerals Are Reserved In SRHA Patent?

Oil and gas,[1] geothermal resources,[2] granite,[3] and sand and gravel[4] have been held by the courts to reserved minerals under the Stock-Raising Homestead Act. Perhaps the case involving sand and gravel is the most significant because sand and gravel have been held to be part of the surface rather than a mineral in many grants and conveyances. The Bureau of Land Management charged Western Nuclear with a trespass for removing gravel from lands patented under the Stock-Raising Homestead Act. A hearing was held before an Administrative Law Judge who determined that sand and gravel was a reserved mineral in such a patent. On appeal, the decision was first affirmed by the Interior Board of Land Appeals and the U.S. District Court for Wyoming. However, the Court of Appeals for the Tenth Circuit reversed the District Court and held that the gravel extracted did not constitute a mineral reserved to the United States. Again on appeal, the United States Supreme Court reversed the 10th Circuit Court and held that gravel is a mineral reserved to the United States in lands patented under the Act. **Watt v. Western Nuclear, Inc.**, 103 S. Ct. 2218 (June 6, 1983). The Supreme Court determined that a SRHA reservation would include substances that:

1. are mineral in character,
2. are inorganic,
3. can be taken from the soil,
4. can be used for commercial purposes,
5. were not intended to be included in the surface estate,
6. have a separate value,
7. are not necessarily metalliferous, and
8. may not necessarily have a definite chemical composition.

The Supreme Court also concluded that gravel is a mineral reserved under the SRHA because (1) gravel has been consistently treated as a mineral under two Federal land-grant statutes which had similar mineral reservations to the United States; and (2) gravel has been treated as a mineral under the mining laws.

Prospecting

Any person qualified to locate and enter mineral deposits or who has acquired the right to mine and remove those mineral deposits has the right to enter upon the lands to prospect for the minerals, providing he complies with the following:

1. Does not injure, damage, or destroy the permanent improvements of the entrymen or patentee.

2. Is liable to compensate the entrymen or patentee for all damages to crops on such lands caused by prospecting activity.

When Bond Is Required

Any activity on land following the location of a claim requires a bond.[5] The rational for this is that since a discovery must precede the location of a claim, there would no longer be any reason to prospect because the next activity should be re-entry for development or mining.

Re-entry After Location

Section 9 of the Act of December 29, 1916, provides that the person who has acquired the mineral deposits from the United States in such lands together with the right to mine and remove the same may re-enter and occupy so much of the surface as may be required for all purposes reasonably incident to the mining or removal of the minerals provided he does one of the following:

1. Secures written consent or waiver from the surface owner,

2. Pays for damages to crops or other tangible improvements to the surface owner where an agreement on the amount can be reached, including value of land for grazing, or

3. If neither of the above can be accomplished, furnishes a bond to the United States for the use and benefit of the owner of the land to secure payment of such damages to the crops or tangible improvements of the owner, including value of land for grazing, as may be determined and fixed in action brought upon the bond or undertaking in a court of competent jurisdiction against the principal sureties.

Liability of Claimant

The amount of the bond does not limit the liability of the mining claimant to the surface owners. The claimant is liable for damages caused to crops or improvements of the surface owner as well any damage that may be caused to the value of the land for grazing by prospecting or mining.[6]

Bond Submission

The Bureau of Land Management is not involved in actions between the surface owner and the claimant until such time as a bond is filed in the proper BLM office. Action by the BLM is necessary only when a bond is filed. The bond with accompanying papers must be filed in the BLM office. There must also be filed with the bond evidence of service of a copy of the bond upon the homestead entryman or owner of the land.

The bond, Form 3814, Bond for Mineral Claimants, must be executed by the person acquiring the mineral deposits, as principal, with two competent individual sureties, or a qualified corporate surety (see 43 CFR 3504.4-2), and must be in the sum of not less than $1,000. All owners of record who have an interest in a mining claim must sign the bond form.

Action on Bond

If the bond meets the above requirements, the BLM is required to take one of the following actions on the claimant's bond:

1. **Approval** - If no objection against the approval of the bond is filed by the surface owner within 30 days after receipt of the bond, the BLM prepares a decision approving the bond.

2. **Objection of Owner** - Disapproval of Bond - When the surface owner files an objection to the approval of the bond within 30 days, the BLM reviews the bond and objections to determine whether the bond should be approved or disapproved. Generally at this point the case is submitted to the field manager for a field examination and report on whether the amount of bond is sufficient. If upon receipt of the field manager's recommendations a determination is made to disapprove the bond, a decision to that effect is sent to the claimant with a copy to the surface owner. If no appeal is filed within 30 days, the BLM must endorse "Disapproved" on the bond and close the case.

3. **Objection of Owner** - Approval of Bond - If the bond is approved over the objections of the surface owner, the authorized officer issues a decision dismissing the surface owner's protest. If no appeal is filed within 30 days, the BLM then issues a decision approving the bond.

Protests by Surface Owner

Most protests by surface owners involve the adequacy of the bond. Exhaustion of the administrative process, including appeal to the Interior Board of Land Appeals, leaves the matter to be settled by parties in a court of competent jurisdiction.

In some protests, the surface owner contends that the mining claimant has not made a discovery under the mining law. In this instance, the protest is dismissed and the surface owner notified that the issue may be determined by the initiation of a private contest in accordance with 43 CFR 4.450. Action on approval or disapproval of the bond is suspended until a final decision on the contest is issued.

Bond Must Cover All Possible Damages within Claim Boundaries

In **William and Pearl Hayes**, 101 IBLA 110 (1988), BLM bonded a company for only the lands to be affected by initial exploration activity - an area of approximately one acre. The Board found that this approach has the potential to restrict the mineral claimant's right to re-entry and fails to adequately protect the surface owner. The Board said the mineral claimant would need to return for further review of the bond amount each time it proposed new mining activities. However the statute states that "upon bond approval the mineral claimant has the right to reenter and occupy so much of the surface * * * as may be required for all purposes reasonably incident to the mining or removal of the * * * minerals." Consequently, the bond amount must be sufficient to cover possible damages within the boundaries of the claim. In other words the bond must be based upon the claims to be entered rather than the area of planned mining operations proposed by the applicant. However, the bond need not be sufficient to cover damages outside the limits of the mining claims.

Surface Owner May Challenge Validity of Claim

One established remedy available to a surface owner to terminate the rights of a mineral claimant is to challenge the validity of a claim. However the surface owner has the burden of preponderating in a private contest.[7] The procedure for a surface owner of land, patented under the Stock-Raising Homestead Act to challenge the validity of a mining claim for lack of discovery of a valuable mineral is by the initiation of a private contest under 43 CFR 4.450.

Surface Owner and Lessee Both Responsible for Trespass Damages

Where the surface owner of a SRHA patent leases sand and gravel to another party, BLM may properly proceed against both parties for the collection of trespass damages.[8]

No Authority to Dispose of Minerals from SRHA Lands

The Interior Department's regulations (43 CFR 3601.1) state that "mineral material disposals" may not be made from "public lands" on which there are "valid existing claims to the land by reason of settlement, entry, or similar rights obtained under the public land laws.

References - Stock-Raising Homestead Act

1. Skeen v. Lynch, 48 F.2d 1044 (10th Cir. 1931).
2. U.S. v. Union Oil Co. of California, 549 F.2d 1271 (9th Cir. 1977), cert. denied 434 U.S. 930, rehearing denied, 435 U.S. 911.
3. Denman Investment Corp., 78 IBLA 31 (1984).
4. Watt v. Western Nuclear, Inc., 103 S. Ct. 2218 (June 6, 1983).
5. Smith Land Company, 15 IBLA 280 (1974).
6. 30 USC 54 (1982).
7. State of California v. Doria Mining and Engineering Corporation, 17 IBLA 380 (1974); Thomas v. Morton, 408 F.Supp. 1361 (DC Ariz. 1976), affirmed sub nom. Thomas v. Andrus, 552 F.2d 871 (9th Cir. 1971).
8. Curtis Sand & Gravel Co., 95 IBLA 144, 152 (1987).

LAND SALES UNDER FLPMA

The Secretary of the Interior is authorized by section 206 of the Federal Land Policy and Management Act of 1976 (43 U.S.C. 1701) to sell public lands where, as a result of land-use planning, such lands are determined to meet specific disposal criteria. Patents and other conveyance documents issued under FLPMA are required to contain a reservation to the United States of all minerals together with the right to prospect for, mine, and remove the minerals under applicable law and such regulations as the Secretary may prescribe. However, section 209(a) of FLPMA allows for the conveyance of minerals with the surface under certain circumstances. See the section on "Conveyance of Federally-Owned Mineral Interests" for more information. Mining claim locations cannot be made on these reserved minerals until the BLM has published rulemaking that would allow location and development. The leasing act minerals may be developed under existing regulations.

EXCHANGES

State and Private Exchanges Under the Taylor Grazing Act

Section 8 of the Taylor Grazing Act of June 28, 1934 (48 Stat. 1272) authorized exchanges of lands between the United States and a state or a private land owner. Either party to an exchange "may make reservations of minerals, easements or right of use. Lands conveyed to the United States through a section 8 exchange become public lands, and therefore open to entry under the United States mining and mineral leasing laws.[1] Restoration orders are mandatory for reconveyances under section 8 exchanges before the new public lands are open to mineral entry.[2]

Exchanges After FLPMA

The Federal Land Policy and Management Act of 1976 repealed a major part of the law that gave the Secretary of the Interior exchange authority and replaced it with a more comprehensive authority granted by section 206 of the Act. Lands and interests in lands acquired by exchange become public land upon acceptance of title by the Federal government. These public lands are not available for location under the mining laws or mineral leasing until a notice of their availability is published in the **Federal Register**.

National Forest Exchange

National forest exchanges are authorized under the provisions of the Act of March 20, 1922, as amended (16 U.S.C. 485) and the Federal Land Policy and Management Act of 1976 (43 U.S.C. 1701 et seq.) and are filed with the U.S. Forest Service. The filing of a notice of an offer for a forest exchange and the notation of the proposed exchange on the public land records serves to segregate the lands from location under the general mining laws but not from the public land laws governing the use of the National Forest system under leases, licenses or permits. The segregative effect of the offer notation on the public land records terminates upon issuance of patent or other document of conveyance to such lands, upon rejection or denial of the exchange offer or 2 years from the date of the notation, whichever occurs first.

Restoration orders are not required under the provisions of FLPMA to open tracts of land acquired by the Secretary of Agriculture under the Forest Exchange Act of March 20, 1922, to mineral leasing and mining claim location.[3] However, the lands do not become part of the National Forest and open to mining claim location until acceptance of title by the Government.[4]

References - Exchange

1. Amax Specialty Metals Corp., 100 IBLA 60, 61 (1987).
2. Petro Leasco, Inc., 42 IBLA 345, 3522 (1979).
3. Id. at 350.
4. 16 USC 486 (1982).

ACQUIRED LANDS

The Interior Board of Land Appeals has defined "acquired lands" as those lands in federal ownership which have been obtained by the Government by purchase, condemnation, or gift, or by exchange for such purchased, condemned or donated lands, or for timber on such lands.[1] The significance of this distinction between "public domain lands" and "acquired lands" is that unappropriated public domain lands are generally available for disposal under the general mining laws of 1872, as amended and the Mineral Leasing Act of 1920, as amended. However, whether minerals may be disposed on acquired lands depends generally on two considerations: (1) the purpose of the acquisition, and (2) the statutory authority for the acquisition.

Acquired Lands Generally Not Open to the Mining and Mineral Leasing Laws

Even though the Mining Law of 1872 declares that lands belonging to the United States are free and open to purchase, there are many types of lands acquired by the United States, especially those acquired for a special purpose, that are not available for mining claim location.[2] There must be an expressed mention in the statute that acquired lands are open to the mining laws or that the disposal is under some specified law. Otherwise no disposal is authorized.[3]

Acquired Lands Leasing Act

All deposits of coal, phosphate, oil, oil shale, gas, sodium, potassium and sulfur in acquired lands may be disposed of under the Acquired Lands Leasing Act of August 7, 1947. 30 U.S.C. 351 (1982).

Leasable Hardrock Minerals

If hardrock minerals are acquired pursuant to one of the acts listed in section 402 of the Reorganization Plan No. 3 of 1946, they are available for leasing under the regulations in 43 CFR 3500. Also, if hardrock minerals are acquired pursuant to an act that expressly mentions that acquired minerals are available for leasing, then these minerals may disposed of under 43 CFR subpart 3500, or by the method mentioned in the act. For example, the Act of September 2, 1958 (16 U.S.C. 521a) gives **Weeks Act** status to certain lands. Specifically, the 1958 Act provides that lands which are acquired under a variety of statutes and are situated within the national forests, have the same status for mineral acquisition purposes as Weeks Act lands. The Authority for leasing of Weeks Act lands comes from the Act of March 4, 1917 (16 U.S.C. 520).

Acquisitions After FLPMA

Section 205(a) of the Federal Land Policy and Management Act of 1976 (43 U.S.C. 1715) authorizes the government to acquire by purchase, exchange, donation or eminent domain lands or interests in lands. Section 205(c) specifies that lands (and minerals) acquired by the Secretary of the Interior shall become public lands for the administration of the public land laws in effect. Section 205(d) provides that lands (and minerals) acquired by the Secretary of Agriculture shall "become National Forest System Lands subject to all the laws, rules, and regulations applicable thereto."

Therefore, lands acquired under section 205 of FLPMA, including acquisitions in the national forest system shall become public lands and be subject to the mining and mineral leasing laws. For example, hardrock minerals would be subject to location under the mining law rather than through a leasing system as are some preFLPMA acquired lands. Of course, a notice of availability of such lands must appear in the Federal Register before mineral locations may be initiated.[4]

References - Acquired Lands

1. Phillips Petroleum Co., 10 IBLA 275, 276 (1973).
2. Junior L. Dennis, 61 IBLA 8, 14 (1981).
3. Oklahoma v. Texas, 258 U.S. 574, 599-600 (1922).
4. Tom Notestine, 73 IBLA 320 (1983).

CONVEYANCE OF FEDERALLY OWNED MINERAL INTERESTS

Section 209(b) of the Federal Land Policy and Management Act of 1976 (43 U.S.C. 1719(b)) authorizes the Secretary of the Interior to convey mineral interests owned by the United States where the surface is or will be in non-Federal ownership if certain conditions are met. Any mineral conveyance under FLPMA must be done under the procedures set forth in section 209(b) and may be accomplished simultaneous with disposal of the surface. This program is also available to surface owners of patents issued under earlier disposal statutes such as the Stock-Raising Homestead Act of 1916 where all minerals were reserved to the United States. The regulations (43 CFR 2720), to implement the statute were made effective February 5, 1979. Section 209(b)(1) authorizes the Secretary to convey mineral interests "if he finds (1) that there are no known mineral values in the land, or (2) that the reservation of the mineral rights in the United States is interfering with or precluding appropriate nonmineral development of the land and that such development is a more beneficial use of the land than mineral development."

Definition of "known Mineral Values"

The term "known mineral values" is defined in the regulations[1] as follows:

> "Known mineral values" means mineral values in lands with underlying geologic formations which are valuable for prospecting for, developing or producing natural mineral deposits. The presence of such mineral deposits in the lands may be known, or geologic conditions may be such as to make the lands prospectively valuable for mineral occurrence.

Case Involving Lands with Known Mineral Values

In **David D. Plater**, 55 IBLA 296 (1981), the Geological Survey stated that a tract was valuable for oil and gas and recommended an exploratory drilling program estimated to cost $5,812,500. In the case the Survey reported "that a gas field is located less than a mile from the tract and a gas-condensate well was completed only 4,000 feet from the tract in 1979."

Form of Application

No specific form is required for an application to acquire Federally-owned mineral interests. However, 43 CFR 2720.1-2 sets forth very detailed information that must be contained in the application. A nonrefundable filing fee of $50 is also required.

Applicant Pays Administrative and Exploration Costs

The regulations[2] require that an application will not be processed until the applicant has deposited the amount of money requested by the BLM to cover administrative costs of processing the application. If an exploration program is required to determine the fair-market value of the tract, the applicant must submit the requested money to cover the cost. There is also a provision for an applicant to obtain consent of the BLM to conduct an exploration program at his own expense to determine the fair-market value of the Federal mineral interests. In this program, an applicant must conduct the exploration under an approved plan of operation and pay all costs of evaluating the exploration data as well as all administrative costs.

Mineral Potential Report to Determine if Exploratory Program Is Necessary

An exploratory program is not required if the BLM determines that "there are no known mineral values in the land." This mineral potential report is prepared by one or more mining engineers or geologists employed by the BLM. Locatable, leasable and salable mineral values are all considered in the BLM report. An exploratory program is not required if lands are classified as prospectively valuable for leasable minerals, but such value is found to be only nominal.[3]

If the exploratory program establishes mineral values, the applicant pays (1) administrative costs, (2) costs of exploratory program, and (3) fair-market value of the Federal mineral interests. The applicant must also show that "the reservation of mineral rights in the United States is interfering with or precluding appropriate nonmineral development of the land and that such development is a more beneficial use of the land than mineral development.

References - Post FLPMA Conveyance of Federally-Owned Mineral Interests

1. 43 CFR 2720.0-5(b).
2. 43 CFR 2720.1-3.
3. 43 CFR 2720.2.

DEFINITION OF A MINERAL

The term "mineral" has been given many definitions, depending on whether the usage or connotation is scientific, practical mining or legal.

Scientific Definitions

Scientific definitions are generally concerned with the origin and the chemical and physical properties of a substance rather than with economic considerations. The **Glossary of Geology**, published by the American Geological Institute, defines "mineral" as follows:

> A naturally occurring inorganic element or compound having an orderly internal structure and characteristic chemical composition, crystal form, and physical properties.

In **A Dictionary of Mining, Mineral, and Related Terms**, published in 1968 by the U.S. Bureau of Mines, Department of the Interior, the term "mineral" is defined in a manner similar to the definition quoted above from the **Glossary of Geology**. However, the Bureau of Mines Dictionary further states:

> In a broad nontechnical sense, the term embraces all inorganic and organic substances that are extracted from the earth for use by man, for example, the mineral fuels.

Thus, the term "mineral" has a much broader legal meaning than technical or scientific meaning. For example, such minerals as building stone, coal, guano, limestone, etc. are typically included in legal definitions but not in scientific definitions.

Statutory or Conveyance Definitions

For legal purposes of determining what is a mineral, a dictionary definition, no matter how authoritative, is of little significance. The controlling factor is how "minerals" are defined in the statute or the conveyance instrument. There are almost as many different definitions of "mineral" as there are conveyance and statutory definitions.

If the wording of a statutory mineral reservation is ambiguous or unclear, the legislative intent of such a reservation may ascertained by studying committee reports, floor debates, successive drafts and the purpose of the legislation. Also, it has long been accepted by courts that in cases where the government grants land, the language of the grant, if unclear, is generally interpreted against the grantee and in favor of the public body. However, the normal rule concerning grant construction is generally interpreted against the grantor.

Court Interpretations of the Term "Mineral"

The courts have held repeatedly that the term "minerals" in a grant or reservation has no general definition and that to determine what is included in the "minerals" definition, one must determine the intent of the parties involved. If the language of the grant or reservation clearly specifies the minerals that are being conveyed or reserved, there is no problem. However, if the grant or reservation only specified that minerals are being granted or reserved, it will be necessary to determine what specific minerals the parties had in mind.

In **Northern Pacific Ry. Co. v. Soderberg**, 188 U.S. 526, 530 (1903), the Supreme Court gave one of the most frequently cited definitions of term mineral:

> The word "mineral" is used in so many senses, dependent upon the context, that the ordinary definitions of the dictionary throw but little light upon its significa- tion in a given case. Thus the scientific division of all matter into the animal, vegetable, or mineral kingdom would be absurd as applied to a grant of lands, since all lands belong to the mineral kingdom, and therefore could be excepted from the grant without being destructive of it.

Almost all definitions of "mineral" would include metallic substances and even some nonmetallic substances such as phos- phate, gypsum, barite, etc. However, certain nonmetallic substances such as oil and gas, geothermal resources, clay, soil, sand and gravel, building stone, peat, water, etc. have always been a problem where such substances were not specifically mentioned in the grant or reservation.

Courts interpret conveyances and reservations to determine what substances are covered by the term minerals. The courts generally attempt to resolve such issues by determining the intent of the parties involved. In all states except Pennsylvania, the courts have held oil and gas to be minerals. However, the "hard minerals present a much more difficult problem.

The courts have determined whether substances are minerals reserved in a reservation or conveyance by applying one or more of the following criteria:

1. Surface destruction
2. Intention of the parties
3. General rules of statutory construction
4. Ejusdem Generis
5. Nongovernment cases construed against grantor
6. Mining or commercial usage
7. Mining rights unsuited for certain minerals
8. Separate value from surface

Surface Destruction

The general consensus of the courts has been that the parties separating mineral and surface estates would not intend to give one the power to destroy the other.[1] The most litigated minerals are sand and gravel. The courts have generally held that the owner of the surface estate owns the sand and gravel because their removal would cause destruction of the surface.

Intention of the Parties

In order to determine whether a substance is a mineral in a reservation or conveyance, the courts tend to examine the intention of the parties at the time the reservation or conveyance occurred. For example, if the parties were only concerned with gold, non-metallic minerals such as building stone might not be determined to be a mineral.

In **Bumpus v. U.S.**, 325 F.2d 262 (10th Cir. 1963), the Court applied the **ejusdem generis** rule in holding that sand and gravel were not included in a reservation of "oil, gas and other minerals." The reservation was in favor of a private party who had conveyed land to the United States for reservoir purposes. Furthermore, the rule was applied only when the Court determined that the result would be consistent with the intent of the parties to the transaction.

General Rule of Statutory Construction

The general rules of statutory construction must be considered in examining a mineral reservation to the United States.[2] These rules include the following:

1. Mineral reservations in patents are construed according to the intent of Congress at the time of enactment and under the circumstances then present.[3]

110

2. Legislative intent is sought in the history of the legislation as recorded in the legislative record, the committee reports, statements by sponsors, floor debates, as well as the condition of the country at the time and the purpose of Congress.[4]

3. Public legislation is construed broadly in favor of the government which made the grant; no rights pass by implication.[5]

Ejusdem Generis

Where certain minerals are specified and followed by generic terminology, the unspecified minerals are limited to the same kind or class (**ejusdem generis**) of substances listed.[6] For example, a court may hold that a reservation of "gold and other minerals" does not include oil and gas. Under **ejusdem generis**, oil and gas being a fluid, organic mineral is not the same kind or class of mineral as gold.

NonGovernment Cases Interpreted
Against the Grantor

It has long been accepted by the courts that in cases where the government grants land, the language of the grant, if unclear, is generally interpreted in favor of the grantor (government).[7] However, the normal rule concerning grant construction is that the courts generally interpret against the nongovernment grantor.

Mining or Commercial Usage

Courts have on occasion determined whether a substance was a mineral in a reservation or conveyance depending on whether it was regarded as such by the mining or commercial community at the time the reservation or conveyance was created. This rule requires that the interpretation to be given the term "minerals" is dependent upon the popular understanding of what substances were known as minerals at the time of the conveyance.[9]

Mining Rights Unsuited for Certain Minerals

The rights specified in a mineral grant which are necessary for mineral extraction or production may be unsuitable for certain types

111

of minerals. For example, provisions in the grant for underground mining may preclude development of a mineral that can only be extracted by surface methods.

Separate Value from the Surface

One criterion applied by the courts requires that a substance be used in such a way that it has a value separate from the surface. Another aspect of this requirement is that the substance be marketable.[9]

Sand and Gravel

The most significant Federal court cases on sand and gravel involve a mineral reservation in a Federal land grant. The long-standing question of whether sand and gravel are reserved minerals in a Stock-Raising Homestead grant is now fully litigated. In **Watt v. Western Nuclear**, 103 S.Ct. 2218 (1983), the United States Supreme Court held that sand and gravel are reserved minerals. However in several earlier cases the Federal courts have held that sand and gravel were not reserved minerals.

In numerous cases state courts have addressed the issues of whether sand and gravel are minerals in a mineral reservation or conveyance. Although the cases tend to go both ways, there is a predominance of cases where the courts have held that sand and gravel go with the surface estate rather than with the mineral estate. For the most part these cases are decided on the fact that sand and gravel are an integral part of the surface, and to remove the sand and gravel would be destructive of the surface.

Water

Water, like sand and gravel, has been treated inconsistently by the courts; there are cases construing deeds finding water to be a mineral and there are also many to the opposite effect. In a Utah State Supreme Court case,[10] a solution of copper and water was found not to be a mineral in a deed conveying all minerals in or on the land.

The Interior Department long ago held that mineral spring water is not locatable under the general mining law. **Pagosa Springs**, 1 L.D. 562 (1882). In a more recent case involving mineral springs on mining claims, the water was evaporated leaving mineral salts which were then packaged and "hawked" through mineral water. The claims were found to be invalid by the Ninth Circuit Court of Appeals.

In the **Charleston Stone Products** case, the Ninth Circuit Court of Appeals affirmed the District Court and held that water is a locatable mineral. The novelty of the ruling caused the Justice Department to petition for a writ of certiorari, which was granted by the United States Supreme Court. On this limited issue, the Supreme Court reversed the Ninth Circuit in a decision reported at 436 U.S. 604 (1978). The Supreme Court held that although "water is a mineral in the broadest sense of the word" it is not a locatable mineral under the 1872 mining law.

Geothermal Resources

Finding an appropriate definition for geothermal resources has been a matter of considerable controversy for state legislatures, the courts and industry. Although most states and the federal government have avoided a statutory definition of geothermal resources, the State of Hawaii claims it as a mineral, the State of Wyoming treats it as water and the states of Idaho, Montana and Washington define geothermal resources as **sui generis** (of its own kind or class or not necessarily a mineral or a water). Apparently the **sui generis** classification gives states the flexibility to treat the resource as a water and/or a mineral.

Whether geothermal resources went to the surface owner of a Stock-Raising Homestead patent, or remained with reserved mineral rights was the subject of a ruling by the Ninth Circuit Court of Appeals on January 31, 1977. In that case, **United States v. Union Oil Company of California**, 549 F.2d 1271, the court held that potentially valuable subsurface steam, used to power electric generators, is the property of the owner of the mineral rights and not necessarily the owner of the surface rights.

Reference - Definition of a Mineral

1. Farrel v. Sayre, 270 P.2d 190 (Sup. Ct. Colo 1954); Smith v. Moore, 474 P.2d 794 (Sup. Ct. of Colo 1970).
2. Watt v. Western Nuclear, Inc., 103 Sup. Ct. 2218 (1983).
3. Moor v. County of Alameda, 411 U.S. 693, 709; U.S. v. Stewart, 311 U.S. 60, 69 (1940).
4. Winona & St. Peter R.R. v. Barney, 113 U.S. 618, 625 (1885).
5. U.S. v. Union Pacific R.R. Co., 353 U.S. 112, 116 (1957).
6. Bumpus v. U.S., 325 F.2d 264 (10th Cir. 1963); State Land Board v. State Department of Fish & Game, 408 P.2d 707 (1965).

113

7. U.S. v. Union Pacific R.R. Co., supra.
8. New Mexico & Arizona Land Company v. Elkins, 137 F.Supp. 767 (DNM 1956).
9. Texaco, Inc., 59 IBLA 155 (1981).
10. Stephens Hays Estate, Inc., v. Togliatti, 38 P.2d 1066 (1934).

MINERAL INTERESTS

Fee Simple Absolute Title

A fee simple absolute title is the highest type of private owner-ship of land. It gives the exclusive perpetual right to the posses-sion of land and is subject only to police power.

Fee Interest

A fee interest generally refers to ownership of both the surface interest and the mineral interest for an infinite duration.

Mineral Fee Interest

A mineral fee interest includes not only the ownership of the minerals, but also includes other implied rights necessary to remove and enjoy the minerals, such as right of access and use of the surface. The owner of the mineral interest can separately convey or reserve some of the incidents of mineral ownership.

Surface Fee Interest

The surface interest may be defined as all rights to property other than the mineral interest. As a general rule, the rights to use of the surface by the surface interest owner are subject to the right of the mineral interest owner to use the surface for exploration, development and production activities incidental to the enjoyment of the mineral interest. In other words the rights of the surface owner are servient to the rights of the mineral interest owner.

Severed Titles

Mineral rights may be separated into independent mineral estates by grant and reservation. If the mineral rights have not been specifically reserved or granted, any conveyance of the land will include the minerals. If the surface is separated from the minerals, the two estates are independent and either one can be conveyed with no concern for the other. The separation or severance of the mineral estate from the surface (or part of the minerals from the surface and remaining minerals) is accomplished by one of the following approaches:

1. Execution of a **mineral deed** to convey the entire mineral estate of the grantor or to convey a part of the mineral estate owned by the grantor.

2. **Surface deed** - to grant a surface deed would leave the grantor with the mineral estate.

3. **Mineral reservation** - includes a reservation of all or a portion of the mineral interests in conveyance of the fee.

In such cases mineral interests, whether granted or reserved should be carefully defined. For example, in a Stock-Raising Homestead grant, the mineral interest is severed from the fee interest by a reservation to the United States of the mineral interest.

Division of Mineral Rights

A mineral grant may convey only part of the mineral rights. These mineral rights may be subdivided by (1) types of minerals; (2) depth; (3) time; (4) an undivided fraction of the mineral rights; and (5) a separation of the rights of ownership.

Oil and gas rights are commonly divided on a horizontal basis in both the mineral grant and assignments. This division should be described by separating at the base or top surface of a specified formation. It is poor procedure to divide on a depth basis because a single producing formation could exist above and below the specified depth.

Mineral Grants and Reservations

A mineral grant or reservation should be carefully written to take into consideration the special technical and legal circumstances in each case. It is important to remember that every mineral property has a unique geologic environment and mineral resource potential. Typically, the mineral grant in a conveyance specifies the substances covered by the conveyance and the types of uses or rights necessary to benefit from removal of the substances.

If it is intended that every possible mineral be included in a mineral grant or reservation, one should include a phrase such as "all minerals of every kind and description including but not

116

limited to..." Because the courts tend to exclude minerals such as sand and gravel that occur at or near the surface and must be extracted by surface mining methods, it is recommended that language be included in the grant that specifically allows extraction by surface mining methods.

Conversely, if the parties wish to limit the grant or reservation to specific minerals, the term "only" should be attached to the specified mineral such as "coal only." Also, if it is intended that certain types of development or mining operations be restricted, this should be specified. For example, heap leaching, solution mining or surface mining could specifically be prohibited.

Generic Language and Specific Language

Mineral grants and reservations have three common types of language: (1) generic language such as minerals, mineral rights and other minerals; (2) specific language such as coal, oil and gas, gold and copper; and (3) and a combination of generic and specific language. Generic language is generally used where there is no particular mineral of concern; whereas, when specific minerals are cited, the opposite is generally true.

Grants or reservations with certain specified minerals followed by "and other minerals" tend to be a source of much litigation. The problem is to establish whether or not the phrase "or other minerals" includes a mineral subsequently found that is not included in the list of specified minerals. For example, "coal and other minerals" may exclude oil and gas because specification of certain minerals tends to exclude those not on the list. In a case with a reservation of "oil, gas and other minerals," the court[1] expressly excluded metallic minerals.

Relative Rights of Surface Owner
and Mineral Owner

The mineral owner has the dominant estate and the surface owner has the servient estate. Even though the surface estate is inferior to the mineral estate, the extent of the mineral owner's surface rights is determined on a case-by-case basis and depends on the language in the reservation or conveyance, the intentions of the parties and the mining customs and technology at the date and place of the severance.[2] The right of the owner of the mineral estate to enter, traverse, occupy, and utilize the surface, even where

117

such right is merely implied, has been held to be in the nature of an easement where the mineral estate is dominant and the surface estate is servient. Such implied rights of entry and development are based on the logical assumption that the mineral estate was reserved for the purpose of retaining the rights to develop the mineral in the grantor. Of course, the owner of the mineral estate owes certain duties to the surface owner as well, such as the duty not to commit waste and to refrain from unreasonable interference with the surface owner's right of enjoyment of his property.[3]

Conveyances

A conveyance is an instrument used to pass ownership in land; it must be a written instrument and include the following elements: (1) grantor and grantee, (2) description of the grant, (3) description of the subject land, and (4) a proper execution. The more common types of conveyances are described as follows:

1. **Deeds** - The various forms of deeds include (1) the general warranty deed which transfers the interest stated in it and warrants title against all adverse claims; (2) the bargain and sale deed which conveys the stated interest but does not warrant title; and (3) the quitclaim deed conveys only that interest the grantor presently owns in the described property.

2. **Options** - An option agreement generally gives the transferee a set period of time to either purchase or lease the described property. An option period may be used to determine if the seller has marketable title or has a property valuable for minerals. Some leases also grant the lessee the option to purchase the leased land. Some courts have held that options unlimited in time are void under the rule against perpetuities.

3. **Less than Freehold Interests** - These interests include such conveyances as right-of-way deeds, leases and easements.

Term Interests

Term interests are not freeholds because they are intended to last for a specified period of time. The interest of the grantor which comes into possession after the end of the term interest is called a "reversionary interest." Some of the more common types of term interests are (1) leaseholds, (2) independent royalty interests and (3) mineral term interests.

There are a number of incorporeal interests in land which are generally also termed interests but are not real property. The interests include (1) a profit a Prendre, (2) a license and (3) easements and rights-of-way.

Leasehold

A leasehold is a term interest that generally provides for a fixed term during which the lessee may get the property under production. Most leases provide for the primary term to be extended indefinitely so long as there is commercial production.

Independent Royalty Interest

An independent royalty interest is a share of the mineral production, free of the cost of production, and carved out of the mineral interest. The independent royalty owner is entitled to the stated share of production without regard to lease terms. These royalty interests are typically created by mineral owners who sell most of their rights but retain an overriding royalty. Independent royalty interests have the following characteristics:

1. May be separated from the mineral title before or after leasing.

2. May exist in perpetuity.

3. Non-expense-bearing interests in gross production.

4. No participation in bonuses, rentals, etc.

5. No executive power to possession, leasing or development.

6. Language refers to participation in production rather than ownership of minerals in place.

To create a hard mineral royalty, it is desirable to call the interest "royalty" and specifically deny ownership of minerals in place and also exclude from the interest all executive powers and participation benefits.

Term Mineral Interests

Term mineral interests are generally created by grant or reservation in a deed for a fixed term of years and "so long thereafter as oil or gas is produced from the land." Term mineral interests are very similar to leasehold interests.

Characteristics of **term mineral interests**:
1. no development obligations
2. generally no royalty
3. full incidents of fee ownership
4. may execute leases and develop
5. not subject to abandonment
6. may be construed against grantor

Characteristics of **Leasehold interests**:
1. development obligations
2. subject to royalty reservation
3. construed against lessee
4. forfeiture for noncompliance

Profit a Prendre

A profit is a right to remove and acquire title to severed ore. It is primarily used in states that do not recognize in-place ownership. All states except Louisiana allow possessory estates in hard minerals to be separated in ownership from the surface; however, with oil and gas, a number of states do not allow estates in oil and gas minerals to be separated in ownership from the surface. In states where in-place ownership is not recognized, a profit is indicated by language of use; whereas, a fee interest is indicated by language of possession. Characteristics of profit are:

1. Gives right of enjoyment rather than possessory right.
2. Subject to abandonment.
3. Commercial rather than personal.

License

A license is a transitory right to enter upon the land. It is personal, nonassignable and revocable. A license has the following characteristics:

1. creates a privilege, not a right
2. grantor retains all rights of ownership

3. licensee's interest is tenuous and is maintained
   at the pleasure of the grantor
4. nonassignable without owner's consent
5. nonexclusive use
6. it is personal (personal use), not commercial

Easements and Rights-of-Way

Easements and rights-of-way are rights to enter upon or have access to land for a specific purpose; these rights may also place constraints on the use of land. Easements and rights-of-way may be perpetual, assignable and inheritable, but may be lost by abandonment.

Fractional Mineral Fee

The conveyance of fractional mineral and royalty interests by owners of fee mineral interests generally have a negative effect on mineral development. As a result titles become complex, difficult to abstract and lose their marketability. One solution to this is to limit fractional interests to a fixed term, and so long as minerals are produced in paying quantities.

Sales of undivided interests are commonly used to finance mineral ventures. Grants or reservations of undivided interests create co-owners with common rights to possess and develop the entire mineral estate.

The most important aspect of undivided interests is to make clear in the conveyance how each fraction relates to the total fee interest, and also show how each fraction relates to the other fraction. Also if the grantor owns only a factional mineral interest and conveys a fractional interest deed, it may be unclear whether he is granting a fraction of his fraction, or a fraction of the entire interest.

In oil and gas, it is common to use the number of undivided mineral acres to the total acres. For example, the sale of 16 mineral acres would give the grantee one-tenth undivided interest of production if the total property includes 160 acres. If both the fraction and the mineral acreage are included in the deed, there could be a problem if the total acreage varies. For example, if the SE 1/4 of section 6 was actually 156 acres rather than 160 acres, there would be a discrepancy between the two interests. Where there is doubt, the courts generally attribute the interest conveyed in the second conveyance to the entire mineral estate rather than the fraction owned by the grantor of the second fraction.

Mineral Interests Versus Royalty Interests

In mineral leasing arrangements there is frequently much confusion over what is a mineral interest and what is a royalty interest. Whether you have a mineral interest or a royalty interest has a strong bearing on how the proceeds from a mineral lease are allocated.

A mineral interest is ownership of all incidents of mineral ownership; it is also an interest in the minerals in place and is subject to the costs of extraction. For example, the lessee in a mineral leasing arrangement holds a "working interest" or an "operating mineral interest" and is responsible for all production costs.

A royalty interest is the right to receive a cost-free share of any mineral actually produced or right to a share of the production. The royalty interest holder has no right to develop - only the mineral interest owner can extract the mineral. The royalty interest generally gives no right to bonuses or rentals.

It is better to have a 1/10 royalty interest than a 1/10 mineral interest because the royalty interest is cost free. For example, it may cost 85 percent of the value of a mineral commodity to get it produced.   So if the mineral production amounted $1,000, a 1/10 royalty interest would be $(1/10)(\$1,000) = \$100$; whereas, a 1/10 mineral interest would be worth $(.15)(1/10)(\$1,000) = \$15$.

Non-ownership Theory

The courts responsible for development of the non-ownership theory held that the owner of the oil and gas rights did not acquire title to the oil and gas until it was produced or captured in a well. In other words, the owner of a severed oil and gas interest has the right to explore, develop and produce oil and gas from the land. There is no present right to possess the oil and gas in place. This right to explore, develop and produce oil and gas is called a **profit a prendre**. Louisiana, Oklahoma, Wyoming, California and several other states follow the non-ownership theory.

Space Formerly Occupied by Minerals Reverts to Surface Owner

Once minerals have removed from the soil, the space occupied by the minerals revert to the surface owner by operation of law. This rule is based on the general interpretation of a mineral grant as giving the grantee the right to explore for, produce, and reduce to possession if found, the minerals granted, but not the rock containing the minerals.

Ownership in Place Theory

The ownership in place theory allows the owner of the severed oil and gas interest to not only the right to use land for exploration, development and production of oil and gas, but also the right to present possession of the oil and gas in place. Texas, Colorado, Mississippi, Kansas and New Mexico are among the states that follow the ownership theory.

Corporeal Interests

A corporeal interest in land includes the right of possession of the land. Thus rights to oil and gas are corporeal in "ownership" states. An incorporeal interest in land includes only the right to use the land rather than possess the land - thus the rights to oil and gas are incorporeal in "nonownership" states. A royalty interest, which is a share of the oil and gas produced free of production, is always considered to be an incorporeal right regardless of the state because there is no present right of possession.

Rule of Capture

The law of capture means that the owner of a tract of land has title to all oil and gas produced from wells drilled on his tracts. This is true even if the produced oil had migrated from another tract under a different ownership. An important aspect of this rule is that there is no liability for draining the neighboring tract. Of course the rule of capture is somewhat limited by various state oil and gas conservation statutes as well as the doctrine of correlative rights.

Correlative Rights Doctrine

The correlative rights doctrine provides that the rights of an owner to capture oil and gas under his property is subject to the requirement that the oil and gas be removed without waste or negligence. If a producer causes oil and gas to be wasted through negligent practices, there is no shield from liability by the rule of capture. The purpose of this doctrine is to allow separate owners producing from a common reservoir an opportunity to remove an amount of oil in proportion to their ownership.

Doctrine of Ad Coelum

The **Ad Coelum** doctrine is based on the common law doctrine that a property owner has title to everything from the heavens to the core of the earth. Although this doctrine has application to "hard" minerals, fugacious minerals have the capacity to migrate through permeable reservoirs, it is generally impossible to ascertain their original position in the subsurface.

Adverse Possession

Adverse possession occurs where a person is in open and notorious possession of the land which is hostile and adverse to the interests of the true owner for a long period of time. The person in adverse possession was presumed to be in possession under a lost grant. The various states have adopted statutes of limitation which prevent actions to recover possession of land by persons out of possession for more than the period of time specified by the statute. A co-owner is not allowed to acquire title against another co-owner by adverse possession unless it can be shown that his possession is hostile and adverse to the claim of his co-tenant.

Adverse Possession of Severed Minerals

Title to severed mineral interests can be perfected only by actual possession. Therefore, the owner of the severed mineral interest cannot show possession of the mineral interest by possession of the surface. The period of adverse possession can start only after the person in possession of the surface initiates possession of the minerals by exploration, development or production of such minerals.

MINERAL LEASE CLAUSES

Granting Clause

The granting clause sets forth what rights are given by the lessor to the lessee. The most significant rights include (1) the substances covered by the lease, (2) a description of the lands, and (3) the types of uses permitted by the lease. A lease generally gives an implied right to use the surface of the land for uses incidental to mining. The "accommodation doctrine" is based on the principle that both the surface owner and the mineral owner would be required to accommodate their use of the surface if possible.

The mineral grant should address a number of considerations that are unique for each mineral deposit. In other words, the spatial distribution of the reserves, the geology, mineralogy and geography are all significant in determining the type and extent of surface facilities and transportation systems necessary to establish a commercial mine. The following concerns should be addressed in the mineral grant:

1. Specify minerals or mineral categories.

2. Legal description - verify that it covers the appropriate lands; excess land means excess liability; attempt to include potential extension of ore body or potential reserves.

3. Right of ingress and egress for power, transportation, water, etc.

4. Right to construct necessary facilities, particularly specialized facilities that may be needed.

5. Include all rights necessary to explore, mine and remove the mineral deposit.

6. In addition to conventional mining rights, it may be important to specifically provide in the grant that unconventional recovery methods such as **in situ** solution mining or heap leaching may be conducted on the leased premises.

Mother Hubbard Clause

The mother hubbard clause usually follows the land description and provides that the parties intend to pass all other lands of the grantor, contiguous to the tract described and located in a specified section or county. This clause is used to protect against ambiguities in the description and make certain the entire property is conveyed. The land owner should be aware that the mother hubbard clause could cause the lease to cover portions of his land that were intentionally omitted from the description.

Rentals

Rentals are a fixed amount for each acre per year for the right to use the land. They are generally paid in advance on the anniversary date of the lease. Although rental payments are normally not related to production, some leases allow payment of production royalties to satisfy the rental payment requirement. In this respect, rental payments may be similar to advance royalty payments. However, rental payments are not credited towards future production royalties as are **advance royalties**.

Escalating rentals are required in some leases for the purpose of encouraging development or to discourage speculative holding of leases. An escalating rental clause generally provides for an increased rental payment in successive years during the primary term to the extent that holding such a lease without production can be a severe financial burden on the lessee.

The **delay rental** is a payment from the lessee to the lessor to maintain the lease without drilling during the primary term. **Delay rental** payments are generally required on an annual basis.

Bonus Payments

A **bonus payment** is generally a lump-sum, one-time payment made at the date the lease agreement is executed. This payment, which is normally not related to any future royalty payment, is based either on (1) an appraisal of the property, or (2) the rental rate for the first year.

In the acquisition of government leases, competitive leasing generally involves the selling of a mineral property at public auction to the bidder who offers the highest bonus bid. The bonus bid is generally a lumpsum offer for each acre of the tract and the bid is made at public auction.

Royalties

Royalty is a share of the mineral production free of the costs of production to be paid by the lessor to the lessee. A royalty interest is a nonoperating interest and gives no right to lease or share in rental or bonus payments. Royalty rates vary considerably, depending on the commodity involved, the type of mine and the mining method. Each mineral deposit is unique; consequently, mining costs and profits vary accordingly.

Royalty rates are assessed (1) on the basis of volume (e.g. sand & gravel at 40 cents per cubic yard), (2) on the basis of weight (e.g. coal at $2.50 per long or short ton), and (3) a percentage of the gross or net value of the mineral produced from the leased premises (e.g. 1/8 of the production of oil and gas). It is a good practice to define weight terms such as "wet ton," "dry ton," "short ton" and "long ton." When using volume measurements one should consider the difference between "in place" or "bank" measurements and "loose" measurements. This is significant because some materials swell over 30 percent after extraction. Other terms that should be defined include "gross proceeds," "net proceeds" and "net smelter returns." The royalty clause should also contain a complete list of deductible expenses.

Land management agencies generally assess a higher royalty rate of a commodity mined by surface methods than the same commodity mined by underground methods. The reason for this is twofold - underground mining is generally more expensive and surface mining may preclude future use of the land.

Royalties have always been difficult to collect from placer gold and gem mining operations. The likely reason is that the miner recovers gold or gems having an exceptionally high market value before processing operations are necessary.

Technical Aspects of the Ore Body that Should Affect Royalty Rate

1. Amount of overburden
2. Shape of the orebody
3. Reserves: potential for additional reserves

127

4. Grade of ore
5. Metallurgical problems
6. Geotechnical problems and mineability
7. Environmental problems including reclamation
8. Proximity to market; access; power; etc.
9. Marketability

Royalty Based on Net Proceeds

One disadvantage of a royalty based on net proceeds is the possibility that the lessee will inflate the costs of the mining operation with nonessential costs, so as to reduce the net profits. For example, the lessee may be tempted to reduce his net profits by utilizing a variety of complex accounting procedures or by commingling activities on the lease with other mining or business activities. However, the lessor can control this practice by carefully defining the allowable cost items so that there will be no opportunity for the lessee to reduce the net profits by claiming mining costs that are not essential and directly related to the mining operation.

Another possible problem in connection with the lessor taking a share of the net proceeds might arise if the lessee's company were inefficiently operated. In such a case the net proceeds would be lower than one would receive from a well managed company because, of course, net proceeds are directly related to the efficiency of the operation. This problem could be minimized by leasing to companies with a proven management record.

Captive Market

A common problem related to a royalty based on net smelter returns occurs where an integrated company does not sell its ores to an independent mill or smelter (captive market) and it is necessary to establish a fair-market value for the ores even though no actual sale is made. For example, suppose the mill or buying station is not purchasing ores from independent operators in the district because the ores are shipped to a buying station or mill owned wholly or in part by the lessee. Establishing a market value for the ores in a captive market may be determined by computation of the market value of the ore as based upon the assay value of the ore(s) and applicable market price quotation for the month of production, less any processing and transportation costs incurred after departure of the ore from the mining property. **Engineering** and **Mining Journal, Metals Week**, or some other trade publication, which the lessor and lessee agree upon, may be used as the basis for the price quotation. The royalty due is determined by multiplying the appropriate ore value per ton times the royalty rate in the lease.

Renegotiation of Royalty

Renegotiation of lease terms, especially royalty rates, is another method for the lessor to maintain fair-market value in light of the changing technology and economic conditions. However, the possibility of renegotiation of terms is also a problem to the lessee. For the purposes of mine design and production planning, the lessee needs to anticipate future costs.

Excess Reserves

If a single lessee acquires vast acreages of mineral property, he has in effect a monopoly. A lessee has excessive reserves when the total reserves exceed what can reasonably be produced in the foreseeable future at the present rate of production. The purpose for acquiring such excessive reserves is to control the market by eliminating the competition. From the position of a lessor, it is mismanagement to allow a lessee to hold mineral property for speculative purposes. Consequently, there have been many methods devised to require a lessee to develop a lease in a timely manner and to ensure that the lessee does not hold too much land. These methods include:

1. Diligent development requirements

2. Advance royalties

3. Escalating rentals, and

4. Maximum acreage and leasehold requirements.

High-Grading

High-grading occurs when the high-valued ore is removed early to maximize profits during the early stages of a mining operation and recover costs as rapidly as possible. The lessor, however, is generally left with a large quantity of subeconomic ore that is not feasible to mine. In many cases, it could be possible to extract a much greater part of the resource by proper planning and mining. High-grading may be avoided by requiring a proposed plan operations prior to initiation of mining. An escalating royalty provision may also be beneficial in minimizing high-grading because an excessively high royalty rate may encourage high-grading.

Logical Mining Units

There is generally a minimum amount of reserves that will justify a company investing in mining equipment and processing facilities. In such a situation one should apply diligent development and maximum leasehold requirements with good judgement. It is more prudent to have minerals leased to a company who has the plant and capability to ultimately develop the resource rather than a speculator who is not capable of developing the property.

Royalties on Associated By-Products

Although a lessee acquires a lease to develop and produce certain minerals, associated minerals may also be profitably recovered. A royalty clause should be designed to cover any by-product mineral that may be recovered in future operations under the lease. Generally it is beneficial to both lessor and lessee to have a lower royalty rate for by-product minerals to encourage the lessee to recover them so that both parties may profit.

Advance Minimum Royalty

Advance minimum royalty may be required in the lease while there is no production for the lease in paying quantities. In the event the lease comes under production, the payment of advance royalties may be credited towards the payment of production royalties. If the lease never comes under production, the advance minimum royalties are generally forfeited.

Sliding Scale or Escalating Royalty

Sliding scale or escalating royalty provisions are designed so that the higher the grade or value of the ore per ton, the higher will be the production royalty rate. The advantage of this approach is that it encourages maximum extraction of the ore body and minimizes the need for the lessee to high-grade the ore body. The lessee is more likely to produce a low-value ore if the royalty rate is set low as an inducement.

Royalty in Kind

A provision in the lease that allows the lessor to take "royalty in kind" rather than a royalty payment derived from the sale of the lessor's share of the production gives the lessor added flexibility. This method gives the lessor the opportunity to take actual possession of his share of the mineral production before it is marketed. Some leases provide that "royalty in kind" may be paid rather than royalty payments at the option of the lessee. Such an arrangement could present a monumental problem to the lessor if oil and gas were delivered rather than conventional payments.

Overriding Royalty

An overriding royalty is a cost-free share of the production, carved out of the lessee's interest in a lease. Of course, termination of the lease also terminates any overriding royalty interest. The services of landsmen and geologists are commonly compensated by overriding royalty interests. In many leases, overriding royalties are limited to a total of 2 to 5 percent of the gross value of the production. The lessor has an interest in limiting overriding royalties because such royalties represent additional costs for the lessee and may cause the property to lose its commercial value.

Royalty Payments

The royalty clause should detail the time, place and frequency royalty payments are to be tendered. It should also indicate the consequences of failure to make timely payments.

Term Clause

The term clause establishes a set period of time for the rights given in the granting clause. Most leases provide for a primary term of one to 20 years (most commonly 10 years) to get a property into production. Once production is obtained within the primary term, the lease term is automatically extended so long as commercial production is continued. If a lease should continue beyond the primary term by means of production or other operations, the lease would be in the secondary term. The most important consideration in establishing the length of the primary term is to allow sufficient time to get the lease into production.

Provisions in the lease that allow it to continue beyond the primary term must be properly defined in the lease. This is accomplished by defining the term "in paying quantities" as a minimum amount of royalty payment that would constitute sufficient production that would allow the lease to continue beyond its primary term.

Oil and gas leases commonly require that if drilling operations are not started within one year after the effective date of the lease, the lease will terminate unless **delay rentals** are paid to the lessor. A **delay rental** is a payment from lessee to lessor due on each anniversary date of the lease to maintain the lease during the primary term. If production is not established by the end of the primary term, the lease will terminate. If production is established, the lease will continue into its secondary term and continue until production ceases. A lease should specify how long it can maintain producing status if there is a cessation of production. For example, the lease could specify that a cessation of production for a period in excess of 180 consecutive days will automatically remove the lease from producing status.

Assignment Clause

The assignment clause generally allows the lessee and (or) the lessor to assign their rights under the lease. It is to the advantage of the lessor to prohibit assignment of the lease without written consent of the lessor. Most lessors would like the opportunity to verify that an assignee is capable of performing the terms and conditions of the lease. If written consent is not required, the lessor should most certainly require notification of any assignment within a specified time period.

Many leases, particularly government leases, prohibit assignments of undivided interests. Also assignments of less than 40-acre subdivisions are commonly prohibited. Such divided tracts would not likely be developed because they would not represent logical mining or drilling units.

Diligent Development Clause

Diligent development clauses are included in leases to prevent speculative holding of leases. This may be accomplished by specific mandatory annual work requirements or, by such indefinite language as "lessee shall use reasonable diligence in prospecting and developing minerals." These provisions should be based on the nature of the mineral deposit and the needs of the parties involved. It is generally a good practice to spell out in detail the type of work and the amount of work to be accomplished in a specified time period to avoid later misunderstanding. The lease may provide that minimum royalty payments may substitute for certain work. Conversely, the Federal geothermal resources lease allows for exploration work to substitute for escalating rentals.

Shut-In Clause

The shut-in clause allows the lessee to maintain a lease even though there is no production from a well capable of producing. The effect of this provision is to classify a shut-in well as a producing well which would cause the lease to continue indefinitely during the primary or secondary term. Typically, a lease will require that shut-in royalties be paid annually to keep the lease in effect. The shut-in clause may specify a time limit on how long the lease may continue into the secondary term without actual production. Some leases specify the circumstances under which a shut-in clause may be effective, such as lack of market or unavailable transportation.

Pooling Clause

The pooling clause allows the lessee to combine a leased tract with adjoining leased tracts for development purposes. The purpose of this provision is to consolidate under one operator all the landowners having an interest in a common reservoir. Therefore, the optimum number of wells are positioned in such a way as to maximize recovery and efficiency.

There are two types of pooling arrangements: (1) voluntary pooling by lease agreement; and (2) compulsory pooling or forced pooling by administrative agency under authority of state law or regulations. Although statutory pooling cannot be avoided, it is to the lessor's advantage to require written consent to pool. This would give the lessor an opportunity to review a specific proposal to pool and ascertain the effect on his retained royalty interest. Once a lease is included in a pool area, many of the lease provisions may be drastically changed to conform with other leases in the pool.

Pugh Clause

A pugh clause may be included in an oil and gas lease where less than all of the leased land is pooled. The pugh clause would cause the portion of the lease in the pool to be severed and considered as another lease separate and distinct from the original lease.

Right of Inspection Clause

The right of inspection clause authorizes the lessor to inspect the records, books and accounts pertaining to the leased mineral property. It may be important for the lessor to verify such items as production, taxation, assays, reserve calculations and other matters that would affect royalty.

Reports

Some leases require that the lessee file monthly, quarterly or annual reports with the lessor on a specified date. These reports generally include the total production during the report period as well as the price received at the first point of sale. Maps may also be required to show all workings, improvements and the distribution of the ore deposit.

Force Majeure Clause

If a lessee is prevented from performing the terms of the lease because of **force majeure** clause should specifically identify the circumstances under which **force majeure** could be invoked. The types of circumstances normally listed are those problems that occur which are beyond the reasonable control of the lessee. Perhaps the most significant effect on a lease title would occur if **force majeure** allowed a lease to continue beyond its primary term without the necessity of production.

Warranty Clause

The warranty clause is a provision in a lease where the lessor guarantees that his title has no defect and agrees to defend the title in case of a dispute. Because the warranty clause benefits only the lessee, a prudent lessor may attempt to have the clause deleted. In some cases the lessor has been held liable for the amount expended by the lessee on the lease.

Hold Harmless

Hold harmless clauses are incorporated in leases to require the lessee to indemnify and hold the lessor harmless from any liability claims, losses or damages cause by operations of the lessee or lessee's assignees on the leased premises.

Surface Protection

Unless the lease specifies that the lessor is liable for damages to the surface estate, there may be no obligation for the lessee to restore the surface area. Of course, if the lessee causes unnecessary damage through negligence, such a lessee could be liable for damages. An operating and reclamation plan may be agreed upon by the lessor and lessee. Satisfactory performance under such plans could be guaranteed by a bond.

Sampling and Assaying

The lease should contain a procedure for weighing, sampling, assaying and moisture determination. Sampling should be done as often as possible. If ores from separate ownerships are commingled in the same concentration operation, the ore should be sampled and assayed prior to commingling.

Establish the Point Royalty Is Payable

It is important to establish the point that royalties are payable in the royalty clause. The following items should be considered:

1. Provision for ore severed from ground, but not shipped or sold.

2. Cost added by manufacture should be deductible because the greater the refinement, the greater the gross income.

3. Consider sales to subsidiaries or captive markets.

4. Lease could provide that royalty payments are made when the lessee receives payment for product.

Options

The option agreement generally contains an exclusive right to explore and evaluate the lands during the option period. The option period is a set period of time stated in the agreement during which the mining company may cancel the agreement without obligation to lease or purchase the property. The option period generally is based on the length of time necessary for a company to evaluate a property. The length of time will of course be variable, depending on the nature of the project. It is essential that the agreement allow for adequate exploration time and the right to

conduct the necessary exploration activities. At the end of the option period the lands may be purchased or leased at the price stated in the option agreement. The terms and conditions of the purchase contract or lease should be incorporated into the option agreement in order to avoid future misunderstandings.

Options are used primarily to keep the front-end investment in a mineral property as low as possible so that scarce exploration money may be spent to evaluate the property rather than to acquire the property. If the property does not prove out, then it may be dropped with no obligation for further payment. One shortcoming of the option agreement for the mining company is that the purchase price or lease rentals and royalties are established with the assumption that the mineral property will prove economic. It is obvious that a property may be acquired by outright purchase at a lower price when the mineral potential is unknown. The owner or the optionor of the property is protected to the extent that the optionee has a specific period during which he must explore the property, therefore lessening the possibility that the property may be held for speculative purposes.

FEDERAL MINERAL LEASING

The Mineral Leasing Act of 1920, as amended (30 U.S.C. 181 et seq.) provides that "deposits of coal, phosphate, sodium, potassium, oil, oil shale, native asphalt, solid and semisolid bitumen, and bituminous rock (including oil-impregnated rock or sands from which oil is recoverable only by special treatment after the deposit is mined or quarried) or gas, and lands containing such deposits owned by the United States" may be acquired only through a leasing system. For the most up-to-date and detailed requirements concerning Federal leasable minerals one should consult the most recent volume of Title 43 of the **Code of Federal Regulations**. Because these regulations are under constant revision, it is also a good practice to check the **Cumulative List of Sections Affected** which gives a monthly update on new regulations, and the **Cumulative List of Parts Affected** which appears in each issue of the Federal Register. Federal leasable minerals are covered in the following parts of the **Code of Federal Regulations**:

Part 3100 - **Oil and Gas Leasing**

Part 3200 - **Geothermal Resources Leasing**

Part 3300 - **Outer Continental Shelf Minerals**

Part 3400 - **Coal Management**

Part 3500 - **Leasing of Minerals other than the above**

OIL AND GAS LEASING

Oil and gas leasing on Federal lands is administered by the Bureau of Land Management through a competitive and noncompetitive leasing system. Oil and gas leases are issued for public domain lands under the authority of the Mineral Leasing Act of February 25, 1920, as amended (30 U.S.C. 181 et seq.). Authority for leasing on acquired lands comes from the Leasing Act for Acquired Lands enacted on August 7, 1947. Upon passage of the Federal Onshore Oil and Gas Leasing Reform Act of 1987 (Pub. L. 100-203), the Bureau of Land Management made a major revision of the Federal oil and gas regulations in 43 CFR 3100. Made effective on June 17, 1988, the new regulations cover competitive and noncompetitive onshore oil and gas leasing.

Competitive Leasing

All lands available for leasing are to be offered for competitive oral bidding. Each BLM state office is required to hold sales for such lands at least quarterly. At the day of the auction, the minimum acceptable bid of $2 per acre, the total first years rental and a $75 administrative fee must be paid. The remainder of the bonus bid moneys for each parcel is due within 10 working days.[1]

Competitive leases shall have a primary term of 5 years. The lands offered in leasing units will be a maximum of 2560 acres per lease. As an exception, in Alaska the leases may be up to 5,760 acres in size.[2]

At least 45 days before a competitive auction, lands to be offered for competitive lease sale as included in a List of Lands Available for Competitive Nominations or in a Notice of Competitive Lease Sale are posted in the BLM state office. Lands included in the List of Lands Available for Competitive Nominations which are not nominated are not included in a Notice of Competitive Lease Sale. These lands are available for a 2-year period for noncompetitive leasing.[3]

Noncompetitive Leasing

Only lands that have been offered competitively and receive no bid are made available for noncompetitive leasing. These lands become available for a period of 2 years beginning on the first business day following the last day of the competitive oral auction, or when formal nominations have been requested, or the first business day following the posting of the Notice of Competitive Lease Sale. Lease applications receive priority as of the date and time of filing. However all noncompetitive offers are considered simultaneously filed if received in the BLM office during the first business day following the last day of competitive oral auction, or when formal nominations have been requested, or the first business day following the posting of the Notice of Competitive Lease Sale.[4]

Lease offers are not made for less than 640 acres (2,560 acres in Alaska) and may not include more than 10,240 acres. All noncompetitive leases are issued for a primary term of 10 years.[5]

Each competitive or noncompetitive lease offer must be accompanied by full payment of the first years rental based on the total acreage. The amount of rental for all leases issued after December 22, 1987, shall be $1.50 per acre for the first 5 years of the lease term and $2 per acre for any subsequent year. A royalty rate of 12 1/2 percent on all leases is required on the amount or value of the production removed or sold.[6]

Reference - Oil and Gas Leasing

1. 43 CFR 3120.
2. 43 CFR 3120.2-3.
3. 43 CFR 3120.3-6.
4. 43 CFR 3120.2.
5. 43 CFR 3120.3-1.
6. 43 CFR 3120.3-1.

GEOTHERMAL RESOURCES LEASING

Leasing Authority

Leasing of geothermal resources in Federal lands is authorized by the Geothermal Steam Act of 1970 (30 U.S.C. 1001-1025). In order to administer this law, regulations contained in 43 CFR 3200 were published December 21, 1973, and made effective January 1, 1974. These regulations are administered by the Bureau of Land Management.

Geothermal Resources: a Definition

From the standpoint of lease administration, geothermal resources and by-products are defined by 43 CFR 3200.0-5 as follows:

"**Geothermal resources**" means geothermal steam and associated geothermal resources which include: (1) All products of geothermal processes embracing indigenous steam, hot water and hot brines; (2)steam and other gases, hot water and hot brines resulting from water, gas or other fluids artificially introduced into geothermal formations; (3) heat or other associated energy found in geothermal formations; and (4) any by-products derived from them.

"**By-product**" means (1) any mineral or minerals (exclusive of oil, hydrocarbon gas, and helium) which are found in solution or in association with geothermal steam and which have a value of less than 75 per centum of the value of the geothermal steam or are not, because of the quantity, quality, or technical difficulties in extraction and production, of sufficient value to warrant extraction and production by themselves, and (2) commercially demineralized water.

Known Geothermal Resources Areas

Similar to oil and gas leasing, the issuance of geothermal resources leases is administered by the Bureau of Land Management through a "competitive" and a "noncompetitive" system. All lands within a "known geothermal resources area" (KGRA) are issued only through competitive bidding. The BLM is also responsible for the classification of land as KGRAs.

A "known geothermal resource area" is defined in 43 CFR 3200.0-55 (K) as:

"an area in which the geology, nearby discoveries, competitive interests, or other indicia would, in the opinion of the Secretary, engender a belief in men who are experienced in the subject matter that the prospects for extraction of geothermal steam or associated geothermal resources are good enough to warrant expenditures of money for that purpose."

One of the most controversial ways a KGRA may be established is by competitive interest. Competitive interest occurs in the entire area covered by an application if at least one half of the lands covered by that application are also covered by another application which was filed during the same filing period.

Geophysical Exploration

Although geophysical exploration is allowed on a geothermal resources lease, a person must obtain a permit to conduct exploration operations on Federal lands not under a lease. A "notice of intent" describing the proposed exploration operations and a $5,000 bond to insure compliance with the terms of the permit is filed with the BLM district manager in the district in which the operations are planned. The district manager has 30 days to either approve or disapprove the permit. When exploration operations are completed, a "notice of completion of explorations" is filed with the district manager. The district manager then has 90 days to notify the permittee whether or not the conditions of the permit are satisfied.

Filing Applications (Noncompetitive)

Applications filed for lands outside any KGRA must be submitted in sealed envelopes and be accompanied by a nonrefundable $50 filing fee and the first year's rental. Each calendar month is a separate filing period. When the application is filed, the date of filing is stamped on the envelope to document the filing period. The first working day of the following month, all applications are opened. They are platted to determine if overlapping applications cause a KGRA due to competitive interests. All applications that do not fall within a KGRA are assigned priority according to the filing date.

Lease Size and Acreage Limitation

A single lease must not exceed 2,560 acres or contain less than 640 acres. The lease must also fit within an area of six miles

square or within an area of six surveyed sections in length or
width. A single lessee may hold a maximum of 20,480 acres per
state.

Term

Leases are issued for a primary term of 10 years and so long
thereafter as steam is produced in paying quantities, up to 40
additional years. If the lease is producing at the end of this 40-
year term, another 40-year term may be allowed.

Royalty

A royalty rate of between 10 and 15 percent of the value of the
steam is required upon production. By-products from production
are subject to a royalty rate of not more than 5 percent; however
by-product minerals subject to the Mineral Leasing Act of 1920, as
amended, are under a different royalty rate.

Competitive Leases

Lands within a KGRA may be leased only through competitive
bidding. Tracts within a KGRA may be put up for a competitive
lease sale either by nominations from the public or by the BLM's
own initiative. At the discretion of the Secretary of the Interior,
notice of a lease sale is published in a newspaper of general
circulation in the area in which the lands are situated. The notice
contains such information as the time and place of sale, description
of the lands, procedure for submitting bids, terms and conditions of
the sale, with required rental and royalty rates. A separate sealed
bid is submitted for each lease tract together with one-half of the
amount bid and a statement of qualifications. Leases are offered to
the highest qualified bidder.

COAL LEASING

Coal Acquired under the Coal Lands Act of 1873

Coal has never been subject to the Mining Law of 1872. Acquisition of fee title to lands known to be valuable for coal, or the development of coal deposits, was pursuant to the Coal Lands Act of 1873. The Mineral Leasing Act of 1920, as amended (30 U.S.C. 181 et seq.) established coal as a leasing act mineral on February 25, 1920.

With enactment of the Federal Coal Leasing Amendments Act of 1976 (30 U.S.C. 201), the Federal procedures for leasing coal were substantially changed. For the most part, coal is now available through a competitive leasing system. The major elements of the competitive coal leasing system are land use planning, setting regional leasing targets, coal activity planning and coal lease sale scheduling. The detailed requirements for acquiring coal exploration licenses and leases are found in 43 CFR Part 3400. This portion of the **Code of Federal Regulations** should be examined for more information because there has been a constant stream of regulatory changes in the area of coal management. Noncompetitive leases are available only to preference right lease applications based on prospecting permits issued prior to August 4, 1976.

Bids Must Be Fair Market Value

No bid will be accepted if it is less than the fair market value determined by the Secretary. Prior to the determination of fair market value, the Secretary will receive and consider public comment on the fair market value.

To Obtain New Leases, Old Leases Must Be Producing in Ten Years

No new coal lease shall be issued to any lessee who holds a lease or leases issued by the United States for Coal deposits if the lease or leases have been held for a period of ten years and are not producing coal in commercial quantities. The ten-year period may be extended if operations under the lease were interrupted by strikes, casualties or the elements at no fault of the lessee.

Land-Use Plan Required
Prior to Lease Sale

No lease sale shall be held unless the lands containing the coal deposits have been included in a comprehensive land-use plan and sale is determined to be compatible with the plan. The Secretary of the Interior shall prepare land-use plans on lands under his administration and will notify the Secretary of Agriculture if plans are required for National Forest lands. If there should be a lack of Federal interest in the surface or insufficient coal resources to justify the costs of a Federal comprehensive land-use plan, the lease sale can still be held if the lands containing the coal deposits have been included in a land-use plan by the state in which the lands are located. If any person should have an interest adversely affected by the adoption of the plan prepared by the state, a public hearing shall be held on the proposed plan prior to adoption.

Surface Management Agency Other Than
Department of the Interior

Leases covering lands that are under the surface management of any Federal agency other than the Department of the Interior will be issued only upon consent of that agency and subject to such conditions as that agency may request.

Public Hearing and Notice
Prior to Lease Sale

Prior to the lease sale, the Secretary of the Interior shall hold public hearings in the area which would be affected by the mining under such a lease. Also, no lease sale shall be held until after the notice of the proposed offering for lease has been given once a week for three consecutive weeks in a newspaper of general circulation in the county in which the leases are located.

Coal Exploration License

No person is allowed to conduct coal exploration for commercial purposes without an exploration license. An exploration license has a term not to exceed two years and does not confer rights to a lease. A separate exploration license is required in each state. Each application for an exploration license must identify the general area and the probable methods of exploration. The license will include conditions to protect the environment. The licensee is allowed to remove only such quantities of coal necessary for analysis and study. If the license should cover lands under the administration of a surface management agency other than the Department of the Interior, that agency may prescribe additional conditions to protect the surface resources.

All geological, geophysical and core drilling information obtained by the licensee during exploration must be furnished to the Secretary. All such data shall be considered confidential so as to protect the competitive position of the licensee.

A person who willfully conducts coal exploration for commercial purposes without an exploration license shall be subject to a fine not to exceed $1,000 for each day of violation.

Logical Mining Unit

If the maximum economic recovery of a coal deposit may be improved by the consolidation of coal leases into a logical mining unit, the Secretary may approve such a consolidation. However, a public hearing must be held if requested by a person whose interest is or may be adversely affected. A logical mining unit is an area of land in which the coal resources can be developed in an efficient, economical, and orderly manner as a unit, with consideration to the conservation of coal reserves and other resources. Although a logical mining unit may include one or more Federal leases, the lands must be capable of being developed and operated as a single operation. It is also required that the reserves of the entire unit be mined within forty years or a lesser period of time if required by the Secretary. Any lease included within a logical unit shall be amended so as to be consistent with the logical mining unit. The total acreage of a logical mining unit shall not exceed 25,000 acres, including both Federal and nonfederal lands.

Terms of Coal Lease

A coal lease shall be for a term of twenty years and for so long thereafter as coal is produced annually in commercial quantities from that lease; however, any lease not producing in commercial quantities at the end of ten years shall be terminated.

145

Minimum Royalty

Coal leases require a minimum royalty of 12 1/2 percent of the value of the coal; however, a lesser royalty may be required for coal recovered by underground operations.

Readjustment of Lease Conditions

Rentals, royalties and other conditions of the lease will be subject to readjustment at the end of the primary term of twenty years and at the end of each following ten-year period if the lease is extended.

Diligent Development

Coal leases are subject to requirements of diligent development and continuous operation unless such operations under the lease are interrupted by strikes, the elements or casualties through no fault of the lessee. However, the lessee must pay advanced royalties which shall be no less than the production royalty for the extended period.

UPLAND MINERAL LEASING
(excluding oil and gas, coal and geothermal resources)

Leasable Minerals - Public Domain

The mineral Leasing Act of 1920, as amended authorizes that specific minerals shall be disposed of through a leasing system. Minerals designated as leasable under this law include:

1. Phosphate;

2. Native asphalt, solid and semisolid bitumen and bituminous rock including oil-impregnated rock or sands from which oil is recoverable only by special treatment after the deposit is mined;

3. Sulphur in the states of Louisiana and New Mexico; and

4. Chlorides, sulfates, carbonates, borates, silicates, or nitrates of potassium and sodium.

Leasable Minerals in Acquired Lands

Leasable minerals in acquired lands may be leased pursuant to the Mineral Leasing Act for Acquired Lands (30 U.S.C. 351-359), enacted on August 7, 1947. All minerals that now qualify as locatable minerals in public domain lands (see chapter on Acquired Lands) may in some cases be obtained through a mineral lease on acquired lands. Leasable minerals in this category would include gold, silver, copper, gems, uranium, etc.

Department of Agriculture Lands

The issuance of leases and permits on National Forest Lands and other lands under the surface management of the Department of Agriculture is subject to the discretion of the Secretary of Agriculture. Mineral leases will not be issued without the consent of the Secretary of Agriculture. If a lease or permit is authorized, the right to explore, develop, and mine is subject to any stipulations that may be attached to protect surface resources. Lessees and permittees are required also to comply with any additional regulations that the Secretary of Agriculture requires.

Filing Procedure

Application for leases or permits are filed with the appropriate fees in the land office of the Bureau of Land Management of the state in which the permits or leases are sought. When an application is received in the land office, it is date-stamped to establish priority and a serial number is assigned. In the event of conflicting applications, priority of applications is established by the time and date of filing. Conflicting applications received by mail or filed over the counter at the same time are resolved by public drawing.

Prospecting Permit

A prospecting permit allows the permittee an exclusive right to prospect and explore within a permit area to establish the existence of valuable minerals. The permittee is allowed to remove only such deposits as necessary to conduct experimental studies and must keep a record of all minerals removed. A prospecting permit does not authorize mining in commercial quantities.

Prospecting permits are normally issued for a term of two years; however, a permit may be extended for a period of four years if certain conditions are met.

Applications for a preference-right lease must be filed in the land office not later than 30 days after the prospecting permit expires.

Lease Term

Leases are issued for a primary term of 20 years and are subject to readjustment of terms if the lease is to be renewed. Asphalt leases are issued for a primary term of 10 years. Hardrock mineral leases for acquired lands have a term which is established by the BLM but cannot exceed 20 years.

SALABLE MINERALS IN BLM ADMINISTERED LANDS

The Materials Act of July 31, 1947 (61 Stat. 681), as amended by the Acts of July 23, 1955 (69 Stat. 367) and September 28, 1962 (P.L. 87-713), authorized that certain mineral materials be disposed either through a contract of sale or a free use permit. This group of mineral materials, commonly known as "salable minerals" includes, but is not limited to petrified wood and common varieties of sand, stone, gravel, pumicite, cinders and clay on public land of the United States.[1] This material sale program is administered under procedures in 43 CFR Part 3600.

Effect on Mining Claims and Other Surface Uses

Mineral material disposals are not made where there are valid existing claims. Any subsequent mining location or mineral lease covering lands under a contract of sale for mineral materials is subject to the outstanding contract of sale. The United States reserves the right to continue to use the surface of lands under contract of sale for leases, licenses and permits concerning other resources; however, these subsequent leases must not interfere with the extraction or removal of the mineral material. Removal of materials from the public lands without authorization is an act of trespass.

Community Pits Closed to Mineral Entry

The regulations[2] provide for the establishment of community pits to be used by the general public to remove small amounts of material after a obtaining a nonexclusive permit from the district office of the BLM. A fee is charged for each cubic yard or ton of gravel removed plus an amount necessary to reclaim the site upon depletion of the pit. The regulations in 43 CFR 3600.0-5(g) state that the "establishment of a community pit, when noted on the appropriate Bureau of Land Management records or posted on the ground, constitutes a superior right to remove material as against any subsequent claim or entry of the lands."

Common Use Areas

Common use areas, like community pits, are established for nonexclusive disposals of mineral materials where the removal of materials would cause only a negligible surface disturbance. However, the establishment of a common use area does not create a superior right to remove material as against any subsequent claim or entry of the lands.[3]

Appraisal of Mineral Materials

Mineral materials are not sold at less than the appraised value. Also, a reappraisal is necessary every two years.[4]

Noncompetitive Sales

Noncompetitive sales may be made where it is impracticable to obtain competition and it is in the public interest. Individual sales, not to exceed 100,000 cubic yards may be made without advertising or calling for bids. The total aggregate of sales to an individual must not exceed 200,000 cubic yards in any one state during a twelve month period. The term of contract for noncompetitive sales is not to exceed five years excluding extension and removal periods. However, the noncompetitive sale of unlimited amounts of mineral materials is made where competition is not possible under the circumstances or there exists an emergency situation that threatens public property, health or safety.[5]

Competitive Sales

All sales are made through competitive bidding unless excluded for the reasons above. Sales are advertised in a newspaper of general circulation in the area where the material is located. A notice of sale is published once a week for two consecutive weeks giving the location of the lands, the material offered, type of materials, quantities, appraised price and the procedure for bidding. Written sealed bids, oral bids or both may be required, together with a bid deposit of not less than 10 percent of the appraised value of the mineral materials. The contract is awarded to the highest qualified bidder. The term for competitive contracts is not to exceed 10 years, excluding extension or removal periods.[6]

Free Use Permits

Free use permits are issued for a period not to exceed one year; however, a maximum term of 10 years is allowed for government agencies and municipalities. Material acquired under a free use permit must be for the permittee's own use and may not be traded or sold. There is no limitation on the number of permits or the amount or value of the material if the permit is issued to a government agency or municipality for use on a public project. A free use permit issued to a non-profit association or corporation must not allow disposal of more than 5,000 cubic yards in any period of twelve consecutive months.[7]

Free Use of Petrified Wood

The Act of September 28, 1962 (76 Stat. 652) removed petrified wood from the locatable mineral category and provided that it be available to the public on a free use basis in limited quantities. The Act defined petrified wood as "agatized, opalized, petrified, or silicified wood, or any material formed by the replacement of wood by silica or other matter." This free use program applies to all public lands administered by the Bureau of Land Management and a portion of the lands administered by the Bureau of Reclamation. No permit for free use is required for specimens over 250 pounds in weight. Specimens over 250 pounds may be used only for museum purposes. Collections of petrified wood on a free use basis is subject to the following rules;

1. One person is allowed to remove a maximum of 25 pounds plus one piece of petrified wood per day. However, that person may not remove more than 250 pounds in a calendar year.

2. No explosives or mechanized equipment may be used for the excavation or removal of petrified wood. Light trucks, up to one-ton capacity, used as a principal means of transportation, may be used for hauling purposes.

3. Free use petrified wood may not be bartered or sold to commercial dealers.

4. Extraction and removal of specimens must be done in a manner that avoids damage to the surface.

References - Salable Minerals in BLM Administered Lands

1. 30 USC 601 (1982).
2. 43 CFR 3604.1.
3. 43 CFR 3600.0-5(h).
4. 43 CFR 3610.1-2.
5. 43 CFR 3610.2-4.
6. 43 CFR 3610.3.
7. 43 CFR 3621.1.

SALABLE MINERALS IN FOREST SERVICE ADMINISTERED LANDS

Authority for the disposal of mineral materials (petrified wood and common varieties of sand, gravel, stone, pumice, pumicite, cinders, clay and other similar materials) in the National Forests is provided by the Materials Act of July 31, 1947, as amended by the Acts of August 31, 1950, July 23, 1955, and September 25, 1962 (30 U.S.C. 601-603). This material sale program comes under comprehensive regulations made effective July 24, 1984 and applies to both public domain and acquired lands within the National Forest system (36 CFR 228.40).

Disposal of Mineral Materials from Unpatented Claims

In contrast to the Bureau of Land Management regulations, the Forest Service regulations[1] provide for disposal of mineral materials from lands embraced by unpatented mining claims. However, no disposal is authorized from claims where the United States does not have the right to manage the surface resources. Also, the claimants must be given prior notice and the removal must not materially interfere with mining operations incidental to the claims.

Appraisal

Prior to sale, all mineral materials must be appraised to determine fair-market value. A sale must not be made at less than the appraised value.[2]

Duration of Contract

In general, a contract or permit may not exceed one year from the effective date of the contract or permit. Extensions are possible under certain circumstances.[3]

Prospecting Permits

On acquired national forest lands, prospecting permits may be issued. These permits grant the permittee the exclusive rights to prospect for mineral material deposits; however material may only be taken for testing. Commercial quantities may not be removed. A prospecting permit may not cover more than 640 acres and may not be issued for a period exceeding 24 months.[4]

Competitive Sales

Mineral material sales which exceed 25,000 cubic yards may be sold by competitive bidding. The sale must be advertised on the same day once a week for two consecutive weeks in a newspaper of general circulation. The advertisement of sale must specify the location of the tract, the kind of material, quantity of material, appraised price, time and place of bid and special stipulations.[5]

Negotiated or Noncompetitive Sales

When it is in the public interest and when it is impracticable to obtain competition, mineral materials not exceeding 100,000 cubic yards may be sold at any one sale. These sales are made at the appraised price without advertising or calling for bids. Furthermore, a single applicant may not acquire more than 200,000 cubic yards in any one state in any period of 12 consecutive months.[6]

Preference Right Negotiated Sales

A preference right negotiated sale may be made to a permittee who has discovered suitable mineral materials within an area covered by a prospecting permit. The application must be made before the expiration date of the prospecting permit. Preference right negotiated sales are exempt from volume limitations and the contract time must not exceed five years.[7]

Free-Use Permits

Free-use permits may be issued to any local, state, federal or Territorial agency, unit or subdivision, including municipalities and county road districts for periods up to 10 years. There is no limitation on the number of permits or the value of the material.

Free-use permits may also be made to settlers, miners, residents, prospectors and nonprofit organizations for other than commercial purposes. These permits are limited to 5000 cubic yards during any period of 12 consecutive months.[8]

Petrified Wood

A free-use permit may be issued to amateur collectors and scientists to take limited quantities of petrified wood for personal use. This material may not be bartered or sold.[9]

References - Salable Minerals in Forest Service Administered Lands

1. 36 CFR 228.41(b)(3).
2. 36 CFR 228.4
3. 36 CFR 228.53.
4. 36 CFR 228.60.
5. 36 CFR 228.58.
6. 36 CFR 228.59.
7. 36 CFR 228.61.
8. 36 CFR 228.62.
9. 36 CFR 228.62(e).

LANDS AND MINERALS SUBJECT TO LOCATION

Minerals Locatable under the Mining Laws

The Federal mining law states that "except as otherwise provided, all valuable mineral deposits in lands belonging to the United States, both surveyed and unsurveyed, shall be free and open to exploration and purchase..." (30 U.S.C. 22). The Federal regulations further define a locatable mineral as "whatever is recognized as a mineral by the standard authorities, whether metallic or other substance, when found in public lands in quantity and quality sufficient to render the lands valuable on account thereof, is treated as coming within the purview of the mining laws." 43 CFR 3812.1.

The above definitions of a locatable mineral are somewhat vague but undoubtedly could be applied to almost any mineral with sufficient value that it could be extracted and marketed at a profit. There is no such thing as a list of locatable minerals because of the requirement for value. For example, some deposits of gold, uranium and gemstones are valuable, whereas other deposits are not. Whether or not a particular mineral deposit is locatable depends on such factors as quality, quantity, mineability, demand, marketability, etc.

Minerals Not Locatable

Rather than attempting to establish what minerals are locatable, it may be more practical to discuss what minerals are definitely not locatable. The number of locatable minerals authorized by the 1872 Mining Law has been substantially reduced by several subsequent Federal laws.

The Mineral Leasing Act of 1920, as amended, authorized that deposits of oil, gas, coal, potassium, sodium, phosphate, oil shale, native asphalt, solid and semisolid bitumen and bituminous rock including oil-impregnated rock or sands from which oil is recoverable only by special treatment after the deposit is mined or quarried, the deposits of sulphur in Louisiana and New Mexico may be acquired only through a mineral leasing system.

The Materials Act of July 31, 1947 amended by the Act of July 23, 1955, excluded common varieties of sand, stone, gravel, pumice, pumicite, cinders and clay. However, uncommon varieties of sand, stone, gravel, pumice, pumicite, cinders and exceptional clay are locatable. The Act of September 28, 1962, removed petrified wood from the locatable mineral category.

Locatable Type Minerals Associated with Leasable-Type Minerals

For a deposit of minerals to be leasable, the lands must contain valuable deposits of the leasable minerals and be chiefly valuable for the leasable minerals. 30 U.S.C. 262. 282 (1982). Conversely, for a deposit of minerals to be locatable, there must be a discovery of locatable-type minerals. This means the locatable minerals must be present in sufficient quality and quantity to constitute a discovery. A mining claim for locatable minerals must be able to stand on its own on the basis of production of locatable-type minerals.

Where leasable minerals without commercial value are associated with locatable minerals that do have commercial value, the deposit should be appropriated under the mining law rather than the mineral leasing laws. **Foot Mineral Co. v. U.S.**, 228 Ct. Cl. 230 (1981), 654 F.2d 81. If both locatable and leasable-type minerals coexist in the same deposit and neither the locatable nor the leasable minerals are worth producing alone, the deposit is not available under a lease or mining claim. This is true even if the locatable and leasable minerals can be profitable mined together. This is based on the principle that one type of mineral (locatable or leasable) cannot be bootstrapped into profitability by mining both types of minerals. Again, the profits from one type of mineral cannot be aggregated with the profits of another to make a viable operation.

Minerals Never Locatable

Even before the Materials Act of 1947 was enacted, many mineral materials were never locatable even though they could be marketed at a profit. In fact the Materials Act of 1947 was enacted to provide a means to dispose of them. Material in this category includes ordinary deposits of clay, limestone, fill material, etc. Non-locatable minerals generally have a normal quality and a value for ordinary uses. Federal court and Departmental decisions have found that such minerals as decomposed rhyolite, blow sand, peat moss, sand and gravel, if suitable only as fill, soil conditioners or other low-value purposes were never locatable.

Lands Open to Exploration

The 1872 mining law states that "except as otherwise provided, all valuable mineral deposits in lands belonging to the United States, both surveyed and unsurveyed, shall be free and open to exploration and purchase..."[1] Mining claims may be located on unreserved, unappropriated lands administered by the Bureau of Land Management and the unreserved, unappropriated public domain land in the National Forest administered by the Forest Service. Mining locations may be made in the states of Alaska, Arizona, Arkansas, California, Colorado, Florida, Idaho, Louisiana, Mississippi, Montana, Nebraska, Nevada, New Mexico, North Dakota, Oregon, South Dakota, Utah, Washington and Wyoming.[2]

Lands patented under the Stock-Raising Homestead Law or other land disposal laws that reserved locatable minerals to the United States are subject to mineral location. The effect of the mineral reservation in the patent is to separate the land into a surface estate and a mineral estate. The mineral estate is subject to location under the general mining laws in the same manner as are vacant, unappropriated public lands. However, the surface owner is entitled to compensation for any damages resulting from exploration or mining.

Lands Closed to Location

The national parks and national monuments are closed to mining location; however, valid mining claims existing at the date a national park or monument was established are entitled to certain grandfather rights. Included among areas closed to mining location are Indian reservations, military reservations, most reclamation projects, Federal wildlife refuges, and land segregated under the Classification and Multiple Use Act.

A great variety of withdrawals or land classifications have served to segregate the public lands from mineral location.[3] Before locating a mining claim, the public land records of the BLM should be examined to determine if the area of interest is available for mineral entry. A mineral location on lands segregated from mineral entry would not only be a waste of time and money, but would also be an unauthorized trespass.

Mining Claims Located Prior to Withdrawal

In many cases, lands withdrawn from mineral entry embrace mining claims existing at the date of withdrawal. Such lands are subject to the valid existing rights of the claimants, and in order to have valid existing rights, a claim must contain a discovery as of the date of the withdrawal as well as at the date of determination.[4] Evidence obtained after the date of the withdrawal by drilling, sampling and other exploratory activities cannot be considered for evidence of a discovery made before the date of withdrawal. If a discovery is not physically exposed within the limits of the claim before the date of withdrawal, the claim is void.[5]

Mining Claims Located After Date of Withdrawal

Mining claims located at a time when the land is withdrawn from mineral entry are null and void ab initio and may be so declared without a hearing. However if the record indicates that part of the claim was not located on withdrawn land, the entire claim cannot be declared null and void ab initio without contest proceedings.[6]

Lands which have been withdrawn from entry under the public land laws remain so withdrawn until there is a formal revocation or modification of the order of withdrawal. Merely because the lands are not presently being used for the purpose of the withdrawal does not affect the status of the withdrawal. Mining claims located on lands withdrawn from mineral entry are null and void ab initio and will not be validated by the modification or revocation of the order of withdrawal to open the lands to mineral entry.[7]

References - Lands and Minerals Subject to Location

1. Act of May 10, 1872; 17 Stat. 91; 30 USC 22 (1982).
2. 43 CFR 3811.2-1(a).
3. Lockhart v. Johnson, 181 U.S. 516 (1901).
4. U.S. v. Almgren, 17 IBLA 295 (1974).
5. U.S. v. Gunsight Mining Co., 5 IBLA 62 (1972).
6. Brace C. Curtis, 11 IBLA 30 (1973).
7. David W. Harper, A-30719, 74 ID 141 (1967).

GENERAL LOCATION REQUIREMENTS

Location by Agent

The law does not prohibit an agent from locating a mining claim.[1] A corporation or an individual may employ an agent to locate claims, either in state or out of state.[2] Furthermore, an agent who locates in the name of a principal need not be a qualified locator.[3]

Location by Minors

Minors who are citizens may locate mining claims.[4] Also parents of minors may locate claims on behalf of their children.[5]

Location by Aliens

Section 1 of the Mining Law of 1872 states that "all valuable mineral deposits in lands belonging to the United States....shall be free and open to exploration and purchase, and the lands in which they are found to occupation and purchase, by citizens of the United States."[6] Section 7 of the 1872 Act further provides that "[p]roof of citizenship...may consist...in the case of a corporation organized under the laws of the United States, or any State or Territory thereof, by the filing of a certified copy of their charter or certificate of incorporation."[7]

If an alien should locate a claim, his rights to the claim are not void but voidable, as he is subject to losing his rights only by government action.[8] A locator who stakes a claim over a prior locator who is an alien, is not entitled to assert priority.[9] If a mining claim is located by an alien and the alien subsequently declares his intention to become a citizen and no adverse rights have been initiated, such declaration relates back to the date of location or acquisition of the alien's interest and validates the location.[10]

If an alien conveys a claim to a citizen, the citizen has a title good against all persons who had acquired no right before the conveyance.[11] Furthermore, if a citizen and an alien jointly locate a claim not exceeding the area allowed by one locator, the location is valid as to the citizen and a conveyance from the two give a valid title.[12]

According to BLM policy,[13] mining claims or sites held by aliens may be adjudicated by the BLM based upon the official records. The BLM will not summarily challenge mining claimants with a foreign address and will only become involved in the adjudication of citizenship under the following conditions:

1. When a mineral patent application is filed.

2. When the public interest would be served.

3. When third parties challenge the citizenship requirement of a mining claimant.

Claimant Has Burden to Show Ownership by United States Citizen

In a 1983 case[14] involving alien ownership of a mining claim, the Interior Board of Land Appeals held that the claimant has the burden to demonstrate that claims are owned, at least in part, by citizens of the United States. To clarify the ownership, the Board directed the claimant to provide it with a list of the current owners of the claims and their current mailing addresses, to identify those owners who are United States citizens, and to supply evidence of or proof of citizenship. Partial ownership of a claim by a United States citizen is sufficient .

Citizenship Requirements of Stockholders of a Domestic Corporation

A corporation organized under state laws may locate and patent claims irrespective of the ownership of the stock.[15] Section 7 of the Mining Law provides that proof of citizenship can be established for a corporation by filing a certificate of incorporation. Therefore, it is not necessary that the stockholders of a corporation be United States citizens because proof of incorporation in a state is conclusive proof of citizenship by the stockholders.[16]

Federal Requirements for Location

The Mining Law of 1872, allows the miners of each mining district to "make regulations not in conflict with the laws of the United States, or with the laws of the State or Territory in which the district is situated, governing the location, manner of recording amount of work necessary to hold possession of a mining claim." However the following Federal requirements for location must be accomplished:

1. The "location must be distinctly marked on the ground so its boundaries can be readily traced."

2. The location notice must contain the following information:

   a. "the name or names of the locators"
   b. "the date of the location"

161

c. "a description of the claim or claims located by reference to some natural or permanent monument as will identify the claim"

The Federal courts have consistently upheld the right of the states to impose additional location requirements so long as such requirements are not inconsistent with Federal law.

Compliance with Location Requirements to Establish Validity

Compliance with the location requirements of state and Federal law confers no right in the absence of a discovery, but is essential to establish the validity of a claim.[17]

Discovery before Location

Federal law (30 U.S.C. 23; 43 CFR 3841.3-1) requires that "no location of a mining claim shall be made until discovery is made of the vein or lode within the limits of the claim located. Therefore, it is required that a discovery of a valuable mineral deposit must precede the location of a claim. This requirement has been approved by many court decisions. Of course, as a practical matter, most claims are located before discovery and are held under the doctrine of pedis possessio or prediscovery rights.

Location Procedure

The first step before locating a claim is to verify that the lands of interest are open to mineral location. This is accomplished by examining the land status maps and records at the land office of the Bureau of Land Management. The basic steps to location procedure are as follows:

1. discovery of a valuable mineral deposit;

2. posting the claim;

3. discovery work if required;

4. marking the claim boundaries; and

5. recording the notice with the local recorder and BLM.

Discovery Work

Some states require discovery work to be completed on a mining claim within a specified period of time. Discovery work is not to be confused with assessment work. Commonly, prospectors think that by performing the discovery work, they have perfected their discovery of a valuable mineral deposit. This may or may not be true. The main purpose of discovery work is to show that a claim has been worked. This may serve a dual purpose by protecting a claim from rival locators and by requiring a minimum amount of work so that a locator may demonstrate good faith.

There is a trend for states to abandon the long-established requirement of a discovery pit, generally for environmental reasons. Some states require that the point of discovery of both lode and placer claims should be marked by a discovery monument. The Federal regulations (43 CFR 3841.4-5(b)) require a discovery monument for lode claims but not placer claims.

No Limit on Number of Claims Per Locator

There is no limit to the number of claims that one individual or a single corporation may locate or acquire.[18] Furthermore, Congress has not put a limit on the number of mining claims that may be included in a single patent and described by a single survey.[19]

Abandonment of Undivided Interest in Mining Claim

If a co-owner abandons an undivided interest in a mining claim, this abandoned interest does not revert back to the public domain and become available for relocation; instead, it passes to the original owner or owners of the remaining interest.[20]

Mining Claim Sold

If a mining claim has been properly located, the owner may sell all or any part in any way that seems proper without prejudice to his right to hold the remainder.[21]

References - General Location Requirements

1. McCulloch v. Murphy, 125 F. 147.
2. Book v. Justice Mining Co., 58 F. 106 (1893).
3. Gray v. Milner Corp., 64 ID 337, 342-43 (1957).
4. Thompson v. Spray, 14 P. 182 (Cal. 1889); 43 CFR 3832.1.
5. U.S. v. Haskins, 59 IBLA 1, 88 (1981); West v. U.S., 30 F.2d 739 (DC Cir. 1929).
6. 30 USC 22 (1982).
7. 30 USC 24 (1982).
8. Manual v. Wulf, 152 U.S. 505 (1894).
9. Herrington v. Martinez, 45 F.Supp. 543 (DD Cal 1945).
10. Shea v. Nilima, 133 F. 209 (1904).
11. North Noonday Mining Co. v. Orient Mining Co. 1 F. 522 (1880).
12. Id.
13. BLM Manual 3833.62E.
14. J. Garth Woodworth, 78 IBLA 112, 113 (1983).
15. McKinley v. Wheller, 130 U.S. 630, 636 (1889).
16. Doe v. Waterloo Mining Co., 70 F. 455 (9th Cir. 1895); In re Pacific Coast Molybdenum Co., 75 IBLA 16, 38-39 (1983).
17. Skaw v. U.S., 13 Cl Ct. 7, 38 (1987).

18. Last Chance Mining Co. v. Bunker Hill Co., 131 F. 579, 583 (1904), cert. denied 200 U.S. 617.
19. Carson City Gold Mining Co. v. North Star Mining Co., 73 F. 597, 600 (1896), affirmed 83 F. 658; St. Louis Smelting and Refining Co. v. Kemp, 104 U.S. 636 (1882).
20. Laguna Development Co. v. McAlester Fuel Co., 572 P.2d 1252, 91 NM 244 (1977).
21. St. Louis Smelting and Refining Co. v. Kemp, supra.

AUTHORITY FOR STATE AND LOCAL REQUIREMENTS

Status of Mining Districts

Mining district means a section of country usually designated by name, and described or understood as being confined within certain natural boundaries, in which minerals are found in paying quantities, and which is worked and the rules and regulations are prescribed by miners operating within the district.[1] The mining districts are also authorized to make rules and regulations concerning location procedures not in conflict with the laws of the United States.[2] However, to be valid such regulations must not only be in force at the time of location, but must also be in general practice.[3] Local mining customs or local mining rules only have validity through consistent use and obedience of the miners rather than enactment, and they are void whenever disregarded. Very few mining districts are currently active in a regulatory capacity nor have they been for many years. As a practical matter, local customs and the rules of mining districts have now been replaced by state laws.[4]

State Location Requirements

Although Federal law gives several basic requirements for location of a claim, detailed procedures for locating mining claims are provided by state law. These state statutes also contain procedures for maintaining the possessory title through annual filing of assessment work and provisions for amending defective location certificates.

The specific provisions of the state location statutes are so important to persons involved in acquiring or maintaining mining claims that it is essential to thoroughly review the pertinent statute and have a copy available for reference. The best up-to-date convenient compilation of these laws as well as other useful reference material is the **Digest of Mining Claim Laws**, Third Edition, compiled and edited by Robert G. Pruitt, Jr. and published by the Rocky Mountain Mineral Law Foundation, Denver Colorado.

Authorization for Federal, State and Local Regulations

The General Mining Law of 1872 provides that "under regulations prescribed by law, and according to the local customs or rules of miners in the several mining districts, so far as the same are applicable and not inconsistent with the laws of the United States."[5]

As stated in the statute above, the states have the power to regulate the location of mining claims, if such regulations are not in conflict with the Constitution and laws of the United States.[6] However, the miners or state legislatures are not authorized to determine how title to the land may be acquired.[7] For example, mining district rules may diminish the size of claims that may be located,[8] but such action must be in accord with Federal and State statutes.[9]

Claim May Be Invalidated under Federal Law If State Law Not Followed

Failure to follow state requirements may result in the invalidation of a claim under the Federal laws. Claims have been invalidated by both the Federal Courts and the Interior Department for failure to properly monument and locate according to state law.[10]

Supremacy of Federal Law Over State Law

Under the Supremacy Clause of the United States Constitution, Federal law necessarily overrides conflicting State laws with respect to Federal Public lands.[11] State or local laws or regulations must always yield in case of conflict with the exercise by the Federal Government of any power it possesses under the Constitution.[12]

Right of Possession Determined by State Courts

In **Perego v. Dodge**, 163 U.S. 160, 168 (1896), the United States Supreme Court held that the question of the right of possession must be determined by the state courts, however, these state courts have no jurisdiction in determining the rights of a claimant to the public lands. Although a judgment by a state court is not binding on the Government, the Department of the Interior may properly accept and follow the judgment of a court of competent jurisdiction determining the respective rights and interests between contending parties and interests.

References - Authority for State and Local Requirements

1. U.S. v. Smith, 11 F. 487 (1882).
2. Del Monte Mining & Milling Co. v. Last Chance Mining & Milling Co., 171 U.S. 55 (1898).
3. Jupiter Mining Co. v. Bodie Consol Mining Co., 11 F. 66 (1881).
4. North Noonday Mining Co. v. Orient Mining Co., 1 F. 522 (1880).
5. 30 USC 22 (1982).
6. Butte City Water Co. v. Baker, 196 U.S. 119 (1905); U.S. v. Zweifel, 508 F.2d 1150 (10th Cir. 1975).
7. Benson Mining & Smelting Co., 145 U.S. 428 (1892).

8. Northmore v. Simonson, 97 Fed. 386, 388.

9. Jupiter Mining Co. v. Rodie Consol. Mining Co., 11 Fed. 666,673.

10. Roberts v. Morton, 549 F.2d 158, 161-62 (10th Cir. 1977); U.S. v. Haskins, 59 IBLA 1, 34 (1981).

11. U.S. Const., art. VI. cl. 2; Kleppe v. New Mexico, 426 U.S. 529, 543 (1976).

12. Jacobson v. Massachusetts, 197 U.S. 11, 25 (1905).

MARKING CLAIM BOUNDARIES

Introduction

Federal law requires that "the location must be distinctly marked on the ground so that its boundaries can be readily traced." Each state generally has detailed statutory requirements for marking claim boundaries. Most states require that a monument of specific dimensions and material be placed at each corner of the claim. Placer claims located by legal subdivision generally do not require corner monuments unless required by state law. Materials used for monuments include posts, blazed trees and piled rocks; however, by far the most common monument is the 4-inch square post.

It is very important to clearly mark the claim boundaries with durable monuments because the position of the monument on the ground will generally prevail over the recorded description. The more difficult it is to move or destroy a monument, the less likely the claim will be overstaked. It is generally preferable to slightly overlap claims than to inadvertently omit desired land.

Claim Boundaries Must Be Marked or Claim Is Invalid

Numerous cases have upheld the statutory requirement that the location of a mining claim must be distinctly marked on the ground so that the boundaries may be readily traced.[1] In a case affirmed by the Ninth Circuit Court of Appeals,[2] it was stated that "the mere fact that the descriptions in the recorded location certificates of three of defendants' claims may have been adequate was unimportant, for a locator may not acquire a claim merely by walking into the recorder's office and filing a location certificate no matter how perfect the description of the location may be." Even if the terrain is steep and difficult to work, the locator is still required to mark the boundaries.

If mining claims are not marked on the ground, they are not valid. A mining claim may not be acquired by merely recording a location notice, no matter how accurate the description of the claim.[3] Furthermore, the posting of a location notice without marking the boundaries is not a sufficient location.[4]

Standards and Procedures for Marking Boundaries

In order to trace the boundaries of a location, one may be expected to have a practical knowledge of surveying and surveying instruments. However, a locator is not expected to understand or follow a metes-and-bounds description.[5]

The boundaries of a location may be marked by blazing trees along boundaries or at the corners, making a trail around the boundary, establishing stakes, posts, piles of stone and blazing stumps.[6] A good general rule for marking a claim on the ground so that its boundaries can be traced is that the markings must be positioned, so that an individual accustomed to tracing the lines of mining claims can readily find all the monuments.[7]

Obviously many more markings (monuments, blazed trees, stakes, etc.) would be required where the claim surface is irregular and covered with dense vegetation than where the surface is flat and barren of vegetation. Under normal circumstances a monument placed at each corner of the location is sufficient.[8] Some states require or recommend end-center and side-center monuments.[9]

Relocator May Use Original Monuments

A relocator of a prior location may use the original boundary markings and monuments regardless if he is relocating his own location or that of another.[10]

Monument May Be Placed on Valid Location of Another

If a locator inadvertently places one or two of his monuments on lands under valid location, that portion of the location not in conflict is still valid presuming a discovery exists within the portion of the claim not in conflict.[11]

Markings on Ground Control over Description in the Notice

Where the monuments are found on the ground, or their position or location can be determined with reasonable certainty, the monuments control over the description in the location notice.[12]

Short Staking Claim Boundaries

The practice of short staking involves marking shorter distances on the ground than are recited in the location notice. The purpose of short staking is to avoid leaving small fractions as a consequence of laying out side lines or end lines that are longer than the statutory maximum of 600 by 1500 feet. Depending upon the accuracy of the method used to measure distances between monuments, the measured distance can be reduced by 10 to 30 feet or more. However, if the measurements are made on steep terrain without compensation for the slope, the measured distances will be shorter than the actual horizontal distance. When locating a large claim block by short staking, it may be difficult to correlate the map with the claim monuments.

Obliteration of Monuments Will Not Affect Validity

Once a location is marked on the ground so that its boundaries may readily traced, the obliteration or destruction of the boundary monuments, marks or notices will not affect the validity of the claim.[13] Of course this presumes that the state law does not require the monuments to be maintained and that the obliteration was accomplished through no fault of the locator.[14] If no monuments are present, it has been held that their position can be established by testimony of a witness who saw them standing after being placed.[15]

Junior Locator Has Burden of Proof

Although a mining claimant bears the responsibility of maintaining markings for mining claims,[16] it has been held that testimony of a junior locator could not prevail over positive testimony of the senior locator. In this case the junior locator said he located over a senior claim because he saw no monuments; whereas, the senior locator asserted that he had erected the monuments.[17]

Senior Locator Has Advantage

Where rival locators are involved in a priority of right conflict, the general rule that applies to all location requirements of state law is that the locator who performs such requirements in good faith will not be deprived of title on some technicality. The senior locator who in good faith performed to the best of his ability is generally protected by the courts.

References - Marking Claim Boundaries

1. Iron Silver Mining Co. v. Eligen Mining & Smelting Co., 118 U.S. 196 (1886).
2. Vevelstad v. Flynn, 230 F.2d 695, 700, 703 (9th Cir. 1956), cert. denied 352 U.S. 827.
3. Id.
4. Doe v. Waterloo Mining Co., 70
5. Oregon King Mining Co. v. Brown, 119 F. 48 (1902).
6. Id.
7. Ledoux v. Forester, 94 F. 600. 602 (1899).
8. Hammer v. Garfield Mining Co., 130 U.S. 291, 299 (1888).
9. Golden Fleece Mining Co. v. Cable Consol. Mining Co., 12 Nev. 312 (1877).
10. Hagan v. Dutton, 181 P. 578 (1919).

11. Perigo v. Erwin, 85 F. 904 (1898), affirmed 93 F. 608.
12. Dye v. Duncan, Diekman & Duncan Mining Co., 164 F.Supp. 747 (1958).
13. Walton v. Wild Goose Mining Co., 123 F. 209 (1903), cert. denied 194 U.S.
    631.
14. U.S. v. Parker, 91 ID 271 (1984).
15. Daggett v. Yreka Mining & Milling Co., 86 P. 968 (1906).
16. U.S. v. Independent Quick Silver Co., 72 ID 367 (1965).
17. U.S. v. Gancarz, 398 P.2d 695, 81 Nev. 64 (1965).

THE LOCATION NOTICE

Federal Regulations Require Information on Notice

Federal regulations[1] specify that certain information must be contained in the location notice. The course and distance from the discovery shaft on the claim to some permanent, well-known object, such as stone monuments, blazed trees, confluence of streams, intersection of roads and prominent mountains, should be described as accurately as practicable. Survey monuments such as brass cap section corners are excellent, especially since the Federal law requires that the location of the claims shall be designated with reference to the lines of the public survey if such claims are situated on surveyed lands. The federal regulations also require that the location notice include the names of adjoining claims, or if nonadjoining, the relative positions of the nearest claims.

Posted and Recorded Notices

Two types of notices have been reviewed by the courts: (1) the "posted" notice that is placed on either a discovery monument or corner monument of the claim as required by state law; and (2) the "recorded" notice which is recorded with the local recorder and the BLM. The general purpose of a posted notice is to give would-be locators information about a new location until the recorded notice is filed. Because the various state laws give 30 to 90 days to record a notice, the claimant has an opportunity to provide better and more accurate information in the recorded notice.

The courts tend to be much more liberal in construing the adequacy of posted location notices. Posted notices have been held to be sufficient even where they contained significant errors and omissions. Recorded notices are held to a much higher standard because the claimant has much more time to rectify any errors.

Regulations Require Corner and Discovery Monuments

The federal regulations require a claimant to "drive a post or erect a monument of stones at each corner of his surface ground, and at the point of discovery or discovery shaft should fix a post, stake, or board, upon which should be designated the name of the lode, the name or names of the locators, the number of feet claimed, and in which direction from the point of discovery."[2] Many of the state laws no longer require a discovery monument. Because the mineral deposits mined today generally do not have a specific discovery point, this is a somewhat obsolete requirement.

172

Description of Claim's Position in Notice

The description of the claim's position on the location notice must be sufficiently precise so that the claim can be found.[3] If the ground cannot be established with certainty from the description on the location notice, the claim may be void.[4] Furthermore, if the claim description is so vague that the claim may be floated over new ground without changing the description, the notice is not adequate.[5]

Locators should take great care to have an accurate description of the position of the claim. Many claims have such a vague description that they could exist anywhere over a large area. A big problem in connection with such a claim is that it could be moved over a subsequent discovery in the vicinity. Such claims are commonly referred to as "floating claims" and because of an earlier location date could present a serious threat to the locator of a new discovery. If the description of a claim's position in the notice is vague or confusing, it is crucial that the monuments on the ground are in place to give would-be locators actual notice of the claim's existence.

Description of Claim by Reference to Natural Object or Permanent Monument

A known mining claim may be used as a reference to a permanent monument;[6] in other words you can tie one claim to another well-known claim. The courts have held that acceptable permanent monuments include mountains, ridges, hogbacks, lake inlets, bays, open cuts, drifts, tunnels and stone monuments.[7]

A placer claim may be tied to the public land survey system,[8] or the boundaries of the claim may be referred and conformed to the lines of the government survey.[9]

The standard for a description on a location notice is that an intelligent person, with the knowledge of the permanent natural objects and permanent monuments in the vicinity can find the claim by reading the description and finding the marked corners.[10]

Description in Notice of Directions and Bearings

The description on the notice does not necessarily have to give the bearings and distances between monuments with absolute accuracy as it is recognized that prospectors may not have access to surveying equipment. Thus a location is not invalidated on the basis of slight errors or inaccuracies in the bearings and distances so long as the claim boundaries are sufficiently marked.[11]

173

Monuments Prevail Over Description in Notice

If there is a discrepancy between the stakes or markers on the ground of a mining claim and the recorded location notice, the claim as marked on the ground controls over the description in the location notice.[12] However the position of the monuments on the ground prevail only if there is no question as to their position.[13]

Error in Description of Claim in Notice

In **Rasmussen Drilling v. Kerr-McGee Nuclear Corp.**, 571 F2d 1144 (10th Cir. 1978), the Court considered a case where a junior locator filed over claims described in the wrong township. Kerr-McGee, the senior locator, conducted uranium exploration in the South Powder River Basin, Wyoming for several years prior to 1967. The company contacted surface owners and completed staking by December 1967, and filed with the county recorder by December 1967. A clerical error made in the descriptions of the claims on the location notice placed the claims in section 19 rather than 17. Rasmussen Drilling, the junior locator, located claims over the Kerr-McGee claims after Kerr-McGee filed amendments correcting the descriptions and placing the claims in section 17.

The Court decided the case in favor of Kerr-McGee because the junior locator had actual notice from the activity on the ground and did not need to see a recorded notice. The court also stated the general rule that "a miner who proceeds in good faith to comply with the various requirements applicable to perfection of a valid location is to be treated with indulgence, and the notices required are to receive a liberal construction."

More than One Claim in Location Notice

Unless state law provides otherwise, it is generally not a fatal defect to include more than one claim in a location.[14] Such a defect would be curable by an amended location. However in two different cases the Interior Board of Land Appeals has held claims to be invalid because more than one claim was entered on a location notice.

In a case involving 13 claims in a single location notice filed with the Colorado State Office of the BLM, the Board applied Colorado law to save one claim and found that under State law the remaining 12 claims were "absolutely void."[15] In another case involving claims filed on a single notice in the Idaho State Office of the BLM, the Board invalidated all claims on the notice because Idaho law states that "no location is made by one or several locators, and if it purports to claim more than one location it is absolutely void."[16]

Critical Information to Be Included in Notice

The critical information that must be included in the posted notice includes the name of the locators, date of location and a sufficient description.[17] However, there are cases where the sufficiency of a notice was upheld where one or more of these items were omitted in a posted notice. Strict compliance with the location notice requirements is not required to locate mining claims; a location notice need only contain sufficient information to enable a reasonably intelligent person to located the claim on the ground by referring to the location notice and the marked boundaries.[18] Of course a state may require what additional information it deems necessary.

Position of Notice on Monument

The location notice must be visible, but its position on the monument is not critical.[19] However, the temporary loss or destruction of a posted notice or location monuments does not affect the validity of the claim.[20]

Federal Law Does Not Require Sworn Affidavit

The Federal law does not require that the location notice be a sworn affidavit or a verified certificate.[21] However the location law of some states does require a sworn affidavit.

Senior Locator Has Advantage in Court

In most cases the courts uphold the location notice of a senior locator acting in good faith despite the fact the compliance with state and federal location requirements is minimal.[22] Those junior locators or "claim jumpers" who wish to have the courts adjudicate the right of possession to a mining claim should be aware that the junior locator seldom prevails even though the claim is not monumented and the description of the claim in the location notice is erroneous. However, where a senior locator has a large block of claims with a record of minimal adherence to the state and federal location requirements, a case based on good faith of the senior locator would be unconvincing.

References - The Location Notice

1. 43 CFR 3841.4-5.
2. 43 CFR 3841.4-5.
3. Dennis v. Barnett, 85 P.2d 916 (1938).
4. U.S. v. Sherman, 288 F. 497 (1923).
5. Brown v. Levan, 46 P. 661 (1896).
6. Glacier Mountain Silver Mining Co. v. Willis, 127 U.S. 471 (1888).
7. Meydenbauer v. Stevens, 78 F. 787 (DCD Alaska 1897).

8. McNulty v. Kelly, 346 P.2d 585 (1959).
9. Gird v. California Oil Co., 60 F. 521 (1894).
10. Flynn v. Vevelstad, 119 F.Supp 93 (1954), affirmed 230 F.2d 695, cert. denied 352 U.S. 827.
11. J.E. Riley Inv. Co. v. Sakow, 98 F.2d 8 (1938).
12. Sturtevant v. Vogel, 167 F. 448, 452 (1909).
13. Thallman v. Thomas, 102 F. 935 (1900), affirmed 111 F. 277.
14. Dye v. Duncan Dieckman & Duncan Mining Co., 164 F.Supp. 747 (1958).
15. Waldron Enterprizes Mining, 88 IBLA 54 (1985).
16. Fletcher DeFisher, 93 IBLA 68, 74 (1986).
17. Preston v. Hunter, 67 F. 996 (1895).
18. Dodge v. Amrine, 596 P.2d 71 (1979).
19. Jose v. Houck, 171 F.2d 211 (1948).
20. Gird v. California Oil Co., 60 F. 531, 539 (1894).
21. Hoyt v. Russell, 117 U.S. 401 (1886).
22. Kenney v. Greer, 656 P.2d 857 (Nev 1983).

STATE RECORDATION REQUIREMENTS

Introduction

Most states have laws that provide detailed procedures for recording the notice. The individual state requirements should be checked frequently, because state law is amended from time to time. Because monuments placed in the field are easily lost or destroyed, a copy of the location notice should be recorded in the county recorder's office in the county in which the claim is located as soon as possible, even though the individual states may allow up to several months. In Alaska, the recording office is under the District Magistrate.

Federal Regulations Required Recordation Under State Law

The federal regulations[1] require that "the location must be filed for record in all respects as required by the State or territorial laws, and local rules and regulations, if there be any." In **H.B. Webb**, 34 IBLA 362 1978), the Interior Board of Land Appeals upheld a BLM decision declaring mining claims null and void because the claimant failed to record the claims as required by the Arizona statute until more than three years after the land was withdrawn from mineral entry. This case is unusual because it is very uncommon for the BLM to void a claim for failure to comply with state recordation law.

In a 1985 case,[2] the Board stated that the "United States has a right to require mining claimants' compliance with State law which is applicable to claims on Federal lands. As held by the Court of Appeals for the Tenth Circuit,[3] "substantial or colorable compliance with State location requirements has been enforced even in controversies between the (Federal) Government and private claimants. * * * State requirements have been held by us to apply in such controversies between the Government and mining claimants."

Failure to Record Claim as Required by State Law

Before the passage of the Federal Land Policy and Management Act of 1976, failure to record a mining claim as required by state law did not of itself render a claim invalid.[4] However other events, such as withdrawal or classification of the land prior to recordation by the claimant may operate as an adverse right rendering the claim invalid.

Unless the recording statute under state law expressly prohibited such construction, actual notice (or constructive notice by possession) was an adequate substitute for recordation.[5] In one case the Court held that recording a notice of location can serve only the purpose of notifying others of the facts of location; and if those facts are already known to would-be locators, neither failure to record nor recording of a notice containing an insufficient description affects rights initiated by a senior claimant.

State Recordation and Bad Faith Entry

In **Columbia Standard Corp. v. Ranchers Exploration & Development, Inc.**, 468 F2d 547 (1972), the Court considered a case where the senior locator failed to file location notices with the county within the 90-day period of location as required by the state statute. Columbia Standard Corporation (Columbia), the junior locator, brought suit to enjoin Ranchers Exploration & Development, Inc., (Ranchers), the senior locator, from interfering with its mining operations. Ranchers had staked mining claims over a five-section area in August 1967 and posted and filed location notices; Ranchers also did discovery drilling. However, the affidavits of discovery work were not filed within the 90-day period required by the statute. From 1967 to 1970, Ranchers drilled about 70 deep drill holes and conducted radiometric testing on some of the claims; Ranchers also graded drill sites and prepared geologic maps.

Columbia entered the disputed land and staked 157 lode claims in January of 1972. Columbia was fully aware of all Ranchers claims and exploratory work but located the claims because of the late filing. The Court decided the case in favor of Ranchers on the basis that Columbia's entry was not in good faith.

Recording Period under State Law

Each state code specifies the time allowed after location or posting that a notice of location must be recorded:

Alaska	90 days	New Mexico	90 days
Arizona	90 days	North Dakota	60 days
California	90 days	Oregon	60 days
Colorado	3 months	South Dakota	60 days
Idaho	90 days	Utah	30 days
Montana	60 days	Washington	30 days (placer)
Nevada	90 days		90 days (lode)
Wyoming	60 days		

References - State Recordation Requirements

1. 43 CFR 3841.4-6.
2. H.B. Webb, 34 IBLA 362 (1978).
3. Hugh B. Fate, 86 IBLA 215, 224 (1985).
4. MacDonald v. Best, 186 F.Supp. 217 (1960).
5. Id.
6. Bradshaw v. Miller, 377 P.2d 781, 14 Utah 2d 82 (1963).

RECORDATION OF CLAIMS

Introduction

Although the Federal Land Policy and Management Act of 1976[1] significantly affected activities under the mining law in many ways, perhaps section 314 of the Act is by far the most important. Before the passage of FLPMA, the recordation of mining claims and the maintenance of possessory title through filing annual assessment work was mandated by state law. As a consequence, all records related to mining claims such as location notices, amended location notices, transfers of interest and assessment work affidavits could be found in the county recorder's office in the county in which the claim was located.

The purpose of section 314 was to provide the Bureau of Land Management (BLM) with information on the location and number of unpatented mining claims, mill sites and tunnel sites. Other objectives were to remove the cloud on title to lands where claims were recorded but abandoned and to determine the name and address of the current owner of record.

Failure to file a location notice, assessment work affidavit, or notice of intent to hold as required by section 314 shall be deemed conclusively to constitute an abandonment of the mining claim or mill or tunnel site by the owner. Thousands of appeals have resulted from claims declared abandoned by administrative decisions for failure of the owner to file the proper instrument. Consequently, there have been decisions rendered by the Interior Board of Land Appeals addressing almost every aspect of the mining claim recordation process. On April 1, 1985, the United States Supreme Court held that section 314 of FLPMA is constitutional and that failure to comply with the statutory filing dates automatically voids the claim.[2]

Recordation of Claims Located on Or Before October 21, 1976

Section 314(a) and (b) of FLPMA[3] require that the owner of an unpatented claim located on or before October 21, 1976, shall within the 3-year period following the date of approval of the Act, file a copy of the notice of location for the claim in the proper office of BLM, and also file (1) evidence of the performance of assessment work, (2) a notice of intention to hold the claim, or (3) a detailed report as provided by the Act of September 2, 1958. Section 314(c) of FLPMA[4] provides that the failure to file the instruments mentioned above shall be deemed conclusively to constitute an abandonment of the mining claim, mill site or tunnel site by the owner.

In one case, a claim owned by the Imperial County in California was deemed to be conclusively abandoned and void even though the late filing was caused by an Act of God (earthquake).[5] In many cases valuable mineral properties with producing mining operations were lost on account of failure to record.[6]

Recordation of Claims Located After October 21, 1976

The owner of an unpatented mining claim, mill site, or tunnel site located after October 21, 1976, on Federal land is required to file within 90 days after the date of location of that claim in the proper BLM office. The claimant must file a copy of the official record of the notice or certificate of location of the claim or site filed under state law.

Regulations Give Same Recordation Requirements to Mill and Tunnel Sites as Claims

The owner of mill or tunnel sites located after October 21, 1976, shall file within 90 days after the date of location in the proper BLM office, a copy of the official record of the notice or certificate of location that was or will be filed under state law.

Curable Defects

As a general rule, items required by the regulations, but not the statute, will be treated as curable defects.[8] A claimant who fails to file the supplemental information is notified and given 30 days in which to cure the defect. If the defect is not cured the filing will be rejected by an appealable decision.

Date of Location

The "date of location" represents the initiation of the mining claim title. This date is also that to which a timely filing must relate. Many of the filings which have been rejected due to failure of the claimants to file within the period authorized by statute involved problems with the date of location. By Departmental regulation,[9] as well as decisions of the Board of Land Appeals,[10] the "date of location" of a mining claim is the date determined by state law in the local jurisdiction in which the unpatented mining claim, mill or tunnel site is situated." As a practical matter, the Board of Land Appeals has generally treated the date of location as the date of posting stated in a recorded location certificate.

181

If claimants fail to include a location date with their filing but do so later upon request by the BLM, such claimants must remember that the location date filed with the BLM must be the same as that filed with the county. For example, you could not possibly have a location date on your BLM filing later than the date of filing with the county. Furthermore, a document filed with the BLM must be a copy of the document filed with the county.[11] This means the dates as well as other information should be the same.

Computing the 90-Day Period

FLPMA requires the owner of an unpatented mining claim located after October 21, 1976, to file a copy of the official record of the notice of location with the BLM within 90 days after the date of location. In computing the 90-day period, the date of location is not included but the last day of the period is included.[12] If the 90th day falls on a day when the office is closed to the public, consider the 90th day as the next day the office is open to the public.[13]

Filing in the Proper Office

Filing in the proper office means a document must be received and date stamped in the BLM office which has jurisdiction over the area in which the claim is located.[14] In most states this is the BLM state office rather than a district or area office.[15] In Alaska there are two filing districts - Anchorage and Fairbanks. In one case, the Board of Land appeals held that if a claim is near the dividing line of two filing districts, such as Anchorage and Fairbanks, timely filing in either district is acceptable.[16]

Copy of the Official Record of the Notice of Location

In the Federal regulations the "copy of the official record" is defined as a "legible reproduction or duplicate, except microfilm, of the instrument which was or will be filed under state law in the local jurisdiction where the claim or site is located. It also includes an exact reproduction, duplicate, except microfilm, of an amended instrument which may change or alter the description of the claim or site."[17]

The Board of Land Appeals has held that a handwritten copy of the instrument of recordation is acceptable; and a machine reproduction is not required.[18] It has also held that quitclaim deeds may not be substituted for the location notice unless it can be shown that the location notices are unavailable.[19]

Amended Location Notices Must Be Filed with Local Recording Office and BLM

The filing of amended location certificates with the BLM cannot change the official description of mining claims unless the certificates are also recorded in the county recording office where the originals were recorded.[20]

Recording Claims Existing in National Park System Lands

A mining claim in existence in national park system lands on September 28, 1976 must have been recorded on or before September 28, 1977, or it is conclusively presumed to be abandoned and void as provided by the Act of September 28, 1976.[21]

Relocation Versus Amended Location

An amended location notice that is timely filed may be considered a relocation if the original location notice filed with it is untimely. However, the Board of Land Appeals held that the recordation of an amended location notice for a pre-FLPMA mining claim, where the original claim had never been recorded with the BLM, cannot confer any earlier right to the claim than the date of the amended location.[22] The Board has also held that an amended location notice need not be denoted as such on the location notice in order to qualify as an amended location notice.[23] See the chapter on this subject for more information.

Information to Be Included With the Location Notice

Federal regulations[24] specify information that must either be in the location notice or included as supplemental information:

1. Name or number of claim or site.
2. Name and address of current owner.
3. Type of claim or site.
4. Date of location.
5. Position of claim must be described to within a quarter section (160-acre quadrant): township, range, meridian and state must be included.
6. Claim(s) must be described by narrative or shown on a map with sufficient accuracy for the Government to identify and locate the claim on the ground. More than one claim may be shown on a map.
7. An approved mineral survey in lieu of items (5) and (6) may be filed.

Map and Legal Description

Section 314(b) of FLPMA requires that the official record of the notice of location include a description of the location of the mining claims and sites sufficient to locate the claimed lands on the ground. A mining claim described by legal subdivision, section, township, range, meridian and state fulfills the map requirement.[25] There is no requirement that the owner of a claim employ a professional engineer or surveyor to prepare the map or description. Claims or sites "shall be depicted on either a topographic map published by the U.S. Geological Survey or by a narrative or a sketch describing the claim or site with reference by appropriate tie to some topographic, hydrographic, or man-made feature."[26]

The test as to whether a recorded description is sufficient is whether the claim may in fact be found and identified by following the recorded description.[27] The fact that a township is unsurveyed does not relieve a claimant from describing the approximate location of the claim, to the extent possible, based upon the protracted U.S. Government grid or a U.S. Geological Survey topographic map.[28] Failure to submit an adequate description or map is considered a curable defect.[29] In thousands of cases the Bureau of Land Management has requested supplemental information from claimants to satisfy this requirement. In many of these cases the Board of Land Appeals has affirmed a BLM decision that claims were abandoned and void because the claimants failed upon notice to provide a description which satisfies the regulations.[30]

Accuracy of Claim Map

When mining claimants have submitted a professional survey map of a mining claim, and the claim location indicated on the map is further verified by the location as drawn on a copy of the master title plat, BLM may rely on that information in determining the location of the mining claim. **Kenneth Russell**, 109 IBLA 180, 184 (1989).

Service Charges

Each mining claim, mill site, or tunnel site filed for recordation must be accompanied by a nonrefundable service charge of $10.00.[31] Annual filings, amendments to a previously recorded location notice and transfers of interest must be accompanied by a nonrefundable service charge of $5.00 for each mining claim, mill site, or tunnel site.[32]

Prior to January 1, 1991, filings that are not accompanied by the proper service charges will be noted as being recorded on the date received provided that the claimant submits the proper service charge within 30 days of receipt of such deficiency notice. Failure to submit the proper service charge will cause the filing to be rejected and returned to the claimant/owner.[33] Beginning January 1, 1991, filings that are not accompanied by the proper service charges shall not be accepted and will be returned to the claimant/owner without further action.[34] If the claimants submits insufficient payment for claims recorded under FLPMA, he may select from all the claims those that can be covered by the payment. The remaining claims are declared abandoned and void.[35]

More Than One Claim Included In Location Notice

The Board of Land Appeals has upheld BLM decision declaring claims in Colorado and Idaho abandoned and void because the claimants had included more than one claim on a single location notice. The Board applied Colorado law to save one claim and found that under State law the remaining claims were void.36 In applying Idaho law, the Board found all claims on the single location notice to be void.[37]

Possessory Title Based on Section 38

Claims based on section 38 where no original location notice exists must record under FLPMA or the claims are a nullity; and since all claims must be recorded within 90 days of the date of location, it appears unlikely that any new claims will arise under section 38. Rights of individual ownership of the claim may still be determined by section 38; however, if that claim has not been recorded under FLPMA, it can only be treated as a nullity.[38]

The Board of Land Appeals has determined the type of evidence sufficient to show the holding of a claim for the purposes of the recordation statute.[39] This includes the following: (1) the name under which the claim is presently identified and all other names by which it may have been known to the extent possible; (2) the name and address of the present claimants; (3) an adequate description of the claim; (4) the type of claim; (5) information concerning the time of the state's statute of limitations and a statement by the claimant as to how long the claim has been held and worked, giving if possible the date (or at least the year) of the origin of the claimant's title and facts as to continuation of possession of the claim; and (6) any other information the claimant would have showing the chain of title to him and bearing upon the possession and occupancy of the claim for mining purposes. Other information which BLM deems essential to meet its purposes may also be required.

Filing Location Notice with Both County and BLM

Section 314 of FLPMA requires filing a location notice with both BLM and the local recording office.[40] Undoubtedly, numerous filings are defective because the claimant either (1) filed different documents in both places, or (2) the claimant filed with BLM but not with local recording office. Furthermore, the claimant may never know of this defect until another claimant locates over the same ground. The BLM generally does not check local filings and would not be in a position to advise the claimant of the problem. Failure to file a location notice with both the BLM and the local recording office constitutes abandonment of the claim and is not a curable defect.

References - Recordation of Claims

1. 43 U.S.C. 1744 (1982).
2. U.S. v. Locke, 471 U.S. 84 (1985).
3. 43 U.S.C. 1744(a) and (b) (1982).
4. 43 U.S.C. 1744(c) (1982).
5. County of Imperial, 51 IBLA 25 (1980).
6. Petro-Lewis Corp., 57 IBLA 300 (1981).
7. 43 U.S.C. 1744(b).
8. Topaz Beryllium Co. v. U.S., 649 F.2d 775, 778 (10th Cur. 1981); 43 CFR 3833.4(b).
9. 43 CFR 3833.0-5.
10. Park City Chief Mining Co., 57 IBLA 342 (1981); Lee Resources Management, 50 IBLA 131 (1980); John C. Buchanan, 52 IBLA 387 (1981); Dutch Creek Mining Co., 98 IBLA 241, 248 (1987).
11. Gerald B. Bannon, 63 IBLA 115 (1982).
12. Warren J. Fytem, 58 IBLA 381 (1981).
13. BLM Manual 3833.12A.
14. C.F. Linn, 45 IBLA 156, 157-58 (1980).
15. Santa Fe Nuclear, Inc., 47 IBLA 222 (1980).
16. Jamie S. Nelson, 55 IBLA 291, 292 (1981).
17. 43 CFR 3833.0-5(i).
18. W.C. Miles, 48 IBLA 214, 215-16 (1980).
19. John J. Vikarcik, 58 IBLA 377 (1981).
20. United States Borax & Chemical Corp., 98 IBLA 358, 359 (1987).
21. 16 U.S.C. 1907 (1982); 43 CFR 3833.1-1; 36 CFR 9.5(a).
22. Walter T. Paul, 43 IBLA 119 (1979).
23. Gary S. Posenjak, 63 IBLA 326 (1982).
24. 43 CFR 3833.1-2(b).
25. 43 CFR 3833.1-2(b)(5).
26. Id; Joe Ostrenger, 94 IBLA 229, 234 (1986).
27. Arley Taylor, 90 IBLA 313, 316-17 (1986).
28. Joe Ostrenger, supra at 234.
29. Walter Everly, 52 IBLA 58, 59 (1981); Joe Ostrenger, supra; Outline Oil Corp., 95 IBLA 255, 259 (1987).
30. Id.
31. 43 CFR 3833.1-3(b).
32. 43 CFR 3833.1-3.
33. 43 CFR 3833.1-4(a).
34. 43 CFR 3833.1-4(b).

35. Robert L. Steele, 46 IBLA 80 (1980).
36. Waldron Enterprises Mining, 88 IBLA 54 (1985).
37. Fletcher DeFisher, 93 IBLA 68, 75 (1986).
38. U.S. v. Haskins, 59 IBLA 1, 105-106 (1981).
39. Philip Sayer, 42 IBLA 296, 300-302 (1979).
40. Sidney O. Smith, 62 IBLA 382 (1982).

ANNUAL FILING REQUIREMENTS

Annual Filing Requirements for Claims and Sites Located Prior to October 21, 1976

The owner of an unpatented mining claim, mill site or tunnel site located prior to October 21, 1976, was required by October 21, 1979, and thereafter on or before December 30 of each year thereafter, file one of the following: (1) a notice of intention to hold the mining claim, mill site or tunnel site, (2) an affidavit of assessment work, or (3) a detailed report as described in 30 U.S.C. 28-1 in two places:

a. File for record in the local office where the location notice or certificate is recorded (generally the county recorder's office).

b. File in the proper office of the BLM a copy of the official record of the instrument filed with the county or local recording office.

FLPMA does not require filing of notices or affidavits for tunnel sites or mill sites, but the regulations do.

Annual Filing Requirements for Claims and Sites Located After October 21, 1976

The owner of an unpatented mining claim, mill site or tunnel site located after October 21, 1976, shall on or before December 30 of each year following the calendar year in which the claim or site was located, file one of the following documents: (1) a notice of intention to hold the mining claim, mill site or tunnel site, (2) an affidavit of assessment work, or (3) a detailed report as described in 30 U.S.C. 28-1 in two places:

a. File for record in the office where the location notice or certificate is recorded (generally the county recorder's office).

b. File in the proper office of the BLM a copy of the official record of the instrument filed with the county or local recording district.

Affidavit of Assessment Work

An "affidavit of assessment work" is defined in the regulations[2] as "the instrument required under state law that certifies that assessment work required by 30 U.S.C. 28 has been performed on, or for the benefit of, a mining claim or, if state law does not require the filing of such an instrument, an affidavit evidencing the performance of such assessment work."

"Assessment Year" Distinguished from "Filing Year"

The annual filing requirements of section 314 of FLPMA have absolutely nothing to do with the assessment year. An assessment year is defined at 30 U.S.C 28, which provides that the period within which the work required to be done on all unpatented mineral claims shall commence at 12:00 meridian (local noon) on the 1st day of September. Therefore, the assessment year runs from September 1 to September 1 of the following year. However, the "year" contemplated by section 314 commences on January 1 and ends on December 30.[4]

Filing Period or Filing Year

Where the requirement of filing proof of assessment work or a notice of intention to hold applies, such filing must be made within each calendar year, i.e., on or after January 1, and on or before December 30.[5]

Annual Filing the Calendar Year That Follows Claims and Sites Located After 31 August

For mining claims, tunnel sites, or mill sites located between September 1 and December 31 of a given calendar year, the claimant is required to submit an annual filing on or before December 30, of the following calendar year. This provision of the regulations[6] makes it clear that even though assessment work is not required the following calendar year for claims located between September and December 31 of a given year, an annual filing is still required to satisfy FLPMA filing requirements.

Filing During the Calendar Year Qualifies Regardless of Assessment Year on which the Work Was Fulfilled under State Law

Evidence of assessment work filed between January 1 and the following December 30 of the same calendar year are considered to have been filed during that calendar year, regardless of what assessment year that work fulfilled under state law (43 CFR 3833.2-3(b). This regulation, made effective January 3, 1989, will allow any affidavit of assessment work to satisfy the requirements of FLPMA for the calendar year it is filed, regardless of the assessment year covered.

Claimant May Elect Type of Annual Filing

A notice of intention to hold a mining claim, mill site, or tunnel site may be filed at the election of the owner, regardless of whether the assessment work has been suspended, deferred, or not yet accrued.[7] However, the claimant must file with the BLM the same documents which have been or will be recorded with the local office of recordation.

Filing a Notice of Intention to Hold Does Not Replace Requirement for Assessment Work

Even though a claimant may elect the type of annual filing, the filing of a notice of intention to hold with the BLM will not relieve the owner of complying with Federal and state laws pertaining to the performance of assessment work. Furthermore, whatever document that is filed with the BLM must also be filed with the local recorder. However, there is no requirement to file a notice of intent to hold for a mill site or a tunnel site with the local recordation office (county recorder).[8]

Annual Filing Must Be Postmarked by December 30 and Received by January 19

Although the required date of filing the evidence of annual assessment work has not been changed, regulations[9] issued December 15, 1982, allow the BLM to accept for a period of twenty days from the due date of December 30 any document postmarked by the U.S. Postal Service on or before the due date. The claimant must have completed all annual assessment work and mailed the document evidencing that work to the proper BLM office on or before December 30th. Presumably, if the annual filing is received after the due date and by January 19th, but the date on the postmark is not legible, the document will not be "timely filed." Also, it should be noted that the grace period provided by regulation applies only when that choice of delivery is the U.S. Postal Service.[10]

Private Postage Meter Labels

Under 43 CFR 3833.0-5(m), a document which is mailed will be considered timely filed if it bears a clearly-dated postmark affixed by the U.S. Postal Service on or before the filing deadline. In **Chemical Products Corp.**, 109 IBLA 357 (1989), the claimant's private postage meter label had a date of December 31, 1988. However, he contended that he set the postage meter date one day ahead at the request of the U.S. Postal Service. The Board responded that "even if we were to assume that the filing was mailed on December 30, the fact that it does not bear an official postmark date within the filing period ending December 30, 1988, is fatal to the filing." Id. at 359.

Affidavit Received Before January 19 Deadline

In **Gary Hennis**, 108 IBLA 121 (1989), the BLM issued an abandonment decision on a claim where there was an affidavit received through the mail and datestamped on January 6, 1986. Therefore, BLM at one point had an envelope, which may or may not have displayed a "clearly dated postmark affixed by the United States Postal Service within the period prescribed by law," but that envelope is no longer part of the record. The Board reversed the BLM decision and concluded that the claimant had timely filed his proof of labor in an envelope bearing a United States Postal Service postmark of December 30, 1985 or earlier.

Annual Filing Rejected If Land Is No Longer Public Land

If the land on which a claim is located is conveyed, the Department no longer has jurisdiction over the land and can make no determination as to a claim's validity. Also the annual filing required by section 314 of FLPMA must be rejected when the land is no longer public land under the jurisdiction of the Department.[11]

Notice of Intention to Hold a Mill or Tunnel Site Need Not Be Filed with the Local Recorder

There is no requirement under FLPMA or the regulations for filing a notice of intent to hold a mill site or tunnel site with the local recorder's office.[12]

Contents of the Notice of Intention to Hold a Mining Claim

A notice of intention to hold a mining claim or group of mining claims shall be an exact legible reproduction or duplicate, except microfilm, of an instrument, signed by the owner of the claim or his/her agent, which was or will be filed for record in the local jurisdiction of the State where the claim is located.[13] The instrument must include the BLM serial number assigned to each claim upon filing in the proper BLM office of a copy of the notice or certificate of location. Include also any change in the mailing address, if known, of the owner or owners of the claim.

Notice of Intention to Hold a Mill or Tunnel Site

The notice of intention to hold a mill or tunnel site must be in the form of a letter signed by the owner or owners and must include (1) the serial number assigned by the BLM to each site, and (2) any change in the mailing address.[14]

Notice of Intention to Hold if Deferment of Assessment Work

If a deferment of annual assessment work has been granted by the BLM, a reference to the decision on file in the proper BLM office by date and serial number which granted the deferment should be specified on the notice of intention to hold. If a petition for a deferment of annual assessment work is pending, the date of filing and serial number should be specified on the notice of intention to hold.[15]

Notice of Intention to Hold Must Be Filed as NOIH and Meet Specific Requirements

Whatever the form of a notice of intention to hold (NOIH), it must be filed with BLM as a notice of intent.[16] A notice of intention to hold must satisfy the following requirements:

1. It must indicate that the claim owner continues to have an interest in the claim.[17]

2. It must also be a copy of the document which was or will be recorded in the local office where the claim's location notice has been recorded.[18]

3. The instrument must also include a description of the location of the mining claim sufficient to locate the claimed lands on the ground.[19] Citing the serial number satisfies this requirement.[20]

4. The instrument must include the BLM assigned claim number,[21] or the name of the claim.[22]

Quitclaim Deed Is Not a Notice of Intention to Hold

A quitclaim deed filed with the BLM cannot be considered a notice of intention to hold under the provisions of 43 CFR 3833.2-3. A "quitclaim deed, standing alone, merely evidences 'present ownership,' not an intention to hold in the future." **George McGowan**, 109 IBLA 1, 2 (1989).

No Specific Form for Notice of Intention to Hold

There is no specific form required for a notice of intention to hold. It must be signed by the owner or his agent. A copy of a notice of intention to hold which has been or will be filed in the local recording office is acceptable. Most of the BLM offices have sample NOIH forms available for use by claimants.

Contents of Evidence of Assessment Work

Evidence of assessment work is required to be in one of two forms (43 CFR 3833.2-2):

1. An exact legible reproduction or duplicate except microfilm of the evidence of assessment work which was performed under state law and was or will be filed for record in the local jurisdiction of the state where the claim or group of claims is located. Also required is the BLM serial number assigned to each claim. Any change in the mailing address of the owner of the claim must also be included.

1. An exact legible reproduction or duplicate, except microfilm, of the detailed report concerning geological, geochemical and geophysical surveys provided for by the Act of September 2, 1958 (30 U.S.C. 28-1) which has been or will be filed for record pursuant to section 314(a)(1) of the Act in the local jurisdiction of the state where the claim or group of claims is located. Also required is the BLM serial number assigned to each claim. Any change in the mailing address of the owner of the claim is also required.

Curable Deficiencies in Annual Filing Instruments

Deficiencies under the regulations, but not under FLPMA, are curable.[23] The claimant is normally sent a decision requiring that the supplemental information be furnished to the proper of office of the BLM within 30 days.[24] Failure to provide the information in the stated period will result in loss of the claim.

Claim Name and Serial Number Omitted From Annual Filing

If there is no designation of the claim name, the assigned BLM number or a description in an assessment work affidavit by which a claim may be identified, the claim must be deemed abandoned.[25] Furthermore, the BLM has no authority to permit amendment of the required filing to include omitted claims after the deadline for filing has passed.[26]

Serial Number Must Be Included With the Annual Filing

The serial number assigned by the BLM to each claim at the time of initial recordation must be included with each annual filing of the notice of intention to hold or proof of labor. However, failure to include the serial number with a filing is a curable defect.[27]

Claim Name Acceptable on Annual Filing

The Board of Land Appeals has expanded the types of filings that would be acceptable by including the proper identification of the claim by name as an alternative to the submission of the correct recordation number given by BLM.[28] Failure to include the name of a claim or BLM serial number with the proof of assessment work or a notice of intention to hold causes abandonment of the claim.[29] It is quite common for owners of large blocks of claims to send the annual filing to the BLM on a single document listing all of the claim names in the claim group. If the names of certain claims are inadvertently omitted, such omitted claims become abandoned.

Claim Name Shown on Map but Not on Affidavit

In **Philip Brandl**, 54 IBLA 343 (1981), the Board expanded the types of filings that would be acceptable by including "the proper identification of the claim by name" as an alternative to the submission of the correct recordation number given by BLM. In other words the claimant is required to identify his claim by **name** or **serial number**.

In **Douglas C. Liechty**, 108 IBLA 247 (1989), the claimant depicted on a map the Scotia #3 Lode Mining Claim among other contiguous mining claims that were expressly identified in the affidavit of assessment work. However, the Scotia #3 Lode Mining Claim was omitted from the express listing of claims for which the annual assessment work was performed. Furthermore, the map was not referred to in the affidavit. Consequently, the Board held that because the appellant failed to unambiguously identify the Scotia #3 claim in his affidavit of assessment work by **name** or **serial number**, the claim was properly deemed to be abandoned and void.

Assessment Work Straddling Two Assessment Years

A common practice among mining claimants is to do assessment work on a claim in August and September, a time period that covers or straddles two assessment years. For example, if a claimant did assessment work in August and September of 1988, he would have satisfied the work requirement for the 1988 and 1989 assessment years. However, if he filed both affidavits for the 1988 and 1989 assessment years during calendar year 1988 and made no filing in calendar year 1989, he would lose the claim.[30] It is important to remember that both the BLM and local recording office must receive an annual filing every calendar year.

Filing Copy of Assessment Work for
Wrong Year Is Curable

Where a claimant files with BLM a copy of assessment work for the wrong year, he satisfies the statutory requirement. He should be given an opportunity to file the correct proof of labor for the preceding assessment year.

Notice of Intention to Hold Requirements
for Mill and Tunnel Sites

Failure to file an annual notice of intention to hold a mill site is a curable defect because the filing requirement is in the regulations rather than the statute. Owners of mill and tunnel sites must be given notice of a deficiency and an opportunity to correct it before their mill sites may be deemed void for failure to comply with FLPMA's filing requirement.[31]

The Board of Land Appeals has held that where BLM fails to notify a mill site claimant to cure a defective filing before a subsequent annual filing is made, BLM has effectively waived the defective filing and may not declare a mill site claim abandoned and void based on the absence of that document from the file.[32]

Supplemental Information Required by Regulations
Cannot Be Used to Settle Disputes

The Tenth Circuit Court of Appeals has held that if failure to file the supplemental requirements contained in the regulations cannot be used by BLM to deem a claim abandoned, then it is clear that this failure may not be used by private parties to settle disputes over ownership of mining claims.[33] However, there is little doubt that requirements contained in the section 314 of FLPMA could be used by private parties to settle disputes over ownership of mining claims.

Claim Owners Cannot Avoid Benefit of Their
Filing to Other Interest Holders

An annual filing by an interest holder in a mining claim benefits other minor interest holders in the claim even though the party who filed contends the interests of the minor interest owner should be deemed abandoned. The original filing constitutes a filing on behalf of all of the interest holders for purposes of compliance with the statute and avoids conclusive abandonment of the other interests. [34]

Claims in National Park System Must Be Filed Annually with BLM

Even though unpatented mining claims in the National Park System were recorded as required by 16 U.S.C. 1907 (1982), if a notice of intention to hold was not properly filed with the BLM and the local recording office on or before December 30 of each year, the claim is deemed abandoned and void.[35]

BLM Not Required to Notify Claimant in Advance to File

The Board of Land Appeals has held that BLM is under no obligation to notify a claimant of the need to make the annual filing. Such notification in the past was merely a courtesy.[36]

Annual Filing Left at BLM Office Five Minutes Late

On December 30, 1981, an assessment work affidavit was left in the Arizona State Office of the BLM at 4:20 p.m.[37] The document was date stamped the next business day, December 31, 1981, because it was received after the close of business which was 4:15 p.m. Consequently the BLM declared the claim abandoned and void. This case illustrates how inflexible the filing deadline is. The BLM has absolutely no discretion to extend the deadline by even one minute.

Until Issuance of Final Certificate, Patent Applicant Must File Annually

Unless a final certificate has been issued, an applicant for a patent to a mining claim is not excused, under 43 CFR 3833.2-4, from the requirement to file annually an affidavit of assessment work or notice of intention to hold the claim with BLM under 43 U.S.C. 1744 (1982). This is because "the patent application is not cognizable as a recordation filing under FLPMA, as it was not an "exact legible reproduction or duplicate * * * which has been * * * filed for record * * * in the local jurisdiction of the state." **U.A. Small**, 108 IBLA 102 (1989).

Annual Filing Required After Recision Final Certificate

The regulation, 43 CFR 3833.2-4, provides that evidence of annual assessment work performed or a notice of intention to hold a mining claim need not be filed for an unpatented claim "for which an application for a mineral patent which complies with 43

CFR Part 3860 has been filed and the final certificate has been issued." In **B.J. Londo**, 109 IBLA 353 (1989), the Board considered a case where the BLM issued a final certificate on August 15, 1980, to a claimant who withdrew five mining claims from his patent application during September 1983. The Board held that the claimant was excused from complying with section 314 of FLPMA for 1980 through 1983. Id. at 355. As restated by the Board, "the filing requirements were satisfied for any filing period ending or arising within that time frame." Id. at 355, f.n. 2.

Situation Where Constructive Service Does Not Apply

In **David Robertson**, 107 IBLA 114 (1989), the claimant had arranged for his mail to be picked up by a designated person. However, the Postal Service delivered at least one notice to pick up the claimant's mail to the wrong house and also did not deliver the mail to the designated person. In this case, the Board held that constructive service did not apply because the claimant established error in Postal Service procedure amounting to negligence. Id. at 117.

Acceptable Evidence that Filing Was Received

An example of acceptable evidence demonstrating that a filing was received includes a copy of the affidavit of labor with a datestamp showing receipt by BLM within the proper filing period or a BLM-prepared acknowledgement receipt. **Donald G. Stern**, 109 IBLA 76 (1989).

Supreme Court Holds Section 314 of FLPMA to be Constitutional

On 1 April, 1985, the United States Supreme Court reversed the Federal District Court for Nevada's holding that section 314(a) of the Federal Land Policy and Management Act is unconstitutional. **United States v. Locke**, 471 U.S. 84 (1985). In holding that section 314 is constitutional, the Supreme Court pointed out that a claimant's intent to abandon is irrelevant, and that failure to comply with the statutory filing dates automatically voids the claim.

The Locke case represents an excellent example of a claimant that obviously did not intend to abandon his claims. The case involved 10 sand and gravel claims owned by the Lockes. Since 1960, the claims produced approximately $4,000,000 in materials, with more than $1,000,000 of that being produced during the 1979-80 assessment year. Furthermore, the claims could not be relocated because "common variety" sand and gravel has not been locatable since July 23, 1955 (30 U.S.C. 611).

The Lockes apparently made a diligent effort to make the annual filing. They sent their daughter to the Ely District BLM office to inquire on the filing procedure. There she was allegedly told that the documents must be filed at the BLM office "on or before December 31, 1980." The Lockes chose to hand deliver the documents and made the filing at the Reno BLM office on December 31, 1980. Since the statute requires filing the assessment notices on or before December 30 of each calendar year, they filed one day after the filing deadline.

References - Annual Filing Requirements

1. 43 CFR 3833.2-1(c).
2. 43 CFR 3833.0-5(j).
3. Buck Wilson, 89 IBLA 143, 146 (1985).
4. Ronald Willden, 97 IBLA 40, 44 (1987).
5. James V. Joyce (On Reconsideration), 56 IBLA 327 (1981).
6. 43 CFR 3833.2-3(a).
7. 43 CFR 3833.2-3(a).
8. Id.
9. 43 CFR 3833.0-5(m).
10. Victor Shepherd, 102 IBLA 334, 336 (1988).
11. Charles Renfro, 96 IBLA 311, 314 (1987).
12. Richard Holland, 74 IBLA 167 (1983); 43 CFR 3833.2-3(c).
13. 43 CFR 3833.2-3(b).
14. 43 CFR 3833.2-3(c).
15. 43 CFR 3833.2-3(b).
16. Add-Ventures, Ltd., 95 IBLA 44, 49 (1986).
17. 43 CFR 3833.0-5(i).
18. 43 U.S.C. 1744(a) (1982); 43 CFR 3833.2-3; Ronald Willden, 60 IBLA 173; Ted Dilday, 88 I.D. 682 (1981).
19. 43 U.S.C. 1744(a)(2).
20. 43 CFR 3833.2-3(b)(1)(i).
21. Id.
22. Arley Taylor, 90 IBLA 313, 314 (1986).
23. 43 CFR 3833.4(b); Ted Dilday, 56 IBLA 337 (1981).
24. Id.
25. Arley Taylor, 90 IBLA 313, 314 (1986).
26. Ethel Bilotte, 99 IBLA 159, 162 (1987).
27. David V. Udy, 45 IBLA 389 (1980).
28. Philip Brandl, 54 IBLA 343 (1981).
29. Arley Taylor, supra.
30. Red Top Mercury Mines, Inc., 96 IBLA 391 (1987); Ronald Willden, 97 IBLA 40 (1987).
31. Ptarmigan Co., Inc., 91 IBLA 113, 118 (1986).
32. James J. Kohring, 89 IBLA 345 (1985).
33. Jackson v. Robertson, 763 F.2d 1176, 1180 (10th Cir. 1985).
34. Id.
35. Riter Ekker, 58 IBLA 251 (1981).
36. Fawn Rupp, 65 IBLA 277, 280 (1982).
37. U.S. v. Ballas, 87 IBLA 88 (1985).

MISCELLANEOUS RECORDATION PROBLEMS

Federal Records of Mining Claims Are Not Official Depositories

Federal records of mining claims are not official depositories of records of mining claims for purposes of examining and establishing record title. Rather, local records control.[1]

BLM Not Required to Determine Legal Status of Claims

BLM does not have an affirmative duty to immediately determine the legal status of every claim filed with the Department and to notify claimants of its conclusions in time to permit them to correct their filings where there are deadlines to be met.[2]

BLM May Delay Abandonment Decision

BLM may declare an unpatented mining claim abandoned and void for failure to make an annual filing even though BLM has delayed issuing such a declaration for a number of years.[3]

Problems with Mail

In numerous cases claimants have alleged that they mailed documents to the BLM of which the BLM has no record. Undoubtedly in some cases the Postal Service or BLM may have lost or misplaced the documents. However, there have been so many cases of this type that it is also likely that some of the instruments were never mailed.[4]

Erroneous Information

There have been many cases where the claimant has alleged that BLM employees had provided erroneous or incomplete information which resulted in the loss of claims. However the Board of Land Appeals has consistently held that reliance upon erroneous advice provided by BLM does not relieve claimants from compliance with the statute or regulations.[5]

No Hearing Required

In many cases the claimant has challenged the constitutionality of FLPMA and the regulations because there is no provision for a hearing prior to a declaration of abandonment. The hearing requirement is satisfied by a claimant's right of appeal to the Interior Board of Land Appeals.[6]   Furthermore, no evidentiary hearing is required where the validity of a claim depends upon the legal effect to be given uncontested facts of record.

BLM Cannot Void Claim If Claimant Does Not Submit Information Not Required by Regulations

Neither the statute nor regulations require a mineral locator to submit evidence of title other than a location notice.[7]   BLM does not have authority to require a claimant to submit documentation establishing a chain of title, and cannot declare claims void either on the basis of the documents of title supplied or for failure to supply them.[8]

Statutory Authority for Regulations

The Tenth Circuit Court of Appeals has held that the regulations promulgated under FLPMA were not in excess of statutory jurisdiction, authority, or limitation, or short of the statutory right under the Act.[9]

Fraudulent Documents

A person who knowingly files false, fictitious, or fraudulent documents is subject to criminal action by the United States under 18 U.S.C. 1001.   Examples of this problem might be filing an affidavit that assessment work or certain location work was done when it was not.

Thirty-Day Appeal Period

The regulations require that a notice of appeal must be filed within 30 days after the person taking the appeal is served with the decision from which the appeal is taken.   43 CFR 4.411(a). Timely filing of a notice of appeal is required to establish the jurisdiction of the Interior Board of Land Appeals to review the decision.[10]   Failure to file the appeal within the time allowed mandates dismissal of the appeal.   The purpose of the 30-day rule is to establish a definite time when administrative proceedings regarding a claim are at an end, in order to protect other parties to the proceedings and the public interest.[11]

Notice of Transfer of Interest

The regulations[12] require that whenever the owner of an unpatented mining claim, mill site or tunnel site   sells, assigns or otherwise conveys all or any part of his interest in the claim, his transferee shall file the transfer of interest in the proper BLM office within 60 days after the completion of transfer. Also, new owners acquiring their interest through inheritance must file the notice in 60 days. The "notice of transfer of interest" must include the assigned serial number and the name and address of the new owner.

The BLM does not consider the failure to file a notice of transfer of interest within the 60-day period to constitute a conclusive presumption of abandonment of the claim or site. Rather, it insures that the present claim owner will receive a notice of contest action or some other action affecting the claim.[13]

Rival Claimants

BLM must accept all proper recordings, including those from rival claimants. Disputes over property rights must be resolved by private settlement, mediation or litigation because the BLM is without authority to determine the question of right of possession to claims between rival claimants.[14] The proper method of resolving such disputes is a suit filed in a court of competent jurisdiction.[15] Therefore, BLM may not refuse to accept and record a notice of location merely because a rival claimant to the same ground protests the filing.[16]

BLM Must Not Determine Standing of Claim at Request of Rival Claimant

The BLM must not make determinations regarding the sufficiency of mining claim recordation documents in response to third party requests.[17] The BLM is constantly requested to give an opinion (verbal or written) on the validity of a claim or to issue an abandonment decision on a mining claim by a rival claimant.[18] Claimants naturally prefer the BLM to solve their rival claimant problem rather than filing suit in a court of competent jurisdiction. However the BLM is strictly prohibited from rendering an opinion or issuing a decision as to the standing of a mining claimant at the insistence of a rival claimant.[19] As the Board of Land Appeals has stated, the "right of possession can be determined from the record, and a cancellation letter by BLM will not serve to 'quiet title' to appellant's claims."[20]

Mining Claim Records Maintained Under Section 314 of FLPMA

Before FLPMA, title records concerning unpatented mining claims were generally available only through the county or local recorder as required by state statute.   With the advent of a Federal computerized system for the maintenance of mining claim records it is now possible to examine up-to-date microfiche containing the basic elements of a mining claim title.   The microfiche as well as copies of the actual case files may be examined either in the public room of the BLM state office or ordered for home or office review.   For example, one may wish to monitor mining claims in certain geographic areas to determine if they are properly maintained under the annual filing requirements.   With updated microfiche copies available every two or three months, it is now possible to ascertain that an area is open to mineral entry with a fair degree of confidence before expending exploration money or staking a claim.   Of course, it is still necessary to examine local records because FLPMA requires that location notices and annual filing documents also be recorded with the local recorder.   Failure to file such documents with the local recorder is fatal to the claim even though the BLM records are properly maintained.

Documents on File with BLM and Available For Inspection or Purchase

1. Case File Documents (organized by serial number):
   Location notices
   Amended location notices
   Transfers of interest
   Receipt for service fee
   Notices of intention to hold
   Geological, geochemical or geophysical reports
   Assessment work affidavits
   Deferment of assessment work
   Claim map or narrative description
   Correspondence
   Administrative decisions and other actions
   Notice of patent application

2. Microfiche Indices:
   Claimant index - alphabetical order
   Claim index - alphabetical order by claim name
   Geographic index - legal description by quarter
   section
   Serial number - reference number for each case file

3. Information on Indices:
   Claim name
   Claimant's name and address
   Serial number of each claim
   County book and page or instrument number
   Claim location date

Date of latest assessment year filing
Date case closed
Type of claim

References - Miscellaneous Recordation Problems

1. United States Borax & Chemical Company, 98 IBLA 358, 359 (1987); 43 CFR 3833.0-1(d).
2. Joseph L. Frankmore, 101 IBLA 202 (1988).
3. Donald E. Stewart, 104 IBLA 202 (1988).
4. Henry D. Friedman, 49 IBLA 97, 98-99 (1980); Fawn Rupp, 65 IBLA 277, 279 (1982).
5. John Murphy, 58 IBLA 75 (1981).
6. Sidney O. Smith, 62 IBLA 378, 382 (1982).
7. Add-Ventures, Ltd., 95 IBLA 44, 48 (1986).
8. Id.
9. Topaz Beryllium Co. v. U.S., 649 F.2d 775 (10th Cir. 1981).
10. R.W. Dodds, 62 IBLA 241 (1982).
11. Id.
12. 43 CFR 3833.3.
13. Topaz Beryllium Co. v. U.S., supra at 779.
14. W.W. Allstead, 58 IBLA 46, 48 (1981).
15. John R. Medows, 43 IBLA 35 (1979).
16. W.W. Allstead, supra at 48.
17. Sandra Memmott (On Reconsideration), 93 IBLA 113, 115 (1986).
18. Gold Depository and Loan Co. v. Mary Brock, 69 IBLA 194 (1982); IMCO Services, 73 IBLA 374 (1983).
19. Sandra Memmott, 88 IBLA 379 (1985).
20. IMCO Services, supra at 376.

LODE CLAIMS

No Limit to Size of Vein

There is no limit to the size of a mineral-bearing vein to make it subject to location. A vein may be wider than the maximum, width of a lode mining claim (600 feet).[1]

Shape and Dimensions of Lode Claims

The Mining law of 1872,[1] in addition to providing that "no location of a mining claim shall be made until discovery of the vein or lode within the limits of the claim located" gives the following requirements concerning the shape and dimensions of lode claims:

1. The claim "may equal, but shall not exceed, one thousand five hundred feet in length along the vein or lode."

2. "No claim shall extend more than three hundred feet on each side of the middle of the vein at the surface."

3. No claim shall "be limited by any mining regulation to less than twenty-five feet on each side of the middle of the vein at the surface."

4. "The end lines of each claim shall be parallel to each other."

Length and Width of Lode Claim

The Federal law and regulations both provide that under no circumstances can a location of a vein or lode made after May 10, 1872, exceed 1500 feet along the course of the vein. Although the law has long provided that a lode claim cannot exceed 300 feet in width on each side of the middle of the vein or lode, a 1986 Solicitor's Opinion[3] now indicates the only width restriction on a lode claim is that it not exceed 600 feet.

Location Parallel to Course of Vein

If possible, the locator should lay out a lode mining claim so that the vein is parallel with the length of the claim and that the center line of the claim is also the center line of the vein.[4] The federal regulations[5] require that prior to locating a claim, if the vein cannot be traced on the surface, sufficient underground workings must be developed to discover the mineral-bearing vein or lode. When the general course of the vein is established, the boundaries of the claim can be marked properly.

Vein May Deviate from Center Line

The above-mentioned Solicitor's Opinion[6] provides that the "relationship between the actual course of the lode and the position of the mining claim's lateral boundaries and center line does not affect the validity of the claim. Original claim boundaries need not be adjusted, even where the lode materially deviates from the center line, so long as the claim has been located in good faith for mining purposes." Also, "no portion of the claim shall be considered excessive where the statutory dimensions, 1500 feet by 600 feet, are not exceeded." Originally the Department had no power to issue a mineral patent to any surface ground exceeding 300 feet in width on each side of the middle of the vein or lode. Now the only requirement is that a discovery is physically exposed somewhere within the limits of the claim.

Oversized Load Claims

If a claim marked in good faith exceeds 1500 feet in length or 600 feet in width, the location is not void in its entirety, but the excess is void.[7] However, if the error is large enough to imply fraud, the entire claim is invalid.[8]

Boundary Lines Must Not Be Irregular

The vein or lode lines of a location are not to be established in an irregular and zigzag manner for the purpose of controlling the length of the exterior lines of the location to suit the convenience of the locator.[9] For example, one may not locate a mining claim as an octagon or a curved figure. End lines should not be broken or curved, but must be laid out as straight lines.[10]

Subparallel Lines Do Not Invalidate Claim

Failure to locate a mining claim with parallel lines does not invalidate the location; subparallel lines are considered sufficient.[11] However, a lode claim should be located in the shape of a parallelogram, with end lines approximately parallel crossing the strike at right angles and the side lines approximately parallel to the strike of the vein and equidistant from the center of the lode.[12]

Parallel End Lines Required for Extralateral Rights

End lines must be parallel in order to acquire underground extralateral rights. Extensions of the parallel end lines serve to bound the underground portion of the vein.[13] The Parallel end lines give the right to follow the downward dip of the vein outside of the side lines of the location.[14]

Boundary Lines of Lode Claim May Extend Onto Withdrawn or Patented Land

The side and end lines of a lode claim may extend onto withdrawn or private land for the purpose of defining extralateral rights to veins or lodes which apex within the claim.[15] Of course the locator does not acquire rights to use the surface of the withdrawn land and may or may not acquire rights to the minerals underneath.[16] However if the lode claim is entirely within the withdrawn or patented land, and is conclusively shown to be so according the location notice and the map, the BLM may declare it null and void ab intio.[17]

Lode Claim Separated into Two Noncontiguous Tracts

An unpatented lode claim separated into two noncontiguous tracts by a patented lode claim may be valid.[18] Furthermore, a lode claim separated into two noncontiguous tracts by a patented placer claim may be patented as a single claim because there is no presumption that the patented claim does not contain a mineral vein.[19]

A lode claim may be separated into two noncontiguous parcels by an intervening patented mill site or other nonmineral patent, provided the lode or vein upon which the location is based has been discovered in both parts of the lode.[20] Both parcels must have the exposed vein because it can not be presumed that the vein discovered on part of the lode passed through the mill site.[21]

References - Lode Claims

1. Carson City Gold Mining Co., v. North Star Mining Co., 73 F. 597, 601 (1896), affirmed 83 F. 658, cert. denied 171 U.S. 687.
2. 30 U.S.C. 23 (1982).
3. Apex and Extralateral Rights Issues Raised by the Stillwater Mineral Patent, 93 I.D. 369 (April 18, 1986).
4. Argentine Mining Co. v. Terrible Mountain Mining Co., 122 U.S. 478, 485 (1887).
5. 43 CFR 3841.3-2.
6. Apex and Extralateral Rights Issues Raised by the Stillwater Mineral Patent, supra at 371.
7. Melvin N. Barry, 97 IBLA 359, 362 (1987); Waskey v. Hammer, 223 U.S. 85, 90 (1885).
8. Haws v. Victoria Copper Mining Co., 160 U.S. 303, 315 (1895).
9. Belligerent and Other Lode Mining Claims, 35 L.D. 22 (1906).
10. Walrath v. Champion Mining Co., 171 U.S. 293 (1898).
11. Grant v. Pilgim, 75 F.2d 562 (1938).
12. Meydenbauer v. Stevens, 78 F. 787 (1897).
13. Del Monte Mining & Milling Co. v. Last Chance Mining & Milling Co., 171 U.S. 55 (1898).
14. Id.
15. Outline Oil Corp., 95 IBLA 255, 257 (1987).

16. Nancy Lee Mines, Inc., 89 IBLA 257 (1985).
17. United States Borax & Chemical Corp., 98 IBLA 259 (1987).
18. Patten Extension Lode, 15 L.D. 133 (1892); Del Monte Mining & Milling Co.
    v. Lost Chance Mining & Milling Co., 171 U.S. 55 (1898).
19. Raymond E. Johnson, 57 L.D. 63 (1939).
20. Id. at 65.
21. Id.

PLACER CLAIMS

Placer Deposits Defined

Placer deposits are defined in the statute[1] as "including all forms of deposit, excepting veins of quartz, or other rock in place." In other words every deposit, not located with a lode claim, should be appropriated by a placer location. Because many mineral deposits do not fall readily into either category, the courts have interpreted this definition in many cases.

Maximum Claim Size

No location of a placer claim shall include more than 20 acres for each individual claimant. However, an association of two locators may locate 40 acres; three may locate 60 acres, and so on. The maximum area that may be embraced by a single placer claim is 160 acres and such a claim must be located by an association of at least eight persons. Corporations count as an individual claimant and are limited to 20-acre claims. For example, a 20-acre placer claim might be described as being the N1/2 NE1/4 NW1/4, Section 5, T.6 N., R.3 W., Boise Meridian.

Placer Claims Must Conform to United States Surveys

All placer mining claims must conform as nearly as practicable with the United States system of public land surveys and the rectangular subdivisions of such surveys, even though the claims are located on unsurveyed lands. If the claims conform to such legal subdivisions, no further survey or plat is required for patent.[2]

Curing Defects in Claim Form

A placer location which does not qualify for patent in its original form because of nonconformity with the public land survey system, is not void; but the defect, in the absence of an adverse claim to the added land, is curable either by amendment or relocation, provided the acreage limitation is observed.[3]

Placer Claims on Unsurveyed Lands

On unsurveyed land and in certain situations on surveyed lands, placer claims must be located by metes and bounds.[4] Regardless of whether placer claims are upon surveyed or unsurveyed lands, they must conform as nearly as practicable with the rectangular subdivision of the public land survey system.[5] Claims must be rectangular in form and of dimensions corresponding to appropriate legal subdivisions, and with east-and-west and north-and-south boundary lines.[6]

Placer Claims Described by Fractional Lots

If an area has been surveyed, the cadastral survey will plat fractional lots in a section that cannot be described by aliquot parts. These lots are generally located on the north and west sides of a township, or adjacent to meandered lakes or rivers. Where a placer claim is located over a lot and it embraces the entire lot (or more than one if necessary), the lot is identified in the legal description of the claim and a mineral survey is not be required when the claim is patented. However, if the claim does not embrace the entire lot, the claim cannot be described by legal subdivision; therefore it must be described by metes and bounds. Moreover, if a claim described by lot number has portions disqualified because one or more of the 10-acre tracts are not found to be mineral in character during the patent application process, a metes and bounds survey may be required to describe the actual land that may be patented.

Exceptions to the Rule of Conformity

Conformity to the public land surveys and the rectangular subdivisions is not required if such compliance would necessitate running the boundaries of the claim over other prior locations or where the claims are surrounded by prior locations.[7] Federal regulations[8] provide that "where a placer location by one or two persons can be entirely included within a square 40-acre tract, by three or four persons within two square 40-acre tracts placed end to end, by five or six persons within three square 40-acre tracts, such locations will be regarded as within the requirements where strict conformity is impracticable." For example, the Secretary of the Interior has held that a 10-acre placer claim consisting of a string of four contiguous 2.5-acre tracts straddling three regular 10-acre subdivisions is in conformity with the public land surveys.[9]

Lack of Conformity Is a Question of Fact

According to Interior Department regulations,[10] "whether a placer location conforms reasonably with the legal subdivisions of the public survey is a question of fact to be determined in each case." Therefore in the event of alleged unconformity in connection with a patent application, a hearing would be required before the application could be rejected. However, the most appropriate way to handle such a problem is to require a claimant to amend the claim so that it does conform as nearly as practicable with the rectangular system of survey.[11]

Gulch Placers

A "gulch" placer, which cannot, by reason of its environment, practicably be conformed to the system of public land surveys, may, upon sufficient and satisfactory showing, be patented in a shape approximating the public survey system as nearly as the conditions will reasonably permit.[12]   Gulch placers may be allowed with a mineral deposit confined within a narrow strip of land in the bed and on the banks of a small stream in a canyon flanked by abrupt walls or rocky slopes on each side, containing no mineral, agricultural, or timber value.[13]   It is almost always to the advantage of the claimant as well as the government to locate placer claims by legal subdivision or in a compact, rectangular form if the lands are not surveyed.

Lands Covered by Placer Claim Must Be Contiguous

It is well established that lands covered by a single placer claim must be contiguous; two separate tracts that corner are not contiguous and cannot be included in a single location.[14]   In the event that a claimant has a location consisting of two separate tracts which corner, he can select one of the two tracts to maintain under the original location.   The other tract may be covered by a new location providing the land is available for a new location.[15]

Oversized Placer Claims

As a general rule, an oversized placer mining claim is not completely void; only the excess portion is void.[16]   The owner of the excess claim is given a reasonable period of time to select the portion of the claim he is entitled to retain.   Any person who makes a location over any part of the oversized claim is a trespasser and his location is void.[17]   Upon identifying an oversized or irregularly-shaped claim while doing status adjudication on mining claim files, the BLM notifies the claimant to correct the defect within a specified time period.

Rule of Approximation

In 1913 the Secretary of the Interior established the "rule of approximation" for placer claims as had been previously applied to entries under the homestead laws.[18]   The "rule of approximation" concerns the situation where a claimant wishes to patent a slightly oversized placer claim on lands described by legal subdivision on surveyed lands.   Based on a formula, a slightly oversized claim may be patented.

The Ten Acre Rule

The Interior Department has established a rule, that when challenged, the claimant must show that each ten-acre tract on a claim contains a valuable mineral and that each ten acre tract must be mineral in character.[19]   The rule is applied equally to individual and association placer claims.[20]   Use of the rule is not restricted to validity examinations in connection with patent proceedings, but is also applied on all validity examinations of placer mining claims.[21]

Ten-Acre Tracts May Include Nonmineral Land

If a placer location is made to conform as nearly as practicable to the system of public land surveys and the rectangular subdivisions of such surveys embrace small portions of land not valuable for placer mining, it is still appropriate to conform the location to legal subdivisions.[22]

Advantages of Association Placer Claims

A single discovery of a valuable mineral deposit is sufficient to validate a placer location, whether it be 20 acres by an individual, or 160 acres or less by an association of persons.   However, each 10-acre subdivision with the claim must be mineral in character. Furthermore, only one hundred dollars worth of assessment work is required per claim, regardless of size.   There are other advantages such as savings in recordation and filing fees with fewer claims.

Subdivision of Placer Claims into 10-Acre Parcels

A placer claims must be laid out in square 10-acre parcels to determine whether each 10-acre portion of the claim is mineral in character, regardless of whether the claim conforms to the system of public land surveys.   In a 1984 case,[23] the Interior Board of Land Appeals gave the rules for subdividing a placer claim into square 10-acre parcels in situations where such claims are not in conformity with the public land surveys.

In applying the 10-acre rule, each claim must be subdivided along the axis in which it was laid out on the ground.   Inasmuch as it is presumed by the statute that a placer claim shall conform to the public land survey, the 10-acre rule is properly applied by subdividing a claim into parcels as nearly square as possible.

If a claim should consist of two or more 10-acre parcels aligned in a direction that deviates from north-south or east-west, the claim is subdivided in the following manner:

1. Draw an imaginary center line parallel to the long axis of the claim.

2. Subdivide the claim along the center line to create as many 10-acre parcels as possible.

3. Parcels should be as nearly square as possible.

Although the situation where a claim may be greater than 660-feet wide was not addressed in the case, it may be necessary to establish two or more contiguous rows of claims. This could be accomplished by subdividing the claim along the short axis into sections of equal length approximately 660 feet apart (a 10-acre square parcel is 660 feet on each side). Then construct lines parallel to the long axis of the claim and through the points of subdivision.

The objective is to establish 10-acre parcels that are not more than 10-acres in size, but are as close to that size as possible. Again, parcels should be as nearly square as possible. Of course there will be many situations where these rules will not provide a means to completely cover a claim with square, 10-acre parcels. As a result some parcels may be of variable size with side dimensions more or less than 660 feet.

Combining Two 20-Acre Claims

A placer location for 20 acres cannot be enlarged to 40 acres by means of an amended location notice. Such an amendment would create a new location.[24]

Dummy Locators

Ever since 1870 when the mining law first provided for association placer, locators have used the names of employees, relatives or friends as dummies to obtain more land than they are entitled to possess by law. This is particularly attractive because the law provides for eight locators to appropriate up to 160 acres in a single claim. Regardless of whether the claim is 20 acres or 160 acres, one discovery is required, and $100 worth of labor is required each year. For more than 100 years the courts have dealt with the issue of dummy locators, generally only hearing the most blatant or obvious cases. Such cases are normally exposed during the examination of title documents as required by the mineral patent process.[25] It is quite likely that most of such cases go undetected because of the lack of record information concerning the relationships among the individual parties.

Perhaps the most common example of dummy locators is where all the locators of an association placer claim are officers in the same corporation.[26] Because a corporation has the status of an individual claimant, a corporation is only entitled to locate 20-acre claims. If a locator has knowledge of a concealed interest and is a

212

party to the use of dummy locators, the location is deemed fraudulent and is invalid in its entirety.[27] However, whether a claim is located by dummy locators is a question of fact that must be determined at a hearing.[28]

Discovery Required Before Transfer of Association Placer Claim

Although it permissible for an individual to acquire an association placer claim more than 20 acres in size, it is essential that there were sufficient individuals to make the original location, and furthermore that a discovery was made within the limits of the claim prior to the date of transfer. In many cases, corporations have purchased association placer claims from associations of persons.[29] If the association claim does not have a discovery established prior to the date of conveyance, a subsequent discovery will only entitle the corporation to a 20-acre patent.

No Limit to Number of Contiguous Claims Included in a Patent Application

There is no limit to the number of association placer claims that may be included in a patent application.[30] Of course the claims must be contiguous.[31]

Building Stone Placer Act

Locatable deposits of building stone may be located with placer-type claims as authorized by the Act of August 4, 1892.[32] The law requires that building stone placers may be located only on lands "that are chiefly valuable for building stone." The Act of July 23, 1955, withdrew common varieties of building stone from entry under the mining laws.

Monumenting Placer Claims

If a placer claim is located on surveyed lands according to legal subdivisions, there is no requirement to monument the corners and mark the boundaries.[33] However, if the state law requires that placer claims located by legal subdivision be monumented, the federal courts will uphold that requirement.

References - Placer Claims

1. 30 U.S.C. 35 (1982).
2. Id.; Snow Flake Fraction Placer, 32 L.D. 198 (1903); Hanson v. Craig, 170 F. 62 (1909).
3. Fred B. Ortman, 52 L.D. 468 (1928).
4. 30 U.S.C. 35 (1982).
5. Miller Placer Claim, 30 L.D. 225 (1900).
6. Laughing Water Placer, 34 L.D. 56 (1905).
7. 43 CFR 3842.1-5(b).
8. 43 CFR 3842.1-5(c).
9. U.S. v. Henrikson, A-28763 (June 4, 1963).
10. 43 CFR 33842.1-5(d).
11. U.S. v. Haskins, 59 IBLA 1, 99 (1981).
12. Wood Placer Mining Co., 32 L.D. 363 (1903).
13. Willaim F. Carr, 53 I.D. 431 (1931).
14. W.G. Singleton, 75 IBLA 168 (1983); Stenfjeld v. Espe, 171 F. 825 (9th Cir. 1909); 30 U.S.C. 36 (1982).
15. Tomera Placer Claim, 33 L.D. 560-61 (1905).
16. Zimmerman v. Funchion, 161 F. 859, 860 (CCA Alaska 1908).
17. Jones v. Wild Goose Mining Co., 177 F. 95 (CCA Alaska 1910).
18. Ventura Coast Oil Company, 42 L.D. 453 (1913).
19. McCall v. Andrus, 628 F.2d 1185, 1188 (9th Cir. 1980), cert. denied, 450 U.S. 996.
20. Lara v. Secretary of the Interior, 820 F. 2d 1535, 1538 (9th Cir. 1987).
21. Id.
22. Hogan and Idaho Placer Mining Claims, 34 L.D. 42 (1905).
23. U.S. v. Lara (On Reconsideration), 80 IBLA 215, 216 (1984), affirmed Lara v. Secretary of the Interior, supra.
24. Charles H. Head, 40 L.D. 135 (1911).
25. Cook v. Klonos, 164 F. 529, 538 (9th Cir. 1908); Nome & Sinook Co. Snyder, 187 F. 385 (9th Cir. 1911); U.S. v. Brookshire Oil Co., 242 f. 718 (DCSD Cal 1917).
26. Big Horn Limestone Co., 46 IBLA 99, 100 (1980).
27. Donald D. Hall, 95 IBLA 33 (1986).
28. Big Horn Limestone Co., supra at 100.
29. Brittain Contractors, Inc., 37 IBLA 233, 239 (1978).
30. Tucker v. Masser, 113 U.S. 203 (1885).
31. St. Louis Smelting and Refining co., 104 U.S. 636 (1882).
32. 30 U.S.C. 161 (1982); U.S. v. Henri (On Judicial Remand), 104 IBLA 93, 100 (1988).
33. Kern Oil Co. v. Crawford, 76 P 1111, 143 Cal 298 (1903).

MILL SITES

The location and patenting of lands for mill site purposes is authorized by the Mining Law of 1872, as amended by the Act of March 18, 1960 (30 U.S.C. 42; 43 CFR 3844 and 3864). The Federal law provides for three types of mill sites: (1) mill sites in connection with lode claims, (2) independent mill sites, and (3) mill sites in connection with placer claims.

Mill Sites Dependent on Lode Claims

The Federal law provides that "where nonmineral land not contiguous to the vein or lode is used or occupied by the proprietor of such vein or lode for mining or milling purposes, such nonadjacent surface ground may be embraced and included in an application for a patent for such vein or lode, and the same may be patented therewith, subject to the same preliminary requirements as to survey and notice as are applicable to veins or lodes."[1]

Mill Sites Dependent on Placer Claims

The Act of March 18, 1960 authorizes that "where nonmineral land is needed by the proprietor of a placer claim for mining, milling, processing, beneficiation, or other operations in connection with such claims, and is used or occupied by the proprietor for such purposes, such land may be included in an application for a patent for such claim and may be patented therewith subject to the same requirements as to survey and notice as are applicable to placers."

Independent Mill Sites

The Federal law provides that "the owner of a quartz mill or reduction works, not owning a mine in connection therewith, may also receive a patent for his mill site."[2]

Procedure for Locating Mill Sites

There is no specific direction in the Federal law or regulations concerning how a mill site may be located or how many mill sites may be located. However, the applicable case law and Interior Department policy indicate that mill sites may be located by legal subdivision if on surveyed lands and by metes and bounds if on unsurveyed lands, regardless of the type of mill site. Each individual mill site, however, is limited to five acres. Also, there is no limitation to the number of mill sites that may be located as long as each mill site is properly "used or occupied" for "mining or milling purposes." Of course, mill sites, like lode and placer claims, should be located (monumented, posted, recorded, etc.) as required by the applicable state law.

Lands Open to Mill Site Location

In order to locate a mill site claim, the land must be unappropriated, and must be open to location under the mining laws.[3] Lands where the United States owns the surface but not the mineral rights is not open to entry.[4] However, the Department does not approve of mill sites on lands where the United States owns the minerals but not the surface. Mill sites cannot be located on lands where only the mineral estate is owned by the United States, such as Stock-Raising Homesteads.[5]

Pickett Act withdrawals which are open to the location of metalliferous minerals are also open to dependent mill site locations in connection to metalliferous mineral locations.[6]

Mill sites could not be located on lands known to be valuable for leasing act minerals or lands under lease or permit before the Multiple Mineral Development Act of 1954. The Act allowed the location of mill sites on such lands.[7]

Mill Sites Must Be Nonmineral Land

The statute requires that land located for mill sites must be "nonmineral in character"[8] (for more information on this subject, please refer to the chapter on "Mineral in Character"). In a 1979 case,[9] a mill site patent applicant's mill site location was contested because the Forest Service mineral examiner found that mill tailings on the property contained sufficient mineral value to be "mineral in character." On appeal, the Interior Board of Land Appeals noted that land can be mineral in character so as to invalidate a mill site; yet there may be insufficient evidence of discovery to validate a mining claim.

Mill Site on End Line or Side Line of a Lode

The provision of the law where only "nonmineral land, not contiguous to the vein or lode," may be acquired for mining or milling purposes in connection with a lode mining claim is intended to prevent a mill site locator from appropriating part of the vein or lode. A mill site may be located adjoining the end line or side line of a lode claim providing that it can clearly be shown that the lode or vein (ore body) terminates inside the lode claim and does not cross the side or end line adjoining the mill site.[10] For example, where a mill site is contiguous to the end line of a lode claim, the Government may require core drilling on the mill site near the end line of the lode claim to establish the nonmineral character of the mill site before issuance of the patent because the normal proofs of geologic inference will not suffice.[11]

Section 38 Applies to Mill Sites

A mill site may be established like a mining claim without a formal location where the mill site is held and worked for a period equal to the statute of limitations of the State in which the land is located.[12]

Public Law 167 Applies to Mill Sites

The owner of a valid mill site location with surface rights under section 4 of the Act of July 23, 1955, may cut and remove the timber on the claim for the purpose of constructing a mill, reduction works and other accessories required in the development of mineral interests. In other words, surface resources may be used for mining or milling purposes, but may not be used for resale, even if the money from the sale is used for purchase of mining or milling equipment or supplies.[13]

Good Faith Use of Mill Site

The fact that land in a national forest is located in such a manner as to give the most possible frontage on the main highway and to adjoin land owned and used for recreational and camping purposes may give serious doubt as to the good faith of a locator, particularly if there is little mining or milling activity.[14] However, the question of relative values with respect to lands within a national forest, whether chiefly valuable as a recreational site or for mining and milling purposes, is not a crucial test of its locatability. The occupation of a mill site for mining or milling purposes must be demonstrated by outward and visible signs of good faith by the claimant.[15]

Owner of Valid Claim May Not Be Entitled to Mill Site

The owner of a patented or patentable mining claim is not entitled to a mill site if the mill site claimant does not show that the mill site is being occupied or used for mining or milling purposes.[16]

Mill Site Used in Connection with Invalid Claim Is Invalid

The validity of a mill site that is used in connection with a mining operation on a lode claim is necessarily dependent upon the validity of such lode claim.[17]   Presumably this rule is also applicable to placer claims, although there is no case authority.

Mining Claim in Connection with Dependent Mill Site Must Also Be Examined

To determine the validity of a dependent mill site, the validity of the mining claim that it is associated with must also be verified.[18] Therefore, in order to receive a patent for a mill site dependent on an unpatented lode claim, the applicant for patent must show a discovery on the associated lode claim. Even if the mining claim has been patented, it is necessary to show mining operations on the associated patented claim.[19]

Lode Claim Located Over Existing Mill Site

If a lode claim is located in such a manner that it overlaps an existing mill site, the owner of the lode claim has no right to remove minerals from the land embraced by the mill site location.[20]

Mill Site Located Over Senior Location

The location of a mill site over a valid mining claim is void and cannot become valid, even if the senior location becomes forfeited or abandoned.[21]

Mill Site and Subsequent Lode Claim

A mill site location becomes valid at the time it is actually used or occupied for mining and milling purposes, rather than the date of location. By comparison, a mining claim becomes valid at the time of discovery which likewise might occur at the time of location or sometime later. However, where there is no conflict, the initiation of a claimant's rights or title to the mining claim relates back to the date of location. Therefore where a mining claim is staked over a mill site, the question of mineral character of the mill site should be addressed at the mill site's location date or the date the mill site became valid rather than the date when the mining claim was located. Otherwise, improvements and expenditures upon the mill site would not be protected.[22]

How to Determine Validity of Dependent Mill Site if Occupancy But No Present Use

While "use" necessarily implies present mining or milling activities, it has long been noted that land may be "occupied" under the statute even in the absence of present "use" of the land for mining or milling purposes.[23] If there is no present "use" of the land for mining or milling purposes, "the claimant must show an occupation, by improvements or otherwise, as evidences an intended use of the tract in good faith for mining or milling purposes." The Board of Land Appeals recently specified the elements that must be considered to determine whether a dependent mill site is occupied but not used for mining or milling purposes:[24]

1. The validity of the claim if unpatented.
2. The extent of mineral reserves on a patented claim.
3. The length of nonuse and amount of time that might reasonably be expected to be consumed in putting the mill site to use. This would be consistent with the scope of foreseeable activities.

In the 1986 case of **United States v. Swanson**, 21 years had past since Swanson had acquired the mill sites. Other than a single 30-day test run, no production from the mill had occurred during this time. However, the Board held that good faith was indicated by extensive valuable improvements and the expenditure of several million dollars in an effort to get the mill in operation.

Past and Future Use

A mill site that might once have been valid can lose that validity, and conversely, a mill site located for future use is not valid. The Board of Land Appeals has held that past use does not qualify where a portable mill was used on the claim in the past but was removed and only a small amount of ore is stockpiled on the mill site.[25] It has also held that planned future use for mining purposes was not sufficient where, although improvements were on the site, present use was merely for prospecting activities.[26]

Intention to Use or Occupy Mill Site In the Future Is Not Sufficient

The Interior Department has consistently held that an intention to use a mill site in the future is not sufficient to establish use or occupancy. The use of improvements on a mill site as a base for occasional sampling or testing activities on associated claims and the intent to use a mill site in the future when and if market conditions are favorable do not satisfy the requirements of use or occupancy.[27]

Use or Occupancy of All Land in a Mill Site: the 2.5 Acre Rule

A mill site patent applicant may be granted less than a five-acre tract if all the land within the tract is not proved to be needed for mining and milling purposes. If each 2.5 acre aliquot part of a 5 acre mill site does not show the element of either use or occupancy, it is excess and must be excluded.[28]

Alternative Method of Omitting Portions of Multiple Mill Sites

Where portions of multiple mill sites are used or occupied for mining or milling purposes, the claimant may be required to omit portions of several mill sites to arrive at the minimum number of mill sites that can embrace all the lands used or occupied.[29]

If Associated Mining Claims Not Operated, Mill Site Cannot Be Used for Mining Purposes

If none of the associated mining claims are being operated, a claimant cannot be using the mill sites for mining purposes. Mill sites have been held to be invalid with improvements such as a 40 by 60 foot metal building, trommel with feed and discharge conveyors, holding reservoirs, 7 trailer space hook-ups, underground water, sewer, and electric lines, septic disposal tank and a well with storage tank because the associated mining claims were not being operated.[30]

Proper Use or Occupancy of a Dependent Mill Site

The following list of uses held to validate a mill site have been approved by numerous Interior and Federal Court decision:

1. Depositing tailings and overburden.[31]

2. Stockpiling or storing ore.[32]

3. Tailings ponds.[33]

4. Blacksmith shop and tool or machine shops.[34]

5. Offices and living quarters for workmen.[35] However, the use of a cabin as a base of operations while engaged in prospecting activities will not validate a mill site.[36]

6. Improvements used to develop water such as wells, springs (if improved) and pumping stations.[37] Although the mere appropriation of water does not validate a mill site, where water is essential for the working of the mine or an associated mill site, works required in the development of the water will validate a mill site.[38]

Use or Occupancy that Does Not Validate a Dependent Mill Site

The Interior Department has determined that the following types of use or occupancy do not validate a dependent mill site:

1. Ditches or pipes for the conveyance or conducting of water from one place to another.[39] Such water conveyances must be established under a right-of-way.

2. Access roads needed for mining or milling operations, including roads for ore haulage.[40]

3. Reclamation work.[41]

Type of Mineral Processed by Independent Mill Site

The minerals processed by a "quartz mill" or "reduction works" must come from a vein or lode. Furthermore, mill sites of this category may not be used as custom works to beneficiate material from placer claims. As a general rule, only metallic minerals in veins or lodes may be processed by a "quartz mill" or "reduction works."

Independent Mill Site: Acceptable Improvements

The Mining Law[42] provides for the location and patent of an independent mill site by "the owner of a quartz mill or reduction works..." A quartz mill or reduction works is the only kind of improvement contemplated by the statute because these improvements are distinctly named and there is no mention of any other kind of improvement.[43] The Secretary of the Interior has held that a mill to crush gypsum to a smaller size is neither a "quartz mill" or a "reduction works" that would qualify an independent mill site for patent.[44] However, he indicated that possible future advances in the mining and milling industry may allow nonmetallic minerals to be processed with a "reduction works." In a 1978 case,[45] the Board of Land Appeals defined the following terms:

Quartz mill: A machine or establishment for pulverizing quartz ore, in order that the gold or silver it contains may be separated by chemical means; a stamp mill.

Reduction works: Works for reducing metals from their ores, as a smelting works, cyanide plant, etc.

The Interior Board of Land Appeals has held that an independent mill site may not be used as a custom works to beneficiate material from placer claims.[46]

Continuous Operation Required for Independent Mill Sites

Coupled with good faith and the existence of an operable mill or reduction works, there must also be evidence of an ongoing and more or less continuous operation for custom work on the mill site.[47] The custom mill must be in continuous operation to satisfy a present demand for milling services.[48]

Independent Mill Site Occupied but Not Used

Where an independent mill site is occupied but not used for mining or milling purposes, the Interior Board of Land Appeals has held that one must apply a test of reasonableness to determine whether the period of nonuse demonstrates invalidity.[49] Within the concept of reasonableness, the Board specified a number of relevant factors:

1. The time of nonuse.
2. The condition of the mill.
3. The potential sources of ore to be run through the mill.
4. The marketing conditions.
5. The costs of operations, including labor and transportation.
6. All factors bearing upon the economic feasibility of a milling operation being conducted on the site.

Dual Use of Mill Site

A mill site may be used as both a dependent mill site and custom or independent mill site.[50]

No Assessment Work or Expenditures for Mill Site

Mill sites do not require annual assessment work; nor do they require $500 worth of work to qualify for patent.[51] However, work done on a dependent mill site can qualify as assessment work on the associated claim(s).

Validity of Mill Sites at Date of Withdrawal

A mill site located prior to a withdrawal must be valid both at the date of the withdrawal and must continue to be valid without interruption from that date forward.[52] A mill site, like a mining claim, may be located on lands withdrawn under authority of the Pickett Act which allows entry for metalliferous minerals.[53] However, a mill site located on land subject to a reclamation withdrawal, or any other withdrawal that closes the land to entry under the mining laws, initiates no rights in the locator and is void from its purported inception.[54]

Improvements Added After Withdrawal Cannot Retroactively Validate Mill Site

Improvements constructed after the date of a withdrawal cannot serve to retroactively validate an otherwise invalid mill site.[55]

Contest Procedures Are Same for Mill Site Locations as Lode and Placer Claims

A mill site is a claim to property which may not be declared invalid without proper notice and opportunity for adequate hearing in accordance with due process.[56]   Consequently, contest procedures are the same for mill site locations as lode and placer claims.[57]

Prima Facie Case Based on No Use or Occupancy

A prima facie case that a mill site is not used or occupied for a significant period of time is not a weak case.[58] Evidence that land has not been used or occupied for mining or milling purposes goes to the very heart of a mill site's validity.[59]

Dependent Mill Site May Be Contested without Contesting Validity of Associated Claim

A dependent mill site may be contested without contesting the validity of a claim with which it is connected.[60] A mill site can be contested separately and declared invalid when evidence establishes it is not being used for mining and milling purposes independent of the issue of the validity of the mining claims.[61]

Survey Requirements

If the lands in a patent application are described by legal subdivision and are situated in surveyed lands, no mineral survey is required regardless of whether the mill sites are independent or located in connection with lode or placer claims. However, if a mill site is described as a portion of an irregular lot or is described by metes and bounds, and is not accompanied by the official survey, the application must be rejected.[62]

Used or Occupied at the Date
Final Certificate Issued

The older Interior cases indicate that the land covered by a mill site location must be used or occupied for mining or milling purposes at the date of patent application.[63] However, a recent case indicates that the critical date for establishing the validity of a mining claim in a patent application is the date final certificate is issued.[64] The date final certificate issues is the date equitable title has passed. Of course, any time after issuance of the final certificate until issuance of patent the Department of the Interior may inquire into the validity of a mining claim.[65]

Mill Site Patent Application Must Not Be Held
Up for Possible Adverse Environmental Effects

The Government does not have the discretion to hold up a mill site patent application on the basis of possible adverse environmental effects.[66] The National Environmental Policy Act (NEPA) does not apply to the patent process because if a claimant has met the requirements for patent, the Government has no discretion to deny issuance.[67]

Dependent Mill Site Is Not Patented Before
Associated Claim Is Patented

A dependent mill site may only be patented if the mining claim to which it is associated is either already patented or a patent is granted simultaneously with the mill site patent.[68] Therefore, a dependent mill site may not be taken to patent at any time before an associated lode or placer mining claim is patented.[69]

Dependent Mill Site May Be Located and
Patented after Claim Is Patented

A dependent mill site may be located after the lode claim is patented.[70] Even years after a mining claim is patented, a dependent mill site may be located and taken to patent.

Requirements to Patent Mill Sites Associated
with Lode Claims Are Similar to Those Associated
with Placer Claims

The language authorizing the patenting of mill sites associated with placer claims was added in 1960 to amend the mining law. Although the type of activity needed to qualify a mill site associated with a lode claim is different from that required for placer claim, the language should be construed similarly.[71]

Ownership of Lode Claim Does Not Disqualify Independent Mill Site Patent Application

A mill site may be patented as an independent location even though the applicant also owns a lode claim. Of course, the use must be proper for an independent mill site.[72]

Applications for Multiple Mill Sites

A separate mill site is not necessarily complemental to each lode location;[73] nor does the mining law necessarily provide for a mill site to be patented for a group of contiguous lode claims held and worked in common.[74] However, if needed and used for mill site purposes, there is no restriction on the number of mill sites that may be included in a patent application.[75]

Adverse Claims

A mill site claimant may not file an adverse claim against a mineral patent applicant but should instead file a protest. The reason for this is that only the Interior Department has the authority to determine whether a discovery exists or that the land is nonmineral in character. An adverse claim should only be filed where a priority of right is involved, such as with two conflicting mill sites.

References - Mill Sites

1. 30 U.S.C. 42(a) (1982).
2. 30 U.S.C. 42(b) (1982).
3. Robert C. LeFaivre, 13 IBLA 289, 290 (1973).
4. Id. at 291; See Eagle Peak Copper Mining Co., 54 I.D. 251 (1933).
5. BLM Manual 3864.11C.
6. Coeur d'Alene Cresent Mining Co., 53 I.D. 531, 533 (1931).
7. See Kasey v. Molybdenum Corp of America, 336 F.2d 560, 563 (9th Cir. 1964).
8. 30 U.S. C. 42 (11982).
9. U.S. v. Silver Chief Mining Co., Inc., 40 IBLA 214 (1979).
10. Montana-Illinois Copper Mining Co., 42 L.D. 434 (1913).
11. Coeur d' Alene Cresent Mining Co., 53 L.D. 531 (1931).
12. Feldsite Corporation of America, 56 IBLA 78, 79 (1981).
13. Effect of Section 4 of the Act of July 23, 1955 on Mill Sites, 64 I.D. 301 (1957).
14. U.S. v. Langmade and Mistler, 52 L.D. 701 (1929).
15. Hecla Co., 12 L.D. 75.
16. U.S. National Motor Service Co., 15 IBLA 22 (1974).
17. U.S. v. Coston, A-30825 (February 23, 1968).
18. U.S. v. Dean, 14 IBLA 107, 109 (1973).
19. U.S. v. Wedertz, 71 I.D. 368, 373 (1964).
20. Cleary v. Skiffich, 65 P. 59 (1901).
21. Kershner v. Trinidad Mill & Mining Co., 201 P. 1055 (1921).
22. Cleary v. Skiffich, supra at 62.
23. U.S. v. Swanson, 93 IBLA 21-22 (1986).
24. Id.
25. U.S. v. Dietmann, 26 IBLA 364 (1976).

26. U.S. v. Wedertz, 71 I.D. 368 (1964).
27. U.S. v. Osmer, Jr., 76 IBLA 59 (1983).
28. U.S. v. Swanson, supra.
29. Id at 35-36.
30. Pine Valley Builders, Inc., 103 IBLA 384 (1988).
31. Utah International, Inc., 36 IBLA 219, 225-26 (1978).; U.S. v. Swanson, supra.
32. Id.
33. Id.
34. Alaska Mildred Gold Mining Co., 42 L.D. 255 (1913); U.S. v. Dean, 14 IBLA
       107, 109 (1973).
35. Satisfaction Extension Mill Site, 14 L.D. 173 (1892); Swanson v. Andrus, Civil
       No. 78-4045 (June 3, 1982).
36. U.S. v. SMP Mining Co., 67 I.D. 141 (1960); U.S. v. W.E. Polk, A-30859
       (April 17, 1968).
37. Howard C. Brown, 73 I.D. 172 (1966); U.S. v. Swanson, 93 I.D. 5, 20 (1986).
38. Sierra Grand Mining Co. v. Crawford, 11 I.D. 338 (1980).
39. Hales v. Symons, 51 L.D. 123 (1925); U.S. v. Swanson, 93 IBLA 1, 29-30
       (1986).
40. Hales v. Symons, supra.
41. Utah International, Inc., supra at 77.
42. 30 U.S.C. 42 (1982).
43. Pacific Portland Cement Company, 51 L.D. 459, 460-61 (1926).
44. Id.
45. U.S. v. Paden, 33 IBLA 380, 383 (1978).
46. Id.
47. U.S. v. Paden, 44 IBLA 257 (1979).
48. Id.
49. U.S. v. Cuneo, 15 IBLA 304 (1974).
50 U.S. v. Parsons, 33 IBLA 326, 337 (1978); U.S. v. Dean, 14 IBLA 107, 109
       (1973).
51. Alta Mill Site, 8 L.D. 195, 196 (1889).
52. U.S. v. Almgren, 17 IBLA 295, 299-301 (1974).
53. Coeur d'Alene Cresent Mining Co., 53 I.D. 531 (1931).
54. J.P. Hinds, A-29239 (March 8, 1962).
55. U.S. v. Swanson, 93 I.D. 21 (1986).
56. U.S. v. O'Leary, 63 I.D. 341 (1956).
57. U.S. v. Paden, 33 IBLA 383 (1978).
58. U.S. v. Swanson, 93 I.D. 5, 15 (1986).
59. Id.
60. U.S. v. Dean, 14 IBLA 109 (1973).
61. U.S. v. Polk, A-30859 (April 17, 1968).
62. U.S. v. Buch, 11 IBLA 307 (1973).
63. Hudson Mining Company, 14 L.D. 544 (1892).
64. U.S. v. Whitaker (On Reconsideration), 102 IBLA 162 (1988).
65. Cameron v. U.S., 252 U.S. 450, 460 (1920); Michigan Land & Lumber Co. v.
       Rust, 168 U.S. 589, 593 (1897).
66. Utah International, Inc., 36 IBLA 219, 226 (1978).
67. Id.
68. Pine Valley Builders, Inc., 103 IBLA 384, 388 (1988); Eclipse Mill Site, 22
       L.D. 496, 551 (1896).
69. Pine Valley Builders, Inc., supra at 388.
70. Eclipse Mill Site, supra at 551.
71. Pine Valley Builders, Inc., supra at 389.
72. U.S. v. Parsons, 33 IBLA 326 (1978).
73. Alaska Copper Co., 32 L.D. 128 (1903).
74. Helena Co. v. Dailey, 36 I.D. 144 (1907).
75. Alaska Copper Co., supra; Hard Cash and Other Mill Site Claims, 34 L.D. 325,
       327-28 (1905); U.S. v. Swanson, 14 IBLA 158 (1974).
76. Snyder v. Walker, 25 L.D. 7, 8 (1907); Helena Co. v. Dailey, supra at 148.
77. Ebner Gold Mining Co. v. Hallum, 47 L.D. 32, 35 (1919).

TUNNEL SITES

Introduction

The authority to locate tunnel sites to prospect for veins or lodes is given in the Act of May 10, 1872.[1] The law states that "where a tunnel is run for the development of a vein or lode, or for the discovery of mines, the owners of such tunnel shall have the right of possession of all veins or lodes within three thousand feet from the face of such tunnel on the line thereof, not previously known to exist, discovered in such tunnel, to the same extent as if discovered from the surface." The phrase "not previously known to exist" refers to the date of location the tunnel was started and not to the date of the discovery of veins in the tunnel.[2]

Tunnel locations are made by erecting a substantial post or monument at the face or point where the tunnel is started, and stakes are placed along the line of the tunnel for 3,000 feet. The owner of a mining tunnel shall have the possessory right to 1500 feet of any blind lodes cut, discovered, or intersected by such tunnel.

Location by Others Prohibited

The law (30 U.S.C. 27) provides that "locations on the line of such tunnel of veins or lodes not appearing on the surface, made by other parties after commencement of the tunnel, and while the same is being prosecuted with reasonable diligence, shall be invalid." This gives the locator of the tunnel exclusive right to prospect 3,000 feet along the line of the tunnel, while work on the tunnel is being prosecuted with reasonable diligence.

"Face" Defined

The term "face," means the first working face formed in the tunnel, and to signify the point at which the tunnel actually enters cover. From the face, prospecting by other parties is prohibited for 3,000 feet along the line of the tunnel.[3]

Line of Tunnel

The "line" of the tunnel is actually wider than a line; it is the width of the bore of the tunnel.[4] Because only the "line" of the tunnel is off limits to mining claim location after commencement of the tunnel, the line of the tunnel should be delineated at the surface to notify prospective lode claimants of the area that is not open to location as long as the tunnel is diligently prosecuted.

227

Procedure for Locating Tunnel Sites

The federal regulations (43 CFR 3843.2) give the following specific procedures for locating tunnel sites:

1. Erect a substantial post, board, or monument at the face or point of commencement of the tunnel.

2. Post a notice on the monument containing the following information:

   a. names of the parties or company claiming the tunnel right;

   b. the actual or proposed course or direction of the tunnel;

   c. the height and width of the tunnel; and

   d. the course and distance from such face or point of commencement to some permanent well-known objects in the vicinity so as to establish the position of the tunnel site.

3. Establish the boundary lines of the tunnel site by placing stakes or monuments along the lines at proper intervals, to the terminus of the 3,000 feet from the face or point of commencement of the tunnel. These marked lines will serve to delineate the boundaries around the line within which prospecting for lodes not previously known to exist is prohibited while work on the tunnel is being prosecuted with reasonable diligence. In other words, the line of stakes should follow a line made by the intersection of the surface with imaginary vertical planes around the perimeter of the tunnel bore.

Recording of Notices

Federal regulations[5] require that a copy of the notice of location defining the tunnel site be filed with the mining recorder of the district (or county) and the Bureau of Land Management. A sworn statement or declaration of the owners of the tunnel must be attached to the location setting forth the following facts:

1. The amount expended by themselves and their predecessors in interest in prosecuting the work.

2. The extent of the work performed.

3. State that it is bona fide their intention to prosecute work on the tunnel so located and described with reasonable diligence for the development of a vein or lode, or for the discovery of mines, or both.

Tunnel Sites Are Not Mining Claims And Cannot Be Amended to Lode Claims

The United States Supreme Court has held that a tunnel site is not a mining claim, but is only a means of exploration.[6] The Interior Board of Land Appeals has held that tunnel sites cannot be amended to lode claims because they are rights-of-way rather than mining claims.[7]

Tunnel Site Must Be Prosecuted With Reasonable Diligence

The Federal law provides that "failure to prosecute the work on the tunnel for six months shall be considered as an abandonment of the right to all undiscovered veins on the line of such tunnel."[8] The Eighth Circuit Court of Appeals has said that a tunnel owner cannot "preserve his rights to undiscovered veins by lazy and perfunctory work....and the prompt and energetic prosecutor of a tunnel will receive the just rewards..."[9]

Limitation on Rights of Tunnel Owner

Although no discovery of mineral is essential to create a tunnel right or to maintain possession of it, The tunnel owner has a possessory right only to veins that strike the line of the tunnel and only those veins that are discovered in the tunnel. As the Eighth Circuit Court of appeals has said, "others may discover and hold all veins within 1,500 feet of the line of the tunnel that do not strike or cross its line, and all that do strike it that are not discovered it." Furthermore, a tunnel site cannot be patented.[10]

Right to Vein Discovered in Tunnel Dates Back to Location Date of Tunnel

The right to a vein discovered in the tunnel dates back to the time of the location of the tunnel site. And also, the right of locating a lode claim to the vein occurs at the time of discovery of the vein in the tunnel.[11] Although there is no requirement to locate a lode claim at the time of discovery in the tunnel in order possess and extract the vein,[12] it is recommended to do so.[13] Because a vein commonly occurs in association with other veins which might or might not cross the tunnel, a lode location would appropriate all the associated veins that would be appropriated by the tunnel site location. Furthermore, a lode location would give rights to establish a dependent mill site if one were needed for mining or milling purposes.

Lode Claim Senior to Tunnel Site

A prior surface location which contains the apex of a blind lode within its surface boundaries does not go to a tunnel site location, even though the blind lode was not known at the date of the tunnel site location.[14]

Tunnel Owner May Locate Claim on Either Side of the Tunnel

The tunnel owner is entitled to locate 1,500 feet on either side of the line of the tunnel. This right goes to the discovery of a vein in the tunnel.[15]

Horizontal Drill Hole May Qualify As Tunnel

By Policy, the Bureau of Land Management has determined that a horizontal drill hole would qualify as a "tunnel" under the tunnel site section of the mining law. Of course this BLM policy would not necessarily apply to lands in the National Forest System.

A tunnel site location is somewhat of an anachronism. Since the advent of drilling technology many years ago, driving a tunnel for exploration purposes has for the most part been terminated. Diamond core drilling can be accomplished in a fraction of the time and cost it would take to drive a tunnel. A tunnel site location presumes at least a year or two of diligent prosecution on a tunnel. A more modern approach would be to locate a lode claim and hold it under pedis possessio for several weeks until the drilling program is completed.

Validity of Tunnel Site Locations

The Interior Department is authorized to determine the validity of tunnel site claims in the same way it determines the validity of lode and placer claims. An important aspect of validity is whether a tunnel was commenced at or near the time the tunnel site was located. The Interior Board of Land Appeals has held that adits or workings that existed at the date of the tunnel site location do not qualify.[16] The Board pointed out that the importance of commencing a tunnel "is that it serves to define the starting point of the line of the tunnel, and, thus any possible veins or lodes, intersecting that line which the tunnel-site claimant would in the future have a right to appropriate. Until the tunnel is begun, the claimant has not established conclusively the direction in which the tunnel is to be run. Existing adits simply do not serve that purpose because a claimant can then continue in any of several directions." The Board also held that the tunnel-site locations were void because the owners "did not commence a tunnel on any of their tunnel site claims at or near the time they located the tunnel-site claims."

Effect of Withdrawal on a Tunnel Site

Once a discovery is made in a tunnel, even though accomplished many years after the withdrawal date, such discovery would relate back to the location date of the tunnel site. Therefore, a discovery many years after the effective date of a withdrawal would predate the withdrawal because the claim would be based on a right of appropriation which related back to the date of location of the tunnel site.[17]

Tunnel sites cannot be based on preexisting adits or other workings.[18] Instead, a tunnel must be commenced at or near the time a tunnel site is located or the tunnel site must be considered void.[19] Consequently, a tunnel site without a tunnel commenced between the location date and the withdrawal date should be considered void.

Tunnel Rights Are Not Reserved in Lode Patents

There is no statutory authority for placing in a patent to a lode claimant any limitation of title by a reservation of tunnel rights.[20] That does not mean that the owner of a prior tunnel site location could not, by discovery of a vein in his tunnel, have a prior right to the vein even if it was within the boundaries of the patented lode claim.

Owner of Tunnel Site Not Required to Adverse Lode Patent Applicant

Until a tunnel owner makes a discovery in the tunnel, he cannot adverse a lode patent application. Even if patent issues, the tunnel owner would have a right to any blind vein discovered in the tunnel years after the patent issues. However, once a discovery is made in the tunnel, a tunnel owner may file an adverse claim regardless of whether or not he filed a lode location. If a tunnel owner with a discovery in the tunnel does not file an adverse claim during the publication period of a conflicting lode patent application, the right to the vein discovered in the tunnel would be lost.[21]

References - Tunnel Sites

1. 30 U.S. 27 (1982).
2. Enterprise Mining Co. v. Rico Aspen Mining Co., 66 F. 200, 205 (1985), affirmed 167 U.S. 108.
3. 43 CFR 3843.1.
4. Corning Tunnel Co. v. Pell, 4 Colo 507 (1878).
5. 43 CFR 3843.3 and 3833.1-2.
6. Creede & Cripple Creek Mining & Milling Co. v. Uinta Tunnel Mining & Transportation Co., 196 U.S. 337, 359 (1905).
7. Elsworth Loveland, 89 IBLA 205, 207 (1985).
8. 30 U.S.C. 27 (1982).
9. Enterprise Mining Co. v. Rico-Aspen Consolidated Mining Co., 167 U.S. 108 (1895).
10. Id. at 206.
11. Enterprise Mining Co. v. Rico-Aspen Consolidated Mining Co., 167 U.S. 108 (1895).
12. Campbell v. Ellet, 167 U.S. 116, 120 (1897).
13. Creede v. Cripple Creek Mining & Milling Co. v. Uinta Tunnel Mining & Transportation Co., supra.
14. Calhoun Gold Mining Co. v. Ajax Gold Mining Co., 59 P. 607 (18909), affirmed 182 U.S. 499.
15. Enterprise Mining Co. v. Rico-Aspen Consolidated Mining Co., supra at 113.
16. U.S. v. Parker, 91 I.D. 271 (1984).
17. Id.
18. Calhoun Gold Mining Co. v. Ajax Gold Mining Co., 182 U.S. 499, 508 (1901).
19. U.S. v. Parker, supra.
20. Creede & Cripple Creek Mining & Milling Co. v. Uinta Tunnel Mining & Transportation Co., supra.
21. Id. at 360.

PROPER TYPE OF LOCATION: LODE OR PLACER

One of the most poorly defined areas of the mining law concerns the question of whether a deposit should be located as a placer or lode. The statute, which is not helpful in many cases, has in turn been interpreted by numerous confusing and conflicting Interior and Federal court decisions. Most of these decisions concerning the proper type of location resulted from litigation between conflicting claimants over the right of possession rather than through initiation of contest action by the Interior Department. Unfortunately such cases offer little consistent direction that can be used by the prospector in the field.

Although in many cases a particular deposit can readily be classified as either a lode or placer, there is a continuing trend for the opposite situation to be the case. Part of the problem relates to the type of mineral deposits worked during the passage of the mining law and the subsequent early case law. These early deposits typically consisted of classic veins and recent stream placers that could be easily categorized under the statutory definition by even the most unsophisticated early miner. However, in recent years, discoveries are commonly for deposits such as industrial minerals and disseminated ore bodies with no predictable form or character.

Statutory Definition of Placer

The statute[1] defines placers as "including all forms of deposit, excepting veins of quartz, or other rock in place..." Therefore, the statutory definition of a placer includes essentially every type of deposit that is not a lode.

Statutory Definition of Lode

The mining law[2] states that a lode location may be made "upon veins or lodes of quartz or other rock in place bearing gold, silver, cinnabar, lead, tin, copper, or other valuable deposits..." Upon comparing the statutory definition of a lode with that of a placer, it appears the critical distinction between the two is that a lode should be rock in place, whereas, a placer should be a deposit that is not rock in place. However, the confusion began when the courts held certain hardrock deposits consisting of rock in place to be placers.[3]

233

Importance of Making Proper Location

The importance of making the proper location over a mineral discovery has been clearly stated by the United States Supreme Court. In **Cole v. Ralph**, 252 U.S. 286, 295-96 1920), the Court held that "a placer discovery will not sustain a lode location, nor a lode discovery a placer location." Therefore, a placer location will not appropriate a lode deposit and a lode location will not appropriate a placer deposit.

Placer Building Stone Act

The Placer Building Stone Act of August 4, 1892,[4] was enacted to clear up confusion which had been generated by various decisions of the Interior Department concerning the proper method of location for building stone deposits. The Act requires that lands chiefly valuable for building stone must be entered as placer claims.

No Rule of Thumb Definition

Another problem with precedents established by earlier court cases involving the question of whether a specific deposit should be located by lode or placer claim is that each ore deposit is unique. It has not worked well to apply a precedent established in one case to another case where the deposit in question may differ greatly from any other. As Lindley, the well-known early authority on mining law, said, "there can be no unyielding rule of thumb definition of a vein or lode; each case must be decided with reference to its own peculiar facts."[5]

Lode Versus Placer Is a Question of Fact

The determination of whether a deposit should be located by a lode or placer claim is a question of fact that must be established at a hearing.[6]

Scientific Definitions Do Not Apply To Veins or Lodes

The courts have, with few exceptions, determined that the meaning of the terms vein and lode is determined by the manner in which they are used by the practical miner rather than scientific definitions by geologists.[7] The courts have also determined that it is not important for a locator to have knowledge of the origin of a mineral deposit because the form and character of the deposit control the type of location. There is a good reason for scientific definitions to not control the type of location because the origin of a deposit is in many cases not clear even to experienced geologists.

Nonmetallic Minerals May Be Located As Lodes

Both metallic and nonmetallic minerals may be located as lodes providing they are in the right form.[8] For example, perlite, which is a valuable rock in itself, is a lode even though it does not contain or bear valuable minerals. In **U.S. v. Estate of Arthur C.W. Bowen, Deceased**, 38 IBLA 390, 400 (1979), it was held that a horizontal blanket of perlite is properly located as a lode if sandwiched between two other rock layers, even if the upper layer is partially eroded away leaving the perlite exposed. It is not disqualifying that a lode consists of nonmetallic minerals of such a nature that the entire body of ore has commercial value. For many years much confusion existed about the proper type of claim to locate limestone. However, limestone, unless used as a building stone, is located no differently than any other mineral; the proper location depends on the form or character of the deposit.

Good Faith Location Should Be Protected

In cases involving the right of possession to a mining claim, whether the issue be marking claim boundaries, posting a notice, recording the notice or assessment work, the courts generally rule in favor of the senior locator, if such locator attempted to perfect the location and maintain it in good faith. This is also true for the original locator who acts in good faith and locates the wrong type of claim.

Early writers such as Lindley have proposed that the courts "recognize the rights of the original discoverer who has acted in good faith, regardless of whether he locates as a lode or as a placer."[9] This approach has been more or less followed by the courts and is about the only solution to the inherent ambiguity in determining whether a deposit is a lode or placer.[10] In all but the most simple case where you have either a well-formed vein or a deposit of stream gravel, even the experts have difficulty in determining the proper type of claim. Furthermore, the case law is conflicting and does not lend itself for use in developing a list of characteristics by which a claimant can select the proper type of location to fit a particular deposit.

Lode is Variation of the Word "Lead"

A practical test of what constitutes a lode would be what a miner might follow to find ore (a lead).[11] The term "lode" simply means the formation by which a miner can be led or guided and is an alteration of the verb "lead."[12] One court, upon determination that the word "lode" is a variation of the word "lead," stated that the term includes "mineralization in place...as distinguished from float or imported material,...of such significance that a practical, experienced miner of prudence and judgment would deem it advisable to pursue the vein or lead."[13]

Form and Character of a Lode Deposit

The courts have identified the following characteristics of lode deposits:

1. The quartz or other rock must be "in place." This means it must be suspended between, or lie within, or be enclosed by walls of rock constituting the general mass of the earth's crust.[14]

2. A lode may lie on the surface, or in other words may not have a hanging wall because of exposure to erosion.[15]

3. Although the ore may be loose and friable, the enclosing walls must be country rock; the enclosing walls may also be highly faulted and broken.[16]

4. The mining law makes no limitation on the width, length or depth of a lode; although a lode may pinch and swell, it must be continuous.[17]

5. A lode may be variable in mineralization, ranging from low grade or barren to rich pay streaks.[18]

6. A lode may consist of sedimentary rock. For example a bed of mineralized sedimentary rock of purely sedimentary origin enclosed between nonmineralized sedimentary strata is a lode.[19]

7. A lode may consist entirely of valuable nonmetallic minerals.[20]

Boundaries of Lodes Determined by Assay Value

If a vein or deposit is not visibly distinguished from the rock enclosing it by well-defined boundaries, such boundaries may be established by assay value.[20] The Tenth Circuit Court of Appeals gave approval to establishing boundaries of lodes by assay analysis and further allowed some mineral in the country rock so long as the mineral content of the lode is significantly greater than the surrounding rock.[21] This important precedent can be applied to large disseminated deposits where the cut-off grade (grade of ore that cannot be mined and processed at a profit) is conventionally established by assay value or chemical analysis.

Form and Character of Placer Deposits

The courts have specified the following characteristics as indicative of a placer deposit:

1. Placers are superficial deposits, occupying the beds of ancient rivers or valleys, washed down from some vein or lode.[23] These include sand, gravel, cobbles and boulders lying on the earth's surface without any walls.

2. A loose, scattered, or disseminated deposit of sand and gravel.[24]

3. A bed of gravel from which particles of gold may be recovered by traditional placer processing methods is not a lode even though the gravel may be enclosed within defined boundaries.[25]

Cases Where Igneous Rock in Place Held to Be Placer

The Tenth Circuit Court of Appeals determined that a mineral deposit consisting of pyroxenite, an igneous rock, should be located by placer location.[26] This deposit covers approximately 8 to 10 square miles and is shapeless with no known dimensions or boundaries. Although the deposit is in place, it has historically been considered a placer deposit and has been mined by placer methods.

In a 1986 case involving the proper type of location for a feldspar gemstone deposit, the Oregon Federal District Court held that the deposit was properly located with placer claims by the senior locator.[27] The claims were originally located as placer claims and then later overstaked by a rival locator with lode claims. The deposit consisted of feldspar crystals disseminated throughout a hydrothermally-altered igneous dike that was in place. There were also placer deposits of crystals on the claim which the original claimant had successfully recovered using placer mining methods. The Court was further convinced that the crystals could not be removed from the unaltered portion of the dike without shattering them.

Name Change of Claim

It is well established that once a claim has been determined to be invalid on the basis of a lack of discovery rather than as an improper type of location, the claimant cannot change the type of location and depend on the same mineral deposit for his discovery.[28]

Section 38 Remedy for Wrong Type of Claim

One possible remedy for those who have located the wrong type of claim for a particular deposit is to establish that they held and worked the claims prior to an intervening right (withdrawal or another claimant) for a period of time equal to the state's statute of limitations.[29] Under the appropriate circumstances, holding and working may be the legal equivalent of proof of location, recording and transfer of mining claim. Of course, such claim must be properly recorded and maintained under section 314 of the Federal Land Policy and Management Act.

References - Proper Type of Location: Lode or Placer

1. 30 U.S.C. 23 (1982).
2. Id.
3. Titanium Actynite Industries v. McLennan, 272 F.2d 667 (10th Cir 1960).
4. 30 U.S.C. 161 (1982).
5. Lindley on Mines, Vol. 1, 3rd Ed., sec. 289; quoted with approval in Titanium Actynite Industries v. McLennan, supra.
6. Estate of Arthur C.W. Bowen, 18 IBLA 383 (1975).
7. Eureka Consolidated Mining Co. v. Richmond Mining Co., 8 F. Cas. 819, 823 (CCD Nev. 1881) aff'd 103 U.S. 839; Duffield v. San Francisco Chemical Co., 205 F. 480, 485 (9th Cir. 1913).
8. Webb v. American Asphaltum Mining Co., 157 F. 203 (1907).
9. Lindley on Mines, Vol 2, Sec. 425(B), p.1005 (3rd ed.).
10. Bowen v. Chemi-Cote Perlite Corporation, 423 P.2d 104 (1967).
11. King Soloman Tunnel & Development Co. v. Mary Verna Mining Company, 127 P. 129 (1912).
12. Eureka Consol. Mining Co. v. Richmond Mining Co., Fed Case No. 4,548 (1877) affirmed 103 U.S. 839.
13. Rummell v. Bailey, 7 Utah 137, 320 P.2d 653 (1958).
14. Meydenbauer v. Stevens, 78 F. 787, 790, 791 (DCD Alaska 1897).
15. Bowen v. Sil-Flo Corporation, 451 P.2d 626 (Ct. App. Ariz. 1969).
16. Tabor v. Dexler, 23 Fed. Cas. No. 13,723 (CC Colo 1878).
17. Bowen v. Chemi-Cote Perlite Corporation, 432 P.2d 104 (1967).
18. Meydenbauer v. Stevens, supra.
19. Mike & Starr Gold & Silver Mining, 12 S.Ct. at 544 (1892); Duggan v. Davey, 26 NW 887 (1886).
20. Bowen v. Sil-Flo Corporation, 451 P.2d 626 (Ct. App. Ariz. 1969).
21. Golden v. Murphy, 103 P. 394 (1909).
22. Titanium Actynite Industries v. McLennon, 272 F.2d 667, 671 (10th Cir. 1960).
23. North Pacific Railroad Co. v. Soderberg, 188 U.S. 526 (1903).
24. U.S. v. Iron Silver Mining Company, 128 U.S. 673, 679 (1888).
25. Gregory v. Pershbakers, 14 P. 401 (1887).
26. Titanium Actynite Industries v. McLennan, supra.
27. Weightman v. Gray, Civ. No. 83-1235 (D.Or. 1986).
28. U.S. v. Haskins, 505 F.2d 249 (9th Cir. 1974).
29. U.S. v. Haskins, 51 IBLA 1 (1981).

COEXISTENCE OF LODE CLAIMS, PLACER CLAIMS AND MILL SITES

Can You Stake a Lode Claim Over a Placer Claim Or a Placer Claim Over a Lode Claim?

This has probably been the most frequently asked question in the area of mining law during the last few years. One reason people find this subject confusing is because the answer depends on whether they are interested in (1) locating a lode claim over their own placer claim, or locating a placer claim over their own lode claim (no conflicting locator), or (2) locating a lode or placer claim over another persons lode or placer claim (two or more conflicting locators). Therefore when you read this chapter keep in mind the significance of the two categories. Another part of the confusion stems from the fact that this is a somewhat unsettled area of the mining law.

Proper Sequence for Locating Lode and Placer Claims on Same Lands by One Individual

Several recent court cases have upheld the right of an individual claimant to locate both lode and placer claims over the same lands. In 1987 the Federal District Court in Nevada indicated that location of both types of claims would not constitute abandonment of either type of claim. In other words, both types of claims could exist on the same lands under the same ownership. **Amax Exploration, Inc. v. Ross Mosher**, Civil R-85-162 BRT (March 2, 1987). The Court indicated this would be an approach to follow before discovery; however, once a discovery was made a choice might be required. In **U.S. v. Haskins**, No. 72-246-JWC (C.D. Cal. 1972), the Court said that "both types of claims can, of course, co-exist, even though in different ownership."

Some writers have suggested that there is a preferred sequence of location. They say that the proper sequence is to locate the placer claim first because to locate a placer claim over your prior lode claim might be deemed an abandonment of the lode claim. The rationale for this sequence appears to be based in part on the patent section of the Mining Law (30 U.S.C. 37) which requires that known lodes must be identified and surveyed when making application for a placer claim. The reason Federal law requires that known lodes must be identified when making application for a placer claim is merely because Congress believed that since a lode deposit goes to a greater depth than a placer, the surface area of a lode claim should be charged at a higher rate ($5) than a placer ($2.50). **Reynolds v. Morrissey**, 116 U.S. 687 (1886).

Section 37 is frequently cited as authority for locating lode claims over placer claims. The law provides that if a known lode exists within the boundaries of a placer claim, 25 feet of surface on each side of the **vein** or **lode** must be surveyed out of the placer claim. However, there is no requirement in the statute to locate a lode **claim** over the placer claim for the purpose of including a known vein or lode in the patent application. **Sullivan v. The Iron Silver Mining Co.**, 143 U.S. 431 (1892); **Railroad Lode v. Noyes Placer**, 9 L.D. 26 (1889). The United States Supreme Court has said that a "known vein" is not synonymous with a "located vein." **The Iron Silver Mining Company v. The Mike & Starr Gold and Silver Mining Company**, 143 U.S. 374 (1888). Again, the main purpose of the requirement to identify known lodes in placer claims under application for patent is to have the applicant pay for the vein or lode at the rate of $5.00 rather than the placer rate of $2.50 because a vein is deeper and more valuable. Consequently, section 37 is not authority to locate lode claims over placer claims, or authority for any sequence of location; it establishes a procedure to delineate the lode deposit within a placer claim so that the Government can be compensated for the lode deposit at the lode rate of $5.00.

It is a common misconception that a lode claim ranks differently than a placer claim because the law requires that known lodes be surveyed out or reserved from the placer patent. However, the mining law states that placer claims are subject to entry and patent "under like circumstances and conditions, and upon similar proceedings, as are provided for vein or lode claims." The United States Supreme Court has interpreted this statement "to place the location of placer claims on an equality both in procedure and rights with lode claims." **Clipper Mining Company v. Eli Mining & Land Company**, 194 U.S. 220 (1904). Therefore it appears that if anything the statute supports the position that no preferred sequence is necessary because both lode claims and placer claims are equal in rights and procedures.

It is a logical rule that to locate a second lode claim over your prior lode claim is an implied admission that the prior lode claim has problems. Furthermore, because both lode claims would be appropriating the same lode deposit, the location of the second lode claim could be deemed an abandonment of the prior lode claim. However, the location of a lode claim over a placer claim or the location of a placer claim over a lode claim may represent an attempt to appropriate two different types of mineral deposits. For example, if you discovered a vein and appropriated it with a lode claim and then some time later discovered a placer deposit within the boundaries of the lode claim, the subsequent location of a placer location over your prior lode claim could hardly be deemed abandonment.

The law of abandonment as it relates to mining law includes relinquishment of possession together with the subjective intent to abandon. To show abandonment, the intent of the claimant to abandon must be demonstrated. For example, if a claimant maintained title on a claim performing annual assessment work and making timely annual filings with both the BLM and the local recorder, such actions could hardly indicate abandonment. As the Court said in **Fuller v. Harris**, 29 F. 814, 818-19 (D. Alaska 1887), "a claimant who relocates the same ground does not evidence an intent to abandon the prior claim." Furthermore, a relocation negates the intent to abandon the ground. **Hartman Gold Mining Co. v. Warning**, 11 P.2d 854, 856 (1932). The advantage of this rule is that if an attempted relocation fails, the claimant may still maintain the rights he had under the first location. **Peach v. Frisco Gold Mines Co.**, 204 F. 659 (D. Ariz. 1913). As a general rule abandonment must be established by clear and convincing evidence. **U.S. v. Eaton Shale Co.**, 433 F.Supp. 1256, 1274 (D. Colo. 1977). The location of a placer claim over a lode claim would hardly be clear and convincing evidence of abandonment of the former lode claim, particularly where annual assessment work and the requisite annual filings were timely accomplished.

Because it seems to be the prevailing opinion of many writers in mining law that placer claims should be located before lode claims, it is probably a good procedure to do so, regardless of reasons. Another option is to locate both the lode and placer claims on the same day, implying discovery was made at the same time However, if you have an existing lode claim and decide to cover the same property with a placer claim, it is probably inadvisable to relinquish or abandon the lode claim just to establish the lode-over-placer sequence. In general, I have found the arguments for a preferred sequence to be unconvincing.

Model Situations for Sequence of Location

To illustrate your available options when locating both lode and placer claims, four situations are given below. As you can see, the recommended sequence of location depends upon the special circumstances in each situation:

1. You have located a placer claim over a deposit that is properly located with a placer claim such as gold-bearing gravel. Then you discover a vein of gold or suspect one exists within the boundaries of your placer claim.

241

In this situation most authorities would recommend that you locate a lode claim over your placer claim to appropriate the lode deposit.

2. You have located a lode claim over a deposit that is properly located with a lode claim such as a gold-bearing quartz vein.
Then you discovery a deposit of gold-bearing gravel and wish to protect your new find with a placer location.

In this situation I would advise that you violate the "lode-over-placer" sequence and locate a placer claim over your prior lode. Here you have two different types of deposits -a lode deposit and a placer deposit. Location of a placer claim over your prior lode cannot be deemed abandonment of the lode claim because the lode claim was intended to appropriate the lode deposit, whereas the placer claim was intended to appropriate a completely different deposit.

3. You have not made a discovery of either lode or placer minerals but based on geological inference or some other basis you would like to appropriate an area with lode and placer claims while you conduct exploratory drilling. Of course, without a discovery you will be holding the claims under prediscovery rights or pedis possessio.

In this situation follow the conventional practice by first locating a placer claim followed by a lode claim.

4. You have just discovered a mineral deposit such as limestone or perlite and are uncertain as to whether a lode location or a placer location would be most appropriate because the deposit does not clearly fit into either category. You are also aware that "a placer discovery will not sustain a lode location, nor a lode discovery a placer location." **Cole v. Ralph**, 252 U.S. 286 (1920). In this situation you are at the core of the "sequence of location" controversy, because here it is advisable to locate both lode and placer claims to make certain that you appropriate the deposit. There is an important distinction between this case and the three cases described above. Here we are only concerned with one type of deposit, whereas in the other three situations we were describing the existence of both lode and placer deposits within the same claim.

As in situation #3, first locate a placer claim and then a lode claim. Even if there is no basis for locating lode over placer rather than placer over lode, it is advisable to do so if only because so many people believe it is important.

242

Lode Claims May Not Be Located on Prior Valid Placer Location and Vice Versa

No person, other than the owner, has the right to enter upon an unoccupied valid placer claim for the purpose of discovering and locating lodes. To do so without the placer claim owner's consent or acquiescence is a trespass. This rule is supported by many Federal court cases, including the United States Supreme Court. **Clipper Mining Co. v. Eli Mining & Land Co.**, 194 U.S. 220, 229-30 (1904). Although there are few supporting cases, the rule should also apply to the situation where the prior location is a lode claim. As the Supreme Court said in the **Clipper Mining Co.** case, "by the statute the right of exclusive possession and enjoyment is given to a locator, whether his location be of a lode claim or a placer claim."

Without Discovery a Claim Must Be Protected by Pedis Possessio

Until a discovery is made within the boundaries of either a lode or placer claim, the protection against trespass does not apply. However, the prospector has some possessory rights against forcible, fraudulent, or clandestine intrusions by actual and continuous occupancy while diligently seeking a discovery.1

But a placer or lode claim that contains no discovery and is not protected under the doctrine of pedis possessio is open to entry and relocation by the first claimant to make a discovery.[2] The courts have long held that until a discovery is made there is no location.[3] Under pedis possessio the courts require actual physical occupancy of each claim on a continuous basis.[4] In conclusion, whether the claim be lode or placer, without a discovery or protection under pedis possessio, the land is open to location as though it had never been appropriated. **Amax v. Mosher**, supra.

Coexistence of Mill Sites with Mining Claims

Lode claims can coexist on the same property with placer claims even though in different ownership because both placer and lode deposits may be found in the same land.[5] However, mill sites are not compatible with mining claims because the statute requires that mill sites must be "nonmineral land" whereas mining claims require the discovery of "valuable mineral deposits." Therefore, the subsequent location of a mill site over your prior placer or lode claim could be deemed an abandonment of the mining claim. Conversely, the subsequent location of a mining claim over your prior mill site could be deemed an abandonment of the mill site.

As the Secretary stated in **U.S. v. Morehead**, 59 I.D. 192 (1946):

> The mill site must be located on nonmineral land. By changing the location to a lode claim because it was ascertained that the land therein was mineralized, it was thereby admitted that the mill site was void from its inception, and no mining title can be held to relate back to the inception of a void location.

Location of Placer Claim over Tailings on Mill Site Claim

Tailings and ore become personal property once severed from the ground. Mill tailings are not available for appropriation until abandonment of such tailings is established by showing both intention to abandon and actual relinquishment.[6] However, if such tailings are moved to lands owned by another through natural processes such as erosion, they become the property of that owner; or, if the tailings are deposited on unappropriated public lands, they may be acquired by placer locations.[7]

Although it may be appropriate to locate abandoned mine tailings with placer claims, it very unlikely that such placer claims could be patented. Aside from the fact that mill tailings are not naturally deposited, to allow a claimant to patent a tract of land by merely placing valuable tailings on it would create an enormous loophole in the mining law. Furthermore, it should also be mentioned that the acquisition of mill tailings may be accompanied by unwanted liability for toxic substances.

Discovery Made After Placer Patent Issues Goes to Patentee

If veins or lodes within a placer claim are not known at the date of application, they will go with the placer patent; only veins or lodes that are known but not applied and paid for are reserved in the placer patent. Any subsequent discovery of a vein or lode not known at the date of application goes to the benefit of the patentee.[8]

References - Coexistence of Lode Claims, Placer Claims and Mill Sites

1. Duguid v. Best, 291 F.2d 235 (1961), cert. denied, 372 U.S. 906.
2. Geomet Exploration v. Lucky McUranium Corp., Ariz, 601 P.2d 1339 (1979).
3. Uinta Tunnel, Mining & Transportation Co. v. Ajax Gold Mining Co., 141 F. 563 (1905).
4. Amax Exploration, Inc. v. Ross Mosher, Civil R-85-162 BRT (March 2, 1987).
5. U.S. v. Haskins, 51 IBLA 1, 90 (1981); U.S. v. Haskins, No. 72-246-JWC (C.D. Cal 1972).
6. U.S., George B. Conway, Intervenor v. Grosso, 53 L.D. 115, 125-26 (1930).
7. Id.
8. Clipper Mining Co. v. Eli Mining & Land Co., 194 U.S. 220 at 231 (1904).

AMENDED LOCATION VERSUS RELOCATION

There is no mention of the term "amended" location in the original mining law of the United States. From the earliest locations it was not unusual for an original location notice to contain errors or defects, particularly in the description of the physical location of the claim. Many states passed laws which allowed amended certificates of location and as early as 1885 the Federal courts recognized the right of a claimant to amend his location.

There is no specific direction in the Federal statute concerning procedures and rights to amend or relocate claims. The state statutes although brief and inadequate in many respects, should be consulted for specific direction on how to relocate or amend a claim as required by state law. Decisions of the state and Federal courts and the Interior Department currently provide most of the specific direction necessary to properly relocate or amend a location.

Definition of Amended Location and Relocation By Interior Board of Land Appeals

An "amended location" of a claim is a subsequent location intended to further the rights acquired by the earlier locator while making some change in the location, such as changing the name of the claim or its owners of record (as where the original claim has been sold) or excluding excess acreage. In contrast to a "relocation," an "amended location" relates back to the date of the filing of the original notice of location, so that the filer receives the rights associated with the earlier location, including its superiority to subsequent withdrawals. The amended location merely furthers rights acquired by a prior subsisting location, and does not include any new land.[1]

Amended Location: Definition by Regulation (1989)

"Amended location" means a location that is in furtherance of an earlier valid location and that may or may not take in different or additional unappropriated ground. An amendment may:
(1) Correct or clarify defects or omissions in the original notice or certificate of location; or
(2) Change the legal description, mining claim name, position of discovery or boundary monuments, or similar items.

An amended location notice relates back to the original location notice date. No amendment is possible if the original location is void.[2]

Relocation: Definition by Regulation (1989)

"Relocation" means the establishment of a new mining claim, mill site, or tunnel site. A relocation may not be established by the use of an "amended location notice," but requires a new original location notice or certificate as prescribed by state law.

This definition, established by regulations made effective January 3, 1989, appears to preclude the use of a mining claim location certificate filed to fill the dual role of both an amendment and a relocation certificate.[3]

Location Notices Captioned as Both Amendment And Relocation Certificate

In many cases claimants have attempted to file a location certificate which would fill a dual role - to serve as both an amended location and a relocation. Presumably if the claimant did not have present title and the certificate could not relate back as an amendment, it could function as a relocation or an original location. However by policy[4] and regulation (see definition of "relocation" above), the BLM does not maintain two files on the same mining claim which purport to carry parallel and continuing rights. There is only one official record of any entitlement maintained against the United States. Any conflicting rights must be adjudicated so that only one set of entitlements exist for each claimant of the public lands.

Dual Captioned Location Certificates Are Treated as Amendments

When the BLM receives a dual captioned location certificate without a statement from the owner as to how the document should be treated, it will be processed as an amended location certificate. If the certificate is dual captioned or is unclear as to whether it is an amendment or a relocation, the claimant will be requested to choose whether it is an amendment or a relocation. If the claimant does not respond, the document will be processed as an amendment.[5]

No Amendments to Original Locations Not Recorded Under FLPMA

If an original location notice is not recorded under section 314 of the Federal Land Policy and Management Act of 1976, the claim is presumptively abandoned and cannot be later brought back to life by amendment.[6]

Present Title Is Prerequisite To Amend Claim

In order to have the right to amend a claim, one must have present title to the claim. If such title is lacking, an individual is not claiming through a prior location, but rather is initiating a claim adverse to the original location.[7]

Gaps in Chain of Title and Documentation

In order to amend an original location, a present owner who is not the claim owner designated in the original location notice must be able to document each transfer of interest so as to show present title to the claim.[8] For example if a claimant should attempt to amend a claim to show his name as the sole owner and the claim was originally located by another person or located by him and other persons, the claimant must be able to document the transfer of interest to him from all other interest holders.[9]

No Requirement That Amended Location or Relocation Be Designated on Certificate

The Interior Board of Land Appeals has held in several cases that there is no requirement to designate on a certificate whether it is an amended location or a relocation.[10]

Original and Amended Certificates Must Be Construed Together

In determining the sufficiency of an amendment, the original and amended certificate of location must be construed together. If the two documents are sufficient when construed together, the location record will be valid, even though neither standing alone would be sufficient.[11]

Amended Location Is Relocation If Not Timely Filed

If the original location notice is not timely filed with the BLM during the 90-day period, the timely filing of an amended location will be considered a relocation of the claim at the date of the amendment, provided of course that no rights of the United States or of third parties have intervened, and the requirements of law pertaining to relocations by the same claimant have otherwise been met.[12] It is important to point out that a copy of such amended location held to be a relocation must also be recorded with the county recorder, otherwise the amended location will be deemed to have been abandoned.

Hearing to Determine if Amended Location Is a Relocation

Under certain circumstances, the determination of whether a notice represents a relocation or an amendment is a disputed issue of fact and a hearing must be held before the claims are declared null and void.[13] The purpose of the hearing is to allow a claimant to establish an unbroken chain of title back to the original location so as to predate a withdrawal.[14] A hearing is held where there is a disputed issue of fact whether the interests of the present mining claimant are adverse to the interests of prior locators.[15]

Right to Amend After Withdrawal

A claim embraced by a withdrawn area may only be amended under certain circumstances: (1)the claim must have been valid and existing at the date of the withdrawal; (2) there must be no break in the validity of the claim; (3) the amender must be able to demonstrate present title; and (4) the location may not be enlarged by adding new land.[16]

Purpose of Amended Location Need Not Be Specified

The general rule is that an amended certificate need not state the specific purpose of the amendment. A general statement that the purpose of the amendment is to cure errors or defects will be sufficient.[17]

New Names in Amended Notices

Where an amended notice of location contains names other than those mentioned in the original notice, it cannot be taken advantage of by other parties. The amended notice may be treated as an original notice to the persons whose names do not appear on the first, and as an amended notice to the names that appear on both notices.[18]

Discovery Required Before Dropping Locator

If the name of one of eight locators of a 160 acre association placer is deleted in an amended location, the Interior Department may properly inquire into the existence of a discovery at the time of the amendment.[19]

Claims Cannot Be Moved Long Distances by Amendment

Where claims are moved substantial distances and the claim positions are constantly changed, notices making such changes in position cannot be considered amendments. However a locator has the right to adjust boundary lines by amendment so long as the intervening rights of others are not impaired. The general rule is that you cannot change boundary lines to take in new land which was either located by another or withdrawn by Federal land action subsequent to your original location.[20]

Placer Location Cannot Be Amended To Lode Location

A placer location cannot be amended to a lode location and a lode location cannot be amended to a placer location because the two types of claims are located for different reasons.[21]

Lode Claims Are Amended Like Placer Claims

For the purpose of curing imperfections or defects in the original location, the same latitude of amendment should be allowed for both lode and placer claims.[22]

Oral Transfers of Interest

Where a claimant can only demonstrate that present title is based on an oral transfer of a mining claim, such oral transfers do not alone cause an amended location to be invalid. The validity of such an amendment is a question of fact that may be resolved at an administrative hearing.[23]

Most states, however, have a statute of frauds which requires that for a conveyance of real property (such as a mining claim) to be valid, it must be in writing. Furthermore, the United States, as owner of the land subject to the alleged conveyance, is equally entitled to the protection of the statute. Therefore, the United States may apply the statute of frauds to challenge the validity of an oral conveyance of a mining claim.[24]

Court Approved Reasons for Amendments

The courts have the supported validity of amendments for a variety of purposes. Among these are the following:

1. A change in the record owners of a claim where such change is reflective of an existing fact.[25]

249

2. Successor in interest to the original locator made amendment to location notice which contained indefinite description of discovery shaft.[26]

3. Defects in the location notice.[27]

4. Amendment to location notice which contained no reference to a natural object or monument.[28]

5. A change in the name of the claim.[29]

6. Amendment to location notice which described claim in wrong section.[30]

References - Amended Location Versus Relocation

1. American Resources Ltd., 44 IBLA 220, 223 (1979).
2. 43 CFR 3833.0-5.
3. 43 CFR 3833.0-5.
4. Instruction Memorandum, No. 87-607 (July 10, 1987).
5. Id.
6. American Resources, 52 IBLA 290, 295 (1981).
7. Tibbetts v. BLM, 62 IBLA 124 at 132 (1982); American Resources, supra at 294-95.
8. Fairfield Mining Co., Inc., 66 IBLA 115 (1982)..
9. Id.
10. R. Gail Tibbetts, 86 IBLA (1979).
11. Estate of Van Doolah, 95 IBLA 132, 134 (1987).
12. Walter T. Paul, 43 IBLA 119, 120 (1979).
13. U.S. v. Consolidated Mines & Smelting Co., 455 F.2d 432, 441 (1971).
14. Fairfield Mining Co., Inc., 66 IBLA 119 (1982).
15. Id.
16. R. Gail Tibbetts, supra at 543.
17. R. Gail Tibbetts, supra at 547; Tonopah & Salt Lake Mining Co. v. Tonopah Mining Co., 125 F. 389, 397 (1903.
18. Id.
19. R. Gail Tibbetts, supra.
20. R. Gail Tibbetts v. BLM, 62 IBLA 124 (1982).
21. Paul Vaillant, 90 IBLA 249, 253 (1986); Hiram Webb, 105 IBLA 290, 300 (1988).
22. Fred B. Ortman, 52 L.D. 467 (1928).
23. R. Gail Tibbetts, 86 I.D. 538, 546-47.
24. Id.
25. U.S. v. Consolidated Mines & Smelting Co., 455 F.2d 432, 442 (9th Cir. 1971).
26. Hagerman v. Thompson, 235 P.2d 750, 757-58 (Wyo 1951).
27. Rassmussen Drilling, Inc. v. Kerr McGee Nuclear Corp., 571 F.2d 1144, 1156-57 (10th Cir 1978), cert. denied, 439 U.S. 862 (1978).
28. Nyland v. Ward, 67 Colo. 108, 187 P. 514, 515-16 (1920).
29. Butte Consolidated Mining Co. v. Barker, 35 Mont. 327, 89 P. 302, aff'd on rehearing, 9 P. 177 (1907).
30. McEvoy v. Human, 25 F. 596, 599-600 (CCD Colo 1885).

CLAIM LOCATION
UNDER SECTION 38

The primary effect of section 38 (30 U.S.C. 38) is to provide that possession of a claim for a period of time equal to the state's statute of limitation is equivalent to making a location by posting and recording a notice of location.[1]

Possession Must Be Actual, Open and Exclusive

The holding and working of a claim for a period of time equal to the state's statute of limitations may be the legal equivalent of proof of acts of location, recording and transfer providing there was actual, open and exclusive possession.[2] Marking the boundaries of the claim so as to afford actual notice of the extent and boundaries of the claim, coupled with actual possession and exclusion of all adverse claimants is required.

Land Must Be Open to Entry

In order to establish a right to patent by holding and working a claim prescribed by the state statute of limitations, the land must be open to entry at the time the claimant initiated his possessory title.[4] Furthermore, the period equal to the time prescribed by the statute of limitations for mining claims of the state or territory where the claim is situated must run while the lands are open to mineral entry.[5]

Unbroken Chain of Title

One must maintain actual, unbroken possession of a specifically defined locality in order to constitute actual, exclusive and continuous adverse possession to acquire title under section 38.[6] An assignee or successor in interest may also qualify for patent where the original locator acquired a claim through provisions of section 38.[7] It has been held that a patent applicant may tack the predecessor's period of possession to its own if there was a privity of interest between them which was demonstrated by any agreement, conveyance or understanding, where the purpose was to transfer the right and possession of the previous adverse claimant to the successor, and this is accompanied by actual delivery of possession.[8]

Requirement That Claim Be "Held and Worked"

Under section 38, the claimant serves notice to the world that the land is appropriated by showing that the land is "held and worked."[9]   The cases indicate holding and working involve two separate concepts. The performance of assessment work has been generally accepted as fulfilling the requirement that the claim be "worked."[10]   However, holding or actual possession of a claim requires more than simply performing assessment work.[11]

Assessment Work to Show Claim Was "Worked"

Performance of assessment work is a necessary prerequisite to demonstrate that a claim was "worked" within the meaning of 30 U.S.C. 38 (1982). The claimant has the burden to establish that the required work had been accomplished during the period of the years the state statute of limitations was "worked."[12]

The failure to record proof of assessment work as opposed to failure to perform assessment work is not fatal to a possessory claim under section 38. However, an absence of recorded proof of labor for a substantial period of time prior to a relocation of the claims followed by a resumption of filings is probative of whether the land was held and worked as a claim at the time.

"Held and Worked" Requires Development

The requirement that a claim be held and worked under section 38 requires possession by the claimant that goes beyond the mere performance of assessment work. It includes the actual, open, and exclusive possession of the claim by the claimant, coupled with development.[13]

Association Placer: All Co-locators Must Have Held and Worked Claim

In association placer claims, all co-locators must have "held and worked" their claims for a period prescribed by the statute of limitations in order that the 20 acres for each locator to be valid.[14]

Discovery Required

Even though a claimant has held and worked a claim for a period equal to the time prescribed by the statute of limitation for mining claims of the state or territory in which the claim is located, the requirements for discovery must still be satisfied.[15] Section 38 does not establish an independent means of acquiring title to a mining claim, nor does it dispense with the requirement that there be a discovery on each claim.[16]

Lode Rights Cannot Be Converted to Placer Rights through Section 38

Any claim asserted under the provisions of section 38 must have been recorded as required by section 314(b) of the Federal Land Policy and Management Act of 1976 or it will be deemed conclusively to be abandoned and void.[17] However the recordation of lode location notices with the County Recorder's office is inadequate to record any placer claim asserted under section 38.[18] In other words, placer rights cannot inure to a lode location under section 38.[19]

Section 38 Claims Must Be Recorded under FLPMA

The recordation provisions of FLPMA required the recording of all claims located prior to October 21, 1976, no matter how located, on or before October 22, 1979, or the claims would be deemed conclusively to be abandoned and void. Since FLPMA also required the recording of new claims within 90 days of their location, it is unlikely that any new claims can rely on a section 38 location.[20] Rights of individual ownership of the claim may still be determined by section 38, but if that claim has not been recorded under FLPMA, it is treated as a nullity.[21]

Requirements to Record a Section 38 Claim under FLPMA

In order to record a preFLPMA claim under section 38 (where claimant cannot show proof that a notice of location was recorded with the local recorder), the Interior Board of Land Appeals[22] has suggested a list of requirements that can be used until regulations are issued specifically addressing the problem. All claims in this category must have been recorded with the BLM on or before October 22, 1979. BLM is also authorized to require any additional information deemed essential to meet its purposes. This would include the following:

1. the name under which the claim is presently identified and all other names by which it may have been known to the extent possible;

2. the name and address of the present claimants;

3. an adequate description of the claim;

4. type of claim;

5. information concerning the time of the state's statute of limitations and a statement by the claimant as to how long the claim has been held and worked, giving, if possible, the date (or at least the year) of the origin of the claim-

253

ant's title and fact as to continuation of possession of the claim; and

6. any other information the claimant would have showing the chain of title to him and bearing upon the possession and occupancy of the claim for mining purposes.

References - Claim Location under Section 38

1. Humphreys v. Idaho Gold Mine Development Co., 120 P. 823, 21 Idaho 126 (1912).
2. U.S. v. Johnson, 100 IBLA 322, 335 (1987).
3. Humphreys v. Idaho Gold Mine Development Co., supra at 827.
4. U.S. v. Midway Northern Oil Co., 232 F. 619 (D.C. Cal 1916).
5. U.S. v. Consolidated Mines & Smelting Co. 455 F.2d 432 (CA Wash 1971).
6. Pacific Coal & Transportation Co. v. Pioneer Mining Co., 205 F. 577. 591 (1913).
7. St. Louis Smelting & Re Co. v. Kemp, 104 U.S. 636 (1882).
8. Alaska Placer Co., 33 IE A 187 (1977).
9. U.S. v. Haskins, 59 IBL 1, 90 (1981).
10. Id.
11. Id.; Law v. Fowler, 261 P. 667, 670 (Idaho 1927).
12. Ernest Higbee (On Reconsideration), 79 IBLA 380, 387 (1984); U.S. v. Haskins, supra at 52-53.
13. U.S. v. Henri (On Judicial Remand), 104 IBLA 93, 102 (1988); U.S. v. Johnson, 100 IBLA 322, 334 (1987).
14. U.S. v. Haskins, 59 IBLA 1, 90 (1981).
15. Multiple Use Inc. v. Morton, 504 F.2d 448 (CA Ariz 1974).
16. Cole v. Ralph, 252 U.S. 286 (1920).
17. Hiram Webb, 105 IBLA 290, 302 (1988).
18. Id. at 305.
19. Id. at 303.
20. U.S. v. Haskins, supra at 105-106.
21. Id.
22. Philip Sayer, 42 IBLA 296, 300-302 (1979).

CONFLICTING LOCATIONS

Court Determines Right of Possession

In many cases where claimants have conflicting locations, they often seek help from the Bureau of Land Management to resolve the ownership rights. However, The United States Supreme Court has held that the question of the right of possession is to be determined by the courts and that the United States is not a party to the proceedings."[1] Therefore the BLM is prohibited from getting involved in any conflict between two claimants over the same lands.

Relocation Over Valid Existing Location

Land under the possession of one who has a valid discovery and location is not subject to location by another until after abandonment or forfeiture.[2] However, if a claim is not located and recorded according to state law, the claim may be subject to location.[3] Once a valid location is made, possessory title vests in the locator. Removal or obliteration of evidence of the location on the ground will not divest the original locator of possessory title.[4]

The courts have ruled consistently in numerous cases that a mining claim located over a valid existing location has no effect and is void. No new location can be established until the prior claim is abandoned.[5]

Although Valid Claim Segregates, Junior Locator May Obtain Patent

Although a valid mining claim segregates the area it encompasses from the acquisition of competing rights under the mineral patenting procedures, it remains possible for a junior locator to obtain a patent if the senior does not file an adverse claim.[6]

Discovery Must Be on Unappropriated Land

To have a valid mining location, the discovery must physically exposed on unappropriated public domain.[7] The fact that the corners of a mining claim are not placed on unappropriated land subject to location, does not render the location entirely void. The part of the claim that is within the marked boundaries and on unappropriated land is valid.[8]

Amended Location

An amended location may be filed only if the original location was valid and had a curable deficiency.[9] Although a mining location may be amended without loss of any rights acquired under the original location, the amendment cannot be used to acquire rights already established by other locations made between the dates of the original and amended location.[9] For example, a locator cannot amend a claim to cover additional ground that was acquired by an intervening locator.

References - Conflicting Locations

1. Perego v. Dodge, 163 U.S. 160, 168 (1896).
2. Belk v. Meagher, 104 U.S. 279 (1881).
3. Zerres v. Vanina, 150 F. 564, 565 (1907).
4. Tonopah & Salt Lake Mining Co. v. Tonopah Mining Co., 125 F 389, 400, 408 (1903).
5. Belk v. Meagher, supra at 284; Gwillim v. Donnellan, 115 U.S. 45, 49; Del Monte Mining & Milling Co. v. Last Chance Mining & Milling Co., 171 U.S. 78-79 (1898).
6. Scott Burnham, 100 IBLA 94, 108 (1987).
7. Cram v. Church, 340 P2d 1116 (1959).
8. McElligott v. Krogh, 90 P. 823 (1907).
9. Sullivan v. Sharp, 90 P. 1054 (1905).
10. Bunker Hill Co. v. Empire State Co., 134 F. 268 (1903).

MINERALS NEVER LOCATABLE

Even before the Materials Act of 1947, many minerals were never locatable even though they could be marketed at a profit. In fact the Materials Act of 1947 was passed to provide a means to dispose of them. Material in this category includes ordinary deposits of clay, rock, sand and gravel, etc. Nonlocatable minerals generally have a normal quality, a value for ordinary uses and are widespread. Most minerals held to be nonlocatable have received such treatment because of the use to which they were put. If the earth material is used in a manner that practically any material could satisfy, then it is not locatable. Material which is principally valuable for use as fill, sub-base, ballast, riprap, or barrow was never locatable.

List of Minerals Never Locatable

Among the more unusual minerals held to be not locatable before the Materials Act of 1947 are the following examples:

1. Peat, peat moss and sedge peat.[1]
2. Stalactites, stalagmites, geodes, crystalline deposits and formations valuable as natural curiosities.[2]
3. Minerals held in solution in springs and other waters.[3]
4. Trace elements of minerals for use as agricultural additives.[4]
5. Clay used as mud for facial cosmetics.[5]
6. A mine deriving revenue only through paid admission of persons desiring to breathe radon gas released by decaying uranium and said to have therapeutic value.[6]
7. Fossil remains of prehistoric animals.[7]

Caliche Is Not Locatable

In 1986 the Tenth Circuit Court of Appeals held that caliche is not a locatable mineral for the following reasons:

> [Caliche] is of the most common occurrence generally and extensively in very large areas in Southeastern New Mexico, Texas and Arizona and there in towns and cities. It is present on many square miles of the land in issue on the surface or under a few inches of other dirt or range grass. It has value as fill dirt and surfacing by reason of its geographical location to the road work where it is used, and a market for this use exists. Nothing can be extracted from it nor derived from it. It is used by reason of its physical characteristics only.

References - Minerals Never Locatable

1. U.S. v. Toole, 224 F.Supp. 440 (1963).
2. South Dakota Mining Co. v. McDonald, 30 L.D. 357 (1900).
3. Pagosa Springs, 1 L.D. 562 (1882).
4. U.S. v. Toole, supra.
5. U.S. v. Springer, 8 IBLA 123 (1972).
6. U.S. v. Elkhorn Mining Co., 2 IBLA 383 (1971), aff'd., Elkhorn Mining Co. v. Morton, Civil No. 211 (D. Mont., filed January 19, 1973).
7. Earl Douglas, 44 L.D. 325 (1915).
8. Poverty Flats Land & Cattle Co. v. U.S., 788 F.2d 676 (10th Cir. 1986).

DISCOVERY UNDER THE MINING LAW OF 1872

Statutory Definition of Discovery

The Act of May 10, 1872[1] provides that "all valuable mineral deposits in lands belonging to the United States...shall be free and open to exploration and purchase..." Although the statutes do not prescribe a test for determining what constitutes a discovery of a valuable mineral deposit, the Department and the courts have established a test through almost a century of decisions. These decisions seem to assume that Congress intended that "valuable mineral deposits" be valuable in an economic sense or could be worked as a paying mine. A profitable mining operation has always been considered as the best evidence of the discovery of a valuable mineral deposit.

Prudent Person Test of Discovery

The most durable and famous test of discovery was the Interior Department case of **Castle v. Womble**, 19 L.D. 455 (1894), in which the Secretary stated:

> ...where minerals have been found and the evidence is of such a character that a person of ordinary prudence would be justified in the further expenditure of his labor and means, with a reasonable prospect of success, in developing a valuable mine, the requirements of the statutes have been met.

This test, known as the "prudent person test" has been approved by the Supreme Court of the United States in many cases.[2]

What Has Been Done Successfully

The most persuasive evidence as to what a person of ordinary prudence would do with a particular mining claim is what people have actually done, not what a witness is willing to state that a prudent person would do.[3] For example, a mining claimant would be justified in initiating actual mining operations on mineral showings that are the same or very nearly the same as those where actual mining operations have been successfully brought to fruition by others.[4]

Cost Analysis Required in Prudent Man Determination

The Interior Board of Land Appeals recently gave an example of why a cost analysis plays a crucial role in the prudent man determination.[5] The Board said the "determination that a valuable mineral exists on a property is only the first step in the 'prudent man' determination. One analysis of the earth's crust noted that the gold contained in seawater represents the largest known 'reserve' of gold in the world. However, the cost of extracting gold from seawater is far greater than the value of the gold that would be recovered. A prudent man, therefore, would not expend his time and means to evaporate sea water and process the solids to recover the gold. A mineral deposit becomes an ore deposit only if the cost of removal and rendering the minerals contained in the deposit suitable for sale is less than the sales price. Cost of extraction must, therefore, be examined."[6]

Insufficient Evidence for Discovery

Not long after enactment of the General Mining Law of 1872, the courts began to develop a definition of what constitutes a discovery of a "valuable mineral deposit." The following quotations were excerpted from three different turn-of-the-century cases:

> ...such applications should not be granted unless the existence of mineral in such quantities as would justify expenditure in the effort to obtain it is established as a present fact. **Davis v. Weibbold**, 139 U.S. 507 (1891).

> ...so, here, the amount of the ore, the facility for reaching and working it, as well as the product per ton, are all to be considered in determining whether the vein is one which justified exploitation and working... **Iron Silver Mining Company v. Mike & Starr Gold and Silver Mining Company**, 143 U.S. 394 (1892).

> It is not enough that there may have been some indications by outcroppings on the surface, of the existence of lodes or veins of rock in place bearing gold or silver or other metal, to justify their designation as "known" veins or lodes. To meet that designation the lodes or veins must be clearly ascertained, and be of such extent as to render the land more valuable on that account, and justify their exploitation. **Chrisman v. Miller**, 197 U.S. 313 (1905).

In order for a mining claim to be valid, there must be a discovery of a valuable mineral deposit within the limits of the claim. Although many prospects show mineralization and are worthy of further exploration, a discovery has not been made. In a recent case[7] involving a claim the Interior Board of Land Appeals found to lack a discovery, 1985 tons of ore was exposed, an amount that could be exhausted in 27 working days. The net price for the 1985 tons would be only a fraction of the fixed costs of $600,000 required to initiate mining operations. The remainder of the fixed costs could be recovered only by further exploration leading to the exposure of thousands of tons of more minable ore than has been exposed.

Paying Mine Need Not Be Demonstrated

Although a mining claimant may be required to demonstrate he has what could be developed into a profitable mine under present economic conditions, it is not required that he demonstrate a paying mine as an accomplished fact.[8] In many cases the courts have held that actual successful exploitation of a mining claim is not required to satisfy the prudent man test. What the test requires is that with actual mining operations under proper management a profitable venture may reasonably be expected to result.

Claimant Has Burden of Proof Discovery Exists

It is important for the claimant to understand that the role of the government mineral examiner is merely to verify the existence of an established, physically-exposed discovery. The claimant has the ultimate burden of proof that a discovery exists.[9] The prudent man rule requires the claimant to submit proof that a prudent man would develop a mine.[10] One of the most common means of demonstrating what a prudent man would do is through the testimony of expert witnesses who have examined the property and express their opinions, as experts, that the evidence supports a determination that further development is warranted. To have an expert in the field examine the property and render a decision is, itself, an exercise of prudence.[11]

No Discovery If Deposit Warrants Additional Exploration

In a 1981 Interior Department case,[12] a geologist (White) employed by the claimant had sampled at the same points tested by the government and also sampled using a suction dredge. The assay values of White's report indicated lower values for gold than assays taken by the government. Because the appellant indicated at the hearing that he accepted the findings of the report, the Board focused on the conclusions of the report where White said "there is sufficient gold present in those Denny placers examined by me, to justify the continued expenditure of time, effort and money in the search for the fabled golden fleece." Concerning the effect of White's report on the case, the Board said "Whites conclusion (quoted above) expresses an often-cited principle of mining law. That principle is that mineralization which may warrant further exploration or prospecting in an effort to ascertain whether sufficient mineralization might be found to justify mining or development does not constitute a valuable mineral deposit. That is, a valuable mineral deposit has not been discovered because a search for such a deposit might be indicated.[13]

It is a common pitfall for a claimant or his expert witness to reveal at the hearing that the deposit is mineralized to the extent that it justifies additional exploration or prospecting to find a commercial deposit. The hearing officer considers this to be an admission by the claimant that there is no discovery. This does not meet the present court interpretation of discovery which requires that the valuable mineral deposit has been found and ready for development and mining. With discovery, no more prospecting or exploration work to find the deposit would be necessary.

Exploration Versus Development

Numerous Departmental and court decisions have held that in order to qualify as a discovery it must be established that the mineral deposit can be mined and sold at a profit and that development and mining operations may proceed with reasonable confidence. If the deposit requires additional exploration to delineate the ore reserves and determine grade or quality before development may be confidently started, a discovery has not been made. The Interior Board of Land Appeals[14] has distinguished between "exploration" and "development" as follows:

> **Exploration** is the process of searching for a valuable mineral deposit. The finding of mineralization of sufficient value to encourage further exploration does not successfully conclude the exploratory process or constitute a discovery. Exploration work includes such activities as geophysical or geochemical prospecting, diamond drilling, sinking an exploratory shaft or driving an exploratory adit. It is that work which is done prior to a discovery in an effort to determine whether the land is valuable for minerals.

> **Development** refers to the physical work incident to the excavation of a mine for the extraction of the mineral values discovered. After discovery, certain exploratory activities incident to the actual production of the minerals values discovered. After discovery, certain exploratory activities incident to the actual production of the minerals are regarded as "development" rather than as "exploration." These would include the blocking out of the orebody, testing for engineering feasibility, determining the strike and dip of the vein beyond the extent of the qualifying knowledge, and related activities.

Loss of Discovery

Worked-out claims do not qualify as valid mining claims. Although a mining claim may have been valid in the past because of a discovery on the claim of a valuable mineral deposit, the claim will lose its validity if the deposit ceases to be valuable because of a change in economic conditions, or the mineral deposit is depleted.

Discovery in Each Claim

The discovery of minerals on one claim will not support rights to another claim or group of claims even though the claims are contiguous.[15] In contest proceedings involving more than one claim, the test of discovery is applied to each claim individually, since "[a] discovery without the limits of the claim, no matter what its proximity, does not suffice." **Waskey v. Hammer**, 223 U.S. 85, 91 (1912).

In order to be valid each claim in a claim group must have a discovery within its boundaries. However, under certain circumstances the government has taken a broad look at the requirement. For example, in the case of large, low-grade, porphyry-copper deposits which by necessity require hundreds of claims to cover the mineralized area, it is obvious that any one claim could not stand by itself as a paying mine. The entire deposit must be available in order to be economically feasible. In acknowledging this fact, the government has issued mining patents on numerous such claims. In recognition of this reality, the Interior Board of Land Appeals issued the **Schlosser v. Pierce** decision.

Each Claim Need Not Support Independent Mine

In **Schlosser v. Pierce**, 93 I.D. 211 (1986), the Board held that a mining claimant is not required to show "the profitability of each claim in a group as a potentially viable independent mine." Although the mineral in this case was bentonite, this ruling would apply to any high-tonnage, low-grade mineral deposit appropriated with a group of mining claims. This is true even though an individual claim of the group might not contain ore of sufficient quantity and quality to support a discovery. Under the following circumstances, there is no requirement that each claim be independently capable of being mined and marketed at a profit:

1. A group of mining claims must be located over a high-tonnage, low-grade deposit.

2. Ore can be extracted profitably from each claim under a single large mining operation; or

3. To be valid, each claim must contain sufficient quality and quantity of mineral to be extracted profitably under an overall mining plan.

This claim group approach to validity is necessary in light of the predominance of large-tonnage, low-grade deposits being mined during the last several decades. In many cases, the large equipment and scale of operations needed to keep unit costs low in such deposits would normally be far too costly for the amount of reserves that could exist within the boundaries of a single claim.

The economic analysis may be based on the claim block as a whole rather than on each individual claim. In **Pacific Coast Moly**, 90 I.D. 352 (1983), the costs for developing a single mine were estimated and apportioned to each claim.

Contiguous or Nearby Claims

Contiguous or nearby claims are required to satisfy group development. The basis for this is that such claims lend themselves to group development because of economic reasons.[16]

Group Development

Under the concept of "mine" development where operations may be established on a group of contiguous claims, the existence of reserves on adjacent mining properties controlled by the claimant is relevant to the question of whether there is a reasonable prospect of developing a paying mine.[17]

Group Development of Building Stone Claims

In a case where the claimant attempted to apply the benefits of "group development" to numerous claims, widely scattered through out the Phoenix area, the Board of Land Appeals[18] rejected the argument. The location of a group of building stone claims to have under claim the greatest possible range of colors and gradations of stone in order to afford customers the widest possible range of choices does not constitute group development as defined in **Schlosser**.

Test of Discovery: Patent Versus Contest

The test of discovery is the same whether a patent is applied for by the mining claimant or the claim is being contested by the United States.[19] The test is also the same regardless of the surface values involved.

Severed Claims and Discovery

For a claim to be valid, a discovery must exist within the boundary of a mining claim; and if a claim is severed, only those portions that contain a discovery are valid.[20] A mining claim intersected and separated by land patented as nonmineral (including mill site claims) requires two discoveries - one on each tract.[21] However, if such intersected mining claim is separated by a patented mineral land, one discovery is sufficient.[22]

Discovery Must Not Be Split to Validate Two Claims

A discovery must be treated as an entirety and the basis of but one location. For example, a single discovery may not be split at the common end lines of two claims to validate the two claims.[23]

Comparison of Values

The Act of 1872 contains no language that limits mining claim locations, except that they must be valuable mineral deposits. The Act of 1892, relating to building stone, however requires as an additional prerequisite for a valid claim for building stone that the lands embraced within such claims must be chiefly valuable for the located mineral. Therefore in the case of building stone, Congress has expressly mandated a comparison of values approach.

If a discovery exists, a claim is valid even if there are more beneficial uses to the land, including a greater value for agriculture. Even in a case involving the issuance of a mineral patent embracing lands in the Misty Fjords National Monument, the IBLA held that the "test of discovery is the same whether the land be unreserved public domain, land in a national forest, or even land in a national park.[24]

Other Values Require Clear and Convincing Evidence

Where the discovery of a valuable mineral deposit is claimed on land known to be valuable for purposes other than mining, the Department requires clear and convincing evidence that the land is valuable for mineral.[25] The existence of other values may be considered in assessing the weight and credibility to be accorded the locator's testimony and may be an issue in evaluating his bona fide intention to develop a mining operation.[26]

Contests Between Claimant and U.S. Require More Stringent Discovery Than Contests Between Locators

The prudent man test, complemented by the marketability test is to be applied with varying degrees of strictness depending on the relative positions of the parties to the case. For example the test is applied with greater strictness in contests between the claimant and the United States Government than in contests between two claimants.[27]

Lower Standard of Discovery in Contests between Rival Claimants

As a general rule the courts make an effort to protect the senior locator operating in good faith in priority of rights contests between rival claimants.[28] As a consequence, the test of discovery has not been stringent for the senior locator. It is extremely rare for a court to rule in behalf of a junior locator because the senior locator did not make a discovery. Note the exceptions to this rule in the chapter on "Prediscovery Rights or Pedis Possessio."

Conflicting Claimants Held to Prudent Man Discovery

The 1987 Nevada Federal District Court case of **Amax Exploration, Inc. v. Ross Mosher**, supra, represents a significant departure from the general rule that the test of discovery is less stringent in a contest between two rival locators than in a contest between a locator and the United States Government. The Federal District Court of Nevada held both the senior and junior claimants to the prudent man discovery standard commonly required of mining claimants by the Department of the Interior. In this case, Amax staked both lode and placer claims over placer claims owned by Ross Mosher on the basis that Mosher had not discovered a valuable placer mineral. Although the Court acknowledged that courts typically view the evidence of discovery more in favor of the senior locator in a dispute between rival claimants, it held that the advantage of being the senior locator cannot displace the need to prove the elements of a discovery. As the Court said, the senior locators "have failed to prove credibly, with respect to each particular claim, placer mineralization which would lead a reasonable and prudent miner to conclude that there is a reasonable prospect of developing a profitable mine." After holding that none of the parties in the case had made a discovery, the Court declared "that the land remains in the public domain open to peaceable exploration by the parties or by any other citizen. The Court took this position even though it agreed that the claims of both parties are procedurally proper.

The Court also found that Amax had not proven a discovery of gold within any of its claims even though gold was found in many samples taken by surface sampling. Amax geologists also used biogeochemical and geomicrobial sampling, resistivity/inverse-polarization geophysical testing, ground magnetic testing and gravimetric testing methods. On this basis Amax geologists extrapolated "a geologic inference that there is excellent potential for discovery of minable deposits." The Court concluded that "at best, this means the area has promising potential for exploration. That falls short of a legal discovery on each Amax claim.

Comparison of Deposits to Determine
Prospect of Success

In **U.S. v. Walper**, 77 IBLA 90 (1983, 35 lode claims covering a large disseminated molybdenum deposit (Nunatak Deposit) were declared null and void for lack of discovery of a valuable mineral deposit. The Board concluded that the testimony of the government mineral examiners was sufficient to establish a prima facie case of invalidity. The mineral examiners relied on a 1978 U.S. Geological Survey report on the Nunatak deposit. The report indicated that the deposit "as presently known" is "between the 50th and 90th percentile in size and just below the 10th percentile in grade," when compared with known porphyry-molybdenum deposits of the world. The report also stated that "in evaluating the mineral resource potential of this favorable area, we assume that the minimum size and grade deposit that would attract serious interest would have at least ... 100 million tons ... of resources containing between 0.15 and 0.20 percent molybdenum ..."

The mineral examiners sampled core segments left behind by the drilling and four assays were taken. The four assays indicated an average grade of molybdenum sulfide of 0.1 percent. This grade is lower than the minimum exploitable grade at the Urad-Henderson mine in Colorado which is 0.2 percent.

The significance of the Government's prima facie case is that the mineral examiners made no estimate of the quantity of ore available on the claims and had not developed the costs of extracting, removing and marketing the ore. Instead the examiners partly determined the Nunatak deposit could not be operated at a profit by comparing its reserves and grade with the minimum ore grade at the Urad-Henderson Mine. Although the Board approved this method, it is clear that the comparison approach in lieu of estimating mining costs to determine profitability should be used only in special cases.

Recitals of Discovery in Location Notice

It is not uncommon for locators to indicate on the location certificate that a discovery exists within the claim boundaries and that such discovery was made on a specified date. The United States Supreme Court[29] has held that such assertions on the location affidavit does not constitute evidence of discovery.

Federal Versus State Discovery Requirements

In a contest between the U.S. Government and a claimant, a state law which provides for a presumption of discovery in favor of the locator would not apply.[30] State mining laws relating to discovery may only add to the Federal mining law; such laws cannot diminish the Federal requirements for the discovery of a valuable mineral deposit on a mining claim located on Federal lands.[31]

Location of Claim Confers No Right If No Discovery

A mining claim location does not give the presumption of a discovery.[32] In **Cole v. Ralph**, 252 U.S. 286, 294-96 (1920), the Supreme Court held that "location is the act or series of acts whereby the boundaries of the claim are marked, etc., but it confers no right in the absence of discovery, both being essential to a valid claim."

Discovery Precedes Location

Although the statute requires that discovery precede location, the order may be reversed provided there is no intervening right established. In **Cole v. Ralph**, supra, the Supreme Court said:

> In practice, discovery usually precedes location, and the statute treats it as the initial act. But, in the absence of an intervening right, it is no objection that the usual and statutory order is reversed. In such a case the location becomes effective from the date of discovery; but in the presence of an intervening right it must remain of no effect.

Assessment Work May Not Substitute for Discovery

The performance of assessment work has no relationship to discovery. It is a common belief among claimants that the longer they have held a claim and done their annual assessment work, the better the title of the claim. However, in **Cole v. Ralph**, the Supreme Court has said that assessment work does not take the place of discovery "for the requirement relating to such work is in the nature of a condition subsequent to a perfected and valid claim and has nothing to do with locating or holding a claim before discovery."

Bad Faith Can Invalidate a Claim

In a 1984 case[33] the Interior Board of Land Appeals held that claims were invalid because they were not located in good faith. During the five years the claimants occupied the lands embraced by the claims, they built two cabins, a water system and cut 50 trees. From the time of location until the hearing, the claimants had done no work on the claims other than take a few samples. Although the owners indicated the claims were valuable for gold, assays indicated a value of only $0.025 per cubic yard using a gold price of $700 per ounce. The claimants also maintained that a discovery existed on the claims for fire clay; however they provided no information on purity, costs of production and marketability. The Board said that even if a discovery can be shown to exist, proof of bad faith can invalidate a claim, since in such a situation the mineral values are incidental to the purpose for which the land is claimed. However it is important to note that where the issue of bad faith is raised, the government bears the ultimate burden of proof.."[34]

Department May Not Adjudicate Validity After Conveyance

Once title to land is conveyed out of Federal ownership, the Interior Department loses jurisdiction. Therefore the validity of mining claims or mill sites can no longer be adjudicated.[35]

Validity at Date of Patent Application

Lode and placer mining claims and mill site claims must be valid at the date of patent application.[36] This means a mill site must be used or occupied for mining or milling purposes and a mining claim must have a discovery at the date of patent application.

Validity at Date of Withdrawal and Date of Hearing

When land is closed to location under the mining laws subsequent to the location of a mining claim, the claim cannot be recognized as valid unless all requirements of the mining laws, including discovery of a valuable mineral deposit, were met at the time of the withdrawal and the claim presently, i.e., at the time of the hearing, meets the requirements of the law.[37] This means that where land occupied by a mining claim has been withdrawn from operation of the mining laws, the validity of the claim must be tested as of the date[38] of the withdrawal, as well as of the date of the hearing. Even though there may have been a discovery at the time of a withdrawal or some other time in the past, a mining claim cannot be considered valid unless the claim has been continuously supported by the same discovery to the present.[39]

Access to Prove Discovery After Withdrawal

Claims are not properly declared null and void for lack of discovery where the mineral claimants are effectively foreclosed from proving that a discovery exists.[40] In cases of withdrawal of the land, such withdrawal entitles the Government to restrict the development of a claim, but restrictions must be reasonable.[41] Of course, a discovery must be judged by what has been exposed on a mining claim at the time of a withdrawal, and a claimant is not entitled to go onto a claim thereafter for the purpose of exposing new veins or lodes.[42]

Exposure of New Reserves or Increase in Mineral Price after Withdrawal

If a discovery did not exist on a claim at the date of a withdrawal, a later discovery established by subsequent mineral exposures or rise in mineral commodity prices would not give a claim validity at the date of a hearing.[43]

If Disclosure of Mineral before Withdrawal, Sampling After Withdrawal May Prove Discovery

The acts of sampling and assaying are acts which either confirm or disprove the existence of a discovery. Therefore, if there was an exposure of mineral at the date of withdrawal, that exposure is a discovery of valuable mineral if subsequent sampling, assaying, and testing confirm the fact that the exposed mineral is valuable.[44] Furthermore, assay results from diamond-drill intercepts of the mineralized zone will support a conclusion that there was an exposure of valuable mineral if reasonable geologic projection leads to a conclusion that the intercept and the exposure are from the same mineralized structure.[45]

References - Discovery

1. 30 U.S.C. 22 (1982).
2. Chrisman v. Miller, 197 U.S. 313 (1905); Best v. Humboldt Placer Mining Company, 371 U.S. 334 (1963); and U.S. v. Coleman, 390 U.S. 599 (1968).
3. U.S. v. Flurry, A-30887 (March 5, 1968).
4. 16 IBLA 126
5. U.S. v. Foresyth, 100 IBLA 185 (1987).
6. Id. at 211.
7. U.S. v. McKenzie, 29 IBLA 270 (1977).
8. Adams v. U.S., 318 F.2d (9th Cir. 1963).
9. Lara v. Secretary of the Interior, 820 F.2d 1535, 1542 (9th Cir 1987).
10. U.S. v. Foresyth, supra.
11. Id.
12. U.S. v. Arbo, 70 IBLA 244 (1983).
13. Converse v. Udall, 399 F.2d 616 (9th Cir. 1968), cert. denied, 393 U.S. 1025 (1969).
14. U.S. v. New Mexico Mines, Inc., 3 IBLA 101 (1971).
15. Ranchers Exploration & Development Co. v. Anaconda Co., 248 F.Supp. 708 (D.C. Utah 1965).
16. U.S. Melluzzo, 105 IBLA 252, 258 (1988).
17. U.S. v. New York Mines, 105 IBLA 171, 191 (1988).
18. U.S. Melluzzo, supra at 258.
19. U.S. v. Higbee, A-31063 (April 1, 1970); U.S. v. Carlile, 67 I.D. 417 (1960); Mulkern v. Hammill, 326 F.2d 896, 898 (9th Cir. 1964).
20. U.S. v. Higbee, supra.
21. Paul Jones Lode, 31 L.D. 359.
22. Hydee Lode, 30 L.D. 420.
23. 16 L.D. 1.
24. In re Pacific Coast Molybdenum Co., 75 IBLA 16 (1983).
25. U.S. v. Wells, A-30805.
26. U.S. v. Kosanke Sand Corporation (On Reconsideration), 80 I.D. 538, 547 (1973).
27. Converse v. Udall, 399 F.2d 616, 619-20 (9th Cir. 1969), cert. denied, 393 U.S. 1025 (1969).
28. Boscarino v. Gibson, 672 P2d 1119 (Mont. 1983); Silver Jet Mines, Inc. v. Schwark, 41 St. Rptr. 933 (Mont. 1984).
29. Cole v. Ralph, 252 U.S. 286, 303 (1920).
30. U.S. v. Ramsey, 14 IBLA 154 (1974).
31. U.S. v. Tappan, 25 IBLA 1 (1976).
32. Ranchers Exploration and Development Co. v. Anaconda Co., 248 F.Supp. 708 (1965).
33. U.S. v. Zimmers, 81 IBLA 41 (1984).
34. In re Pacific Coast Molybdenum Co., supra; U.S. v. Prowell, 52 IBLA 256 (1981).

35. Ed Bilderback, 89 IBLA 263 (1985).
36. Pruess v. Udall, 286 F.Supp. 138 (1968), affirmed, 410 F.2d 750, cert. denied, 396 U.S. 967; Best v. Humboldt Placer Mining Co., 371 U.S. 334, 336.
37. U.S. v. Netherlin, 33 IBLA 86 (1977).
38. U.S. v. Chappell, 42 IBLA 74 (1979).
39. U.S. v. Clemans, 45 IBLA 64, 71-72 (1980).
40. U.S. v. Parker, 91 I.D. 271, 294 (1984).
41. U.S. v. Neice, 77 IBLA 205, 207-08, n. 3 (1983).
42. U.S. v. Parker, supra.
43. U.S. v. Lara, supra at 57.
44. U.S. v. Foresyth, 100 IBLA 185, 207 (1987).
45. Id at 211.

THE MARKETABILITY TEST

Introduction

The marketability test has been followed by the Department of the Interior since **Layman v. Ellis**, 52 L.D. 714 (1929). The application of the test was expressly upheld in **Foster v. Seaton**, 271 F.2d 836 (D.C. Cir. 1959). It was further approved by the United States Supreme Court as a complement to the prudent man test in **United States v. Coleman**, 390 U.S. 602 (1968). In **Foster v. Seaton**, the Court stated the marketability test as follows:

> With respect to widespread non-metallic minerals such as sand and gravel, however, the Department has stressed the additional requirement of present marketability in order to prevent the misappropriation of lands containing these minerals by persons seeking to acquire such lands for purposes other than mining. Thus, such a "mineral locator or applicant, to justify his possession, must show that by reason of accessibility, bona fides in development, proximity to market, existence of present demand, and other factors, the deposit is of such value that it can be mined, removed and disposed of at a profit."

The Coleman Case

In **U.S. v. Coleman,** the United States Supreme Court approved the requirement of the Secretary that "the mineral can be extracted, removed and marketed at a profit - the so-called marketability test."[1] Essentially, in **Coleman** the Court determined that non-metallic minerals of widespread occurrence must be marketable at a profit.

Marketability Applies to All Minerals

The question of whether the marketability test is applicable to intrinsically valuable minerals such as base and precious metals has been considered in many cases.[2] In the 1968 case of **Converse v. Udall**, the Ninth Circuit Court of Appeals[3] held that the marketability test, including the profit factor, was applicable to all mining claims including those containing precious metals. However, the marketability test is more stringent for common materials such as limestone.

Present Marketability or Profitability

Since **Coleman**, the test of discovery has, in certain cases required that a mine could be operated at a profit under present economic conditions.[4] The expectation of future profitability under the prudent man test must be based upon present economic circumstances known then and not upon mere speculation as to possible substantial changes in the market place. You cannot locate claims upon public lands and then simply wait until the minerals are in sufficient demand to be marketed at a profit.

Presently Marketable at a Profit: a Definition

The Interior Board of Land Appeals has significantly refined the prudent-man test by defining "presently marketable at a profit" to mean that the claimant "must show that as a present fact, considering historic price and cost factors and assuming that they will continue, there is a reasonable likelihood of success that a paying mine can be developed." **In re Pacific Coast Molybdenum**, 90 I.D. 352. 360 (1983). This new definition was made in response to large fluctuations in mineral commodity prices that occurred during the preceding five years.

Now a claimant does not necessarily have to use the latest market price of a commodity, but instead may average prices over an appropriate period of time. However the Board did caution that "situations can occur in which structural economic changes or technological breakthroughs invalidate historical conditions as a guide to present marketability." For example, mineral prices elevated artificially by Government price supports would not be relevant to the question of present marketability. Also the possibility that a future stockpiling program might someday be initiated would be "essentially speculative and could not serve as a predicate upon which a prudent man would have proceeded to expend time and money with a reasonable hope of success."

Market Value of Claim Does Not Relate to Validity

The Interior Board of Land Appeals[5] has held that "the market value of a mining claim is not the test for discovery of a valuable mineral deposit." However, it is difficult to accept that Congress did not intend to include as "valuable mineral deposits" those large mineral deposits including operating mines that have a market value of many millions of dollars, but that cannot be operated at a profit during a temporary low in the economic cycle. For example, during the early 1980s some of the largest mines in the United States could not be operated at a profit.

Present Marketability Does Not Apply to Oil Shale Claims

In **Andrus v. Shell Oil Co.**, 446 U.S. 657 (1980), the United States Supreme Court ruled that pre-1920 oil shale mining claims are an exception to the general principles for establishing a discovery . The Court held that the Department could not impose the present marketability test on oil shale placer claims as of 1920.

Injunctions and Marketability

If a claimant is restrained from operating a claim by a court order, such an injunction may not be used by the Government to establish that a claimant has not made a showing of marketability.[6]

Proof of Profitable Market

A mining claimant is not required to prove a discovery by showing that he is actually engaged in profitable mining operations or even that profitable operations are assured; but it does require a showing of a prospect of profit which is sufficient to invite reasonable men to expend their means in attempting to reap that profit by extracting and marketing the mineral.[7]

Amount of Profit

One of the most common question by claimants concerning the profitability requirement is how much profit is necessary to validate a claim. In several cases the Interior Department addressed the profitability requirement in terms of the amount of profit necessary to establish a discovery. In a 1968 case[8] the Board held that a profit as low as $245 per year would not satisfy the prudent man test of discovery. In a 1973 case,[9] the Board indicated that although a sale of $1.00 could represent a profit to a claimant, it would not meet the prudent-man test.

Effect of Lack of Development on a Claim's Validity

The Interior Department and the courts have long held that where, over a sustained period of several years, the claimant has failed to engage in productive extraction of mineral from a claim, a presumption is raised that there has been no discovery of a valuable mineral deposit or that the market value of the discovered minerals was not sufficient to justify the costs of extraction.[10] This rule reflects the principle that, in varying economic conditions present during a period of years, the claims will be developed if there is mineralization on them and if it is commercially feasible to do so at a profit. Evidence of absence of production or sale from mining claims over a period of years is sufficient without more, to establish a prima facie case of invalidity. However, lack of marketability is not conclusive proof of invalidity of a claim.[12]

However, under certain circumstances it is prudent and reasonable to locate and hold minerals in reserve without development on a particularly claim. For example in one case where there was a history of problems with material sources, the expansion of business, 25 years of continued operation and the amount of invested capital, the Board of Land Appeals[13] held that it would be prudent and reasonable to locate and hold a source of supply in reserve.

Proof or Evidence of Sales Records

In a number of Interior Department and Federal Court cases, it has been held that it is the responsibility of the claimant to maintain adequate business records relating to both sales of the mineral product and costs of production. As the Board of Land Appeals said[14] "a mining claimant cannot meet this burden by failing to keep adequate records or other means of proof. Or, if he has kept such records, he cannot be relieved of his burden if his records are lost or destroyed and he has only infirm or inconsistent recollection to substitute. * * * [H]e cannot expect the validity of his claim to be established by his default."

The case of **United States v. Arbo**, 70 IBLA 244 (1983) is an excellent example of where a claimant had no record of sales. Although the appellant supplied a number of receipts indicating sales of gold to several different companies, he was not able to show the costs of producing the gold or even to document that the gold came from the contested claim. It is not uncommon for the owner of a placer gold claim to have a poor record of receipts in some cases because the gold is recovered in a highly marketable condition and there may be a temptation to market the gold in such a manner so as to avoid income taxes. However as the Board indicated, you cannot have it both ways, i.e., get credit for sales in a contest action for which there is no income tax record of sales. This situation can be avoided if a claimant maintains detailed records of all sales and costs and how they are applied to each claim.

Mineral Examiner Must Be Expert on Marketability of Specific Mineral

In **Rodgers v. United States**, 726 F.2d 1376 (9th Cir. 1984), a case involving the gem mineral "sunstones," it was held that the Government failed to present evidence on marketability sufficient to make out a prima facie case of invalidity. The Court focused on the qualifications and testimony of the Government's expert witnesses.

One of the most significant aspects of this case is the Court's holding "that the testifying mineral examiner must be an expert as to the marketability of the particular mineral." As the Court pointed out, the two government mineral examiners stated that they had no expertise regarding gemstones or the market for those stones. Conversely, testimony by the claimant's witnesses included a geologist for the State of Oregon, an amateur faceter, the original locator of the claims, a mineral commodities marketing specialist and an eminent mineralogist.

Market too Small for Profitable Operation

The Interior Board of Land Appeals has determined that even though there is a market for chemical-grade limestone, the claims are not valid if this market could not support an operation of the size necessary to establish a profitable operation.[15]

Claimant Has Burden to Show Potential Buyers And Price They Would Pay

The claimant has the burden to demonstrate that there is a reasonable prospect that someone will buy his minerals at a price higher than the cost of extraction.[16] Therefore the claimant is responsible for submitting evidence regarding the existence of potential buyers of the product and the price they would be willing to pay.[17]

Marketability Must Not Depend on Value Added by Manufacture

It is well established that the marketability of a mineral must be based on the mineral in its raw state rather than depend on value added by manufacture. Any determination of validity must rest on the marketability of the mineral in its rough or unprocessed form and not upon any enhanced value from subsequent processing or craft work.[18]

Profitability Must Be Based on Locatable Minerals

Sales of minerals from a mining claim for unqualified or non-locatable uses such as fill material cannot be considered in determining the marketability of the material, even if the material could meet the specifications for locatable-type uses.[19]

Aggregation of Profits

You cannot aggregate the profits from the sale of a nonlocatable mineral such as sand and gravel with the profits from the sale of a locatable mineral such as gold. The validity of a claim must rest entirely on the marketability and profitability of the locatable mineral.[20]

Marketability of Comparable Material

The claimant cannot rely solely on the fact that comparable material is being marketed. Rather, the claimant must establish that his material was of a quality that would have met the existing demand, and that it was marketable at a profit.[21] Proof that material from neighboring claims is being marketed is relevant to determining a claim's marketability, but such proof alone does not overcome evidence that the market was well supplied. Thus, even though comparable claims are being mined, a new claim may be unprofitable because the market has reached such a point of saturation that a new entrant cannot make a profit.[22]

Supply and Demand

Minerals that are not intrinsically valuable such as many of the construction or building materials are extremely vulnerable to the "law of supply and demand." Most of the cases in which the Interior Department or the Federal courts have considered the problem of supply and demand as it applies to the marketability test involved sand and gravel, building stone and cinders or pumice.

Where a market is saturated by a super-abundance of top quality materials from competitive sources at prices near the irreducible minimum, the advent of a new supplier will be viewed with a jaundiced eye.[23] Similarly, where demand is limited to a very few consumers who supply their needs from their own sources, so that the market is "closed" or "captive," a mining claimant must prove that the consumers will buy the materials of his claim at a profit.[24] With respect to supply, a hypothetical market must be created which includes all potential sources of supply. If the amount of material would be such a superabundance that the price would be lowered below a profitable level, then the claim cannot compete and would not be valid.[25]

Prospective Market or Reserves with No Market

In many parts of the west, minerals subject to the mining law are covered by large claim groups. Where such minerals are widespread with vast reserves, it is not uncommon for the claims or claim groups to cover substantially more reserves than the market could ever absorb. These minerals tend to be nonmetallic minerals without intrinsic value such as building stone, sand and gravel, bentonite, silica sand, pumice, perlite and many other constructions materials.

As the Ninth Circuit Court has said in several cases,[26] a hypothetical market in which the claimant's material is the only unmarketed material taken into account is hardly a useful supposition. If the claimant's material can be marketed, then so can that from all potentially competitive sources. To exclude all unmarketed material save that of the claimant could result in the unrealistic conclusion that all such material considered claim by claim, is marketable at a profit. However, if all the claims had been actively operated, none could have done so profitably. Furthermore, you

277

cannot locate claims upon the public lands and then simply wait until the minerals are in sufficient demand to be marketed at a profit.

The Baker Case

Although the administrative and Federal court cases are unanimous in holding that claims located for more material than a market could conceivably accommodate are nonmineral in character, **Baker v. United States**, 613 F.2d 224 (9th Cir. 1980) cert denied, 101 S.Ct. 332 (1980) stands out as an unexplainable aberration, especially since the same Court ruled on almost the same issues five months later in the **McCall** case (see below) in a manner consistent with existing case law. Because the **Baker** case represents such a deviation from existing precedent and was followed by the **McCall** case, the Interior Department is ignoring **Baker** and following the rationale in **McCall.** See **Oneida Perlite**, 57 IBLA 167 (1981).

Baker had located claims covering 15 million tons of cinders with sales over an 18 year period amounting to about one million tons. However most of the sales were for fill or other nonlocatable uses. The maximum gross income for the period averaged $5,555 per year. Baker's 15 million tons of cinders gave him a reserve supply that could last more than 400 years. The Government contested four claims on the basis that they held reserves with no market and thus no value. The Ninth Circuit Court overruled and said there can be no such thing as an "excess reserves test" or a "too much test."

The McCall Case

McCall had 26 association placer claims of 80 acres each located for sand and gravel on a tract adjoining the City of Las Vegas. Some of the claims had been developed and two patents had already issued for 230 acres covering parts of five claims. The remaining 170 acres of the land in the five claims were never contested for being nonmineral in character.

Evidence showed that sand and gravel of similar quality but more easily recovered exists over many square miles in the Las Vegas valley. Furthermore, the 230 acres previously patented contained more than 3.5 million cubic yards of sand and gravel sufficient for a reserve supply for 100 years. The contested portions of the claims were held to be "nonmineral in character" even though the material on the contested portions was of the same type and quality as the patented portions.

The Government's holding was based on the finding that (1) there was a limited ability of the market to absorb the material, (2) the vast local abundance of sand and gravel, (3) there are numerous competitive suppliers and (4) the claimants already received patent to a 100-year supply. The Court of Appeals was of the opinion that the claimants had a market for some material but were asserting claims to more land and mineral than could profitably be exploited. **McCall v. Andrus**, 628 F.2d 1185, cert. denied 49 USLW 3710 (March 23, 1981).

Oneida Perlite Case

Oneida Perlite[27] involved a patent application for 15 association placer claims embracing 2,000 acres in the Caribou National Forest of Idaho. The forest service mineral examiner recommended patent on an area that contained 5,300,000 tons of commercial perlite, which based on the applicants annual production, would provide a reserve that would last more than 1,000 years. The total reserves on the claims were estimated at between 200 and 300 million tons. This was estimated to be sufficient to supply the entire needs of the United States for 200 to 300 years at the present consumption rate.

Excess and Reasonable Reserves Defined

In the **Oneida Perlite** case, the Interior Board of Land Appeals define "excess reserves" and "reasonable reserves" as follows:

> **Excess reserves** describes the location of claims for far more land and mineral than reason and prudence would allow because there is such a superabundance of the material that the market simply cannot accept all of it at a profit. Therefore, some of the deposits must be regarded as not valuable in an economic sense. * * * [In making the determination that minerals are not presently marketable at a profit], it is appropriate to consider the quantity of the claimant's other holdings of this same mineral, and the limitations of the market, and the claimant's share of that market. It is also appropriate to consider the magnitude and sources of other supplies of the mineral to the same market.

> **Reasonable Reserves**: And, as also related above, reasonable reserves, liberally projected for many years into the future, have been consistently approved by this Department as legitimately within the scope and purpose of the general mining law. What amount of reserves is "reasonable" is a determination to be decided on the basis of the evidence in each case. The nature of the mineral, its unit value, the extent of the market, and whether it is expanding or diminishing, the amount of similar mineral which can supply that market from other sources, might all bear on the question of whether the location of additional claims for the same mineral was justified as the act of a prudent man in the reasonable belief that by the expenditure of his labor and means a valuable mine might be developed on each such claim.

ACT OF JULY 23, 1955

Hypothetical Market at a Critical Date

The Act of July 23, 1955, as well as many withdrawal actions have caused certain minerals to be no longer open to location under the mining law. However, valid existing claims for such minerals at the date of the withdrawal, remain valid so long as a discovery existed at the critical date and continues to the present. When the United States investigates the validity of such claims, it is necessary to apply the marketability test at both the critical date and the present. In cases where minerals from a claim were never mined and marketed at or since the critical date, it must be determined that if minerals were produced, could they fill a theoretical void in a hypothetical market.[28]

Continuous Operation Is Not Required
During Critical Period

Failure of a claimant to maintain continuous operations or make sales during the critical period, though relevant, will not alone support a finding of unmarketability and nondiscovery. A critical period refers to that period of time between the date of withdrawal and the present time during which a showing of marketability must be maintained. When there is little or no evidence of pre-1955 sales, a court should consider costs of extraction, preparation and transport as well as the level of then-existent market demand. There is a presumption of non-marketability raised by the lack of development and sales; however, such a presumption may be overcome be credible evidence that the claimant could have extracted and sold material at the critical date.

Reasonably Continuous Market Required

In order for a mining claim for a common variety of mineral located prior to the Act of July 23, 1955, to be valid, the prudent man/marketability test of discovery must have been met at the time of the Act and reasonably continuously thereafter up to and including the time of a contest hearing.[29] However, it is clear that sales are not absolutely necessary to establish the marketability of material from a claim.[30]

Evidence of Marketability

The Interior Board of Land Appeals[31] has held that the following factors can show a lack of credible positive evidence of marketability:

1. Lack of experience and equipment of claimant as both relate to production of a mineral.

2. Aerial photographic evidence established a lack of surface disturbance on a claim before and after the critical date.

3. No evidence of costs of production or profits from sales.

4. Very little material marketed from the claims prior to July 23, 1955.

5. No evidence of a demand for material as of July 23, 1955.

References - Marketability Test

1. U.S. v. Coleman, 390 U.S. 600, 602-03 (1968).
2. U.S. v. Denison, A-29884 (April 24, 1964); U.S. v. Pekovich, A-30868 (Sept. 27, 1968).
3. Converse v. Udall, 399 F.2d 616 (1968).
4. U.S. v. Estate of Alvis F. Denison, 76 I.D. 233 (1969); Hollenbeck v. Kleppe, 590 F.2d 852 (1979); and U.S. v. Smith, 66 IBLA 182, 190 (1982).
5. U.S. v. Winegar, 81 I.D. 370 at 388 (1974).
6. U.S. v. Foresyth, 15 IBLA 43, 61 (1974).
7. U.S. v. Gould, A-30990 (May 7, 1969).
8. U.S. v. Barrows, 76 I.D. 299 (1969).
9. U.S. v. Penrose, 10 IBLA 334 (1973).
10. U.S. v. Barrows, supra at 306.
11. U.S. v. Rosenberger, 71 IBLA 195, 200 (1983).
12. U.S. v. Rodgers, 726 F.2d 1326 (9th Cir. 1984).
13. U.S. v. Harenberg, 9 IBLA 77 (1973).
14. U.S. v. Barrows, supra.
15. U.S. v. Husman, 81 IBLA 271, 278 (1984).
16. U.S. v. Foresyth, 100 IBLA 185, 228-29.
17. Id.
18. U.S. v. Mansfield, 35 IBLA 95 (1978).
19. U.S. v. Osborn, 10 IBLA 23, 25 (1972).
20. U.S. v. Prowel, 52 IBLA 256 (1981).
21. Melluzzo v. Morton, 534 F.2d 704, 707 (9th Cir. (1984).
22. Dredge corp. v. Conn., 733 F.2d 704, 707 (9th Cir. 1984).
23. U.S. v. Gibb, 13 IBLA 382, 393 (1973).
24. Id.
25. U.S. v. Melluzzo (Supp. on Judicial Remand), 32 IBLA 51.
26. Melluzzo v. Morton, supra at 864.
27. Oneida Perlite, 57, IBLA 167 (1981).
28. U.S. v. Penrose, 10 IBLA 332, 334 (1973).
29. U.S. v. Johnson, 100 IBLA 322, 338 (1987).
30. Rawls v. U.S., 566 F.2d 1373 (1978).
31. U.S. v. Melluzzo, 105 IBLA 252, 258 (1988).

COMMON AND UNCOMMON VARIETIES

Statutory Authority for Common Variety Minerals

Section 601 of Title 30 of the United States Code authorizes the Secretary of the Interior to sell "common varieties" of "sand, stone, gravel, pumice, pumicite, cinders and clay." On July 23, 1955, Public Law 167 (30 U.S.C. 611) was passed to, among other things, prohibit further location of common variety minerals. The Act stated in part:

> No deposit of common varieties of sand, stone, gravel, pumice, pumicite, or cinders and no deposit of petrified wood shall be deemed a valuable mineral deposit within the meaning of the mining laws of the United States so as to give effective validity to any mining claim hereafter located under such mining laws.

However, the Act went on to provide for an exception to "uncommon variety" minerals at 30 U.S.C. 611:

> "Common varieties" as used in sections 601, 603, and 611 to 615 of this title does not include deposits of such materials which are valuable because the deposit has some property giving it distinct and special value and does not include so-called "block pumice" which occurs in nature in pieces having one dimension of two inches or more.

Therefore, the statute clearly implies that "uncommon varieties" of such materials exist and are still locatable under the mining law. Uncommon varieties are "valuable because the deposit has some property giving it distinct and special value..."

The remainder of this chapter is primarily devoted to what the Federal Courts and Interior Department have interpreted the phrase "property giving it distinct and special value" to mean so as to provide a basis for determining under what circumstances a deposit of "sand, stone, gravel, pumice, pumicite or cinders" may be located.

The Interior Department has attempted, with little success, to define "common varieties" by regulation (43 CFR 3711.1(b)):

> "Common varieties" includes deposits which, although they may have value for use in trade, manufacture, the sciences, or in the mechanical or ornamental arts, do not possess a distinct, special economic value for such use over and above the normal uses of the general run of such deposits. Mineral materials which occur commonly shall not be deemed to be "common varieties" if a particular deposit has distinct and special properties making it commercially valuable for use in a manufacturing, industrial, or processing operation. In the determination of commercial value, such factors may be considered as quality and quantity of the deposit, geographical location, proximity to market or point to utilization, accessibility to transportation, requirements for reasonable reserves consistent with usual industry practices to serve existing or proposed manufacturing, industrial, or processing facilities, and feasible methods for mining and removal

of the material. Limestone suitable for use in the production of cement, metallurgical or chemical grade limestone, gypsum, and the like are not "common varieties."

Stone Versus Mineral or Element

Because common varieties of sand, stone, gravel, pumice, pumicite or cinders generally consist of an aggregate of two or more elements and (or) minerals, the properties of each are not particularly significant. It is important to note that in this context we are talking about minerals in the "scientific" sense rather than the "legal" or "economic" sense. In fact, it is quite uncommon for minerals to be used in the scientific sense in any Interior or court decision. However in **U.S. v. Pierce**, 75 I.D. 270 (1968) as well as several other Interior decisions, the Board of Land Appeals did use the term "mineral" as a geologist would.

Scientific definitions are generally concerned with the origin and the chemical and physical properties of a substance rather than with economic and legal considerations. Stone is a general term for rock used in construction. A rock (or stone) is defined as an aggregate of one or more minerals. Examples of stones are limestone, shale, sandstone, granite, basalt, slate, gneiss and schist. These rocks or stones are composed of minerals or elements. A "mineral" is defined by the **Glossary of Geology**, published by the American Geological Institute as follows:

> A **mineral** is a naturally occurring inorganic element or compound having an orderly internal structure and characteristic chemical composition, crystal form, and physical properties.

As an example of how the Board of Land Appeals made a distinction between "stone" and "mineral" in the **Pierce** case, let us use the example of granite (a stone) which is composed of the minerals quartz, feldspar and mica. Suppose that granite is mined for feldspar, one of the component minerals, to be used for a particular purpose that requires the physical and (or) chemical properties of the mineral feldspar. In such a case we do not have a have a common variety situation because feldspar is a mineral like gold. However, if the granite were mined and used as a stone for some purpose such as veneer building stone, then we would have a common variety case.

In general, if the rock is valuable for only an individual mineral or element such as gold, silver feldspar, mica, etc., it is not a common variety question and 30 U.S.C. 611 does not apply; however, if the entire rock is used and the constituent elements or minerals are relatively unimportant, then 30 U.S.C. 611 may apply.

Prior to July 23, 1955 "Specification Material" Was Locatable

Certain mineral products have never been regarded as subject to location under the mining laws even though they might be marketable at a profit. Among these nonlocatable mineral are those used for fill, grade, ballast and subbase.[1] However, prior to the Act of July 23, 1955, an exception to the general rule was applied for certain types of ballast and base for roadbeds which conformed to engineering specifications for such use. Prior to the passage of the Act of July 23, 1955, "specification material" was regarded as locatable on the ground that inferior grades would not suffice.[2] However, even where material was previously regarded as locatable because it met engineering standards for "compaction, hardness, soundness, stability, favorable gradation," etc., in road building and similar work, such materials have been treated as common varieties and were not locatable after passage of the Act of July 23, 1955. The reason for this is materials which meet the standard are of widespread occurrence.[3]

Guidelines to Distinguish between Common And Uncommon Varieties

In **McClarty v. Secretary of the Interior**, 408 F.2d 907, 908 (9th Cir. 1969), the Court set standards to distinguish between common varieties and uncommon varieties:

1. there must be a comparison of the mineral deposit in question with other deposits of such minerals generally;

2. the mineral deposit in question must have a unique property;

3. the unique property must give the deposit a distinct and special value;

4. if the special value is for uses to which ordinary varieties of the mineral are put, the deposit must have some distinct and special value for such use; and

5. the distinct and special value must be reflected by the higher price which the material commands in the market place (or by reduced cost or overhead so that the profit to the claimant would be substantially more).

Lower Overhead and Greater Profits

In **McClarty v. Secretary of the Interior**, the Court also suggested that the distinct and special value of a stone may not be measurable by a comparison with the price of other building stones, and that the unique property of the deposit might allow lower costs of mining and thus greater profits.

Immense Quantities Indicate Common Variety

In the **Coleman** case,[4] the United States Supreme Court said "we believe that the Secretary of the Interior was...correct in ruling that "in view of the immense quantities of identical stone found in the area outside the claims, the stone must be considered a common variety."

Comparison With All Deposits Rather Than Uncommon Varieties

The Interior Board of Land Appeals[5] has held that the comparison of the deposit of stone in question may be with all deposits, or limited to similar deposits. The Board held that the comparison should be with all deposits generally if (1) the deposit is marketable for purposes which are not typical of common variety minerals, and (2) the material is not widespread.

Unique Property Based on Comparison with Deposits Nationwide

In **United States v. Henri (On Judicial Remand)**, 104 IBLA 93 (1988), the Board of Land Appeals indicated that the "unique property" giving stone a distinct and special value is based on a national comparison rather than a local comparison. The testimony in **Henri** suggested that although the stone may be unique in Anchorage and Juneau, it is "very mediocre" if compared to other deposits in the western United States.

Comparison with Other Minerals on Per Unit Basis

Materials must be compared on a per unit basis rather than on volume or quantity of material sold. As the Interior Board of Land Appeals said[6] "if a comparison of the value of materials were not based on a "per unit" basis, then it might be said that coal could be considered more valuable than gold based upon the respective volumes produced and sold."

Unique Properties Distinguished from High Quality Material

Even though the material on a claim is of a better quality than other material found generally in the area, the fact that deposits may have characteristics superior to those of other deposits does not make them an uncommon variety so long as they are used only for the same purposes as other deposits which are widely and readily available. Of course it is assumed that the superior characteristics do not give the deposit a special and distinct value.[7]

Mineral with Readily Available Substitute

A mineral is not unique if there is a readily available substitute. Where there is such a substitute, the particular property which makes the mineral under review more desirable for that purpose cannot be considered unique.[8]

Stone with Market Value but No Unique Property

In **United States v. Henri (On Judicial Remand)**, 104 IBLA 93, 98 (1988), the claimant contended that a micaceous quartzite on his claims was an uncommon variety. The stone easily split along cleavage surfaces so as to make flat-surfaced plates suitable for building stone. The BLM mineral examiner gave testimony asserting that the building stone on the contested claims compared unfavorably with stone in other areas that he had determined to be uncommon varieties. The claimants offered testimony that with respect to cleavability and coloration, the quartzite was unique in the anchorage and Juneau areas.

In conclusion the Board held that while "the deposit of phyllite and quartzite located on the claims clearly has market value as a building stone, we are unable to conclude the stone has a unique property giving it a distinct and special value for use as a building stone which is reflected in either a higher price for the stone or a reduced cost to develop the deposit." The Board gave the following reason for holding that the stone lacked a unique property:

1. Although the stone has good cleavage giving it flat surfaces desirable for masonry work, it was not unique among building stone deposits.

2. When compared with uncommon varieties of veneer building stone, the size diameter of the plates is too small and the spacing of the cleavage caused the plates to be too thick.

3. The coloration of the stone did not continue to depth.

Intrinsic Factors Distinguished from Extrinsic Factors

The Interior Board of Land Appeals has held in a number of cases that unique properties which give a deposit a distinct and special value must be inherent in the deposit. Extrinsic factors such as scarcity,[9] proximity to market,[10] value added by manufacture,[11] availability of water[12] and other external factors unrelated to the deposit itself are not counted towards giving a deposit a distinct and special value.

Transportation Costs

In determining whether a deposit has a distinct and special value for use as a building stone, you cannot give a stone a competitive advantage because shipping costs are less. In other words when comparing the sales price of stone in the market place, you must subtract out transportation costs.

Amount of Profit for Uncommon Variety

In **McClarty v. Secretary of the Interior**, supra, the Court held that for material to be uncommon, the "profit to the claimant would be substantially more."

Gold or Other Locatable Minerals with Common Variety Minerals

The question of whether gold can be claimed if it is contained in common variety material such as sand and gravel was addressed by section 3 of the Act of July 23, !955, which provides as follows:

> That nothing herein shall affect the validity of any mining location based upon discovery of some other mineral occurring in or in association with such a deposit (of a common variety of sand, stone, etc.).

This provision refers to the discovery of some locatable mineral such as gold occurring in a deposit of a common variety sand and gravel. Congress did not intend that the presence of any gold within such a deposit would validate the claim, but that there must be a discovery of the gold within the meaning of the mining laws. The fact that a mineral such as gold occurred in a nonlocatable deposit of sand and gravel would not invalidate the claim if it were otherwise valid because of the discovery of gold under this standard. However, likewise, the value of the sand and gravel would not be considered in evaluating the value of the gold to determine if there was a valuable deposit of the gold.[12]

Here is an example of how cost reduction might effect validity of a claim. Rather than moving and reclaiming sand and gravel, a placer gold operator gives the sand and gravel to a party who transports it from the property and uses it for land fill. The operation would properly be examined in a value determination by calculating the transportation and reclamation costs of the common variety product as a proper cost of the operation.

Aggregation of Profits from Sales of Common and Uncommon Varieties

In many cases a claim may contain deposits of both common and uncommon variety minerals. For example, a claim may embrace layers of very pure metallurgical-grade limestone which are interbedded with layers that are not as pure and do not qualify as metallurgical grade. If the claimant should by necessity mine both grades and sell the lower-grade limestone for some common variety use, he cannot include profits from the sale with profits derived from sale of the metallurgical-grade limestone to show marketability for the claim.[13] Another example of this might be a limestone deposit with more than 95 percent total carbonate used for portland cement which is interbedded with a less pure limestone that could be sold as fill or road material (common variety uses).[14] Deposits of uncommon variety minerals must be profitable entirely on the basis of sales of the locatable minerals. You must treat the common variety limestone as waste with no value, even if it must be mined in order to extract the uncommon variety deposit.[15]

Uncommon Varieties Sold at Common Variety Prices or for Common Uses

Another problem is for uncommon varieties to be sold at common variety prices, or an uncommon variety stone is sold for a common variety use and as a result does not command a premium price.[16] Income from such sales should be disregarded when projecting profitability. If mining costs are reduced as a result of sales or disposal of common variety materials or uncommon varieties used for common variety purposes, the reduced costs should also be disregarded when projecting profitability.

Removal of Common Varieties Is Trespass

The sale or disposal of common variety minerals (or uncommon variety minerals sold for common variety uses or at common variety prices) is an act of trespass. Common variety materials may only be sold under the authority of a material sale contract.

References - Common and Uncommon Varieties

1. U.S. v. Wirz, 89 IBLA 350, 358 (1985).
2. U.S. v. Bienick, 14 IBLA 290, 298.
3. U.S. v. Wirz, supra at 358.
4. U.S. v. Coleman, 390 U.S. 600, 603-04 (1968).
5. U.S. v. Kaycee Bentonite Corp., 64 IBLA 186, 207-09 (1982).
6. U.S. v. McClarty, 17 IBLA 20, 46 (1974).
7. U.S. v. Guzman, 81 I.D. 685 (1974); U.S. v. Harenberg, 9 IBLA 77 (1973).
8. U.S. v. Thomas, 90 IBLA 225 (1986).
9. U.S. v. Melluzzo, 76 I.D. 320 (1968).
10. U.S. v. Smith, 66 IBLA 182, 188 (1982).
11. U.S. v. California Soylaid Products, Inc., 5 IBLA 192 (1972).
12. U.S. v. Basich, A-30017 (Sept. 23, 1964).
13. U.S. v. Pfizer, 76 I.D. 331, 348-49 (1969).
14. U.S. v. Foresyth et al, 100 IBLA 185, 241 (1987).
15. U.S. v. Lease, 6 IBLA 19, 25-26 (1972); U.S. v. Mansfield, 35 IBLA 95 (1978).
16. U.S. v. Foresyth et al., 100 IBLA 185, 247 (1987).
17. Id.

COMMON AND UNCOMMON VARIETIES: SPECIFIC COMMODITIES

Locatable Grades of Limestone

A regulatory definition of "common varieties" given in the previous chapter provides, with respect to limestone, that, "Limestone suitable for use in the manufacture of cement, metallurgical or chemical grade limestone, gypsum, and the like are not 'common varieties.'"[1]

The Interior Board of Land Appeals[2] has held that limestone must contain 95 percent or more calcium and magnesium carbonates for it to be locatable as either a chemical grade, metallurgical grade, or of a grade suitable for the production of cement. In other words, limestone used in the manufacture of cement is an uncommon variety providing it has a purity 95 percent or more of calcium and magnesium carbonates.

Limestone Used As Concrete Aggregate or Soil Additives

Limestone deposits cannot be located after July 23, 1955 for use as concrete aggregate or soil additives (fertilizer). **U.S. v. Alaska Limestone Corp.**, 66 IBLA 316, 324 (1982).

Sand and Gravel Deposits

Sand and gravel used as fill, subbase or ballast have never been locatable.[3] The Department has consistently held that sand and gravel deposits suitable for road base, asphalt-mix and concrete aggregate without expensive processing have not been locatable since July 23, 1955.[4]

The McCormick Case: An Uncommon Variety Sand and Gravel

In **U.S. McCormick**, 27 IBLA 65 (1976), the Board held that the sand and gravel deposit in question was an uncommon variety. This is one of the very few sand and gravel deposits to ever qualify as an uncommon variety, and is an important example of the type of properties and/or uses that make such a mineral locatable even after July 23, 1955. The evidence established the following special characteristics of the deposit which translate directly into special and substantial economic values:

1. No drilling, blasting or ripping is required

2. No primary crushing to reduce the rock is required.

3. Three of the four purchasers testified that no secondary crushing was required.

4. There is little or no overburden.

5. The material is naturally sorted by type; no sorting or classification is required beyond screening to eliminate oversize.

6. The waste factor is very much lower than at other area pits.

7. The material is naturally clean, requiring no washing.

8. No blending of fine or coarse aggregates is necessary to meet specifications.

9. Because the material is significantly lighter in weight than competing aggregates, a ton of the subject material will cover a 20 percent greater area.

10. The material can be used without the addition of expensive lime or commercial anti-stripping agents.

Not only is there a substantial economic advantage to the producer resulting from reduced costs of production, the material also sells at a royalty range of $ 0.15 to 0.26 per cubic yard, whereas the average royalty from other pits in the area is $ 0.10 per cubic yard.

Building Stone Properties

The Interior Board of Land Appeals has held that certain specific properties do not give stone a distinct and special value and would not qualify the stone as an uncommon variety:

1. Deposits large in size and uniform in quality

2. Building stone that with high degree of hardness and resistance to weathering.[5]

3. Coloration is not a unique property.[6] As the Board has said the "beauty of coloration is inherently subjective. One type of coloration from among the infinite variety of nature may appeal to some persons and this coloration may in fact be unusual. However, the fact that one deposit of a material may bear this coloration does not make it unique, as there are often deposits which will do the same job to the full satisfaction of other persons."[7]

4. Good cleavage and flat surfaces are not unique features unless the development of each is exceptional.[8]

5. Each deposit of stone may have unique properties but is not necessarily locatable. It is a widely-accepted truism that nature does not duplicate exactly, i.e., that there are no two identical snowflakes, fingerprints, trees, mountains, etc. Each product of nature may be expected to have some distinct feature or unique characteristic which will distinguish it from others of its kind, and perhaps either enhance its value or render it worthless.[9]

Gem Stones and Gem Minerals

Gem stones such as jasper, opal, obsidian, etc., must be uncommon varieties in order to be locatable; otherwise they would be salable. However gem minerals such as garnets, quartz, topaz, diamonds, beryl (emerald), corundum (ruby & sapphire), mineral specimens, etc., are locatable just like gold and silver and are not subject to the common varieties section of the law (30 U.S.C. 611).

Obsidian Is a Common Variety Mineral

The Interior Board of Land Appeals has determined that the ability of obsidian to take a polish does not make it an uncommon variety.[10] The Board held that obsidian is a common variety mineral because it exists "in almost limitless quantities."

Geodes Are Uncommon Variety Minerals

Geodes are an uncommon variety mineral and should not be compared with other geode deposits but instead should be compared with other stone formations. In **U.S. v. Bolinder**, 28 IBLA 192 (1976), the Board concluded that "deposits of geodes and geodes themselves, have unique properties which give them a special and distinct value. The fact that the geodes may be similar to geodes from other areas which have similar properties and values is not sufficient alone to establish that the deposit of geodes is a common variety of stone within the meaning of the Act of July 23, 1955.

Gemstone Permits Do Not Apply Towards Validity

The mining laws do not authorize the sale of permits to take or enjoy gemstones; and any such sales would not be considered in determining the validity of a claim.[11] In a case involving agate claims the Board indicated that marketing permits rather than minerals is not a mining operation as contemplated by the general mining laws, and the income from its operation could not properly be considered in determining validity.[12]

Value of Gemstones as Found on Claims Rather Than Enhanced Value

Even though many stones will take a polish and have an enhanced value because of it, it is the value of the stone deposit as it is found on the claims that is the important fact. In other words if a gemstone such as jasper is to be an uncommon variety, it is the value of the stone in its uncut or unpolished state that must be compared with other stone formations.

Cinders to Make Cement Blocks

A volcanic cinder deposit used in the manufacture of cement blocks is a common variety mineral. The fact that a deposit has qualities which are particularly well-suited to this purpose does not alter its essential character as common cement block material.

Soil Amendments

It was held in **U.S. v. Bunkowski**, 79 I.D. 43 (1972) that when a mineral is used as a soil amendment, it must cause a chemical change to the soil rather than a physical change. An obvious exception to this rule is limestone. Limestone, a sedimentary rock composed of more than 50 percent by weight of calcium carbonate, is exposed over thousands of square mile on the public lands. Calcium carbonate is highly reactive with any acidic soil so even a low-purity limestone would cause a chemical reaction to many soils. See **U.S. v. Alaska Limestone Corp.**, supra.

References - Common and Uncommon Varieties: Specific Commodities

1. 43 CFR 3711.1(b).
2. U.S. v. Foresyth, 100 IBLA 185, 242 (1987); U.S. v. Chas. Pfizer & Co. Inc., 76 I.D. 331 (1969).
3. U.S. v. Osborn (Supp. on Judicial Remand), 28 IBLA 13 (1976); U.S. v. Harenberg, 11 IBLA 158 (1973).
4. U.S. v. Ramstad, A-30351 (Sept. 24, 1965); U.S. v. Guzman, 81 I.D. 685, 692 (1974).
5. U.S. v. Kincanon, 13 IBLA 165, 171 (1981).
6. U.S. v. Thomas, 90 IBLA 225 (1986).
7. U.S. v. Dunbar Stone Co., 56 IBLA 61, 64-67 (1981).
8. U.S. v. Henri (On Judicial Remand), 104 IBLA 93, 98 (1988).
9. U.S. v. Dunbar Stone Co., supra.
10. U.S. v. Mansfield, 35 IBLA 95 (1978).
11. U.S. v. Stevens, 14 IBLA 380 (1973).
12. Id.
13. Id.
14. U.S. v. Harenberg, 9 IBLA 77 (1973).

CLAYS AND RELATED MINERALS

Introduction

Historically clays have been considered by the Department to be a mineral that was never locatable, even before the Act of July 23, 1955.[1] However, in several Interior decisions, there is recognition that certain clay deposits with special characteristics and special uses may be locatable.[2] The most comprehensive decision concerning the locatability of clay is undoubtedly **U.S. v. Peck**, 84 I.D. 137 (1977). Of particular significance in **Peck** is the Board's distinction between common" or "ordinary" clay, which has not been considered a "valuable mineral deposit," and deposits of clays having exceptional qualities useful for purposes for which common clays cannot be used. "Common clay" deposits are salable and not locatable; whereas, "exceptional clay" deposits are locatable.

Common Clay

In referring to "common clay" which is not locatable under the mining laws, the precedents demonstrate that clay used only for structural brick, tile, and other heavy clay products, and pressed or face brick, falls within that classification. They also demonstrate that clay deposits useful only for pottery, earthenware, or stoneware which cannot meet the refractory and other quality standards for high-grade ceramic products, such as china, come within that classification.

Exceptional Clay

The exceptional qualities that have been recognized as taking a deposit outside the classification of a common or ordinary clay within the meaning of the mining laws are, as mentioned, clays having a sufficiently high refractoriness to meet the standards for products requiring such special qualities. In addition, certain clays with special characteristics making them useful for particular uses, such as in the oil and oil well drilling industries, outside the manufacture of general clay-products, have been considered locatable.

Clay Not Locatable Even If It Meets New Specifications

The fact that a given clay deposit may meet the particular specifications of a large brick and tile manufacturer, whereas many other available deposits would not meet those specifications, does not make the clay exceptional or locatable.[3] Neither does the fact that a particular deposit may be of a better quality for the manufacture of certain other clay products than other widespread clay deposits make it locatable.[4]

The Kaycee Bentonite Case

In **U.S. v. Kaycee Bentonite Corp.**, 64 IBLA 186 (1982), the Board upheld a decision declaring five mining claims null and void and 125 mining claims valid because the claims contain deposits of exceptional clay. The Board held that if a claimant can establish that a deposit of bentonite is marketable for purposes for which common clay cannot be used, the deposit is locatable. Bentonite, the "exceptional clay" in this case is used as a binder in pelletizing taconite. Approximately eighty percent of the steel produced in the United States is made from pellets of taconite.

Between 1946 and 1969, the BLM issued mineral patents for 76,237 acres containing bentonite. In many cases, the only test of locatability was the "taste test." However, as early as 1961 many managers in BLM began to question the locatability of bentonite.

Two-Fold Test to Determine if Zeolites and Other Minerals Are Locatable or Leasable

In **U.S. v. Union Carbide Corp.**, 84 I.D. 310 (1977), the Board considered the question of whether a deposit of zeolites is locatable under the general mining laws or is subject to leasing under the provisions of the Mineral Leasing Act of 1920. The Board held in this case that the particular zeolite deposit in question is locatable; however, another deposit of zeolites with a different composition might conceivably be leasable. The Board gave a two-fold test to determine whether or not a deposit is locatable or leasable. A mineral is leasable if (1) the sodium must be present in sufficient quantity so as to be commercially valuable; and (2) if the presence of sodium or any other material listed in the Mineral Leasing Acts is essential to the existence of the mineral. The significance of the two-fold test is that it can be applied to any mineral that contains "chlorides, sulphates, carbonates, borates, silicates or nitrates of sodium..." (30 U.S.C. 261) to determine if it is locatable or leasable.

References - Clays and Related Minerals

1. Alldritt v. Northern Pacific R.R. Co., 25 L.D. 349 (1897); Holman v. State of Utah, 41 L.D. 314 (1912); Bettomcourt v. Fitzgerald, 40 L.D. 620 (1912); U.S. v. Shannon, 70 I.D. 136 (1963; and U.S. v. O'Callaghan, 8 IBLA 324, 79 I.D. 689 (1972).
2. Fred B. Ortman, 52 L.D. 467, 469 (1928); U.S. v. Bargrover (On Rehearing), 57 I.D. 533, 534 (1942); U.S. v. Gunn, 79 I.D. 588 (1972); U.S. v. Mattey, 67 I.D. 63 (1960).
3. U.S. v. Peck, 84 I.D. 137 (1977).
4. Id.

GEOLOGICAL INFERENCE

Geological Inference to Determine Mineral In Character But Not Discovery

It is well established that geological inference may be used to support a classification of land as "mineral in character" but may not be used to support the existence of a discovery. The reason for this is that a discovery requires actual physical exposure of a mineral deposit within the claim boundaries; whereas, mineral in character may be established by geological inference.[1]

Definition of "Geological Inference"

"Geological inference" of a valuable mineral deposit involves making certain assumptions about a mineral deposit on the basis of geological evidence which may be any level of evidence short of actual physical exposure. Such evidence may include surface indications of minerals, favorable geological environment such as rock types and structures conducive to mineralization, geochemical or geophysical evidence and discoveries in nearby lands. The Board of Land Appeals[2] has said that geological inference is no more than the opinion of a geologist inferred or deduced from known and observed geological evidence.

Geophysical, Geochemical Testing and Geological Mapping

An assumption of mineralization inferred from the results of geological mapping and geophysical and geochemical testing invites further exploration, but is not sufficient to show a discovery of a valuable mineral deposit. Geophysical and geochemical evidence will allow a geological inference that unexposed mineralization exists below the surface and such geological inferences may at best indicate that further exploration is necessary and a discovery has not been established.[3]

Radiometric Measurements Versus Chemical Assays

Radiometric measurements may be used as supporting geological inferences in evaluating a deposit but, alone, they cannot be accepted to prove the existence of a uranium deposit. A sample taken from an exposure of mineralization and chemical assays of the sample may be given greater weight to prove the existence or nonexistence of a valuable uranium ore deposit than radiometric probe measurements of gamma ray emissions.[4]

Evidence of Geological Inference Alone Will Not Validate a Claim

Even though mining claims may be within a favorable geological environment and are adjacent to claims once successfully mined, such evidence will not establish the validity of the claims. There must be a physical exposure of the ore body.[5]

Use of Geologic Inference to Show Discovery

Although geologic inference cannot be relied upon to establish the existence of a mineral deposit, it may be used as evidence to the extent of a deposit.[6] In **U.S. v. Feezor**, 90 I.D. 262 (1983), the Board significantly expanded the use of geologic inference in determining the necessary reserves or quantity of ore necessary to establish the existence of a discovery. The Board held that "to the extent exposures and samples exist which show high values of relative consistency, geologic inference is properly used to determine the reasonable likelihood of the persistence of similar mineralization beyond the areas actually sampled or exposed."

In **Feezor** it was pointed out that "geologic inference is primarily applicable as a basis upon which to show continuity of values" and that isolated and erratic high values cannot be used to infer the existence of better values someplace else on the claim. The Board then held that "where values have been high and relatively consistent, geologic inference can be used to infer sufficient quantity of similar quality mineralization beyond the actual exposed areas, such that a prudent man would be justified in expending labor and means with a reasonable prospect of success in developing a paying mine."

In **Feezor**, the Board examined the type of reserves necessary to support a discovery using definitions given in Principles of Mineral Resources Classification, **Geological Survey Bulletin 1450-A** at A3-A4 are as follows:

Measured - Reserves or resources for which tonnage is computed from dimensions revealed in outcrops, trenches, workings, and drill holes and for which the grade is computed from the results of detailed sampling. The sites for inspection, sampling and measurement are spaced so closely and the geologic character is well defined that size, shape, and mineral content are well established. The computed tonnage and grade are judged to be accurate within limits which are stated, and no such limit is judged to be different from the computed tonnage or grade by more than 20 percent.

Indicated - Reserves or resources for which tonnage and grade are computed partly from specific measurements, samples, or production data and partly from projection for a reasonable distance on geologic evidence. The sites available for inspection, measurement, and sampling are too widely or otherwise inappropriately spaced to permit the mineral bodies to be outlined completely or the grade established throughout.

Demonstrated - A collective term for the sum of measured and indicated reserves or resources.

Inferred - Reserves or resources for which quantitative estimates are based largely on broad knowledge of the geologic character of the deposit and for which there are few, if any, samples or measurements. The estimates are based on an assumed continuity or repetition, of which there is geologic evidence; this evidence may include comparison with deposits of similar type. Bodies that are completely concealed may be included if there is specific geologic evidence of their presence. Estimates of inferred reserves or resources should include a statement of specific limits within which the inferred material may lie.

In **Feezor** the Board held that not only can demonstrated reserves be used to show the quantity of ore necessary to show a discovery, but under certain circumstances "inferred" reserves may also be used to show a discovery. These conditions are given below:

As noted above demonstrated reserves (i.e., measured and indicated) can clearly be used to show the quantity necessary to establish a discovery. We do not, however, believe that any such broad ruling can be made insofar as inferred reserves are concerned. To the extent that such an estimate is based on assumed continuity or repetition for which there is geologic evidence, we feel such a reserve base can properly be considered. Where, however, a body is completely concealed, so that its actual existence must be predicated on geologic inference, use of geologic inference would, in effect, substitute for the exposure of the mineral. Such an exposure, however, is a necessary precondition to a discovery. Therefore, an "inferred" reserve whose existence is dependent solely on geologic inference cannot serve as a predicate for finding quantity and quality sufficient to support a discovery.

Case Where Geological Inference Cannot Be Applied

The **New York Mines**, 105 IBLA 171 (1988) case involved a mined out supergene mineral deposit. This type of deposit occurs below an oxide zone where the minerals are leached by ground water and redeposited at the water table in the zone of supergene enrichment. Below the zone of supergene enrichment is a much lower grade deposit of primary mineralization. This is the lower portion of the deposit.

The Board of Land Appeals held that in the face of such strong evidence that past production came from a zone of supergene enrichment, it would not be prudent to project the size or grade of the ore previously mined to the underlying mineral deposit, where exposures in that deposit show it to be composed of primary mineralization. In other words the facts in this case do not support the downward projection or ore-grade deposits below the water table using geological inference.

References - Geological Inference

1. U.S. v. Hines Gilbert Gold Mines Company, 1 IBLA 296 (1971); U.S. v. Carbon County Land Co., 46 F. 980 (1931), aff'd 284 U.S. 534 (1932).
2. U.S. v. Lundy, A-30724 (June 30, 1967).
3. U.S. v. New Park Mining Co., A-28530 (January 25, 1961).
4. U.S. v. Rigg, 16 IBLA 385 (1974).
5. U.S. v. Milisich, A-30720 (April 13, 1967).
6. U.S. v. Dresselhaus, 81 IBLA 252, 265 (1984).

MINERAL EXAMINATIONS

Objectives of the Examination

The mineral examiner's field examination represents the first step in the validity determination. The validity determination, as far as the mineral examiner is concerned, is a mineral property evaluation or feasibility study to determine if a mineral deposit has a reasonable prospect of sustaining a profitable mining operation. The mineral examiner conducts the study somewhat similar to the way a mining company might make an evaluation of the property, utilizing modern geologic and engineering principles and procedures. Of course, the mineral examiner is not allowed to drill or excavate so as to uncover the deposit as this is considered exploration.

In the case of a validity determination, if the mineral examiner verifies that a discovery exists within the boundary lines of the mining claim, the claimant retains full possessory title; and, in the case of a patent examination, if all other aspects of the case are in order, a patent will issue. However, if the mineral examiner should determine that a discovery does not exist within the limits of the mining claim, contest proceedings are initiated with subsequent Departmental hearings.

Scope of the Examination

The law does not require the Government to make an exhaustive study of the mineral deposit; the law merely requires that the examiner verify and sample the discovery.[1] If a mining claimant charges the Government with failure to examine a particular working, it is incumbent upon the claimant to produce evidence that mineralization of significant value has been exposed at that location.[2]

Notification of Claimant

Although it has long been the policy of the Forest Service and BLM to notify a claimant of a pending field examination, failure to make such notification does not disqualify the Government's evidence. The purpose of the notification is to provide the claimant with an opportunity to show the mineral examiner certain aspects of the deposit that might benefit the claimant, particularly the discovery points that should be sampled. At the same time the claimant has an opportunity to observe the examination procedure in order to verify that the examination is properly conducted.[3]

Refusal to Allow Examination

A mining claimant has no right to prevent the Government mineral examiner from inspecting a claim. The lands within a mining claim are Federal lands unless and until they are patented, and the Government retains the legal title and the right to enter these lands at any time without a search warrant.[4] If a claimant fails to keep his discovery points open and safely available for sampling by the Government's examiner, or declines to accompany the examiner on the claim, he assumes the risk that the Government examiner will be unable to verify the alleged discovery of a valuable mineral deposit.[5]

Placer Claims Open to Bedrock

Although many placer claim owners recognize that the highest values are generally found near bedrock, they are not aware that if the examiner is to sample the best values at bedrock, the placer deposit must be open by trenching or some other method to allow access to the examiner and physically expose the discovery. The IBLA decisions indicate that digging to a depth of four or five feet would involve discovery work that is the responsibility of the claimant. In other words, the requirement for physical exposure means that all overburden or cover must be removed.

The principle of physical exposure also applies to deposits in inaccessible river bottom. In one case the Board of Land Appeals upheld the samples taken by an examiner along a streambank even though the claimant contended the values were in the river bed.

Handbook for Mineral Examiners

The **Handbook for Mineral Examiners** used by mineral examiners in the Forest Service and the Bureau of Land Management for guidance in conducting validity examinations on unpatented mining claims was extensively revised and published in December of 1984, and was again revised in 1989. The new edition was written by Roger A. Haskins and Eugene Carlat of the Bureau of Land Management and Frederic B. Mullin of the U.S. Forest Service.

Interagency Agreement Between BLM and Park Service

On May 1, 1985, an Interagency Agreement between the Bureau of Land Management and the National Park Service was signed. This agreement formalized the current BLM/NPS working relationship where the validity of mining claims in the National Park System must be determined. All BLM regulations, instructions, manuals and handbooks shall be followed in mining claim examination and preparation of mineral reports. Mineral examiners employed by the Park Service may conduct mineral examinations and prepare mineral reports. However, all such reports must be reviewed and approved by the BLM to see that they are technically correct. In the special case of patent applications, BLM conducts the validity examination and prepares the mineral report with the participation of the Park Service.[6]

Interagency Agreement Between BLM and Forest Service

The Forest Service, Department of Agriculture has no adjudicative authority over locatable minerals in the National Forest System under the 1872 Mining Law. However the Forest Service does have an important role in the management of these minerals. A Memorandum of Understanding, executed by the Forest Service and Bureau of Land Management and effective May 3, 1957 (VI BLM Manual 3.1, Illustration 4, June 21, 1962) provides that the Department of the Interior will give the forum for any proper contest proceedings against unpatented mining claims which the Forest Service may wish to initiate. On the basis of this agreement, the Interior Department has no authority to refuse to initiate a contest challenging the validity of a mining claim located in a national forest, if the elements of a contest are present. Under the Memorandum of Understanding, the Forest Service has the authority to initiate contests, to use Department of Agriculture Attorneys in the prosecution of the case and to use Forest Service employees as mineral examiners and witnesses.

If an unauthorized use of a mining claim is believed to exist, the District Ranger submits a request for a mineral examination to the USFS Regional Office. A Forest Service Mineral examiner, after proper authorization, may go on an unpatented claim to make a mineral investigation. The mineral examiner's findings, conclusions, recommendations, together with pictures and maps, will be compiled in a report and sent to the Regional Office for technical review by the Regional Mineral Examiner. This report will be the basis for a decision on whether or not to contest the claim.

Probability of Validity Examination

Possibly, fewer than several hundred mining claims are examined for validity in any single year. If you consider that there are now more than 1.1 million mining claims recorded with the BLM, it is evident that there is a very low probability that any single claim will be examined - about one chance in 10,000. Most of the claims examined by the government fall into one of two categories: (1) the claim is included in a withdrawn area such as a national park; and (2) the claimant is living on the claim but is not actively mining.

Charge of Lack of Good Faith

Although it is common for the Government to include a charge indicating a claim is not held in good faith, the applicable Interior and Federal court decisions generally require that the evidence for such a charge must be clear and convincing.[7] While the existence of other land values does not qualify a locator's rights under the mining law, if he has a valid claim, evidence of such other values may be considered in assessing the weight and credibility to be accorded the locator's testimony in determining whether a discovery has been made. Evidence of other land values may also be a factor in evaluating his bona fide intention to develop a mining operation.[8] The most prevalent evidence of bad faith occurs when a claimant makes improvements on a claim unrelated to mining.[9]

Validity Examinations in the Park System

Section 6 of the Parks Act, 16 U.S.C. 1905 (1982), requires the Secretary of the Interior to determine the validity of all claims in the National Park System within a certain specified time period. The Board has since held that failure of the Government to complete such validity examinations within the statutory period did not preclude the validity examination at a later date.[10]

Examiners Mistakes

Even though a Government mineral examiner errors in the examination procedure or evaluation, the claimant cannot take advantage of such error. And under certain circumstances the claim will be reexamined.[11]

Qualifications of Examiner

In mining claim contests, the qualifications and competence of a Government examiner to investigate a specific type of mineral deposit are commonly challenged. Because there are hundreds of different types of mineral commodities that any one examiner may be responsible for, it is quite likely that even the most experienced examiner will have experience with only a small percent of the total types. However, even though possessing a lack of specific experience, general education and experience coupled with diligent preparation on the deposit in question are sufficient to qualify an examiner to establish a prima facie case of invalidity.[12] Of course the more relevant the experience, the greater the weight will be given to testimony of the examiner.

In one case[13] a claimant asserted that an examiner had no actual work experience as a gold miner and was therefore not qualified. The Board said that the "mineral examiner had sufficient educational background and work experience to testify about gold placer mining. He had examined mining claims for 14 years, his lack of work experience as a gold placer miner does not detract from his expertness."

In another case[14] the claimant asserted that the Government witnesses who examined the claims failed to follow established guidelines for field examination of mining claims. On this issue the Board said "that such standards are merely general guidelines and do not have the force and effect of statutes or regulations. There is no requirement that such guidelines be followed."

Reports as Evidence

In order for a mineral report to be given much weight as evidence, the author must be available for cross examination by the other side.[15] A mineral report, like any other internal government report, has no independent evidentiary weight until the report is admitted as evidence at a hearing initiated by a contest complaint. The only purpose of a mineral report is to inform the authorized officer as to mineral values so an informed decision can be made on whether or not a contest complaint should issue.

Mineral Examiner May Rely on Statements of Claimant

Where the mineral examiner testifies that a mineral claimant or his representative has stated that certain claims are not supported by a discovery, such testimony, unless impeached in cross-examination, is sufficient to constitute a prima facie case that claims are invalid.[16] Of course it must be emphasized that if the claimant or his representative should later, at a hearing, attempt to contradict the substance of the admission, such admission could not be used to establish a prima facie case.

References - Mineral Examinations

1. U.S. v. Swain, A-30926 (December 30, 1968).
2. Russell v. Peterson, 498 F.Supp. 8 (D.C. Idaho 1980).
3. U.S. v. Grigg, 8 IBLA 331 (1972).
4. U.S. v. Gayanich, 36 IBLA 111, 117 (1978).
5. U.S. v. Knecht, 39 IBLA 8, 11-12 (1979); U.S. v. Russell, 40 IBLA 309 (1979), aff'd sub nom Russell v. Peterson, 498 F.Supp. 8 (1980).
6. Information No. 85-251 (June 10, 1985).
7. U.S. v. Dillman, 36 IBLA 358, 360 (1978); U.S. v. Prowell, 52 IBLA 256 (1981).
8. U.S. v. Osborn (Supp. on Judicial Remand), 28 IBLA 43 (1976).
9. U.S. v. Knecht, supra.
10. U.S. v. Alaska Limestone Corp., 66 IBLA 316, 326 (1982).
11. U.S. v. Bunkowski, 79 I.D. 43, 52 (1972); U.S. v. Vaughn, 56 IBLA 247, 252 (1981).
12. U.S. v. Rouse, 56 IBLA 36, 39 (1981).
13. U.S. v. Harling, 32 IBLA 31 (1977).
14. U.S. v. Zweifel, 11 IBLA 89.
15. U.S. v. Williams, 65 IBLA 346, 350 (1982).
16. U.S. v. Copple, 81 IBLA 109 (1984).

SAMPLING AND ASSAYING

Introduction

The sampling and assaying program represents the most important part of the mineral examination. In many cases the claimant selectively samples the highly mineralized portion of the ore body rather than attempting to take a representative sample which reflects the total amount of rock that must be extracted, including both ore and waste. This variance in sampling procedures among claimants often leads to inconsistent assay values for the same ore body. Such problems may be avoided by (1) conducting the sampling program according to recognized engineering standards, (2) adequately describing the sampling procedure, and (3) having the samples processed by competent assayers.

High Assay Values Are Not Sufficient Evidence

The Department has consistently held that high assay reports alone are not evidence of a discovery. The nature of the samples yielding the high values must be considered and the evidence, taken as a whole, must suggest that the assay results are representative of mineralization on the claims.[1] "Other factors must be considered, such as the extent of the mineral deposit, the number of samples assayed which show only a trace of mineral value, and the nature of the samples which yielded the high values. To be meaningful, the samples must be representative of the entire mineral deposit, not simply selective showings of the best mineralization."[2]

Sampling a Minable Width

The Interior Department has, in several cases,[3] required that samples be cut across a "minable width." This requirement is justified and is a standard practice among experienced geologists, engineers and miners. Even though a vein is one foot wide, it would be impossible in most cases to remove only the vein and leave all of the host or waste rock. The "minable width" merely recognizes that in developing underground workings one must provide sufficient space to allow people and equipment to enter the mine and follow the vein. Although the minimum "minable width" is generally four feet wide, it of course may be more or less depending on the circumstances in an individual case. An assay value adjusted to a minable width does not purport to represent the value of the "ore" to be shipped, but demonstrates the diluent effect a vein of less than a minable width has upon the assay value of the vein material.[4] A vein of less than a minable width affects the value of the mineral deposit in a combination of ways - by increasing mining costs through additional handling of barren country rock, both in sorting of barren rock from the ore and in removing the barren rock to get to the vein; and by diluting the ore with the barren country rock.[5]

Overburden Included

It is a standard procedure in the testing of a placer mining claim to take channel samples from top to bottom of a cut, trench or pit, including overburden; also when taking samples by churn or auger drill it is also a standard procedure to include the overburden. The mineral values are then determined on the basis of the cost of removing all material that must be moved during the mining operation.

Adequate Sample Descriptions

The primary purpose of a sampling program is to determine the average quality (grade or assay value) and quantity (reserves) of a mineral deposit. In order for such a program to yield effective results and have a high probative value in an administrative hearing, the samples must be adequately described. A sample without an adequate description of how it was taken is meaningless for establishing the average quality and estimating the quantity of a mineral deposit.[6] A sample properly cut from a mineral deposit should represent the average value of the deposit along the line of the sample.

Among the items that must be addressed in a sampling program include: (1) description of the mineral deposit and the surrounding host rocks; (2) size and shape of the mineral deposit; (3) mineralogic and structural description of the mineral deposit; (4) weight or volume of the sample; (5) dimensions of sample; and (6) mineralogic and structural description along line of sample.

Sampling and Mining with a Suction Dredge

There have been two recent appeals to the IBLA involving validity examinations by the Forest Service where the claimants method of mining was by suction dredge in the bed of active streams. In **U.S. v. Williams**, 65 IBLA 346 (1982), the Forest Service investigated the validity of a gold placer claim. The claim was contested and a prima facie case was established on the basis of the Government examiner using standard sampling techniques, rather than using a section dredge. The claimant submitted evidence showing a recovery of 26 or 27 ounces of gold using a suction dredge. Because the government did not submit evidence

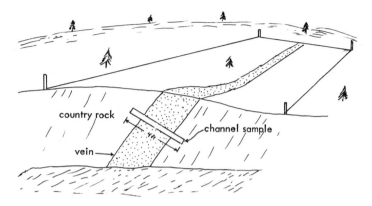

Channel Sample Taken Across Vein for a Minable Width of 4 Feet.

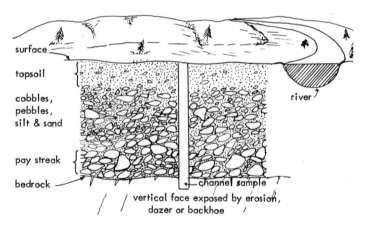

Vertical Channel Sample Cut from Surface to Bedrock Even Though Values Are Concentrated On or Near Bedrock

showing that suction dredging on the claim has not resulted in a discovery, the Board held that the claimant's evidence was sufficient to overcome the Government's prima facie case. The Board determined that the Government's evidence was even more deficient than the claimants because it did not sample using a suction dredge. The Board then stated:

> The record showed that contestees were removing mineral material laid down in the stream bed, concentrating it, and apparently removing enough gold to meet their expenses. The "deposit" consisted of the material laid down in the stream bed by the water. The contestees were removing the material, not the water itself, as Ball testified. The fact that they were mining in an active stream bed did not make the process any less placer mining. Further, the fact that they used a suction dredge (or any other instrumentality) did not make the process any less legitimate, as long as it was economical for them to do so, as measured by the traditional marketability tests.
>
> FS' position that it need not address the economics of suction dredging was evident at the hearing and is now urged upon us as a rule of law. We reject it, and we emphasize that if FS expects to successfully contest the validity of claims such as this one, it must meet its burden of showing, on a case by case basis, that such operations are not economical. It may be necessary for FS to use a suction dredge to take sample tests at the claim in order to so demonstrate.
>
> In any event, FS did not establish that contestees were removing "flood gold." The record contained no evidence that the geological situation described by Wells in his discussion of "flood gold" existed, or that other conditions existed that favored the conclusion that flood gold was being collected. In the absence of evidence of such a showing, we cannot presume that contestees were not actually mining a "river deposit" that had been over-looked because it was within an active stream bed. The record contained evidence showing that no concentrations were present on the banks of the stream, but it did not deal adequately with the stream bed itself. We do not comment on the extent to which such concentrations may exist; we simply hold that it is part of contestant's obligation to address this issue.

However, **Williamson** does not necessarily mean the Government must use the same sampling method as the claimant. If the claimant furnishes evidence that profitable recovery may be made by a method not addressed in the Government's prima facie case, the Government must also provide evidence showing that the new method has not resulted in a discovery.

In **U.S. v. Arbo**, 70 IBLA 244 (1983), the Forest Service Mineral examiner was assigned to conduct a validity examination of a placer property. The examiner noted that the only evidence of recent mining activity appeared to be a small suction dredge in the river. Although the claimant apparently maintained that his discovery was in the bed of the river and requested the examiners to take samples using the dredge, the examiners refused to sample with the dredge. Instead, the examiners selected their own sites for sampling above the river. Asked during the hearing why he did not take samples using the dredge, the examiner replied that he took none because "there was no definable deposit in the river" and based on geologic analysis and inference the examiner gave his opinion that recovery of gold from the river would not be profitable.

The Board concluded that the Government's testimony and exhibits were sufficient to establish a prima facie case of invalidity. The invalidity of the claims was based on the negative results of the sampling rather than the opinion of the Government's witness that the river contained "no definable deposit."

Although the Board did not really address the failure of the mineral examiner to sample the river bottom with the dredge, Judge Harris stated in his concurring opinion:

> It was clear error in the present case for the Government mineral examiner to refuse to sample from appellant's dredge. Appellant's dredge was available. Samples easily could have been taken; however, they were not. I would find that where a mining claimant directs the Government mineral examiner to what the claimant considers as his discovery area, and the examiner refuses to sample, and there is no legitimate basis for that refusal, the Government has not established a prima facie case of lack of discovery of a valuable mineral deposit.

From the standpoint of the mineral examiner, it is very difficult to establish accurate reserve and grade information on a deposit using a suction dredge, particularly if the water is deep, turbulent or murky. However, a suction dredge may be the most appropriate mining method for certain types of river placers, especially it is possible to reach bedrock. If gold should exist in a river bed, the nature of concentration can be diverse. The gold may be concentrated on the surface of the river bed, in one or more layers or paystreaks, disseminated throughout the gravels or concentrated on bedrock. Under the best of circumstances, it is difficult to quantify the reserves and grade of a deposit situated below an active stream or river.

Assayer or Sampler Not at Hearing

Assay reports are generally admitted into evidence even if the reports have major deficiencies; however, the reports will be accorded appropriate weight by the judge or fact finder depending on the circumstances in each case. Normally the assayer is not present at the hearing but the sampler is available to testify. If neither the assayer or sampler are present, the evidentiary value of the report is very low.[7]

Selection of Assayers

Assayers should be selected on the basis of established reputation and registration under state law if required.[8] Many assayers have a poor reputation or no reputation. In most states, there is no requirement at all for an assayer to have any education or experience. For this reason, it is crucial to have a well established and reputable assayer.

Delivery of Samples to Assayer

The procedure for handling samples, from the time they are collected at the outcrop until they are delivered to the assayer is important. In order to maintain the integrity of samples, the sampler is responsible to see that (1) the assay results of one sample will not be confused with the results of another sample, (2) the samples are not damaged, diluted or salted, and (3) the samples are secure at all times and the sampler can fully account for every aspect of the process from sampling to assay.[9]

Grab Samples

Assay reports have limited probative value where there is no evidence as to how and where the samples were taken.[10] The Interior Board of Land Appeals[11] has determined that "grab samples" have little value because (1) they do not represent any attempt to delineate a mineralized zone or ore body, (2) they do not relate to the structure sampled, (3) the location of the sample site has no relevance to the claim or the mineral deposit, and (4) the samples are not representative of a mineral deposit.

Sample Points Must Be Accessible to Mineral Examiner

Minerals are not required to blast or do any extensive discovery work beyond the workings exposed by the claimants in order to satisfy the Government's prima facie burden. It is incumbent upon a mining claimant to keep his discovery points available for inspection by Government mineral examiners. Where he does not, he assumes the risk that the mineral examiner will not be able to verify the discovery of the alleged mineral deposit, and his argument that the samples taken by the examiner are not representative will be rejected.[12]

The claimant has responsibility to keep his workings available for inspection. Accordingly, if the workings are inaccessible because a shaft has caved or is otherwise unsafe, a mineral examiner has no obligation to either imperil himself or retimber the workings.[13] In one case a claimant indicated that his discovery was covered by large boulders and deep water to the extent it was inaccessible.[14] The Board[15] held that since "there was no means of gaining access to the alleged discovery point, this indication was tantamount to an admission that no valuable placer material had been discovered on the claim at the time of these inspections. In

311

these circumstances the mineral examiners were justified in not taking any placer samples, since none could be representative.

Examiners Should Independently Select Sample Sites

Although it is appropriate for a mineral examiner to take a sample at sites recommended by the claimant or the representative of the claimant, examiners should also independently select sample sites in the same manner as they would if unaccompanied by the claimant.[16]

Date of Exposure Versus Date of Sample

In order to establish discovery by a certain date such as a withdrawal, it is essential that the discovery be exposed prior to that date. Then once the discovery is validated by exposure prior to the withdrawal, the sample may be taken at any later time.[17]

Claimant Objects to Government's Sampling Procedure

If a claimant contends that the Government samples his claim improperly, he must be able to offer probative evidence tending to show that the samples taken by the Government failed to adequately represent the mineral value of the land.[18]

Joint Sampling When Discrepancy in Assay Values

In situations where there is a significant discrepancy between the assay values of the Government and the claimant, a joint sampling of the claim may be ordered by the judge to reconcile the conflicting testimony.[19] However, if the claimant fails to submit the requested report in accordance with the hearing examiner's instructions, the claimant's charge, made after issuance of the decision that the Government's mineral examiner failed to sample properly is entitled to no consideration.[20]

Nonstandard Assay Methods

There are numerous methods of assaying minerals; however in most cases there is only one method that is considered most appropriate for a given situation. The Board of Land Appeals[21] has held that a nonstandard method of assay is not entitled to probative weight without a scientific basis. The Board said:

> Finally, we agree with Judge Ratzman's determination that the appellants' expert witness "utilizes unreliable processes, and provides inaccurate information." Appellants' own samples, when tested by the fire assay method failed to show the presence of gold in significant quantities. In apparent explanation of the disparity of results between their fire assays and their nonstandard assays, appellants' expert witness stated that the gold was "clear down in the atoms" of

the associated material. While we do not categorically assert that such pre-Agricolian notions of metallurgy are totally invalid, neither do we believe that such evidence is entitled to probative weight without a showing of its scientific basis.

Fire Assays on Placer Samples

The Department has never accepted fire assays for placer gold samples. The reason for this is that the fire assay will recover more gold than a placer miner would ever recovery by using the most efficient placer mining equipment. It is generally financially prohibitive to smelt the heavy minerals or black sands recovered from a placer gold mining operations. Therefore, a fire assay of a placer sample may result in a higher value than would normally be recovered and could result in the validation of a subeconomic property.[22] In citing BLM Technical Bulletin 4, **Placer Examination: Principles and Practice** by John Wells, Judge Burski said "I think that Government mineral examiners should be put on notice that fire assaying of placer deposits might not, in some future cases, be a sufficient basis upon which to prevail before this Board....In such future cases, it may well be that the assay results obtained through a fire assay will not be accorded the same weight as assay results which are derived from procedures more likely to fairly value placer ground. Against this eventuality, mineral examiners should clearly be on guard."[23]

The preferred method for assaying gold samples is recovery of the free gold by amalgamation.[24] However it is also a standard practice to fire assay the tails to determine if, under any circumstances, it would be worthwhile to recover gold by smelting from the heavy mineral concentrates.

Chemical Assays Given Greater Weight Than Radiometric Measurements of Uranium Ore

Chemical assays of a sample of uranium mineralization may be given greater weight to demonstrate the value of uranium ore than radiometric probe measurements of gamma ray emissions. Radiometric measurements may be used as supporting geological inferences in evaluating a deposit; however, alone, they cannot be accepted to prove the existence of a uranium deposit.[25]

Atomic Absorption Assays Are Recognized Test

Atomic absorption assays have been approved by the Interior Board of Land Appeals[26] as a recognized test for hardrock gold deposits. The Interior Board of Land Appeals has held that "while the atomic absorption method is not as universally accepted in the mining industry as is the standard fire assay, it is, nevertheless, a recognized test of gold content."

Expert Witness Must Have Personal Knowledge of Sampling and Assaying

Testimony regarding the mineral values of ore samples will be held to have no value if the witness has no personal knowledge of the sampling or the testing of the samples.[27]

Assay Values in Old Reports

It is not uncommon for mining claimants to submit assay values mentioned in old reports as evidence that a discovery exists. However, there is seldom sufficient description of such samples to make them useful; furthermore, since publication of the report, the mineral deposit may have been mined out.[28] As the Board says, such reports are not reliable evidence of whether the claims now contain valuable minerals.[29]

Average Grade Calculations Must Be Weighted Average

A report can given little weight where the average grade of a deposit is based on a numeric average. The proper method is to calculate average grade by a weighted average.[30]

References - Sampling and Assaying

1. U.S. v. Lambeth, 37 IBLA 107, 114 (1978).
2. U.S. v. Bechthold, 25 IBLA at 88 (1976); U.S. v. Judd, 68 IBLA 137, 139 (1982).
3. U.S. v. Fitzgerald, A-30973 (July 25, 1969).
4. U.S. v. Crawford, A-30820 (Jan. 29, 1968).
5. U.S. v. Taylor, A-30780 (Oct. 24, 1967).
6. Id.
7. U.S. v. Rukke, 32 IBLA 155 (1977); U.S. v. Burt, 43 IBLA 367, 368 (1979).
8. U.S. v. Gillette, 104 IBLA 269, 275 (1988).
9. U.S. v. Clemans, 45 IBLA 64, 70-71 (1980).
10. U.S. v. Jones, 72 IBLA 52, 57 (1983).
11. U.S. v. Parker, 91 I.D. 271, 282 (1984).
12. U.S. v. Anderson, 57 IBLA 256 (1981); U.S. v. Polashek, 57 IBLA 104 (1981).
13. U.S. v. Copple, 81 IBLA 109, 125 (1984).
14. U.S. v. Cook, 71 IBLA 268 (1983).
15. Id. at 270-71.
16. U.S. v. Rosenberger, 71 IBLA 195 (1983).
17. U.S. v. Page, 43 IBLA 396 (1979).
18. U.S. v. Murdock, 65 IBLA 242, 243 (1982).
19. U.S. v. Signa Lauch, 9 IBLA 66 (1973).
20. U.S. v. King, A-30867 (March 1, 1968).
21. U.S. v. Ramsey, 14 IBLA 156.
22. U.S. v. San Juan Exploration Co., A-30965 (March 27, 1969); U.S. v. Bass, 6 IBLA 113 (1972).
23. U.S. v. Ramsey, 84 IBLA 66, 71-73 (1984).

24. U.S. v. Parker, 91 I.D. 271 (1984); U.S. v. Ramsey, 84 IBLA 66 (1984); U.S. v. Chapman, 87 IBLA 216, 222 (1985).
25. U.S. v. Rigg, 16 IBLA 385 (1974).
26. U.S. v. Pool, 78 IBLA 215, 221-22 (1984).
27. Cactus Mines Limited, 79 IBLA 20, 30 (1984).
28. U.S. v. Vaux, 24 IBLA 289, 299 (1976).
29. U.S. v. Franklin, 99 IBLA 120, 123 (1987).

ECONOMIC ASPECTS
OF VALIDITY

Mining Costs

The costs of extraction, processing and transportation must be considered in determining the validity of a claim. Furthermore, labor and equipment costs must be calculated at a price one would have to pay to hire the work done by others. The purpose of this requirement is to prevent a claimant from appropriating the public land by subsidizing mining operations with his own labor and equipment. Such costs include the amortization cost of the equipment used in the mining operations, even though the claimant by fortuitous circumstance has access to machinery at a cost less than the average prudent person would have to pay.[1] Some of the types of cost factors currently considered in determining the validity of a mining claim under the prudent man rule include:

1. Expected costs of the extraction, beneficiation, and other essential costs of the operation necessary to mine and sell the mineral, including capital and labor costs.[2]

2. Costs to satisfy environmental requirements of Federal, state, and local laws and regulations.[3]

3. Costs such as water supply, additional land, financing must be considered.[4]

4. Quantity of minable mineral on the claims.[5]

5. Average grade or quality of mineral on the claims.[6]

6. Price at which the mineral will be sold, anticipated sales volume, the unit price, the identity and location of prospective purchasers or the cost of delivery to them.[7]

Labor Costs

In numerous cases the Interior Department has held that labor costs must be considered in determining whether a mining operation could be profitable; and furthermore, the value of such labor must be applied in amount that would be sufficient to hire another person. Even in a one man operation, the value of the claimant's labor must be considered in determining whether there has been a discovery of a valuable mineral deposit.[8] In other words, there must be profit left over after the value of the claimant's labor is subtracted from the gross income. The Board of Land Appeals[9] has rejected the argument that a meager yield of income from the claims would constitute a substantial increment to the income of a person living on retirement benefits and would be sufficient to satisfy the amount required to establish a profitable operation.

Basis for Estimating Mining Costs

To satisfy the prudent man test, mining costs may be established by comparison of the estimated costs based on a reliable cost analysis system and by use of a comparison to an operating mine.[10]

What a Prudent Man Might Expect as Mining Costs and Selling Price

It is not necessary for a prudent man to know exactly the cost of producing the product or the exact price he might receive. Rather, based upon a reasonable and rational estimate of the cost of production and a reasonable and rational estimate of the market price for the product, there is a reasonable probability of success in the development of a valuable mine.[11]

Mining Costs Must Be Supported by Specifics

The Board of Land Appeals[12] found that a claimant's profit analysis was of little probative worth because "mining, hauling, and milling costs are unsupported by specifics or realistic cost data. For example, a contract mining cost of $55.25 per ton is posited, but neither the necessary machinery nor man-hours is itemized. Nor is there any mention of other operations which might serve as comparisons."

Earlier Development Costs Not Considered in Determining Validity

Costs associated with developing a deposit should not be considered in determining if an ongoing operation is profitable. Earlier expenses in development of a property such as the cost of constructing cabins, buildings, access roads, purchase of rail and ore cars are not costs that need to be factored into the profitability analysis.[13] However any outstanding debt incurred as a consequence of development work would be considered in the profitability analysis.[14]

Cost Estimation Unnecessary for Prima Facie Case

The Board has held that a cost estimation is not required to establish a prima facie case. However, a prima facie case with no cost estimation would be a very weak case and much easier to overcome by the claimant at the hearing.[15]

Mine Costs and Commodity Prices Taken Date
Final Certificate Issues

Mining costs and commodity prices to be applied in the profitability analysis must be those in effect at the date of final certificate rather than some later date such as the date of a hearing. Where the United States contests the validity of a mining claim after issuance of final certificate, the government is determining whether or not equitable title has already passed. Of course the date of hearing would still be the critical date for validity examinations where no application was involved.[16]

Commodity Prices for Contested Claims

In determining the validity of a mining claim at an administrative hearing, the Department has consistently held that one must use the commodity prices at the date of the hearing as well as the mining costs at the same date. Of course in the case of determining validity of a claim located prior to a withdrawal, one would use the commodity prices and mining costs at both the date of the withdrawal and the date of hearing. As the Board has frequently noted, the validity of a mining claim depends on present prices; the anticipation of future increases in the value of a mineral commodity is not permitted.[17]

Claim Bootstrapped into Validity
by Associated Business

A claim must be validated on the basis of the mineral commodity itself rather than riding on the "coattails" of an associated business. An otherwise invalid mine cannot be bootstrapped into validity because of the profitability of some other business in which a claimant may be engaged.[18]

Closed or Captive Market

The marketability test is not met by a claimant selling minerals in a closed or captive market. A mining claimant must prove willing customers exist to whom the claimant could reasonably expect to sell at a profit.[19]

Value Added by Manufacture

It is well established that the value of a mineral as it relates to the validity of a claim is the value of the mineral after extraction from the mine, but before any additional manufacturing that would significantly raise the value.[20] In other words the value should be based on the mineral in its raw state rather than on the value of subsequent workmanship. For example, the value of gold may be $400 per ounce, whereas, the same ounce of gold, once manufactured into jewelry, might have a value of more than $1,000.

Government Support

During certain periods, the Federal Government has created an artificial market for low-grade ores by paying an incentive price under a stockpiling program. The Interior Board of Land Appeals[21] has held that there is no justification to issue a mineral patent for mining claims containing low-grade manganese ore simply because patents were issued for similar-type claims during the war. In 1966 the Court of Claims has held that the incentive price should not be considered as establishing the value of manganese for the purpose of commodity tariff rates.[22]

Using Market Data from Several Claims to Give One a Discovery

The Department has held in many cases that mineral values obtained from several claims cannot be joined or consolidated to establish a discovery on one of them. For a claimant to meet the evidentiary burden of showing a discovery of a valuable mineral deposit on each claim, cost and production records should be maintained on each individual claim to avoid the problem of "floating production."[23]

Discovery Lost

The Department[24] has held that a once valid claim may lose its discovery and become invalid. A discovery, once made, may be lost through the occurrence of any one of a number of events, including the physical loss of the discovery, the loss of essential transportation facilities, exhaustion of the deposit or a loss of the market for a substantial duration (as distinguished from temporary market fluctuations).

Substitutes for Discovery

Over the years, mining claimants have come up with a number of reasons their claims should be considered valid even though they have not discovered a "valuable mineral deposit" within the boundary lines of their claims. A few examples include the following:

1. Consolidate ownership to keep out other locators.[25]
2. Claim located to provide access to other claims.[26]
3. The Government is not required to establish a prima facie case for every possible mineral that might exist on a claim.[27]

319

Unproven Methods of Mineral Recovery

There have been a number of cases where the claim owners contended that they have a new process to recover gold or other minerals. These cases fall into two general categories:

1. The gold can be detected in standard assays but cannot be recovered by conventional mining or processing methods. In such a case, the claimant asserts that he has a new recovery process that will enable profitable recovery of the gold.[28]

2. The Government determines that only small amounts of gold can be detected by standard assays; however, the claimant contends that additional gold does exist and can be profitably recovered by a secret or unconventional process.[29]

In general, if a claimant asserts that he has a novel and unproven method for recovery of very fine gold which cannot be recovered profitably by conventional methods, it is the claimant's affirmative duty to present evidence that such gold can be recovered at a profit.

References - Economic Aspects of Validity

1. U.S. v. Mannix, 50 IBLA 110, 118 (1980).
2. Id. at 67.
3. U.S. v. Pittsburgh Pacific Co., 30 IBLA 388, 84 I.D. 282 (1977), affirmed 462 F.Supp. 905, 614 F.2d 1190 (1980).
4. Id. at 285.
5. U.S. v. Manniz, supra at 118.
6. Id.
7. U.S. v. Alaska Limestone Corp., 66 IBLA 316, 324 (1982).
8. U.S. v. Gardner, 18 IBLA 175, 179 (1974); U.S. v. White, 72 I.D. 522 (1965), aff'd White v. Udall, 404 F.2d 334 (9th Cir. 1968).
9. U.S. v. Harper, 8 IBLA 357, 365 (1972).
10. U.S. v. Foresyth et al, 100 IBLA 185, 224-25 (1987).
11. Id. at 227.
12. U.S. v. Gillette, 104 IBLA 269 at 275 (1988).
13. U.S. v. Mannix, supra at 119.
14. Id. at 119.
15. U.S. v. Parker, 91 I.D. 271, 284 (1984).
16. U.S. v. Whitaker (On Reconsideration), 102 IBLA 162, 166 (1988).
17. U.S. v. Gold Placers, Inc., 25 IBLA 374, 375 (1976).
18. U.S. v. Beckley, 66 IBLA 357, 364-65 (1982).
19. U.S. v. Taggart, 53 IBLA 357 (1981).
20. U.S. v. Alexander, 17 IBLA 429, 433 (1974).
21. U.S. v. Kinder, A-30916 (November 26, 1968).
22. Northern Pacific Railroad Co. v. U.S., 355 F.2d 601 (Ct. Cl. 1966).
23. U.S. v. Melluzzo (Supp. on Judicial Remand), 32 IBLA 59, 60 (1977).
24. U.S. v. Johnson, 16 IBLA 237, 238 (1974).
25. U.S. v. Grigg, 8 IBLA 331, 343, 79 I.D. 682 (1972).
26. U.S. v. Connett, 36 IBLA 87 (1978).

27. U.S. v. Johnson, supra at 242.
28. U.S. v. Page, 43 IBLA 395 (1979); U.S. v. Segna, 49 IBLA 75 (1980).
29. U.S. v. Swain, A-30926 (1968); U.S. v. California Alluvial Mining Corporation, A-30928 (January 30, 1969).

POSSESSORY TITLE

A Claim Is Property

The discovery of a valuable mineral deposit within the limits of a mining claim located on the public lands in conformance with state and Federal statutes validates the claim; and the locator acquires an exclusive possessory interest in the claim. The classic statement on a mining claim as property is found in the United States Supreme Court case of **Wilbur v. U.S. ex rel. Krushnic**, 280 U.S. 306 (1930). The Supreme Court said:

> When the location of a mining claim is perfected under the law, it has the effect of a grant by the United States of the right of present and exclusive possession. The claim is property in the fullest sense of that term; and may be sold, transferred, mortgaged, and inherited without infringing any right or title of the United States. The right of the owner is taxable by the state; and is "real property," subject to the lien of a judgment recovered against the owner in a state or territorial court. The owner is not required to purchase the claim or secure patent from the United States; but so long as he complies with the provisions of the mining laws, his possessory right, for all practical purposes of the ownership, is as good as though secured by patent.

This possessory interest may be asserted against the United States as well as against third parties,[1] and may not be taken from the claimant by the United States without due compensation,[2] or be declared invalid except in accordance with due process.[3] Fee title remains with the Federal Government until patent issues. The owner of an unpatented claim is entitled to mine, remove and sell all valuable mineral deposits within his claim boundaries that are not subject to extralateral rights of adjacent claim owners. The claimant is also entitled to surface rights necessary for mining operations.

Quiet Title and Trespass Actions

Quiet title actions and trespass actions apply to mining claims as they do real estate.[4] Furthermore a mining claim comes under the statute of limitations.[5]

Transfer of Mining Claims

Mining claims may be transferred by deed.[6] And a locator may convey any portion of a mining claim.[7]

Surface Rights

The Multiple Surface Act of July 23, 1955, was enacted to provide a means for the Federal Government to obtain management rights to surface resources on mining claims locate both before and after the Act. As a result any use of the surface of an unpatented claim for purposes unrelated to mining is unauthorized and subject to trespass action by the surface management agency.

Rights of Co-owners

Where two or more persons locate a mining claim, a tenancy in common arises and each locator has the same rights in respect to his share as a tenant in severalty. But any one of the locators holds his interest independently of the other(s) and may transfer, devise or encumber it separately without the consent of the other co-tenants.[8] Where a mining claim is owned by two or more persons the possession of one is the possession of all, and there can be no abandonment by one owner so long as his co-owner continues in possession.[9]

Inheritance of Mining Claims

Upon the death of the owner of a mining claim, the identical rights and interests of the claimant passes to his heirs by descent. These interests may be sold as other property by an executor or administrator.[10]

Mining Claims Are Subject to Liens

Unpatented mining claims are real property, and as such, are subject to liens.[11]

Due Process

The courts and the Department of the Interior have consistently maintained that a mining claim is an interest in and a claim to property and may not be declared invalid except in accordance with due process.[12] Due process means more than notice and opportunity for hearing. It requires the application of fixed, objective rules to facts, and requires that the claimant have a hearing before being deprived of that right. The Bureau of Land Management must apply the Administrative Procedures Act, sections 551 et seq. and 701 et seq. of Title 5, which also governs the right to judicial review.[13]

Taxes on Ores

When ore becomes detached from the earth, it becomes the personal property of the mine owners and is free from any title of the United States. However, the extracted ore may be subject to taxation by the state and the collection of taxes may be enforced by sale as is any other property.[14]

A state does not have the power to make a lien for taxes levied on ore to be a lien on a mining claim, if such lien in any way affects the title of the United States. A state tax levied on a property right of the United States is void. However, if the tax is levied on the possessory right of the locator and can be collected without affecting title of the United States, it is proper for the state to collect the tax.[15]

Holder of Valid Mining Claim Has Right to Patent

Upon satisfaction of the requirements of the statute, the owner of a valid mining claim has an absolute right to a patent from the United States conveying fee title to the land within the claim. The actions taken by the Secretary of the Interior in processing an application for patent by such claimant are not discretionary and the issuance of a patent can be compelled by court order.[16] Also, the patent may contain no conditions not authorized by law.[17]

There is no requirement for a claimant to apply for a patent to preserve his property right in the claim, but he may continue to extract and remove the locatable minerals until the claim is exhausted, without ever having acquired full legal title to the land.[18] The patent, if issued, conveys fee simple title to the land within the claim, but does nothing to enlarge or diminish the claimant's rights to the locatable mineral reserves.

Until Patent Issues, Government Has Right to Enter Lands

Unless and until the lands within a mining claim are patented to the claimant, they are Federal lands, and the Government retains the right to enter the lands at any time without search warrants, including the right to remove samples from the claim in order to determine whether the land is mineral in character.[19]

References - Possessory Title

1. Best v. Humboldt Placer Mining Co., 371 U.S. 334, 336 (1963).
2. U.S. v. North American Transportation & Trading Co., 253 U.S. 330 (1920).
3. Cameron v. U.S., 252 U.S. 450 (1920).
4. Block v. Elkhorn Mining Co., 49 F. 549, 552 (1892), affirmed, 163 U.S. 443.
5. Lavagnino v. Uhlig, 71 P. 1046 (1903), affirmed, 198 U.S. 443.
6. Roseville Alta Mining Co. v. Iowa Gulch Mining Co., 24 P. 920 (1898).
7. St. Louis Mining Co. v. Montana Mining Co., 171 U.S. 650 (1898).
8. Union Oil Co. of California, A-29560 (Supp.) (July 30, 1965), 72 ID 313.
9. Alaska Dome Mines, 52 L.D. 550.
10. O'Connell v. Pinnacle Gold Mines Co., 140 F. 854 (1905).
11. Bradford v. Morrison, 212 U.S. 389 (1909).
12. Cameron v. U.S., supra.
13. Adams v. Witmer, 271 F.2d 29 (CA Cal. 1959).
14. Forbes v. Gracey, 94 U.S. 762 (1877).

15. Id.
16. Wilbur v. Krushnic, 280 U.S. 306 at 318-19; Roberts v. U.S., 176 U.S. 221, 231 (1900).
17. Deffenback v. Hawke, 115 U.S. 392, 406 (1885).
18. Union City Oil Co. v. Smith, 249 U.S. 337, 348-49 (1919).
19. U.S. v. Knecht, 39 IBLA 8 (1979).

EXTRALATERAL RIGHTS

Extralateral Rights Outside Vertical Side Lines

The statute (30 U.S.C. 26) provides that extralateral rights to veins, lodes and ledges that apex within the boundary lines and dip downward so as to extend outside the vertical planes through the side lines belong to the owner of such lode location. So the extralateral portion of the vein is that part which extends on its downward dip through the vertical planes along the side lines. To qualify for extralateral rights the following criteria must be satisfied:

1. The location must be a lode claim.

2. The vein must be discrete and continuous along its downward course.

3. The vein must be inclined and the top or apex of the vein must lie inside the vertical extension of the boundary lines; however, the terminal edge of the vein need not crop out at the surface.

4. The end lines must be parallel.

5. Extralateral rights are confined to that part of the vein that exists between two vertical planes drawn through the parallel end lines.

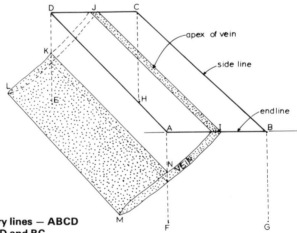

claim boundary lines — ABCD
side lines — AD and BC
end lines — AB and DC
vertical planes drawn through endlines — ABGF and DCHE
vertical planes drawn through sidelines — AFED and BGHC
vein — IMLJ
apex of vein — IJ
extralateral rights — NMLK

Definition of "Apex"

The statute[1] indicates that the "apex" of a vein is the "top" or highest part of all veins, lodes and ledges within the boundary lines. The "apex" or "top" refers to the parts of a vein or lode which come nearest to the surface even though such apex may be well below the surface.[2] At its apex the vein must have both a strike and dip component and not be just an upward projecting spur.[3] An apex does not refer to the highest point in a succession of rolls or folds of a vein; however, the crest of a single anticlinal fold is an apex.

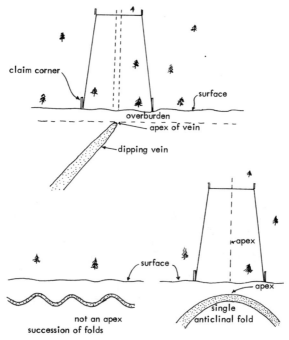

Definition of "Strike" of a Vein

Regardless if the surface is level or inclined, the actual surface outcrop of a vein is taken as the course or strike, rather than the true strike which may be in a different direction.[5] If the vein crops out on the surface, the strike is shown by the course the vein takes on the surface. But the true strike of the vein is its horizontal line - the line of a level run in the vein and lengthwise as to the vein. Therefore, the strike of a vein at the surface determines the location lines and extralateral rights rather than the strike of the vein in the subsurface which may be quite different.[6]

Definition of "Dip"

The term "dip" is synonymous with "downward course" and they both refer to the direction of the vein or lode descends into the earth at right angles to the strike or course of the vein.[7]

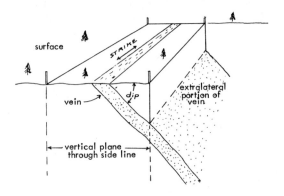

Legal Apex

Where a vein apexes on lands patented as placer claims or patented under the nonmineral laws, and the same vein also extends downward on dip into public lands, the highest part of the vein in the public land shall be considered the "legal apex." The Secretary of the Interior has defined the "legal apex" as "that portion of the vein within the public lands which would constitute its actual apex if the vein has no actual existence in the ground so disposed of."[8]

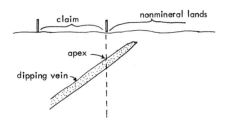

Required Characteristics of Vein for Extralateral Rights

In order for a mineral deposit to constitute a vein and thus qualify for extralateral rights, it is not necessary that it be a clean fissure filled with mineral. But the fissure must have form and be well-defined, with a hanging wall and foot wall.[9]

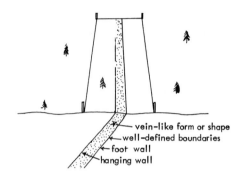

vein-like form or shape
well-defined boundaries
foot wall
hanging wall

Vein Must Be Continuous

To maintain extralateral rights, the vein must be more or less continuous; however, some interruption is acceptable.[10] If the vein is faulted, the extralateral rights terminate.[11] A vein offset 15 feet by faulting was held to be continuous.[12] In another case where a mineralized fault offset a vein, the Court held that because the fault was mineralized, the vein was continuous.[13]

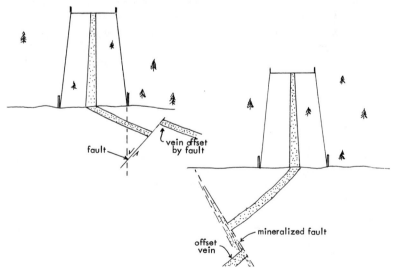

fault
vein offset by fault
offset vein
mineralized fault

329

A claimant is not entitled to follow his vein under another location if the vein is not a single discrete one, but a network of interconnected veins which forms one large lode and unites at depth below the surface of both claims.[14] Perhaps the most practical rule for continuity of a vein is that it can be traced by a miner along its downward course.[15]

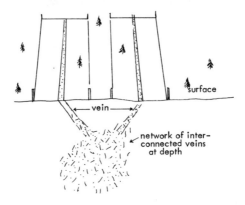

Parallel End Lines Required for Extralateral Rights

The end lines of a lode mining claim must be parallel for the locator to have the right to follow a vein outside the vertical planes drawn through the side lines. This lateral right is confined by statute to such portion of the vein that exists between planes drawn through the end lines and extended along the vein on its downward dip.[16] If the end lines are not parallel, extralateral rights will either converge and diminish or diverge and increase the farther into the earth the vein is followed.[17] Extralateral rights are determined by the location on the ground rather than how the location is shown on the survey plat of a patent.[18]

Secondary Veins

The location lines are generally established relative to the "primary" or "discovery" vein. However, lode locations may also contain a number of "incidental" or "secondary" veins that may have a "strike" and "dip" that is different than the discovery vein.[19] If such secondary veins apex within the location lines, the owner has extralateral rights, providing the secondary veins relate properly to the lines of the location which control extralateral rights.[20] However, a locator may not, under any circumstances, have extralateral rights outside vertical planes run through the end lines, even for secondary veins.[21]

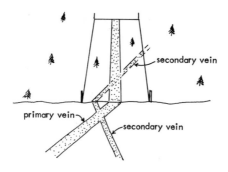

secondary vein

primary vein

secondary vein

Rights to All Ore Except Veins Apexing on Another's Claim

The owner of a mining claim has the right to all ore beneath the surface of his claim, including a vein that does not have its apex within the claims. However, if the apex of such a vein should fall within the limits of a claim owned by another, that claimant has the right to follow the vein downward on its dip.[22]

Junior Claimant May Have Extralateral Rights Under Senior Location

A Junior claimant has the right to follow the extralateral portion of a vein dipping under a senior location if such vein apexes within the claim of the junior locator.[23]

Junior Claimant Has Burden of Proof

In a suit involving extralateral rights between two adjacent claimants, the junior locator has the burden of proving that a vein apexes within his claim and extends in a downward course beneath the surface of the senior locator.[24] A claimant who asserts extralateral rights to a vein penetrating another's claim has the burden of proving that the vein has its apex within the boundaries of his claim. Also the continuity and identity between the vein and surface apex will not be presumed over substantial unexposed distances.[25]

Flat-Lying Veins Have No Extralateral Rights

Even though a flat-lying or horizontal vein is located as a lode, such a location has no extralateral rights and operations must be confined within the boundary lines. The rationale for this is that the right is restricted to following the vein in its course downward so as to extend outside the vertical side lines of such surface location.

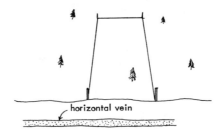

No Extralateral Rights Where
Vein Becomes Horizontal

Extralateral rights do not go to a lode or vein beyond the point outside the side lines where it flattens to a horizontal plane or takes an upward trend for a considerable distance.[26]

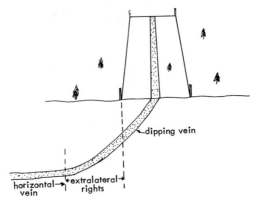

Converging End Lines

If the end lines of a mining claim converge in the direction of the dip, extralateral rights will apply to the extralateral portion of the vein taken within the converging lines.[27]

If two claims overlap along the apex of a vein and their end lines converge and meet, the extralateral rights of the junior location is bounded by the extension of the plane passing through the end line of the senior claim. Therefore the extralateral rights of the junior claim converge in the direction of the dip of the claim.[28]

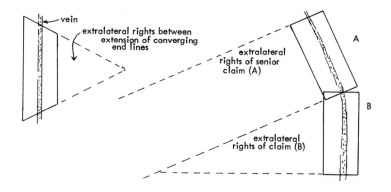

Longitudinally Divided Vein Goes to Senior Locator

If two or more mining claims longitudinally bisect or divide a vein, the right to the entire width of the vein along its downward course goes to the senior locator (A). This is based on the custom of miners to treat a vein as an indivisible unit because it is not practical to separate the vein as it is extracted along the downward course.[29]

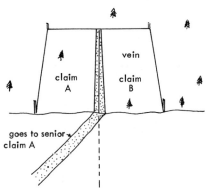

Apex Partly within Two Claims

In the case where a thick vein crosses a common side line between two claims, the apex is partly within both claims for a distance. The entire vein is considered to apexing upon the senior location to the point on the side line (a) where it is entirely within the junior location.[30]

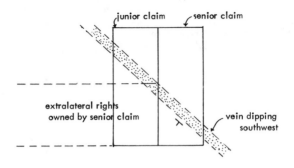

junior claim senior claim

extralateral rights
owned by senior claim

vein dipping
southwest

Extralateral Rights May Apply to Both Side Lines

Extralateral rights for a vein apexing within a claim may apply to one or both side lines.[31] Such a case might exist where there is an anticlinal (folded upward) vein, or two veins both apexing on the claim but dipping in opposite directions.

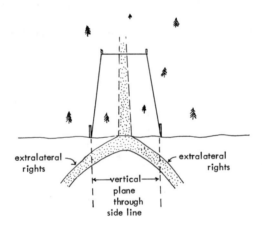

extralateral
rights

extralateral
rights

vertical
plane
through
side line

Vein Passing Through Side Lines

The owner of a location cannot follow the extralateral portion of the vein within the side lines of a prior location, if the prior location has the vein pass through both side lines so as to make them end lines.[32] The Supreme Court considered a case where the vein passed through both side lines rather than the end lines.[33] The Court held that for the purpose of determining extralateral rights it will treat such side lines as end lines and such end lines as side lines. Therefore, under a location where the vein runs through the side lines, the locator may not follow the vein along its strike

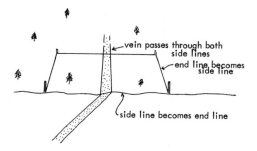

vein passes through both
side lines

end line becomes
side line

side line becomes end line

outside of his end lines. Situations where the side lines become
end lines and end lines become side lines only apply to discovery
veins and not secondary or minor veins apexing within the location.[34]

Length of Apex Limits Length of
Vein Along Strike

When following the extralateral portion of a vein, you are
entitled to no greater dimension along the strike then its dimension
along the apex that is terminated by the two end lines.[35]

Vein Crosses One End Line

If the apex of the vein crosses one end line and one side line
of the claim, the owner may still follow the vein on its dip beyond
the vertical side line; but, the owner must stay within vertical
planes run through extensions of the end lines.[36]

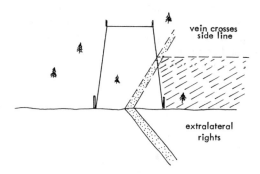

vein crosses
side line

extralateral
rights

Vein Need Not Extend Full Length of Claim

In order to have extralateral rights, it is not essential that the
vein extend the full length of the claim, from end line to end line.[37]
However, a claimant is not entitled to any part of an apex outside
the claim boundary lines. The extralateral portion of the vein is

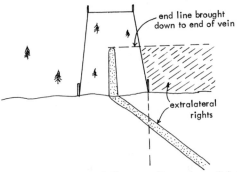

end line brought
down to end of vein

extralateral
rights

determined by placing the end line at the point of intersection of the vein with the side line as shown below. In other words, the end lines may be placed where the lode terminates within the surface lines or where the apex of the lode crosses the side line.[38]

Intersecting or Crossing Veins

According to the mining law (30 U.S.C. 41), "[w]here two or more veins intersect or cross each other, priority of title shall govern, and such prior location shall be entitled to all ore or mineral contained within the space of intersection; but the subsequent location shall have the right-of-way through the space of intersection for the purposes of the convenient working of the mine. And where two or more veins unite, the oldest or prior location shall take the vein below the point of union, including all the space of intersection."

If two veins from two claims belonging to a single owner unite in a single vein and continue down until it intersects with a third vein belonging to another, priority for the zone of intersection belongs to the earlier of the two former claims and that of the third claim.[39]

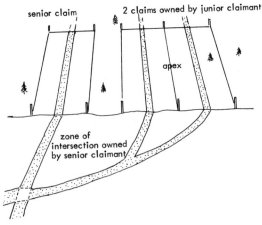

senior claim

2 claims owned by junior claimant

apex

zone of
intersection owned
by senior claimant

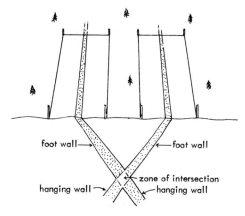

foot wall →   ← foot wall

hanging wall →   ← zone of intersection / ← hanging wall

Ore within the space of intersection refers to the body of ore bounded by the foot and hanging walls of one lode as they extend across the foot and hanging walls of one lode as they extend across the foot and hanging walls of the other lode as they extend along the general course of the vein.[40]

Blind Veins Belong to Prior Lode

Blind veins that apex underneath a prior lode claim belong to such lode claim even though veins are discovered by a tunnel under a subsequent tunnel site location. If the tunnel site location is later than the lode location, the blind vein belongs to the lode claimant.[41]

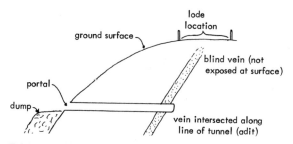

lode location

ground surface

blind vein (not exposed at surface)

portal

dump

vein intersected along line of tunnel (adit)

No Right to Tunnel in Country Rock

A locator has no authority under the mining law to run tunnels through country rock in another claimant's adjoining location for any reason including to cut a vein apexing in his own patented claim.[42] However, under certain circumstances, "easements and rights-of-way necessary for the practical and economical operation of a mine, such as sublateral tunnels, drainage ways and railways, may be acquired by condemnation or otherwise only where permitted by statute.[43]

337

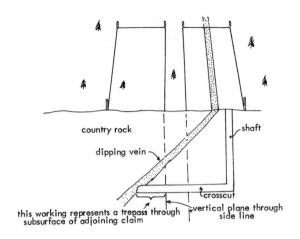

country rock

dipping vein

shaft

crosscut

this working represents a trepass through
subsurface of adjoining claim

vertical plane through
side line

Country Rock May Be Removed with Vein

Extralateral rights include the right to excavate country rock if the vein is too crooked or narrow to follow within its confines so that the surface owner cannot accomplish the necessary excavations.[44]

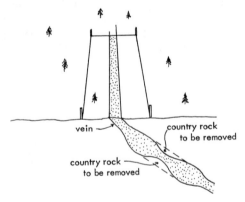

vein

country rock
to be removed

country rock
to be removed

Lines of Junior Location Across Senior Location

The lines of a junior location may be laid within, upon or across the surface of a valid senior location for the purpose of securing extralateral rights for the junior location. However, the extralateral rights of the junior location must not conflict with the senior location.[45]

No Right to Enter Surface of Another Claim

The statute clearly states that no surface rights on adjoining patented or unpatented claims accompany extralateral rights.[46] The cases hold that one is prohibited from entering on the surface of a placer to work an extralateral portion of a vein within the vertical lines of a placer location. Under the same theory one is also precluded from entering upon the surface of a placer claim to explore for vein or lodes.[47] However, the subsurface of a placer claim may be entered by a lode claimant to extract ore from the extralateral portion of the lode claimants vein.[48]

Extralateral Rights Under Patented Lands

The owner of a patented lode claim containing the apex of a vein has the right to follow the downward course along the vein outside the vertical side lines whether or not the right is specified in the patent document.[49] This of course would not be the case if the United States did not own any vein or lode existing beneath the surface of the adjoining claims and having its apex within the patented claim, regardless of whether provided for in the patent.[50]

A valid unpatented mining claim has extralateral rights superior to the subsurface rights later granted by a nonmineral patent. In other words, if a mining claim has valid existing rights at the date of a nonmineral patent for adjacent lands, the claimant will have extralateral rights in the subsurface of the junior nonmineral patent.[51]

Extralateral rights to lands embraced by nonmineral patents such as homestead entries, school lands and railroad grants are only available if a valid mining location was established before the date the agricultural land was patented. On the other hand, "the right of a junior lode claimant, whether his claim be patented or unpatented, to follow the dip of his vein into an adjoining patented or unpatented lode claim, is one which arises under the mining laws."[52]

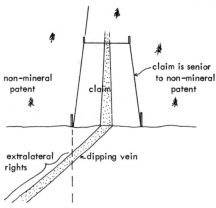

non-mineral patent

claim

claim is senior to non-mineral patent

extralateral rights

dipping vein

For mining claims perfected after issuance of a nonmineral patent, extralateral rights in the subsurface only apply if minerals were known to be valuable at the time of patent issuance. If minerals were known to be valuable at the time of patent issuance, the owner of a subsequent claim will have extralateral rights.[53]

If lands covered by nonmineral patents were not known to be valuable for minerals at the date of patent issuance, all minerals subsequently discovered will go to the nonmineral patentee or his successor in interest.[54]

In order to determine the availability of mineral rights in the subsurface of lands covered by nonmineral patents, one must examine the following:

1. The date of the nonmineral patent and whether such date predated or postdated the claim.

2. The specific language in the patent and statutory authority for the patent.

3. If the location was perfected after the date of patent issuance, were the lands known to be valuable for minerals at the date of issuance.

Claims on Down-Dip Extension of a Vein with Physical Exposure May Be Patented

On July 14, 1982, Manville Products Corp. filed a mineral patent application with the Montana State Office of the Bureau of Land Management. The claims, located for platinum-group metals, cover a part of an ore-grade layer of the igneous Stillwater Complex. Manville had located mining claims over both the apex and along the apparent down-dip extension of the lode. Manville contended that the claims on the down-dip extension of the vein were validated by drilling which exposed ore-grade mineralization in place within the limits of each claim. The drill data suggests but does not confirm that the mineral deposits on the down-dip claims are an extension of the vein that crops out on the up-dip claim.

Following a validity examination of the claims, the Forest Service advised Manville that the claims may be improperly located because the course of the lode deviates from the center lines of the claims. The Forest Service also advised Manville that only those claims located on the exposed outcrop or apex of the lode may be valid; and any claims located over the apparent down-dip extension of the lode are invalid. According to the Forest Service, the down-dip claims are invalid because the extralateral rights attached to the apex claim appropriate the down-dip extension of the lode.

In **Apex & Extralateral Rights Issues Raised by the Stillwater Mineral Patent**, 93 I.D. 369, 383 (1986), Solicitor Tarr described the rights of a lode locator to place locations along the down-dip extension of a lode. A locator is not required to show that the apex of the vein is within the claim boundaries to have a valid location. Solicitor Tarr stated:

> We therefore construe the Mining Law as not limiting a locator to appropriate a discovered mineral vein only by locating claims along the apparent apex. The Mining Law requires an apex as a prerequisite to the exercise of extralateral rights, but not to the validity of a lode mining claim. If there is in fact a true apex with an identifiable descending vein, the claimant may at his option rely solely on locations on the apex and the corresponding extralateral right to appropriate the vein, as well as upon the apex, so long as each claim is supported by an exposure of the valuable mineral deposit.

> Where a claimant chooses to locate claims along the apex and the dip of the vein, the location and maintenance of the claims on the dip is properly viewed as evidencing the claimant's right flowing from the apex locations with regard to the mineral within the boundaries of the down-dip claims.

The existence of an apex within a given lode claim is not essential to validity of the claim, but only the claimant's ability to assert an extralateral right derived from that location.

Side Line Agreements

Two companies having claims adjacent to each other may establish an agreement for subsurface rights beneath the common side lines. Typically such companies execute vertical side line agreements where the division of rights is made by a vertical plane running through the common side lines. Vertical side line agreements are most commonly made where mineral deposits are irregular or consist of a complex network of veins and where the legal-technical problems of ascertaining extralateral rights are insurmountable.

Claims Partially Covering Patented or Withdrawn Lands

In **Zula C. Brinkerhoff**, 75 IBLA 179 (1983), the Board overruled a number of earlier Interior decisions which held that a lode claim partially within prior patented or withdrawn lands is null and void ab initio for that portion within the withdrawn or patented lands. The placement of exterior boundary lines over the surface of withdrawn or patented lands may be done only for the purpose of claiming unappropriated veins through extralateral rights. Of course the extension of boundary lines over withdrawn or patented lands should not be done without permission of the land owner. If such permission is not possible, the claimant may make extension by projection and use of witness corners.[55]

Although a locator may place the exterior boundary lines of his claim over patented or withdrawn lands, the rights that may be acquired by this practice depend on the particular circumstances in each case. For example, it may be possible for a claimant to obtain extralateral rights to veins dipping below or outside patented surface or withdrawn lands.[56]

With the exception of Stock-Raising Homestead patents which reserved minerals to the United States, most patents including placer, mill site, homestead, school grants and railroad grants convey locatable minerals to the grantee. Therefore, in most cases, a claim located after the issuance of a patent will not have extralateral rights within the boundary lines of an adjacent nonmineral patent. Only where the locatable minerals are available for appropriation are such extralateral rights available.[57]

The exterior boundary lines of mill sites and placer claims may not be placed over patented or withdrawn lands. This is because such locations do not give extralateral rights. Therefore, placer claims and mill sites partly located on prior patented or withdrawn lands are null and void to the extent of their encroachment.[58]

Law of the Apex: Present Status

Since the early 1900s, there have been very few significant court cases concerning conflicts over extralateral rights. Several reasons for this lack of legal activity include the following:

1. The early cases have provided direction for most of the possible situations.

2. Many companies solve potential extralateral rights problems by establishing vertical side line agreements.

3. Development costs are so high that companies consolidate mineral properties to avoid such conflicts before starting mining operations.

4. Newly-discovered lode deposits are less likely to be of the classic vein type where extralateral rights would attach. Most new deposits tend to be large, of irregular form and have poorly-defined boundaries.

References - Extralateral Rights

1. 30 U.S.C. 26 (1982).
2. Steven v. Williams, Fed. Cas. Nos. 13,413, 13, 414 (1878).
3. Stewart Mining Co. v. Ontario Mining Co., 132 P. 787 (1913), affirmed 237 U.S. 350.
4. Jim Butler Tonopah Mining Co. v. West End Consol. Mining Co., 158 P. 876 (1916), affirmed 247 U.S. 450.
5. Brugger v. Lee Yim, 55 P2d 564 (1936).
6. Flagstaff Silver Mining Co. v. Tarbet, 98 U.S. 463 (1878).
7. Brugger v. Lee Yim, supra.
8. Woods v. Holden, 26 L.D. 198 (1898).
9. Consolidated Wyoming Gold Mining Co. v. Champion Mining Co., 63 F. 540 (1894).
10. Utah Consol. Mining Co. v. Utah Apex Mining Co., 28 F. 249 (1922), cert. denied, 261 U.S. 617.
11. Wall v. U.S., 232 F. 613 (1905).
12. Original Sixteen to One Mine v. Twenty-One Mining Co., F. 630 (1918).
13. National Mine Syndicate, 205 F. 787, 791 (1912).
14. Colorado Central Consol. Mining Co. v. Turck, 50 R. 588, 592 (1892), On rehearing 54 F. 262, 265, error dismissed 150 U.S. 138.
15. Cooper v. Saratoga, 40 F. 509 (1889).
16. Iron Silver Mining Co. v. Elgin Mining & Smelting Co., 118 U.S. 196 (1896).
17. Del Monte Mining & Milling Co. v. Last Chance Mining & Milling Co., 171 U.S. 55, 85 (1898).
18. Consolidated Wyoming Gold Mining Co. v. Champion Mining Co., supra.
19. Cosmopolitan Mining Co. v. Foot, 101 Fed. 518 (CCD Nev. 1900).
20. Del Monte Mining & Milling Co. v. Last Chance Mining & Milling Co., supra.
21. Walrath v. Champion Mining Co., 171 U.S. 293 (1898).
22. Mammoth Mining Co. v. Grand Central Mining Co., 213 U.S. 72 (1909).
23. Colorado Central Consolidated Mining Co. v. Turck, 54 F. 262 (1893).
24. Butte & Superior Copper Co. v. Clark-Montana Realty Co., 248 F. 609 (1918) cert. denied 247 U.S. 516.
25. Silver Surprize, Inc. v. Sunshine Mining Co., 547 P2d 1240, 15 Wash App. 1 (1976), affirmed 558 P2d 186.
26. Tom Reed Gold Mines Co. v. United Eastern Milling Co., 209 P. 283 (1922), cert. denied, 260 U.S. 744.
27. Grant v. Pilgrim, 95 F2d 562 (1938).
28. Bunker Hill & S. Mining & Concentrating Co. v. Empire State Idaho Mining & Developing Co., 108 F. 189 (1900), affirmed 109 F. 538.
29. Argentine Mining Co. v. Terrible Mining Co., 122 U.S. 478, 484 (1887).
30. St. Louis Mining Co. v. Montana Mining Co., 104 F. 664 (1900) error dismissed 186 U.S. 24, reversed on other grounds 204 U.S. 204.
31. Jim Butler Tonopah Mining Co. v. West End Consol. Mining Co., 247 U.S. 450 (1918).
32. Tyler Mining Co. v. Sweeney, 79 F. 277 (1897).
33. King v. Amy & Silver Smith Copper Mining Co., 152 U.S. 222, 228 (1894).
34. Del Monte Mining & Milling Co. v. Last Chance Mining & Milling Co., 171 U.S. 55 (1898).
35. Tyler Mining Co. v. Last Chance Mining Co., 71 F. 848, 851 (1894).
36. Del Monte Mining & Milling Co. v. Last Chance Mining & Milling Co., 171 U.S. 55 (1898).
37. Tyler Mining Co. v. Sweeney, 54 F. 284 (1893).
38. Id. at 292.
39. Little Josephine Minine Co. v. Fullerton, Colorado, 58 F. 521 (1893).
40. Watervale Mining Co. v. Leach, 33 P. 418, 4 Ariz. 34 (1893), appeal dismissed 159 U.S. 258.
41. Calhoun Gold Mining Company v. Ajax Gold Mining Co., 182 U.S. 497 (1901).

42. St. Louis Mining & Milling Co. v. Montana Mining Co., 194 U.S. 235 (1904).
43. 30 U.S.C. 43 (1982).
44. Twenty-One Mining Co. v. Original Sixteen to One Mine, 265 F. 543 (1920).
45. Del Monte Mining & Milling Co. v. Last Chance Mining & Milling Co., 171 U.S. 55 (1898).
46. 30 U.S.C. 26 (1982).
47. Del Monte Mining & Milling Co. v. Last Chance Mining & Milling Co., supra.
48. Iron Silver Mining Co. v. Reynolds, 124 U.S. 374 (1888).
49. Doe v. Waterloo Mining Co., 54 F. 935 (1893).
50. Empire Star Mines Co. v. Grass Valley Bulletin Mines, 99 F.2d 228 (1938).
51. Hecla Mining Co. v. Atlas Mining Co., 445 P2d 225, 92 Idaho 476 (1968).
52. Reeves v. Oregon Exploration Co., 127 Or. 686, 273 Pac. 389, 391 (1929).
53. Davis v. Weibbold, 139 U.S. 507, 519 (1891).
54. Deffeback v. Hawke, 115 U.S. 392, 404 (1885).
55. Santa Fe Mining Co., Inc., 79 IBLA 48, 50 (1984).
56. Id. at 51.
57. Id. at 50-51.
58. Id. at 51.

PREDISCOVERY RIGHTS
OR PEDIS POSSESSIO

Introduction

The mining laws require that a discovery precede a mineral location. This is an impractical requirement because most mineral deposits which may be discovered today are hidden well below the surface. Therefore, because a discovery may be made, large amounts of exploration money must be expended through geochemical, geophysical and geological surveys in addition to sampling and core-drilling programs. If the claims are not staked prior to the exploration program, rival claimants alerted by the exploration activity might locate claims over the area.

In the mining camps of California, a custom developed which spread throughout the west and was subsequently recognized by the courts. A claimant in actual occupancy of a mining claim, even if he did not have a discovery, could hold against anyone who had no better title, so long as he was diligently engaged in seeking a discovery. The doctrine of **pedis possessio** was founded to provide such protection. However, these possessory rights are limited to protection against adverse locators or the general public. They are of no value against the United States who holds the superior title.

There are now approximately 1.1 million recorded mining claims in the western United States and most do not have a discovery under the mining laws. So, the majority of all mining claimants must operate under the doctrine of pedis possessio to protect their claim.

Law of Possession

The doctrine of pedis possessio, which evolved from the customs of miners, has achieved statutory recognition in the Federal law as the "law of possession," 30 U.S.C. 53 (1982):

No possessory action between persons, in any court of the United States, for the recovery of any mining title, or for damages to any such title, shall be affected by the fact that the paramount title to the land in which such mines lie is in the United States; but each case shall be judged by the law of possession.

Actual Possession Versus Constructive Possession

The literal meaning of "pedis possessio" is a foothold, actual possession. **Black's Law Dictionary**, 1289 (rev. 4th ed. 1968). This actual occupancy must be distinguished from constructive possession, which is based on color of title and has the effect of enlarging the area actually occupied.[1]

Discovery Required for Valid Claim or Rights Against Government

Regardless of compliance with statutory requirements such as monumenting and recordation, one cannot perfect a location, under either Federal or state law, without actual discovery of minerals in place. As was stated in **Union Oil Co. of California v. Smith**, 249 U.S. 337 (1919), "it is clear that in order to create valid rights or initiate a title as against the United States a discovery of mineral is essential."[2] So until discovery, the law of possession determines the right of possession.

The Law and Regulations Require Discovery Before Location

In 30 U.S.C. 23 (1982), it is stated that "no location of a mining claim shall be made until discovery of the vein or lode within the limits of the claim located." Federal regulations (43 CFR 3831.1) also require a discovery before location:

> Rights to mineral lands, owned by the United States, are initiated by prospecting for minerals thereon, and, upon the discovery of mineral, by locating the lands upon which such discovery has been made.

Pedis Possessio and the Supreme Court

The classic discourse on pedis possessio is found in 1919 Supreme Court case of **Union Oil Company of California v. Smith**[3] in which the theory was recognized that if a qualified person peaceably and in good faith enters vacant, unappropriated public domain for the purpose of discovering a valuable mineral under the mining laws - while he is so searching, he may exclusively hold the place where he is working against those having no better right. In other words, to qualify for rights of pedis possessio the claimant must physically occupy the claim while excluding rival claimants and diligently in good faith attempting to make a discovery. As the Supreme Court said, "possession may be maintained only by continued actual occupancy by a qualified locator or his representatives engaged in persistent and diligent prosecution of work looking to the discovery of mineral."[4]

What May Happen If Occupancy Relaxed

Because prediscovery rights may be maintained only by continued actual occupancy, failure to maintain such occupancy may open your claim to location by others. In **Cole v. Ralph**, 252 U.S. 286, 294 (1920), the Supreme Court said that "if his occupancy be relaxed, or be merely incidental to something other than a diligent search for mineral, and another enters peaceably, and not fraudulently or clandestinely, and makes a mineral discovery and location, the location so made is valid and must be respected accordingly."

Discovery Makes Continuous Occupation Unnecessary

For more than one hundred years it has been established that continuous occupation is not necessary to maintain a mining claim, if such claim is protected by discovery. As the Supreme Court said in **Belk v. Meagher**, 104 U.S. 279 (1881), "actual and continuous occupation of a valid mining location based upon discovery is not essential to the preservation of the possessory right. The right is lost only by abandonment, as by nonperformance of the annual labor..."

Geomet Exploration v. Lucky McUranium Corp: A Case on Actual Occupancy

In 1979 the Arizona Supreme Court decided a case where the senior locator, Lucky McUranium Corporation (lucky), detected radiometric anomalies (areas of higher than background for natural radioactivity of rock as measured by a radiation detector in the Artillery Peak Mining District in Yuma County. **Geomet Exploration v. Lucky McUranium**, 601 P.2d 1339 (1979). In November, 1976, Lucky monumented and posted 200 claims, including 4,000 acres. The company then drilled a 10-foot hole on each claim and recorded notices as required by Arizona State law.

Sometime later while Lucky was not occupying the claims, Geomet Exploration (Geomet) peaceably enter the area claimed by Lucky and started drilling operations. Although employees of Geomet were aware of Lucky's claims, they considered them invalid because there had been no discovery of minerals in place and Lucky was not in actual occupancy of the areas Geomet entered and located. The Court held that the claims must not only be actually occupied, but must undergo diligent exploration of minerals.

Even though continuous or actual occupancy has been upheld by the courts through the years as essential in order to maintain prediscovery rights, it is well known that many major companies are holding claims without protection of a discovery under circumstances no different that the claims held by Lucky Mc Uranium Corporation. As was stated in **Davis v. Nelson**, 329 F2d 840 (9th Cir. 1964), "the premature location of such a claim and the recordation of certificates or notices of location cast a cloud upon the title of the United States to the lands, as the law contemplates that discovery must coincide with the physical location of the claims."

Occupancy of Each Claim Versus Occupancy on a Group or Area Basis

Several cases have come before the courts concerning the issue of whether a claimant could, by occupying a small part of a claim group, maintain pedis possessio over the entire claim group. In **Union Oil Co. of California v. Smith**,[5] the Supreme Court rejected pedis possessio on a group bases. In **MacGuire v. Sturgis**, 347 F.Supp. 580, 584 (1971), the Court provided for pedis possessio on a group or area basis under the following circumstances:

1. the geology of the area claimed is similar and the size of the area claimed is reasonable;

2. the discovery (validation) work referred to in Wyo. Stat. sec 30-6 (1957) is completed;

3. an overall work program is in effect for the area claimed;

4. such work program is being diligently pursued, i.e., a significant number of exploratory holes have been systematically drilled; and

5. the nature of the mineral claimed and the cost of development would make it economically impracticable to develop the mineral if the locator is awarded only those claims on which he is actually present and currently working.

However, in **Geomet Exploration v. Lucky Mc Uranium Corp., Ariz.**, the Arizona Supreme Court rejected the **MacGuire v. Sturgis** holding for pedis possessio on a group or area basis and held that "pedis possessio protects only those claims actually occupied" and does not extend to contiguous unoccupied claims on a group or area basis.

Pedis Possessio Requires Physical and Continuous Occupancy of Each Claim

In **Amax Exploration, Inc. v. Ross Mosher**, (Civil R-85-162 BRT, March 2, 1987), the Federal District Court of Nevada indicated that pedis possessio requires that each claim be physically occupied on a continuous basis. The Court held that "assessment work and sampling on the claims in dispute have not brought the parties to the claims with the frequency of an occupation. * * * There is a great difference between this and recognizing some right short of discovery to support contiguous, unoccupied claims located solely upon geologic inferences and an area-wide program of exclusion."

348

Good Faith Effort to Comply with Law

Continental Oil Co. v. Natrona Services, Inc., 588 F.2d 792 (10th Cir. 1978), an important case involving the doctrine of pedis possessio, requires a good faith effort to comply with the law. Continental Oil Company (Conoco) filed a declaratory judgment against Natrona Services, Inc. and John MacGuire to establish Conoco's right to exclusive possession to certain unpatented claims. Conoco alleged that it hired contractors to locate, record and perform the validation work on the claims. Conoco also contended that it had spent $500,000 in service contracts for the purpose of airborne reconnaissance, geophysical work, surface sampling and deep exploratory drilling. The deep exploratory drilling on a portion of the claims allegedly included 40,000 total feet and involved 48 deep holes. Conoco maintained that the claimed area was reasonable in size and that the exploratory work was systematic, diligent and performed in good faith. Although Conoco admitted that it had not actually been present and currently working on a large number of the claims, it was in possession to the extent that it was practical and had asserted its rights to the claims.

Natrona and MacGuire admitted overstaking some of Conoco's claims in 1975 on the basis of their determination that the recorded location certificates were falsely made and that the location and discovery work did not comply with the law.

Natrona and MacGuire counterclaimed to establish that they had superior rights to some 1,200 claims and further sought to establish that Conoco's remaining 840 claims that they had not overstaked were invalid. The U.S. District Court for the District of Wyoming granted a verdict in favor of Conoco for the claims that had not been overstaked by Natrona and MacGuire. On the remaining claims , a jury verdict, which went in favor of Natrona determined the following:

1. Conoco had not completed discovery;
2. there was no overall work program by Conoco in the claimed area;
3. no such work program was diligently pursued; and
4. there was no evidence of a significant number of exploration holes systematically drilled.

Judge Davis of the Tenth Circuit Court of Appeals affirmed the trial court decision. He held that Conoco was able to maintain its rights to the claims that were not overstaked by Natrona because it had demonstrated sufficient good faith effort to comply with the law. The Court pointed out that for the claims overstaked by Natrona, Conoco "had attempted a wholesale location program which could be said to have been designed to tie up large areas of public lands without making any substantial effort to comply with the law." Judge Doyle agreed that there is sufficient evidence to support the jury verdict that Conoco did not (1) have an overall work program, (2) act in good faith, (3) diligently pursue work on the overstaked claims, and (4) substantially comply with the law. However, it is important to note that Judge Doyle qualified his decision by saying the "senior locator who has diligently pursued a claim, but by ignorance or error has failed to fulfill a technical requirement is protected." This principal has been consistently upheld by the courts.

In reference to **MacGuire v. Sturgis**, the Court said that "a reading of the **MacGuire** opinion shows that its standards do not differ from those which were applied here in deciding whether the appellant was entitled to exclusive possession."

References - Prediscovery Rights

1. Geomet Exploration v. Lucky McUranium Corp., Ariz, 601 P.2d 1339 (1979).
2. Best v. Humboldt Placer Mining Co., 371 U.S. 334 (1963).
3. 249 U.S. 346 (1919).
4. Id. at 346-47.
5. Supra.

SURFACE RIGHTS ON MINING CLAIMS

Surface Resources Act (PL-167)

On July 23, 1955, Congress adopted an Act commonly called the Surface Resources Act. 30 U.S.C. 612 (1982). Section 4 provides a means for the United States to manage and dispose of the vegetative surface resources and to manage other resources, except locatable mineral deposits. Claims located before July 23, 1955, may retain surface rights, if such claims are verified as being valid under Sections 5 and 6 of the Act. However, claims located after July 23, 1955 are subject to all provisions of the Act, including the Government's right to manage surface resources. This law was enacted in response to abuses of the mining laws where claims were located for purposes other than mining, such as recreational cabins, fishing and hunting sites, cafes, or for timber, grazing and water rights.

As stated in section 4 of Public Law 167, the claimant of an unpatented mining claim located after July 23, 1955, has the following surface rights:

1. Unpatented mining claims may not be used for purposes other than prospecting, mining or processing operations and related uses.

2. All surface rights of unpatented claims are subject to the right of the United States, its permittees, and licensees to use so much of the surface as necessary or for access to other lands; however, uses by the United States, its permittees or licensees, shall be such as not to materially interfere with mineral-related operations.

3. If the United States should sell timber from the surface of the mining claim which is subsequently needed for mineral-related operations, the claimant is entitled to be supplied free of charge with timber that is equivalent in kind and quantity to the timber taken from the claim.

4. Timber or vegetative resources may not be removed from a claim for other than mineral-related purposes.

Determination of Surface Rights

Mining claims located prior to the date of Public Law 167 may be made subject to the provisions of section 4 of the Act if a determination of surface rights is made according to a procedure given in sections 5 and 6 of the Act. The head of a Federal

351

department or agency which has surface management responsibilities of Federal lands may file with the Secretary of the Interior a request for publication of notice to mining claimants for determination of surface rights. A notice to mining claimants is published in a newspaper having general circulation in the county in which the lands involved are situated. In addition to a field examination, a title search is made in the county recorder's office to determine the existence and ownership of all mining claims in the involved lands. All owners of record are sent a notice by personal service or registered mail.

The notice, which describes the involved lands notifies the owners of unpatented claim that they must file within 150 days from the date of the first publication of the notice a verified statement which includes; (1) the date of the location; (2) the book and page of the recorded location notice or the certificate of location; (3) the legal description of where the claim is situated; and (4) the names and addresses of the owners and others claiming an interest. If any claimant fails to file a verified statement within 150 days as specified above, failure to do so constitutes a waiver and relinquishment of surface rights so that the claimant would have the same rights under section 4 of the Public Law 167 as though the claim were located after July 23, 1955.

If a verified statement is filed, all claims indicated in the statement are examined by a government mineral examiner for a discovery. Proceedings are initiated on those claims that do not appear to have a discovery and a hearing is held to determine whether the claimant or the Government has the right to manage the surface resources. Although, at the hearing, the claim is contested on the grounds of a lack of discovery, the only effect of a determination adverse to the claimant is a restriction of surface rights as stated in section 4 of the Act. The claim is not invalidated and the claimant does not lose any possessory rights to the mineral or his rights to mine and use as much of the surface as necessary to his mining operation. If the determination is made that the claim has a discovery, the claimant retains the same surface rights he had before enactment of Public Law 167.

The claimant may file a waiver of surface rights and avoid a possible hearing. The effect of this action would give the claim the same surface rights as it would have if located after July 23, 1955.

Claims with Surface Rights Under PL-167

What surface rights does a claimant have who acquired such rights pursuant to the verification process provided by Public Law 167 that a claimant without such rights have? Regardless of the status of surface rights, it has long been held that the surface of an unpatented mining claim cannot be used for some purpose other than mining.[1] Although the claimant has the present and exclusive possession for the purpose of mining, the federal government retains fee title and can protect the land and the surface resources from trespass, waste or from uses other than those associated with mining.[2]

Claims without Surface Rights under Public Law 167

In cases involving mining claims located before July 23, 1955, where the Government does not verify a discovery in connection with a section 5 proceeding, the claimant loses certain surface rights, but still retains the mining claim and all the surface rights necessary to develop and mine the mineral resource.[3] In general there is very little benefit to having surface rights to a mining claim. Perhaps the only advantage in most cases is the right to exclude the public from the claim.

How to Determine if a Claim Has Surface Rights

The best way to determine if a claim located before July 23, 1955, has surface rights is to examine the Master Title Plats maintained in the public room of the BLM. If the claim has surface rights, the right side of the plat will be annotated with a listing of all claims in the township carrying surface rights. If you have reason to believe the plat is improperly annotated, you may request the original case file from the BLM for the appropriate Public Law 167 determination area. The plat should give the number for the case file. Such surface rights can be maintained through a succession of owners so long as the claim is properly maintained and the transfers of interest are proper. If there is a break in the chain of title, surface rights are lost and cannot be reacquired through relocation. For example, many claimants lost surface rights because the owner failed to record the claim or make the requisite annual filings under section 314 of the Federal Land Policy and Management Act of 1976. Even though the claimant is able to relocate, the surface rights are lost forever.

Timber May Not Be Taken Unless Necessary for Mining

As early as 1901, the Federal courts required that timber may not be removed from a claim unless the use is reasonably necessary to conduct mining operations. The courts have held that appropriate uses of timber include fuel, support for shafts and tunnels, and the construction of buildings.[4] However timber may not be sold, even to purchase mining supplies or equipment.

Mining Claimant Has No Grazing Rights

Possession of the surface of the land included in an unpatented mining claim does not permit the locator to use the mining claim for grazing purposes or to grant this privilege to others.[5]

High Value of Surface Resources Does Not Change Discovery Requirement

The fact that a mining claim is located in a national forest does not qualify the rights of the locator in any way or increase the mineral values required to establish a discovery. However, because the land on which the claim is situated is known to be valuable for purposes other than mining, the Department requires clear and convincing evidence of the values that are claimed in order to establish the validity of the claim.[7]

Sale of Surface Resources Is a Trespass

The sale of surface resources for use unrelated to mining operations constitutes a trespassory taking, even where the funds raised by such sale are used to finance the legitimate mining operations conducted on the site.[8]

Right of Access to Mining Claim

The right of reasonable access for purposes of prospecting, locating, and mining is provided by the mining law. Such access must be in accordance with the rules and regulations of the Forest Service (36 CFR 228) or the BLM (43 CFR 3809). Although the claimant has the right of access, under these regulations the Government has, under certain circumstances, authority to approve the route and method of access so as to minimize the surface disturbance. However, it is important to emphasize that access to a mining claim is a nondiscretionary right of the miner and is not subject to a right-of-way permit.

No Right-of-Way Across Federal Lands to Patented Claim

There is no legal right-of-way across Federal land to a patented mining claim where there is no use of the claim for mining or related activity. **Bob Strickler**, 106 IBLA 1, 4 (1989).

Right of Access to Claim is Nonexclusive

The United States mining laws give to the owners of mining claims a nonexclusive right of access across the public lands to their for the purposes of maintaining the claims and as a means of removing the minerals.[9]   Although the Department has ruled in several cases that the right of access to a mining claim is nonexclusive, the IBLA has held that where it is in the public interest, multiple locks may be placed on gates to allow entry to only the government and the claimant.[10]

Permit Not Required for Access to Mining Claim

In **Mosch Mining Co.**, 75 IBLA 153 (1983), the Board considered a case where the BLM filed a trespass action against a claimant who constructed an access road to a claim.   In response, Mosch, the claimant, filed an application for an exclusive right-of-way.   Mosch then appealed from a decision offering the right-of-way grant.

The Board pointed out that section 302(b) of the Federal Land Policy and Management Act of 1976 specifies that "no provision of this section or any other section of this Act shall in any way amend the Mining Law of 1872 or impair the rights of any locators or claims under that Act, including, but not limited to, rights of ingress or egress."   The Board further noted that the surface management regulations in 43 CFR 3809 make numerous references to access.   In conclusion, the Board made the following comments on a claimant's right of access:

1. A claimant is not entitled to exclusivity of access.
2. The grant of a right-of-way under Title V of FLPMA is not the appropriate means to establish a claimants access over and to his mining claims.
3. Access to mining claims should be resolved under the surface management regulations.

Although the **Mosch** case involved BLM-administered lands, it seems likely that the same approach would hold true for Forest Service-administered lands, i.e., access roads to mining claims would be regulated under 36 CFR 228 rather than a right-of-way grant or permit.

Right-of-Way Permit Required to
Transport Water to Mining Claim

In **Desert Survivors**, 96 IBLA 193, 196-97 (1987), the Board held that a right-of-way permit issued under Title V of FLPMA must be obtained before transporting water across public land for any mining purpose.   Approval of a right-of-way application is discretionary and the application process is subject to an environmental assessment as required by NEPA.   The Board held that the "implied right of access to mining claims never embraced the right to convey water from outside the claim for use on the claim. This latter right emanated from an express statutory grant in the 1866 mining act. * * * In enacting FLPMA, Congress repealed the 1866 grant of a right-of-way for the construction of ditches and canals (see 706(a) of FLPMA, 90 Stat. 2793) and provided, in section 501(a)(1), 43 U.S.C. 1761(a)(1), for the grant of a right-of-way for the conveyance of water under new procedures."

Although the **Desert Survivors** case involved BLM-administered lands in a wilderness study area, the legal basis for the Board's decision is persuasive that a Title V right-of-way under FLPMA would be required for transporting water across all BLM or Forest Service administered lands.

Power Lines to Mining Claims

Although Congress provided for a right-of-way permit for power lines under Title V of FLPMA as it did for conveyance of water, there was, of course, no mention of power lines in either the 1866 mining act or the mining law of 1872. The BLM and Forest Service surface management regulations (36 CFR 228 and 43 CFR 3809) indicate that water lines and power lines would be authorized under the surface management regulations. At this writing, a power line across federal lands could be authorized by either a right-of-way under Title V of FLPMA or the surface management regulations.

Special Use Permits Do Not Apply to Exploration or Mining Operations

In **U.S. v. Craig**, CR-82-8H (April 16, 1984), the U.S. District for the District of Montana considered a case where a mining claimant appealed from a U.S. Magistrate's judgment finding him guilty of violating the regulations 36 CFR 261.10(a) and 261.12(d). The Forest Service contended that the claimant had damaged a national forest system road and had locked a gate on a forest system road without a special use permit required by 36 CFR 261.

The Montana District Court dismissed the complaints and held that the "appellant was not required to have a special use permit for activities done in connection with mining operations as defined in 36 CFR part 252 (now part 228)." The Court also held that 36 CFR 261 does not apply to a claimant acting under the United States mining laws of 1872 who submitted a proposed plan of operations as required by 36 CFR 228. And any violation of Forest Service regulations should be charged under 36 CFR 228.

Public Access on Unpatented Mining Claims

In **United States v. Curtis-Nevada Mines, Inc.**, 611 F.2d 1277 (9th Cir. 1980), the Court reversed judgment which required members of the general public to have specific written licenses or permits from a state or federal agency in order to gain access to unpatented mining claims for recreational purposes or for entrance to adjacent national forest lands. Since 1970, Curtis-Nevada Mines, Inc. had located 203 mining claims covering approximately 13 square miles on public lands administered by the Bureau of Land Management and on lands within the Toiyabe National Forest administered by the Forest Service. The United States initiated the action to enjoin Curtis-Nevada Mines, Inc., from prohibiting the public access through their unpatented mining claims and public recreational use of the surface of their claims. The Court held that while the BLM or Forest Service may require permits for public use of Federal lands, they need not do so as a prerequisite to public use of surface resources on unpatented mining claims.

In **U.S. v. Curtis-Nevada Mines, Inc.**, the Court also discussed the "exclusive right of possession" to claims located before July 23, 1955. If no determination were ever made or, if the claimant retained surface rights as a result of a determination of surface rights, then the claimant would have the "exclusive right of possession" and would have the right to exclude the general public from his claim. The Court also indicated the Surface Resources Act was passed largely to limit this exclusive possession in order to permit multiple use by the public.

Residency on a Mining Claim

Uses, such as residency, that are not reasonably incident to mining are not permitted on a mining claim, including those claims located before the Surface Resources Act of July 23, 1955. The right of a locator to place buildings for residential purposes on a claim is based on the requirement that such buildings must be directly related and incidental to the mining operation. In **United States v. Nogueira**, 403 F.2d 816 (9th Cir. 1968), the Court held that "the government can prohibit occupation of a mining claim and collect damages for past trespass where the land is not being used for mining purposes, regardless of whether or not the claim was valid." So, according to **Nogueira**, even a valid claim cannot be occupied unless it is being used for mining purposes.

In **United States v. Osterlund**, 505 F.Supp. 165 (DCD Colo. 1981), the Court affirmed **Nogueira** and further held that even if the claims were valid at one time and the structures were used in connection with past mining activities, it would be a trespass to occupy such claims without ongoing mining operations. There is little question that actual continuous exploration or mining operations are required to validate occupancy. Work done just to accomplish assessment work requirements would not qualify. In order to succeed in an action for ejectment, the Government must establish that a claim is invalid, either because the claimant has failed to make a mineral discovery, or because he is not occupying the land in good faith for mining purposes.

Government Remedies for Occupancy Trespass

Even though a claim is valid, the owner has no right to occupy it in the absence of actual and continuous exploration or mining operations. Therefore, it is unnecessary for the government to conduct a validity examination and initiate contest proceedings in order to remove an occupancy trespass. As stated in **Nogueira**, the "court may not deny the United States injunctive relief or damages if trespass upon the public lands is shown." More recently in **United States v. Brown**, 672 F.2d 808, 810 (10th Cir. 1982), the Court said that "people who occupy unpatented mining claims as residences are thus subject to trespass claims and ejectment actions by the United States if the land cannot be patented."

No Rights by Prescription

A claimant who has continuously occupied a mining claim cannot acquire any rights against the government by prescription or adverse possession.[11]

Abandoned Property on Mining Claims

The three types of abandoned property that might exist on a mining claim or mill site include (1) property attached to realty, (2) personal property embedded in the soil, and (3) personal property not embedded in the soil.

1. **Personal property attached to realty** - This type of property includes permanent, nonmovable fixtures attached to the land such as cabins or other buildings. If the mining claim is abandoned, these fixtures become the property of the United States.[12] If the lands embracing the cabin are subsequently located, the new locator has the same rights of exclusive possession to the cabin as he does to the surface resources on the mining claim.[13] Therefore, rights to use a cabin, or a surface resource on an unpatented claim must be directly related and incident to actual mining operations on the claim.

2. **Personal property embedded in the soil** - This type of property, which is not attached to realty, includes such items as mining equipment embedded in the soil but does not exclude

"treasure troves." A treasure trove is defined as "...any gold or silver in coin, plate, or bullion found concealed in the earth, or in a house or other private place, but not lying on the ground, the owner of the discovered treasure being unknown, or the treasure have been hidden so long as to indicate a probability that the owner is dead." Upon abandonment of the claim, this type of property becomes the property of the land owner, the United States.[14] The new locator of this type of abandoned property would have rights to use such property if the use is directly related and incidental to actual mining operations.

3. **Personal property not embedded in the soil** - This type of property, which is found at the surface of realty, includes such items as tools and vehicles. Upon abandonment, such items become the property of the finder rather than the landowner or the United States. However, ownership of such abandoned property can be claimed by the United States under 40 U.S.C. 484 (m). This section requires that the government assert dominion and control over the abandoned property by taking possession of such property. Until the government takes this affirmative action, the abandoned property remains subject to the claims of whoever first finds the objects and claims title. If the new locator of an abandoned claim containing such property asserts possession over these movable items before the United States does so, ownership of the property would vest in the claimant. Furthermore, there is no requirement that such property be used in connection with mining operations because the claimant would hold a legal rather than a possessory title.

Liability for Unlawful Use, Removal or Damage to Abandoned Property

If a relocator should remove, damage or use property left on an abandoned claim, he may be subject to civil and criminal liability. For example, if the property belongs to the United States, such liability would apply if the relocators use or dispose of the property, regardless of whether the relocator actually believed he had a right to the property.

Removal and (or) sale of appurtenances abandoned by a prior location on an unpatented mining claim by a relocator without right can, under certain circumstances, constitute a criminal act under 18 U.S.C. 641. Maximum penalties for theft of government property may be a fine of up to $10,000 and (or) imprisonment for up to 10 years. Unlike the civil remedies, however, not only must government ownership and a trespassory taking be shown, but it must also be shown that the defendant acted with an intent to appropriate property he know to belong to another.

Intentional damage to property left on an unpatented mining claim by a relocator without right can, under certain circumstances, also constitute a criminal act under 18 U.S.C. 1361. Like the criminal theft statute, and unlike the civil remedies, not only must government ownership and trespassory act be shown, but it must also be shown that the defendant acted intentionally (rather than merely negligently) and with knowledge that the property belonged to the United States.[15]

Fish and Fish Habitats Are "Other Surface Resources"

In **Robert E. Shoemaker**, 110 IBLA 39 (1989), the Board held that fish and fish habitats are "other surface resources" which the Department has authority to manage on the surface of mining claims under 4(b) of the Surface Resources Act, 30 U.S.C. 612(b) (1982). However, section 4(b) further provides that "any use of the surface of any such mining claim by the United States, its permittees or licensees, shall be such as not to endanger or materially interfere with prospecting, mining or processing operations or uses reasonably incident thereto * * * ."

If Federal Surface Management Activities Endanger or Materially Interfere with Mining Operations

In the **Shoemaker** case the BLM had installed weirs to enhance the wildlife habitat on a stream embraced by an existing placer claim. The Board had to make a determination as to whether the weirs endanger or materially interfere with the operations conducted by the claim owners. If the weirs do endanger or materially interfere, the "Federal surface management activities must yield to mining as the 'dominant and primary use," the mineral locator having a first and full right to use the surface and surface resources." **Robert E. Shoemaker**, supra at 53. Based on dictionary definitions, the Board determined that "materially interfere" is equivalent to "substantially hinder, impede or clash." The Board then held that the 10 weirs "substantially impede" or "materially interfere" with the appellant's mining operation. Id. at 55.

References - Surface Rights on Mining Claims

1. U.S. v. Rissinelli, 182 Fed. 675 (Idaho 1910).
2. U.S. v. Curtis-Nevada Mines, Inc., 611 F.2d 1277 (9th Cir. 1980).
3. U.S. v. Bartell, 31 IBLA 47 (1977).
4. Teller v. U.S., 113 Fed. 273 (8th Cir. 1901); U.S. v. Deasy, 24 F.2d 108 (Idaho 1928).
5. Id.; Authority of the Bureau of Land Management to Sell Timber on an Unpatented Mining Claim, M-36365 (March 11, 1955).
6. U.S. v. Etcheverry, 230 F.2d 193 (10th Cir. 1956); James G. Brown, 65 I.D. 394 (1958).
7. U.S. v. Wells, A-30805 (Jan. 8, 1968).
8. Teller v. U.S., 113 F. 273 (8th Cir. 1901).
9. Alfred E. Koenig, 78 I.D. 305 (1971).
10. Mosch Mining Co., 75 IBLA 153, 161, f.n. 4 (1983).
11. U.S. v. Osterlund, 505 F.Supp. 165 (DCD Colo. 1981).
12. Brothers v. U.S., 594 F.2d 740 (9th Cir. 1979).
13. McKenzie v. Moore, 176 P. 568 (Ariz. 1918).
14. Alfred v. Biegel, 219 SW 2d 665 (Mo Ct Cl 1949).
15. U.S. v. Simpson, 460 F.2d 515 (9th Cir. 1972).

ASSESSMENT WORK

Purpose of Assessment Work

The purpose of the assessment work requirement is to discourage the speculative holding of mining claims to the exclusion of others and to require a demonstration of good faith in developing a claim.[1] Assessment work is done to assure diligent development of mining claims and prevent speculation by location of many claims and letting them go idle.[2]

There is some precedent for requiring that assessment work cause visible change to the surface so as to notify other potential locators that the ground is being held in good faith. The Tenth Circuit Court of Appeals[3] has held "that the basic federal requirements, the staking, and the assessment work were all acts relating to the ground itself and to create some condition which could be observed by persons seeking to locate claims in the same area..." However, a California State court[4] held that the work "must be of such a character a directly tends to develop and protect the claim and facilitate the extraction of minerals even though such work does not create visible signs." In 1974 the Supreme Court of New Mexico[5] said that the "general rule is that the work must be of such character as directly tends to develop and protect the claim and to facilitate the extraction of minerals.

The Assessment Year

The assessment year or the period during which the work must be done annually "on all unpatented mineral claims located since May 10, 1872, including such claims in the Territory of Alaska, shall commence at 12 o'clock meridian on the 1st day of September succeeding the date of location of such claim." 30 U.S.C. 28 (1982). The Act of August 23, 1958 (72 Stat. 829) changed the period for doing assessment work so that each assessment year begins at noon September 1 instead of noon July 1. Assessment work is not required during the assessment year the claim is located. For example, if a claim were located November 10, 1988, the first assessment work would be required for the assessment year beginning September 1, 1989, and ending September 1, 1990. Assessment work is not required subsequent to issuance of the patent certificate. Of course Section 314 of the Federal Land Policy and Management Act requires that a "notice of intention to hold" be filed with both the BLM and the local recording office during calendar year 1989 even though assessment work is not required.

Amount of Work Required Per Claim

The Federal law requires that "on each claim located after the 10th day of May 1872, and until a patent has been issued therefor, not less than $100 worth of labor shall be performed or improvements made during each year." 30 U.S.C. 28 (1982).

Value of Labor Rather than Price Paid

To determine the amount of work done on a claim, the critical factor is the reasonable value of the work rather than the contract price paid.[6] Other factors that may be taken into consideration in the value of labor is remoteness of the claim from sources of labor, the cost and availability of supplies and the lack of facilities.

Type of Work

The Federal law does not specify the type of work that should qualify for assessment work. However, because the law does require that discovery precede location, any work done must directly relate to the development or extraction of the mineral. Any work expended towards finding a mineral discovery would be exploratory in nature and would not qualify. The following situation represents a hypothetical example. If a geochemical, geophysical anomaly, or a mineralized area is drilled to determine if there is a commercial deposit in the subsurface, such work would be exploratory in nature and thus, would not qualify as assessment work. Even if ore were intersected by the first drill hole and several other holes were necessary to establish that the deposit contained sufficient reserves of ore to justify development, this additional drilling would also be exploratory in nature and may not qualify.

However, once it is established that the deposit is sufficient in quality and quantity to justify commercial development, a discovery is made.[7] Any future drilling to further define the limits or shape of the ore body would, of course, qualify as assessment work.[8] Again, the above is an extreme theoretical situation. The courts have accepted many types of exploratory work and would normally accept most types of drilling.

In a conflict between claimants over right of possession of a mining claim, involving the question of proper assessment work, the question of whether a discovery is made is generally not an issue and probably should not be. The judge is in a poor position to determine a question of fact such as discovery; but the judge is generally quite comfortable with ruling on good faith. Therefore, in most cases, judges have ruled in favor of a senior locator who performed assessment work in good faith, regardless of whether such work consists of exploration type work.

Examples of Work or Improvements that May Qualify as Assessment Work

1. A building that benefits and improves the claim.[9]

2. Reasonable value of meals to miners who receive board in addition to salary.[10]

3. Value of blasting supplies.[11]

4. Construction of road to mining claim.[12]

5. Maintenance of access roads to mining claim;[13] this may not qualify if used year after year.

6. Sinking shafts and running tunnels or drifts.[14]

7. Installation of mining machinery or fixtures.[15]

8. Employment of a watchman when necessary to protect Structures or property used in developing a claim.[16]

9. Drilling and removal of sample from a mining claim;[17] be aware that drilling must be for development purposes rather than exploration.

Examples of Work Courts Have Held Do Not Qualify As Assessment Work

1. Removal of water from a mine for inspection of prospective buyer.[18]

2. Erection of a house outside the boundaries of a claim for the shelter of miners.[19]

3. Eating utensils, groceries and bedding.[20]

4. Amount paid for horses used in development work; however value of their use will qualify.[21]

5. Payment for iron rails or tools, but their value in developing the mine may qualify.[22]

6. Material taken to a claim but not used.[23]

7. Sampling and assaying.[24]

8. Reconnaissance surveys of mining claims.[25]

9. Use of a claim to deposit wastes from other claims and building a flume to carry tailings to claim.[26]

10. Employment of a watchman to prevent relocation;[27] or where there is no valuable improvement or machinery to protect.[28]

Geological, Geochemical and Geophysical Surveys

Until the Act of September 2, 1958, authorized that geological, geochemical and geophysical surveys may be used to fulfill the annual labor assessment requirements, the Federal laws did not describe the type of assessment work that would satisfy the statutory requirement of $100 per claim per year.

If geological, geochemical and geophysical surveys are to be utilized to fulfill the requirement for assessment work as authorized by the Act of September 2, 1958, such survey must be conducted by qualified experts and verified by a detailed report filed in the county in which the claim is located. The report must include: (1) the location of work performed in relation to the point of discovery and boundaries of the claim; (2) type of work, extent and cost; (3) the results of the survey; and (4) the name, address and professional background of the person or persons conducting the work. 30 U.S.C. 28-1 (1982).

In PL 85-876 (30 U.S.C. 28-2 and 43 CFR 3851.2[b]-1) the following definitions are given:

The term "geological surveys" means surveys on the ground for mineral deposits by the proper application of the principles and techniques of the science of geology as they relate to the search for and discovery of mineral deposits; (2) The term "geochemical surveys" means surveys on the ground for mineral deposits by the proper application of the principles and techniques of the science of chemistry as they relate to the search for and discovery of mineral deposits; (3) The term "geophysical surveys" means surveys on the ground for mineral deposits through the employment of generally recognized equipment and methods for measuring physical differences between rock types or discontinuities in geological formations; (4) The term "qualified expert" means an individual qualified by education or experience to conduct geological, geochemical, or geophysical surveys, as the case may be.

Surveys may not be used to satisfy the assessment work requirement for more than two consecutive years or for more than a total of five years on any one claim. No two surveys on the same claim may involve the same type of work. Such surveys may not be applied towards the statutory requirement that $500 must be expended for each claim in order to obtain patent.

Good Faith and Evidence of Work

Good faith may be taken into consideration in determining whether a senior locator has performed the required assessment work.[29] Although annual assessment work on mining claims does not need to be performed openly and notoriously,[30] a lack of visible assessment work after years of occupancy of a claim indicates no such work was done.[31]

Group Assessment Work

Assessment work done on one or more of a group of adjoining claims, or even outside all of them, held in common ownership must be of a character that it would benefit the development of the group as a whole and the value of the labor must be at least $100 for each claim.[32]   Group assessment work is authorized in 30 U.S.C. 28 and 43 CFR 3851.1. The law provides that "where such claims are held in common, such expenditure may be made upon any one claim."[33]

If the assessment work is not done within the claim boundaries, the locator has the burden to show that the work would benefit the development of the claim.[34]   Claims must be contiguous or at least in such a position in relation to the ore body that it is reasonable to conclude that assessment work done on one claim would benefit the others.[35]

Definition of "Contiguous"

If claims of such a group touch only at a common corner, they are not considered contiguous.[36]

The regulations (43 CFR 3851.1) also state that "cornering locations are held not to be contiguous."

Gold Placer Claims May Not Qualify for Group Assessment Work

The United States Supreme Court[37] has held in a case involving placer claims that the labor should be done on each claim because the "general development work being upon and near the surface does not tend to benefit other claims than the one upon which the work is actually done..." Of course ordinary placer claims should qualify for group assessment work if the work benefits each claim.

Compliance with Federal Assessment work Requirement Liberally Construed

The owner of a group of mining claims, when in good faith performs work on one claim to benefit the entire group, is generally given broad latitude by the courts as to how and where such work is done.[38] The Utah Supreme Court[39] said that "when there is an attempt at compliance, however, the law should be construed liberally to prevent a forfeiture."

Assessment Work Off Claim

Assessment work may be performed outside the boundary lines of a claim, or outside the entire contiguous claim group so long as the work benefits the claim. The courts have held that such work may be done on unappropriated public domain or patented lands.[40] However, such work may not qualify if done within the boundaries of a claim owned by another.[41]

It is not essential that labor improvements be made on the claim itself so long as work such as labor to develop water, or to remove waste rock or tailings from a placer claim facilitates the extraction of ore.[42] However, labor expended to obtain water to operate a mill does not qualify.[43] Not only has work in connection with bringing water to a benefitting claim been held to qualify, but also construction of access roads to claims has been held to qualify as assessment work.[44]

Apportionment of Work Among Contiguous Claims

In situations where a claimant performs an insufficient amount of work (less than $100 per claim) to cover all claims in a contiguous group, the courts[45] generally resolve the deficiency in one of three ways:

1. If the assessment work is apportioned equally to each claim, all claims will have insufficient work.[46]

2. The assessment work may be allocated entirely to the claim(s) where the work was performed.[47]

3. The claim owner may select those claims upon which sufficient work was performed.[48]

Work on Patented Claim Applies to Adjacent Unpatented Claim

In a 1984 case the Montana Supreme Court[49] held that assessment work done on patented claims would benefit an unpatented claim. Silver Jet, the senior claimant, had cleared vegetation from 6,000 square yards of land in an area leading to a tunnel on an adjacent patented claim, and had also secured the entrance to a tunnel. The Court held that the cleared area could be used as an operations area to support the unpatented claims, and also indicated that the unpatented claim could possibly be mined from the tunnel.

State Requirements for Assessment Work

Each state has a statute requiring that an affidavit of assessment work be filed. Although all state statutes give specific information that must be included in the affidavit, the states of arkansas, Arizona, Colorado and Idaho include in the statute the exact language to be included in the affidavit. In all states except Wyoming, the statutes provide that the filing of an affidavit of assessment work constitutes prima facie evidence that the work was performed.

Recordation of Assessment Work Affidavit Under State Law

Each state statute provides that the affidavit must be filed by the end of a specified period of time following the assessment year:

State	Period Allowed or Date after Sept. 1
Alaska	90 days
Arizona	before December 31
California	30 days
Colorado	on or before December 30
Idaho	60 days
Montana	90 days
Nevada	on or before Nov. 1
New Mexico	on or before December 30
North Dakota	not required
Oregon	30 days
South Dakota	no form required
Utah	30 days after completing work
Washington	30 days
Wyoming	30 days after completing work

Work for Contiguous Claims in One Affidavit

As a general rule, assessment work covering a contiguous group of claims may be included in a single affidavit unless the state law provides otherwise.

Burden of Proof on Junior Locator that Assessment Work Not Performed

Most courts have held that the Junior locator has the burden of proving by clear and convincing evidence that the senior locator failed to do the required work.[50]

Failure to Perform Assessment Work

In the event a claim owner fails to perform the annual labor, "the claim or mine upon which such failure occurred shall be open to relocation in the same manner as if no location of the same had ever been made, provided that the original locators, their heirs, assigns, or legal representatives, have not resumed work upon the claim after failure and before such location." 30 U.S.C. 28. Failure of a mining claimant to make the expenditure or perform the labor required upon a location will subject a claim to relocation unless the original locator, his heirs, assigns, or legal representatives have resumed work after such failure and before relocation. 43 CFR 3851.3(b).

Performance of Assessment Work Not a Matter of Concern to United States

Historically, assessment work was done to prevent relocation by a rival claimant, and whether or not such work was done was of little concern to the Federal Government.[51] However, in **Hickel v. Oil Shale Corporation**, 400 U.S. 48 (1970), the Supreme Court held that the Secretary of the Interior has authority to declare unpatented mining claims invalid for lack of assessment work. Although the claims in this case were for oil shale, the Secretary, in an effort to extend the requirement to all types of mining claims, adopted the following regulations in 1972 (43 CFR 3851.3[a]:

> Failure of a mining claimant to comply substantially with the requirement of an annual expenditure of $100 in labor or improvements on a claim...will render the claim subject to cancellation.

However, the Interior Department has been reluctant to apply this regulation to mining claims in general. As a general rule, assessment work is required only to preserve the exclusive right to the possession of a valid location on which discovery has been made.

Association Placer Claims

Although placer claims may range in size from 20 acres with one locator and up to 160 acres in an association placer located by at least eight persons, only $100 worth of labor is required by the statute.

Relocation After Expiration of Assessment Year

A relocation on lands covered by a valid location is void. A relocation should not be made until the existing location expires at the end of the assessment year, or 12 o'clock (noon) on September 1.[52] This is true even if the owner of the valid existing location ultimately fails to perform the required work.[53] Of course a claimant could relocated a claim over his own prior claim before the end of the assessment year.

Relocation by Original Locator

A mining claimant may relocate his claim for any purpose except to avoid performing annual assessment work.[54] However if a location has lapsed and is subject to relocation because the annual labor was not performed, the owner of the lapsed claim may relocate.[55] If no intervening rights are established, the original locator may revive his rights by doing the necessary work. Some claim owners have been known to relocate their claims every year shortly after expiration of the assessment year so as to avoid the $100 expenditure for assessment work.[56] There are several pitfalls involved with such a practice: (1) the claim loses its seniority; (2) the claim is open to relocation for a short period of time; and (3) if the claim is properly relocated, the costs involved could exceed the costs of the assessment work.

Work by Agent or Person Who Holds No Interest

Labor or improvement on a claim may be performed by the owner's authorized agent.[57] And the work is still attributable to the required assessment work even if done by a person who holds no interest in the claim.[58]

Threats by Junior Locator

A junior locator cannot acquire any right by forcibly preventing a senior locator from doing assessment work.[59] However, a court has held that threats made seven miles from a claim do not constitute a sufficient excuse for nonperformance.[60]

Fraudulent Acquisition of Title

Title to a mining claim cannot be fraudulently acquired by an agent, trustee, co-owner or any person having confidential relations with the owner of a claim by violation of agreement or trust. Any locator who fraudulently obtains such title by relocating in his own name is considered as a trustee of the rightful owner and acquires no interest in the property by such action.[61] Many cases have occurred where individuals under contract to perform the assessment work have failed to do the work for the purpose of making the ground open to relocation either to themselves or to a third party.[62]

Abandonment and Co-owner

If one co-owner abandons his interest, the entire claim is not abandoned, but the abandoned interest passes to the other cotenants.[63] Abandonment of a mining claim is a question of intent and may be demonstrated only by clear and convincing proof.[64]

There is a general rule that co-owners or co-tenants have a relationship of mutual trust and that one is not allowed to demonstrate hostility to other co-owners by acquiring a separate title from the joint ownership. Any separate or distinct title goes to the benefit of all joint owners.[65] For example, one co-owner may not relocate a claim owned jointly on the basis that the annual work was not done.[66] A co-owner who relocates or patents the claim in his own name, will hold the title in trust for all.[67]

Failure of Co-owners to Contribute to Assessment Work

Co-owners who do not contribute their share of the annual assessment work may lose their interest in the claim through a procedure given in 30 U.S.C. 28 (1976). The law provides that "upon the failure of any one of several co-owners to contribute his proportion of the expenditures required hereby, the co-owners who have performed the labor or made the improvements may, at the expiration of the year, give such delinquent co-owner personal notice in writing or notice by publication in the newspaper published nearest the claim, for at least once a week for ninety days, and if at the expiration of ninety days, after such notice in writing or by publication such delinquent should fail or refuse to contribute his proportion of the expenditure required by this section, his interest in the claim shall become the property of his co-owners who have made the required expenditures. The regulations (43 CFR 3851.4) give directions to the claimant receiving the forfeited interest as follows:

> Where a claimant alleges ownership of a forfeited interest under the foregoing provision, the statement of the publisher as to the facts of publication, giving dates, and a printed copy of the notice published, should be furnished, and the claimant must state that the delinquent co-owner failed to contribute his proper proportion within the period fixed by the statute.

Even though a co-owner is prevented from making the assessment work contribution by occurrence of death during the assessment year, his rights are subject to forfeiture by proper notice to his heirs.[68] Even the disabilities of infancy do not relieve a minor from the obligation to contribute to assessment work on a claim.[69]

The required assessment work contribution of a delinquent co-owner, if made by friends or a third party is valid and prevents forfeiture if agreeable to such delinquent co-owner.[70] Contribution of assessment work from a co-owner cannot be made if such work is not required.[71] Also if a co-owner takes exclusive possession of the claim and prevents the other co-owner from contributing to the assessment work, the co-owner in possession may not forfeit the interests of the excluded co-owner.[72]

Only the co-owner who has performed the required work has the right to give notice to the delinquent co-owner. In order to forfeit a co-owner for failure to contribute to assessment work, the $100 worth of labor or improvements must be expended for each claim.[73] Many cases have occurred where the evidence suggested that the required work was not done and the intent was to extract money or the claims from one or more co-owners.[74]

In order to acquire patent, a co-owner who obtained a forfeiture of the interest of a delinquent co-owner who obtained a forfeiture of the interest of a delinquent co-owner must be able to furnish evidence concerning the delinquent co-owners failure to contribute his part of the required work.[75]

References - Assessment Work

1. Jupiter Mining Co. v. Bodie Consolidated Mining Co. 11 F. 666 (1881).
2. Powell v. Atlas, 615 P.2d 1225 (Utah 1980).
3. Hickle v. Oil Shale Corp., 406 F.2d (10th Circ. 1969), reversed on other grounds, 400 U.S. 48 (1979).
4. Eveleigh v. Darneille, 276 Cal App 2d 638, 81 Cal Repts 301, 303 (1969).
5. Great Eastern Mines, Inc. v. Metals Corp. of America, 527 P2d 112 (1974).
6. McKay v. Neussler, 148 F. 86 (CCA Alaska 1906).
7. Chrisman v. Miller, 197 U.S. 313, 321-22 (1905); Barton v. Morton, 498 F.2d 288 (1974).
8. Schlegal v. Hough, 182 Ore 441, 188 P.2d 158 (1947).
9. Bryan v. McCraig, 10 Colo 309, 15 P. 413 (1887).
10. Fredricks v. Klauser, 52 Or 110 96 P. 679 (1908).
11. Id.
12. U.S. v. 9,947.71 Acres of Land, More or Less, in Clark County, State of Nev., 220 F. Supp. 328 (DC Nev. 1963); Silliman v. Powell, Utah, 642 P.2d 388, 393 (1982).
13. Pinkerton v. Moore, 66 NM 11, 340 P.2d 844 (1959).
14. James v. Krook, 42 Ariz. 322 (1933).
15. Id.
16. Ingersoll v. Scott, 13 Ariz 165, 108 P. 460 (1910).
17. Eveleigh v. Darneille, 81 Cal Rptr 301 (Cal App 1969).
18. Evalina Gold Mining Co. v. Yosemite Gold Mine Co., 15 Cal App 714, 115 P. 946 (1911).
19. Remington v. Baudit, 6 Mont 138, 9 P. 819 (1896).
20. Fredricks v. Klauser, 52 OR 110, 96 P. 679 (1908).
21. Id.
22. Id.
23. Id.
24. Bishop v. Baisley, 28 OR 119, 41 P. 936 (1895).
25. Pinkerton v. Moore, 66 NM 11, 340 P.2d 844 (1959).
26. Jackson v. Roby, 109 U.S. 440 (1883).
27. Justice Mining Co. v. Barclay, 82 F. 554 (CC Nev 1897).
28. James v. Krook, 42 Ariz. 322, 25 P.2d 1026 (1933).
29. Haws v. Victoria Copper Mining Co., 160 U.S. 303 (1895).
30. Great Eastern Mines Inc. v. Metals Corp. of America, supra.
31. U.S. v. Mobley, 45 F.Supp. 407 (D.C. Cal. 1942), Supplemented on other Grounds, 46 F. Supp. 676.
32. St. Louis Smelting and Ry. Co. v. Kemp, 104 U.S. 636 (1881).
33. 30 U.S.C. 28 (1982).
34. Justice Mining Co. v. Barclay, 82 F. 554 (CC Nev. 1897).
35. Powell v. Atlas Corp., 615 P.2d 1225 (Utah 1980); Jackson v. Roby, 109 U.S. 440 (1883).
36. Anvil Hydraulic & Drainage Co. v. Code, 182 F. 205 (CCA Alaska 1910).
37. Union Oil Co. of Cal. v. Smith, 249 U.S. 350, 351-52.
38. Copper Mtn Mining & Smelting Co. v. Butte & Corbin Consolidated Copper and Silver Mining Co., 39 Mont. 487, 104 P. 540 (1909).
39. Silliman v. Powell, 642 P.2d 388, 394 (1982).
40. Anvil Hydraulic Drainage Co. v. Code, 182 Fed. 205 (9th Cir. 1910).
41. Weigle v. Salmino, 49 Idaho 522, 290 Pac. 552 (1930).
42. Smelting Co. v. Kemp, 104 U.S. 636 (1881).

43. DuPrat v. James, 65 Cal 555, 4 P. 562 (1884).
44. Lind v. Baker, 31 Cal App 2d 631, 88 P.2d 777 (1939).
45. 2 American Law of Mining 7.721, p. 128.
46. Duncan v. Eagle Rock Gold Mining & Reduction Co., 48 Colo 569, 111 Pac 588; Platt v. Bogg, 77 Ariz 214, 269 P.2d 715 (1954).
47. Swanson v. Kettler, 17 Id 321, 105 P. 1059 (1910), On rehearing 105 P. 1065, affirmed 224 U.S. 180.
48. Utah Standard Mining Co. v. Tintic Indian Chief Mining & Milling Co., 73 Utah 456, 274 P. 950, 951 (1929).
49. Silver Jet Mines v. Schwark, 41 St. Rptr. 933 (Mont. 1984).
50. Pascoe v. Richards, 20 Cal Reptr 416 (1962); McDermott v. O'Brien, 409 P.2d 588, 2 Ariz App 429 (1966); Velasco v. Mallory, 427 P.2d 540, 5 Ariz. App. 406 (1967).
51. James W. Hansen, 1 IBLA 134 (1970).
52. Belk v. Meagher, 104 U.S. 270 (1881).
53. Rooney v. Barnette, 200 F. 700 (1912); Velasco v. Mallory, 427 P.2d 540, 5 Ariz App. 406 (1967).
54. Lehman v. Sutter, 198 P. 110 (1921).
55. Warnock v. DeWitt, 40 P. 205 (1895), appeal dismissed 18 S. Ct. 949.
56. Belk v. Meagher, 104 U.S. 279 (1881).
57. Richard v. Thompson, 72 F.2d 807 (CCA Alaska 1934).
58. Smelting Co. v. Kemp, 104 U.S. 636 (1881).
59. Ames v. Sullivan, 235 F. 880, 149 CCA 192 (1916).
60. Slavonian Mining Co. v. Perasich, CC Nev. 188, 7 F. 331.
61. Turner v. Sawyer, 150 U.S. 578 (1893).
62. Soule v. Johnson, 201 P. 834 (1921).
63. Crane v. French, 39 Cal App 2d 642, 104 P.2d 53 (1940); Laguna Development Co. v. McAlester Fuel Co., 572 P.2d 1252, 91 NM 244.
64. Loeser v. Gardiner, 1 Alaska 641 (1902).
65. Stevens v. Grand Central Mining Co., 133 F. 28 (1904).
66. Speed v. McCarthy, 181 U.S. 369 (1901).
67. Turner v. Sawyer, supra.
68. Elder v. Horshoe Mining Co., 194 U.S. 248 (1904).
69. Pomeroy v. Sam Thorpe Mining Co., 296 P. 255 (1931).
70. Forderer v. Schmidt, 154 F. 475 (1907).
71. Kline v. Wright, 51 F.2d 564 (DC Id 1931).
72. Becker-Franz Co. v. Shannon Copper Co., 256 F. 522 (CCA Ariz 1919).
73. Pack v. Thompson, 223 F. 635 (CCA Cal 1915).
74. Delnoe v. Long, 88 P. 778 (1907).
75. Turner v. Sawyer, 150 U.S. 578 (1893).

DEFERMENT OF ASSESSMENT WORK

Introduction

The Act of June 21, 1949 (30 U.S.C. 28) authorizes the temporary deferment of annual assessment work under the following circumstances:

> ...upon the submission by the claimant of evidence satisfactory to the Secretary that such mining claim or group of claims is surrounded by lands over which a right-of-way for the performance of such assessment work has been denied or is in litigation or is in the process of acquisition under State law or that other legal impediments exist which affect the right of the claimant to enter upon the surface of such claim or group of claims or to gain access to the boundaries thereof.

Petition Must Be Filed for Deferment

The regulations in 43 CFR 3852.2 give the specific requirements for filing a petition. The petition, which has no particular form, is filed with the state office of the Bureau of Land Management and must have a copy of the "notice to the public" attached to show that the notice was filed with the county recorder or other local office of recordation. The regulations require that the applicant give full details concerning the "legal impediments" preventing access to the claim.[1]

Definition of Legal Impediment

The meaning of the term "legal impediments" was specifically considered in the legislative history of 30 U.S.C. 28(b) and was discussed in the Senate Report No. 405 (May 19, 1949) as follows:

1. Delays in making arrangements with surrounding surface owners due to contested titles, family squabbles, changes of ownership during negotiations, etc.

2. Delays in official approval of bonds to protect the owners of the surface of the claims.

3. Delays in causing legal condemnation of rights-of-way, which can be contested for a long time in the courts.

4. Delays in overcoming by court action the posting of "No Trespassing" signs on roads which have been used by the public for many years but have never been declared public roads.

The Interior Board of Land appeals has ruled on a variety of cases requiring interpretation of the term "legal impediments." The

Board has held that the following actions do not constitute "legal impediments:"

1. Bankruptcy does not restrict physical access.[2]

2. In Stock-Raising Homestead Act cases, the claimant must attempt to get access from the surface owner before he can complain that access is restricted.[3]

3. Delay in approval of plan of operations cannot be used for deferment. Both BLM and Forest Service surface management regulations contain provisions requiring the limited approval of operations which are necessary for meeting the assessment work obligations, pending approval of a plan.[4]

4. Pending government contest is not sufficient basis.[5]

5. A possible or threatened trespass action by the Government does not constitute a legal impediment.[6]

6. The mere pendency of litigation involving mining claims, which gives rise to a risk that any assessment work invested in the claims may be lost as a consequence of an unfavorable court decision is an insufficient basis for a deferment.[7]

The Board has held that an injunction issued by a court is a legal impediment to entry which will justify a deferment.[8] In another case the Board held that the barricading entry to a mining claim by the Government constitutes a legal impediment.[9]

Additional Deferment under Judicial Declaration

Although the two-year deferment is authorized by statute and may not be extended by the Department, in a recent case the Board of Land Appeals pointed out that "if circumstances exist which would warrant a deferment under judicial declarations, then such circumstances may be availed of in appropriate judicial litigation."[10]

Period of Deferment

The statute states that "the initial period shall not exceed one year but may be renewed for a further period of one year if justifiable conditions exist." 30 U.S.C. 28(c). The period begins on the date requested in the petition unless the BLM specifies a different date in the approval. If the circumstances justifying the deferment are removed before the specified termination date, the deferment ends automatically at the end of the earlier date.[11]

The law allows a deferment of assessment work for a maximum period of two years even though the "legal impediment" that prevents access to the claim may exist for a longer period of time. For this reason claimants commonly attempt to obtain a deferment for a third year. However, the Board has consistently held that there is no statutory authority to extend the deferment period even if it were otherwise justifiable.[12]

When Deferred Work Must Be Done

According to the statute "all deferred assessment work shall be performed not later than the end of the assessment year next subsequent to the removal or cessation of the causes for deferment or the expiration of any deferments granted under sections 28(b) to 28(3) of this title and shall be in addition to the annual assessment work required by law in such year." 30 U.S.C. 28(d).

Recordation of Deferment

The statute requires that the "claimant shall file or cause to be filed or recorded in the office where the notice or certificate of location of such claim or group of claims is filed or recorded, a notice to the public of claimant's petition to the Secretary of the Interior for deferment...and of the order or decision disposing of such petition." 30 U.S.C. 28(d). In other words, the claimant must file in the office where he recorded his notice of petition a copy of the decision from the BLM granting the deferment of assessment work.

Deferment of Assessment Work with No Notice of Intention to Hold

A deferment of assessment work authorized by 30 U.S.C. 28 without a timely filed notice of intention to hold a mining claim will not save a mining claim from abandonment under 43 U.S.C. 1744(a). However a notice of intention to hold filed with both the BLM and local recording office before December 31 satisfies the law.[13]

BLM policy allows a deferment of assessment work which is still in effect, or a petition for deferment which has been recorded in the local recording office to serve as a notice of intention to hold.[14]

No Assessment Work Required for Mill Site

The Board of Land Appeals has held that no deferment of assessment work could be granted for a mill site because the law does not require assessment work for mill sites.[15]

Claims Protected from Forfeiture While Owner in Military Service

Section 505 of the Soldiers and Sailors Civil Relief Act of 1940. protects claims from forfeiture for nonperformance of assessment work while the owner serves in the military. Assessment work is not required during the period of the claimant's military service, or until six months after termination of the service.[16] This period of protection also includes the time spent in a hospital as a result of wounds or disability incurred in the line of duty.

The owner of a mining claim who wishes to obtain this deferment must before the end of the assessment year during which military service is entered, file or have filed in the county recording office, a notice that he or she has entered such service and that the mining claim is to be held under section 505 of the Soldiers' and Sailors' Relief Act of 1940.

References - Deferment of Assessment Work

1. A.J. Maurer, Jr., 61 IBLA 39, 41 (1981).
2. Oliver Reese, 34 IBLA 103, 105 (1978).
3. A.J. Maurer, Jr., 36 IBLA 4, 9 (1978).
4. Instruction Memorandum No. 86-191 (Jan 8, 1986).
5. J.R. Eck, 6 IBLA 263 (1972).
6. Charlestone Stone Products, Inc., 32 IBLA 23 (1977).
7. Continental Oil Co., 36 IBLA 65, 68 (1978).
8. Id. at 68.
9. American Resources, 44 IBLA 227 (1979).
10. J.M. Glenn, 73 IBLA 323 (1983).
11. 43 CFR 3852.4.
12. Dredge Corp., 38 IBLA 178 (1978); John S. Herr, 40 IBLA 159 (1979); Charlestone Stone Products, Inc., supra at 24.
13. Marcus D. Schneider, 94 IBLA 239, 241 (1986).
14. BLM Manual 3833.23A.
15. Andew L. Freeze, 50 IBLA 26, 87 I.D. 396 (1980).
16. 43 CFR 2096.2-7.

REGULATIONS ON
NATIONAL FOREST LANDS

Introduction

On September 1, 1974, the U.S. Department of Agriculture made effective regulations (36 CFR Part 228) designed to cover prospecting, exploration and mining activities on National Forest Lands by persons operating under the Mining Law of 1872, as amended. Although these regulations do not constitute a permit to explore or mine as that is already a statutory right under the 1872 mining law, they do provide that such exploration and mining activities be conducted so as to minimize adverse environmental impacts on the National Forest System.

These regulations apply to all operations concerned with prospecting, exploration, development, mining or processing mineral resources, including access roads and other operations whether on or off a mining claim conducted under the U.S. Mining Laws on National Forest land.[1]

Notice of Intent to Operate

Before initiating any operation which might cause disturbance to the surface resources, a notice of intent to operate must be submitted to the district ranger having jurisdiction over the area to be affected. If the district ranger determines that the proposed operation may cause significant disturbance to the surface resources, a proposed plan of operation must be submitted. A notice of intent to operate and a plan of operation are not required in the following situations: (1) operations that do not involve cutting of trees; (2) operations confined to use of vehicles on existing roads; (3) mineral collecting and sampling of a mineral deposit that does not cause a significant disturbance of the surface resources; and (4) location of a mining claim.[2]

The notice of intent to operate must include sufficient information to identify the nature of the proposed activities, the route of access and the method of transport. The district ranger must notify the operator within 15 days whether or not a plan of operations is required.[3]

Plan of Operations

Among other things, the plan of operations must include the name and address of the operators, a map of the proposed site of operation delineating all roads and other areas to be affected, a description of type of operation, including how and where it will take place and environmental and reclamation procedure. If it is not feasible to prepare a complete plan for the entire operation, an initial plan may be submitted and augmented later by supplemental plans as the project develops.[4]

Upon receipt of the proposed plan of operation, the district ranger has thirty days to review the plan and notify the operator that: (1) he has approved the plan; (2) the proposed operations do not require an operating plan; (3) modification of the plan is necessary; (4) more time, not to exceed an additional sixty days is required to review the plan; or (5) the plan will not be approved until a final environmental statement has been prepared and filed with the Council on Environmental Quality, if an EIS is needed. While reviewing the plan of operation, the district ranger makes an environmental analysis to determine whether an environmental statement is required. Certain information in the plan of operation may be designated as confidential and will not be available for public inspection.[5]

Reclamation Requirements

The operator is required to reclaim all lands affected by the mining operation, during the mining operation, if feasible, or within one year after termination of mining operations. Reclamation procedures specifically include: (1) control of erosion and landslides; (2) control of water runoff; (3) removal and control of toxic substances; (4) rehabilitation of fisheries and wildlife habitat; and (5) reshaping and revegetation of disturbed areas, where reasonably practicable. Also, within a reasonable time following a cessation of mining activities, the operator is required to remove all structures and equipment and clean up the site of operation.[6]

Bonding

In certain cases, operators required to file a plan of operations will also be required to furnish a bond conditioned upon reclamation of the site of operations. The basis for determining the amount of bond will be the estimated cost of reclamation of the area of operations. As each portion of the site is reclaimed, the bond may be reduced proportionately.[7]

Residency Covered by Regulations

In **United States v. Langley**, 587 F.Supp. 1258, 1266 (E.D. Cal. 1984), the Court held that the claimant's residence is covered by the Forest Service regulations and must not exist unless approved under an operating plan.

Operating Plan Approval May Require an EIS

In some cases, the approval of an operating plan may require the preparation of an Environmental Impact Statement (EIS). Any major federal action which is likely to have a significant effect on the environment requires such a statement. The need for an EIS is normally identified in the environmental assessment. **Thomas v. Peterson**, 753 F.2d 754 (9th Cir. 1985).

Operating Plan Required for Structures on Mill Site

In **United States v. Brunskill**, 792 F.2d 938 (9th Cir. 1986), the Court required mining claimants "to remove at their expense a cabin, a mill, and other structures from their mill site on Forest Service land and to pay the United States $1,000 to restore the land to its natural state." If the claimants do not remove the structures within one year, the government was given permission by the Court to remove the structures and assess the claimants costs. The Court also found that the claimants "are required to have an approved operating plan for their cabin, mill and other structures because each of those structures constitute a surface disturbance within the meaning of 36 CFR 228.

Terms of Approved Plan Exceeded

In **United States v. Doremus**, 658 F.Supp. 752 (D. Idaho 1987), a miner appealed a conviction in a Court trial before a United States Magistrate for exceeding the terms of an approved operating plan and damaging natural resources on national forest land. United States District Court Judge Ryan affirmed the decision of the magistrate and conviction of the appellants.

The operating plan required by 36 CFR 228.1-228.63 was signed by the appellant in 1985. The plan provided that no more than five trenches be opened at one time and that exploration be confined to the clearout area. The claimants were also prohibited from using live timber and that all amendments be in writing. Apparently more than thirty trenches were opened, some larger than approved in the plan, and live trees were pushed over. Other regulations such as 36 CFR 261.9(a) and 261.10(k) prohibit certain other conduct such as damaging natural features, property of the United States. Criminal Charges for violation of these regulations is authorized by 16 U.S.C. 551. The Court held that 36 CFR 261.9(a) and 261.10(k) are clear and not constitutionally vague.

Loss of Mineral Rights from Unapproved Plan

In **David Doremus v. United States**, Civil No. 88-3103 and 3105 (October 28, 1988), a claimant was enjoined from conducting mining operations in the Gospel Hump Wilderness area until his plan of operations was approved. In this case Doremus had located 23 placer claims and 103 tunnel site claims in a Wilderness area that would be closed to mining on December 31, 1988.

Doremus submitted a plan for Forest Service approval which would allow him an opportunity to make discoveries on his placer claims and to initiate tunnels on his tunnel site claims. In order to establish valid existing rights to the claims and sites, the work must be done by December 1988. Without approval of the operating plan, Doremus would be unable to establish rights that could relate back to before December 31, 1988.

In noting that Doremus is well aware of the requirements to get approval of an operating plan, the Court cited a case where a miner faced the loss of mineral rights if certain actions were not completed by a given date and held that a miner could not claim injury when he had not allowed sufficient time for obtaining permits. **Downstate Stone Co. v. United States**, 651 F.2d 1234, 1241 (7th Cir. 1981).

Appeals Procedure

In response to an adverse action or decision by the district ranger, an appeal may be made in written form setting forth the manner in which the decision is contrary to the facts, law, regulations or is otherwise in error. This written statement must be filed with the district ranger within thirty days of the date of notification of the contested decision. Upon receipt of the statement, the district ranger will forward it, together with his own statement to the forest supervisor. The final administrative appeal may be taken to the regional forester. Upon receiving an adverse decision by the regional forester, the claimant may go directly to the courts for judicial review.[8]

Court Approval of Forest Service Regulations

Although the regulations (36 CFR Part 228) have been challenged numerous times on the basis of insufficient statutory authority, the courts have consistently upheld their validity. Under sections 478 and 551 of Title 16, the Secretary of Agriculture has authority to develop regulations concerning the methods of prospecting and mining in the national forest.

In **United States v. Curtis-Nevada Mines.**, 415 F.Supp. 1373 (DC Cal 1976), affirmed in part, reversed in part on other grounds 611 F.2d 1277 (1980), the Court held that owners of unpatented mining claims located in the national forest are required to file operating plans as required by the regulations in 36 CFR 252, prior to initiating mining operations.

In **United States v. Goldfield Deep Mines Co. of Nev.,** 644
F.2d 1307 (9th Cir. 1981), cert. denied 455 U.S. 907 1982), the
United States sued for trespass, seeking injunctive relief and damages. The Ninth Circuit Court of Appeals affirmed the District
Court's award of the requested relief. Goldfield cut trees, dug
roads and used heavy equipment and machinery in the national
forest in San Bernardino, California and refused to file an operating
plan as required by the regulations (36 CFR Part 228). The United
States Marshall seized the equipment and prevented Goldfield from
further operations. The Government was also awarded damages
totaling $17,560.

Regulations Apply to Wilderness

The regulations (36 CFR 228 and 293) also apply to mineral-
related activities in wilderness and primitive areas. The Act that
created the National Wilderness Preservation system in 1964 (Act
of September 3, 1964) specified that prospecting for minerals and
location of mining claims would be permitted in wilderness areas
through December 31, 1983. Although prospecting and mining are
authorized, they must be conducted in a manner as compatible as
possible with preservation of the wilderness. Therefore, the standards under which the regulations are applied in a wilderness are
somewhat stricter than on other lands. Special limitations and
restrictions have been placed on the use of mechanized equipment.
For example, no operator shall construct roads across a National
Forest Wilderness unless authorized in writing by the Forest Supervisor.[9]

Special Use Permits Do Not Apply to
Exploration or Mining Operations

In **United States v. Craig,** CR-82-8-H (April 16, 1984), the
U.S. District Court for the District of Montana considered a case
where a mining claimant appealed from a U.S. Magistrate's judgment finding him guilty of violating the regulations 36 CFR
261.10(a) and 261.12(d). The Forest Service contended that the
claimant had damaged a national forest system road and had locked
a gate on a forest system road without a special use permit as
required by 36 CFR 261.

The Montana District Court dismissed the complaints and held
that the "appellant was not required to have a special use permit
for activities done in connection with mining operations as defined
in 36 CFR 228. The Court also held that 36 CFR 261 does not
apply to a claimant acting under the United States mining laws of
1872 who submitted a proposed plan of operations as required by
36 CFR 228. And any violation of Forest Service regulations
should be charged under 36 CFR 228.

Violators of Regulations Subject to Criminal Sanctions

In **U.S. v. Langley**, 587 F.Supp. 1258 (1984), the district court enjoined claimants from conducting mining operations using a D-4 caterpillar and maintaining a residence on a claim without obtaining an approved plan of operations as required by 36 CFR 228. The Court noted that "violations of the regulations may subject the violator to criminal sanctions under 16 U.S.C. 551." This section provides that "any violation of the ...rules and regulations (enacted for the protection of national forests) shall be punished by a fine of not more than $500 or imprisonment for not more than six months, or both."

The Granite Rock Case

In **California Coastal Commission v. Granite Rock Company**, 55 LW 43666 (1987), the United States Supreme Court held that Federal law does not preempt reasonable state environmental permitting requirements for mining activity on unpatented mining claims. In 1980, Granite Rock Company submitted to the Forest Service a 5-year plan of operations under the regulations in 36 CFR 228 for a mining operation on unpatented mining claims on National Forest lands near the California coast. The Forest Service sent the plan to the California Coastal Commission for consistency review under the California Coastal Act. The Commission did not respond so the Forest Service approved the plan.

In 1983, the Coastal Commission instructed Granite Rock to apply for a coastal development permit. Granite Rock refused and filed suit in Federal District Court. The District Court denied Granite Rock's motion for summary judgment and dismissed the action. The Ninth Circuit Court of Appeals reversed the District Court and held that an "independent state permit system to enforce state environmental standards would undermine the Forest Service's own permit authority and is preempted." Therefore, Granite Rock Company is not subject to the permit authority of the California Coastal Commission.

The Supreme Court reversed the Ninth Circuit and held that the surface management regulations 36 CFR 228 (Forest Service) and 43 CFR 3809 (BLM) do not preempt state laws and regulations relating to the conduct of operations or reclamation on Federal lands under the mining laws. Furthermore, the Court noted the federal regulations contemplate compliance with state environmental permit requirements. The state's involvement appears to be limited to those areas where the federal law does not regulate. The decision distinguished environmental regulation from land use planning with the assumption that federal land use planning laws preempt state land use planning requirements from applying to federal lands. The decision also indicates that the states may not control use of federal land by land use planning or by denying environmental permits.

References - Regulations on National Forest Lands

1. 36 CFR 228.2.
2. 36 CFR 228.4(1).
3. 36 CFR 228.4(2).
4. Id.
5. 36 CFR 228.5.
6. 36 CFR 228.8.
7. 36 CFR 228.13.
8. 36 CFR 228.14.
9. 36 CFR 228.15(c).

BLM'S SURFACE MANAGEMENT REGULATIONS

Introduction

The Federal Land Policy and Management Act of October 21, 1976 (FLPMA) directed the Secretary of the Interior to take any action necessary by regulation or otherwise to prevent unnecessary or undue degradation of the lands. To implement this part of FLPMA, the Secretary issued proposed "3809 regulations" on December 6, 1976 which were then reproposed March 3, 1980. The final 3809 regulations, made effective January 1, 1981 (45 FR 78902; 43 CFR 3809), apply to surface disturbances made in connection with mining operations conducted under the Mining Law of 1872, as amended. 30 U.S.C. 21-54 (1982).

The compliance process is similar to that authorized by the Forest Service regulations (36 CFR Part 228). The final regulations address three levels of exploration and mining activity: (1) for casual use where mechanized earth-moving equipment and explosives are not used, there is no requirement to contact the BLM; (2) if proposed exploration or mining activities would cause a surface disturbance of five acres or less per year, the operator is required to submit a "notice" to BLM 15 days before starting work; and (3) a plan of operations must be submitted to the BLM if surface disturbance is more than five acres per year, or if the operations are proposed in certain specified environmentally-sensitive areas. The "plan of operations" must contain a detailed description of the proposed mining and reclamation activities. Once submitted to the BLM, the plan is reviewed and processed in much the same manner as plans filed under the Forest Service regulations. All operations, whether casual, under a notice, or under a plan of operation must be reclaimed. 43 CFR 3809.1-1.

Jurisdiction of Regulations

The regulations generally apply to all BLM-administered lands subject to the mining law. The regulations do not cover lands included in the National Park System, the National Forest System, the National Wildlife Refuge System and the Stock-raising Homestead lands or lands where only the mineral interest is reserved to the United States. Lands under Wilderness Review and administered by the BLM are subject to regulations in 43 CFR 3802 and not to the 3809 regulations.

Unnecessary or Undue Degradation

"Unnecessary or Undue Degradation" is defined in 43 CFR 3809.0-5(k) as surface disturbance greater than what would normally result when an activity is being accomplished by a prudent operator in usual, customary, and proficient operations of similar character and taking into consideration the effects of operations on other resources and land uses. Failure to reclaim disturbed areas may also constitute unnecessary and undue degradation.

Casual Use - No Notice or Plan Required

No notification to the BLM is required for casual use, however casual use operations may be monitored to ensure that unnecessary and undue degradation does not occur.[1] The regulations define "casual use" as activities ordinarily resulting in only negligible disturbance of the federal lands and resources.[2] For example the use of mechanized earth moving equipment and explosives is not allowed under casual use.

Notice Required for Disturbance of 5 Acres or Less

Operators on project areas whose operations, including access across federal lands, cause a cumulative surface disturbance of 5 acres or less during any calendar year must file a notice with the Bureau of Land Management.[3] A "project area" is defined[4] as a single tract of land upon which an operator is, or will be, conducting operations. It may include more than one mining claim under one ownership as well as federal lands on which an operator is exploring or prospecting prior to locating a mining claim. Before an operator may conduct additional operations under another notice, all lands disturbed under a previous notice must be reclaimed. "Reclamation" is defined in the regulations[5] as taking such reasonable measures as will prevent unnecessary or undue degradation of the federal lands, including reshaping land disturbed by operations to an appropriate contour. Revegetation of disturbed areas may be necessary so as to provide a diverse vegetative cover.

A written notice of planned activities must be submitted to the BLM at least 15 calendar days before starting operations. The Notice must describe the operations and their location and must contain a statement that the lands will be reclaimed to standards provided in the regulations. No approval or bonding is required, but the BLM may request a meeting with the operator when road construction exceeds certain specifications.[6]

Notice Does Not Require Environmental Assessment

In **Sierra Club v. Penfold**, Civil No. A86-083 (January 29, 1987), the Federal District Court of Alaska held that the filing of a notice is not a Federal "action" under the CEQ regulations (40 CFR 1501.4(b) and 1508.18) because no approval is required before beginning operations. NEPA documents are not required where there is no Federal "action." The Sierra Club had contended that no mining can proceed until an environmental assessment is completed.

Plan of Operations - Disturbance of More Than 5 Acres or Mining in Special Areas

A plan of operations must be submitted to the BLM if surface disturbance exceeds 5 acres for a single calendar year, or if the operations are proposed in the following areas: (1) California Desert Conservation Area; (2) areas designated for potential addition to, or an actual component of the National Wild and Scenic River System; (3) designated areas of critical environmental concern; (4) areas designated as part of the National Wilderness Preservation System which are administered by the BLM; (5) areas withdrawn from operation of the mining laws in which valid existing rights are being exercised; and (6) areas designated as "closed" or "limited" to off-road vehicle use.[7]

A plan of operations must be filed in the District Office of the BLM having jurisdiction over the lands to be affected. The regulations[8] specify the contents of the plan which need not be prepared in any special form. Generally, the plan will describe operators, nature of the operations and a map will be required. The plan must also describe measures to be taken to prevent unnecessary or undue degradation and measures to reclaim disturbed areas.

Plan Approval

Upon submission of a proposed plan of operations, the BLM acknowledges receipt of the plan and has 30 days to approve or require changes in the plan. If changes in the plan are necessary, or additional time is needed to review the plan, an extension of time, not to exceed 60 days, may be required; however, days during which the area of operations is inaccessible for inspection are not counted when computing the 60-day period. The plan cannot be approved until the BLM has complied with section 106 of the National Historic Preservation Act or section 7 of the Endangered Species Act.[9]

Modification of Plan

The regulations[10] provide for modifications of an approved plan. Significant modifications require approval in the same manner as an initial plan. Plan modification may either be required by the BLM or requested by the operator.

Lands Disturbed under Prior Notice Must Be Included in Determining if Plan Required

Deferral of reclamation for certain legitimate mining purposes is allowed by the regulations.[11] However before conducting additional operations under a subsequent notice, the operator shall have completed reclamation of operations which were conducted under any previous notice. Therefore any lands disturbed by mining may be legitimately deferred, but all disturbed land must be included in the computation of surface disturbance for the purpose of determining whether a plan of operations is required. 43 CFR 3809.1-3(a); **Differential Energy, Inc.,** 99 IBLA 225, 231 (1987).

Operating Plans Subject to Stipulations

In **Draco Mines**, 75 IBLA 278 (1983), it was held to be proper for the BLM to condition the approval of a plan of operation on the acceptance of stipulations designed to prevent unnecessary and undue degradation of the public lands. It is also required that such stipulations are reasonable and properly reflect considerations of the public interest.

BLM Discretion in Approving a Plan

BLM may make its approval contingent upon acceptance of various modifications designed to prevent or mitigate undesired impacts. Such modifications may make it more difficult or more expensive for the claimant to develop the property. BLM may require design changes in plan operation or in the route of access. BLM may not, however, absolutely forbid mining or totally bar access to a valid mining claim. **Southwest Resource Council,** 96 IBLA 105, 120 (1987).

Plan Approval May Constitute "Major Federal Action"

The approval of a plan of operations not only is a "Federal action," requiring an environmental assessment, but may also be a "major Federal action" requiring an environmental impact statement. **Southwest Resources Council** at 121.

"Unnecessary and Undue Degradation" Relates to Validity

In **Southwest Resource Council**, the appellant asserted that BLM cannot determine whether unnecessary or undue degradation is occurring without a determination that a valuable mineral deposit has been discovered; or in effect, arguing that any degradation of the federal lands caused by the development is necessarily undue and unnecessary if there exists no right to enter such lands. The Board stated "that the determination of the question whether unnecessary or undue degradation will occur necessarily assumes the validity of the use which is causing the impact," and therefore a validity examination should not necessarily be prerequisite to approval of a plan of operations.

However the Board noted that BLM is not precluded from determining the validity of a claim. If "BLM determined that the claims were not supported by a discovery, the proper course of action would be to initiate a contest as to the claims' validity and suspend consideration of the plan of operations pending the outcome of the proceedings."

Noncompliance for Lack of State Permits

A notice of noncompliance may be based on the failure of an operator to obtain state permits. However, a decision alleging a lack of compliance with state permitting requirements should clearly delineate the permits needed and clearly describe the reasons why each permit is needed. **Bruce W. Crawford**, 86 IBLA 350, 401 (1985).

Plan Approval for Occupancy Not Required

Under the regulations, there is no requirement that a claimant obtain prior approval to establish occupancy. In fact, a claimant could proceed to erect a cabin in the face of BLM's objections and not violate any element of the regulations. **Bruce W. Crawford** at 381 and 391. In the **Crawford** case, the Board pointed out that under the present regulations the BLM must react to rather than anticipate the occupancy activities of a claimant. For example, if BLM determined that the placement of a cabin on a claim constituted unnecessary or undue degradation, it could issue a notice of noncompliance on such grounds. However, the regulations require that such occupancy be duly described in a notice. An occupancy that is described in a notice can be prohibited, only by a showing that such occupancy results in unnecessary or undue degradation.

Hearing Necessary to Determine if Occupancy Is Incidental to Mining

If there is no mining activity on a claim, a determination can be made that occupancy of such a claim is not reasonably incidental to mining. This determination can be made without the benefit of a fact-finding hearing. However, if some mining activity is taking place and the claimant contends that occupancy of the claims is necessary in order to develop the mineral deposits, the effect of an order requiring such a claimant to cease occupancy is tantamount to a taking of the right to mine. Where mining is occurring and the Government seeks to challenge occupancy as not reasonably incident to such mining activities, the Government must provide notice and an opportunity for hearing prior to ordering the cessation of occupancy. **Bruce W. Crawford** at 350, 373 and 401.

Occupancy Is Challenged by Contest

If BLM desires to challenge a claimant's occupancy on the basis that such occupancy is not reasonably related to the mining activities, or that the specific occupancy is causing unnecessary or undue degradation, a contest alleging such grounds should be initiated. **Bruce W. Crawford** at 401.

Two or More Plans of Operation on One Mining Claim

If more than one plan of operation should be filed for a single claim, each plan of operation will be reviewed on its own merits and approved if it complies with the regulations. The reason for this is the Department of the Interior has no authority to become involved in determining right of possession of a mining claim.[12]

Access to Claims Covered by 3809 Regulations Rather than Right-of-Way Permit

Mosch Mining Co., 75 IBLA 153 (1983) was a case where the BLM required a claimant to file an application for a right-of-way permit to construct an access road to a mining claim. On appeal the Board held that "the grant of right-of-way was not the appropriate means of resolving the question" and "the matter should have been resolved under the surface management regulations." Although this case dealt with BLM-administered lands, it seems certain that the Forest Service surface management regulations (36 CFR 228) would cover access to claims in the same manner.

Bonding Requirements

Mining operations conducted under an approved plan may require a bond. The amount of bond is normally based on the estimated cost of reclamation; however, no bond may be required if the operations would cause only minimal disturbance to the land. In lieu of a bond, the operator may deposit and maintain in a Federal depository account of the United States Treasury, a cash bond or negotiable securities of the United States. The regulations also provide for blanket bonds covering statewide or nationwide operations.[13]

Noncompliance

Failure of an operator to file a notice or a plan of operations may result in being served a notice of noncompliance or being enjoined from continuing such operations by a court order. Also, failure to reclaim disturbed areas or follow an approved plan of operation will subject the operator to a notice of noncompliance. Actions specified in a notice of noncompliance must be corrected in 30 days; failure to take necessary actions may be justification for requiring a plan of operations and mandatory bonding.[14]

Appeals

Any operator adversely affected by a decision of the authorized officer has the right of appeal to the State Director of the BLM. The decision of the State Director, when adverse to the appellant, may be appealed to the Board of Land Appeals. The adversed party in a decision of the Board of Land Appeals may then appeal that decision to the federal courts.[15]

Court Approval of BLM Surface Management Regulations

United States District Court Judge Ramirez issued an order to the locators of a mining claim enjoining and restraining them from conducting any mining operations on the claim unless they submit a plan of operations pursuant to 43 CFR 3809 and obtain approval. This is the first federal court requirement that a mining claimant comply with the BLM surface management regulations. **United States v. Bales**, 522 F.Supp. 150 (E.D. Cal. 1981).

References - BLM's Surface Management Regulations

1. 43 CFR 3809.1-2.
2. 43 CFR 3809.0-5(b).
3. 43 CFR 3809.1-3.
4. 43 CFR 3809.0-5(i).
5. 43 CFR 3809.0-5(j).
6. 43 CFR 3809.1-3.
7. 43 CFR 3809.1-4.
8. 43 CFR 3809.1-5.
9. 43 CFR 3809.1-6.
10. 43 CFR 3809.1-7.
11. 43 CFR 3809.1-3(d)(5).
12. Instruction Memorandum No. 81-590 (July 23, 1981).
13. 43 CFR 3809.1-9(d).
14. 43 CFR 3809.3-2.
15. 43 CFR 3809.4.

BLM WILDERNESS STUDY AREAS

Nonimpairment Mandate

Section 603(c) of the Federal Land Policy and Management Act of 1976 says to manage wilderness study areas (WSA) so as "not to impair the suitability of such areas for preservation as wilderness..." Section 603 also provides for exception from the nonimpairment mandate with "grandfather uses." Grandfather uses are referred to in section 603 as follows:

> ....subject however, to the continuation of existing mining and grazing uses and mineral leasing in the same manner and degree in which the same was being conducted on the date of approval of this Act...

Therefore mining uses which existed on October 21, 1976, are restricted to the same "manner and degree." All activities except those exempt must be regulated to prevent impairment. If an activity cannot meet the nonimpairment standard, it will not be permitted. Some temporary uses are permitted even though they cause physical or aesthetic impacts, providing impacts are temporary and can be reclaimed.[1]

Lands in wilderness study areas must be managed to prevent unnecessary and undue degradation. This applies to both grandfather uses and valid existing rights. "Unnecessary and undue degradation" is defined to mean impacts greater than those that would normally be expected from an activity being accomplished in compliance with current standards and regulations and based on sound practices, including use of best reasonably available technology.[2]

Appropriation Under the Mining Laws

Lands under wilderness study are still open to entry; however new locations fall under the nonimpairment standard. A post-FLPMA claim with a discovery has a right to patent, and on receipt of patent, the claimant is no longer subject to the nonimpairment standard.

Grandfather Uses

Existing mining and mineral leasing uses on October 21, 1976, may be continued in the same manner and degree. This means actual physical impacts on the land before October 21, 1976. In **Havlah Group**, 88 I.D. 115 (1981), the Board determined that assessment work alone does not qualify; there must be actual development or mining operations on the claims.

With grandfather rights you can continue operations in the "same manner and degree." This means to expand the scale of the operation at a logical pace and progression (i.e., exploration through development and through mining), with geographic extension until deposit is exhausted. Grandfather uses go with the land and cannot be transferred to other properties. It is the use rather than the claim that is grandfathered. A grandfathered mineral use may continue in the same manner and degree onto adjacent claims owned by the same person. A grandfathered mineral use outside the boundary of a WSA may extend into the area as long as the activity follows the logical pace and progression of development.

Valid Existing Rights

The Department cannot regulate valid existing rights to the nonimpairment standard. The situation is given below for both mining claims and leases:

I. Mining Claims

Mining claims have valid existing rights if a discovery was made on the claim before October 21, 1976, and the claim continues to be supported by a discovery. A claim would also have grandfather rights if it were actively worked as of October 21, 1976. However a claim has a more liberal development standard under valid existing rights. Grandfather uses are unimportant if the claim also has valid existing rights because claimants may proceed even if the activities exceeded the manner and degree that existed on October 21, 1976.

Activities to use and develop a claim must satisfy the nonimpairment criteria unless it would unreasonably interfere with the claimant's rights to use and enjoyment of the claim. If so, the claimant may proceed while regulated to prevent unnecessary or undue degradation.

II. Mineral Leases

Mineral leases have valid existing rights if they were issued before October 21, 1976. Grandfather uses are not applicable to pre-FLPMA mineral leases because such leases enjoy more liberal development standards under valid existing rights.

Activities must satisfy the nonimpairment criteria unless this would unreasonably interfere with the rights provided by the lease. If rights can only be exercised through activities that permanently impair wilderness suitability, such activities will be allowed to proceed, but they will be regulated to prevent unnecessary and undue regulation.[3]

Transfers of Interest

If a claimant or lessee transfers a claim or lease, the same valid existing right is recognized in the new owner. Valid existing rights are tied to a particular claim or lease and cannot be transferred to a different claim or lease, even for the same land.

Nonimpairment Standard May Be Exceeded If Valid Existing Rights

Development of mining claims with valid existing rights prior to FLPMA may, under certain circumstances, exceed the nonimpairment standard; however, such activities will be regulated to prevent unnecessary or undue degradation. The unnecessary and undue degradation criterion authorized by Section 603 c of FLPMA must not be applied to post-FLPMA claims because such claims are subject to the much higher nonimpairment standard. **Ralph E. Pray**, 105 IBLA 44, 46 (1988).

Split Estate Lands May Have WSA Status

In **Sierra Club v. Watt**, 608 F.Supp. 305 (E.C. Cal. 1985), the Court determined that the definition of "public lands" in FLPMA included split estate lands. Therefore the Court ordered the Secretary to restore WSA status to all split estate lands that had been deleted by the order.

Reclamation Deadline Under the Interim Management Policy

Impacts within wilderness study areas (WSA), except for grandfathered uses and those having valid existing rights, must be reclaimed to a condition of being substantially unnoticeable in the WSA as a whole by the time the Secretary of the Interior is scheduled to send his recommendation on that area to the president. Chapter I.B.2, page 10, **Interim Management Plan,** December 12, 1979, as amended July 12, 1983, published by the Bureau of Land Management.

The latest possible date for attaining complete reclamation for all nonimpairing impacts within WSAs scheduled for statewide reporting is the date the Secretary is scheduled to sign the record of decision. To ensure the reclamation timeframe is met, each state establishes a final deadline for having all projects reclaimed within WSA's, regardless of the suitability recommendation on any specific WSA. The reclamation deadline can be no later than October 21, 1991, which is the statutory date by which the Secretary must report all recommendations to the President. From that date until Congress acts, the only activities permissible (other than grandfather uses and valid existing rights) under the Nonimpairment Criteria are temporary uses that create no new surface disturbance. Such uses may continue until Congress acts, so long as they can easily and immediately be terminated at that time, if necessary to manage the area as wilderness. **Instruction Memorandum No. 86-491** (May 22, 1986).

Off-road Vehicles in WSAs

The regulations in 43 CFR 8340.0-5(a), which are the authority for closing areas to off-road vehicle use, make an exception for off-road vehicles used in connection with lawful mining activities. Off-road vehicles may be used for mining purposes if expressly authorized by the appropriate BLM official. 44 FR 34834 (June 15, 1979); **Manville Sales Corp.**, 102 IBLA 385, 388 (1988).

References - BLM Wilderness Study Areas

1. Implement Management Plan Issued December 12, 1979, as amended July 12, 1983, published by the Bureau of Land Management.
2. 43 CFR 3802.
3. Colorado Open Space Council, 73 IBLA 226 (1983).

BLM 3802 REGULATIONS

Final Regulations: April 2, 1980 (45 FR 13968)

Authority: Sections 302 and 603 of FLPMA

Purpose: Procedures established to prevent impairment of the suitability of lands under wilderness review for the inclusion in the wilderness system and to prevent unnecessary and undue degradation.

Operations Existing on October 21, 1976

A plan of operations is not required for operations that were conducted on October 21, 1976, unless the manner and degree of operation on October 21, 1976 is being exceeded.

An approved plan may be requested if operations in the same manner and degree are causing unnecessary and undue degradation. Operations may cover previously undisturbed ground and may take place even if impairment of wilderness suitability should occur.

Plan Approval

The plan approval process is used to determine if the plan will result in wilderness suitability or if parts or all of the plan is based on mining claims with valid existing rights. In **Golden Triangle Exploration Co.**, 76 IBLA 245 (1983), the Board upheld the rejection of a plan of operation because the proposed operation would impair the naturalness of the WSA.

When Plan Is Required

An approved plan of operations is required when one or more of the following actions are involved (43 CFR 3802.1-1):

1. Construction of access including bridges, aircraft landing areas or improving or maintaining access facilities in such a way that changes the alignment, width, gradient, size or character of such facilities. For example, significant alteration and enlargement of an existing access road in a WSA requires approval of a plan of operations;

2. Destruction of trees two or more inches in diameter at the base;

3. Mining operations using tracked vehicles or mechanized earth-moving equipment, such as bulldozers or backhoes;

4. Using motorized vehicles over other than "open use areas and trails;"

5. The construction or placement of any mobile, portable or fixed structure on public land for more than 30 days;

6. Use of explosives; and

7. Changes in a water course.

When Plan Is Not Required

A plan of operations is not required for the following actions (43 CFR 3802.1-2):

1. Searching for and removing mineral samples or specimens;

2. Operating motorized vehicles over "open use areas and trails;"

3. Maintaining or making minor improvements of existing access routes, bridges, landing areas for aircraft or other facilities for access; however, the alignment, width, gradient, size or character of such facilities shall not be altered; and

4. Making geological, radiometric, geochemical, geophysical measurements using instruments or drilling equipment which are transported without using mechanized earthmoving equipment or tracked vehicles.

Proposed Plan Rejected Because Road Cannot Be Reclaimed Before Deadline

In **Manville Sales Corp.**, 102 IBLA 385 (1988), the Board upheld the rejection by BLM of a proposed plan of operation in a WSA. The BLM determined that the impacts of road construction could not be reclaimed to meet the criteria of being substantially unnoticeable in the area as a whole by the time the Secretary was scheduled to make his recommendation to the President.

BLM Cannot Completely Forbid Mining

When considering a proposed plan of operations, BLM cannot completely forbid mining either under the 3802 regulations, **L.C. Artman**, 98 IBLA 164 (1987), or under the 3809 regulations, **Southwest Resource Council**, 96 IBLA 105, 120, 94 I.D. 56 (1987).

Hearing Authorized on Denial of Mining Plan

In **Norman G. Lavery**, 96 IBLA 294 (1987), Mr. Lavery appealed a BLM district decision disallowing his plan of operations because the activities proposed would impair the suitability of the area for preservation as wilderness. The appellant requested that his case be assigned to an administrative law judge for a hearing. The Board exercised its discretionary authority and referred the case to an administrative law judge for a hearing on an issue of fact. An appellant seeking reversal of a decision involving lands in a wilderness study area must show that it was premised either on a clear error of law or a demonstrable error of fact. The burden of persuasion by a preponderance of the evidence rests on the appellant.

Right-of-Way Permit Required to Transport Water to Mining Claim

In **Desert Survivors**, 96 IBLA 193, 196-97 (1987), the Board held that a right-of-way permit must be issued under Title V of FLPMA before transporting water across public land for any mining purpose. Approval of a right-of-way application is discretionary and the application process is subject to an environmental assessment as required by NEPA.

Failure to Notify Owner

If the operator is not notified within the 30-day period or the 60-day extension, operations under the plan may begin. However, this does not constitute approval of a plan of operations. If operations later impair wilderness suitability, the operator is notified of the compliance and a modified plan of operations is requested.

Modification of Plan

In many cases it is not possible to file a plan for the entire life of the operation because certain aspects of the deposit are unknown. The operator files an initial plan and at the appropriate time files a supplemental plan. A supplemental plan is approved in the same manner as the initial plan. The operator either voluntarily submits a significant modification of the plan or is asked to submit a modification.

Bonding

Bonds are not required except in connection with an approved plan of operation. If a plan is not required, a bond is not required. The requirement for a bond is discretionary and depends on -

1. the potential for surface disturbance
2. operator's past record of reclamation

The amount of bond should be based on the estimated cost of reclamation. When a claim is patented or disturbed land is satisfactorily reclaimed, the bond may be reduced proportionately.

Noncompliance

Noncompliance results where the operator -
1. operates without having filed a plan or bond
2. failed to comply with requirements of an approved plan of operations
3. failed to comply with the 3802 regulations

and the noncompliance is causing -
1. impairment of wilderness suitability, or
2. necessary or undue degradation

If the above occurs, the authorized officer shall serve a notice of noncompliance upon the operator. An operator who fails to file a plan of operations and ignores the notice of noncompliance should be enjoined from operating by a court order.

Criminal Penalties

There are no criminal penalties expressly contained in the 3802 regulations. However, operators who fail to obtain proper authorization with an approved plan and continue operations or fail to respond to a notice of noncompliance may be cited for violation of 43 CFR part 8340 or part 8360 or both. The conduct is criminal under these provisions.

Environmental Assessment

Once a plan of operations is filed, an environmental assessment must be prepared within the 30-day period.

Cultural and Paleontological Resources

A cultural resource inventory shall be completed before approval of a plan. Although the operator is not required to do the inventory, he may hire a qualified professional to expedite the process. If the operator discovers cultural resources, he must notify the BLM and leave it intact. Operations can proceed within 10 days after notification.

Notice of Suspension of Operation

Except for seasonal suspension, the operator must notify the BLM within 30 days of a suspension. During periods of suspended operations, the name and mailing address of the operator should be posted on the site.

Cessation of Operation

Within one year following cessation of operations, the operator must remove all structures and equipment and reclaim the site of operation.

Appeals

If adversely affected by a decision of the authorized officer or the State Director, the operator has the right of appeal to the Interior Board of Land Appeals. The adversed party from the IBLA has the right of appeal to the federal courts.

Reference - BLM 3802 Regulations

1. William E. Godwin, 82 IBLA 105 (1984).

DESIGNATED WILDERNESS AREAS ADMINISTERED BY THE BLM

Validity Examinations on BLM-Administered Wilderness Areas

Regulations made effective on March 27, 1985 (43 CFR 8560.4-6(j), give procedures for reviewing plans of operations on unpatented mining claims within wilderness areas administered by the Bureau of Land Management. Before approving plans of operation or allowing previously approved operations to continue on unpatented mining claims (on newly-designated wilderness areas), a mineral examiner will conduct a validity examination to determine whether or not the claim was valid prior to the withdrawal and remains valid. If the mineral report indicates the claim lacks a discovery or is invalid for any reason, the plan of operations will be denied. Existing approved operations will be issued a notice ordering the cessation of operations. In both cases the BLM will initiate contest proceedings to determine the status of the claims conclusively. However, the regulations provide for allowing proposed operations that will cause only insignificant surface disturbance for purposes such as sampling and performing assessment work.

INDEX